Creation
and the
World of Science

CREATION
and the
WORLD OF SCIENCE
The Re-Shaping of Belief

ARTHUR PEACOCKE
Former Director of the Ian Ramsey Centre,
University of Oxford

OXFORD
UNIVERSITY PRESS

OXFORD
UNIVERSITY PRESS

Great Clarendon Street, Oxford OX2 6DP

Oxford University Press is a department of the University of Oxford.
It furthers the University's objective of excellence in research, scholarship,
and education by publishing worldwide in

Oxford New York

Auckland Bangkok Buenos Aires Cape Town Chennai
Dar es Salaam Delhi Hong Kong Istanbul Karachi Kolkata
Kuala Lumpur Madrid Melbourne Mexico City Mumbai Nairobi
São Paulo Shanghai Taipei Tokyo Toronto

Oxford is a registered trade mark of Oxford University Press
in the UK and in certain other countries

Published in the United States
by Oxford University Press Inc., New York

© *A. R. Peacocke 1979, 2004*

The moral rights of the author have been asserted
Database right Oxford University Press (maker)

First published in 1979
Reprinted 1998
First published in paperback 2004

ISBN 0–19–826650–2 (hbk)
ISBN 0–19–927169–0 (pbk)

Printed in Great Britain
by Biddles Ltd,
King's Lynn

To
the memory of
GEOFFREY LAMPE
and
IAN RAMSEY
who encouraged and helped me in this quest

Preface

IT is notable that, although the Bampton Lectures were intended by the testator to 'confirm and establish the Christian Faith' and although the world-view of mankind has in the twentieth century come to be increasingly dominated by that of the sciences, only two of these series of Lectures in this century have so far been at all concerned with the relation of Christian theology and the sciences—those of L. W. Grensted in 1930 (*Psychology and God: a study of the implications of recent psychology for religious belief and practice*, Longmans, Green & Co., London, 1930) and of E. L. Mascall in 1956 (*Christian Theology and Natural Science: some questions on their relations*, Longmans, Green & Co., London, 1956). The latter were magisterial in both the range of the sciences they surveyed and in the breadth of theological learning they brought to bear on these issues from what I am sure Professor Mascall would not mind my describing as a neo-Thomist and orthodox Christian viewpoint.

In the two decades or so since those Lectures, the development of molecular biology has further reinforced our view of living organisms as complex physico-chemical entities and has thereby filled, in principle, one of the major gaps in our understanding of the evolution of the cosmos—namely that between inorganic matter and living organisms. Life may now be regarded as a form of living matter and this crowning of the neo-Darwinian scheme, together with developments in cosmology, ecology, and our understanding of sub-atomic matter, have transformed the setting for discourse about the relation of God and man to nature to an extent which has still yet to be fully absorbed by Christian (or indeed any other) theology.

The universe described by science today is one which is in continual development from the most elusive sub-atomic particles to living organisms on the Earth (and perhaps elsewhere?) some of which appear to have conscious activities very like those predicated of man. Moreover biological, physiological, and psychological studies of man increasingly reveal features of his behaviour which can be discerned in animals. But man nevertheless has his peculiar 'glory', as finely expounded by Professor David Jenkins in his 1966 Bampton Lectures on *The Glory of Man* (SCM Press, London, 1967), so that the impressive nexus of scientific concepts raises even more acutely than in the past those fundamental problems, about the kind of universe in which man finds himself and his relation to it, for which the Christian beliefs of God as Creator, of nature as created, and of man as creature, were the traditional explanations.

These 1978 Bampton Lectures, here presented in a much fuller form than that in which they were originally delivered before the University of Oxford, are principally concerned with discerning how God's relation to the world, including man, may be conceived and explicated in the context of this apparently all-embracing scientific perspective on the world. The study is introduced (I) by an assessment of the current relation between science and Christian faith in the light of its earlier history, of the impact of the social sciences and of more recent philosophical analyses of their respective activities. The Judeo-Christian doctrine of creation is thus seen as a way of satisfying man's need to discern intelligibility and personal meaning in the world, a world now best described in scientific terms.

In succeeding lectures, an examination is made of the implications for the understanding of God's relation to the world of: cosmology and other developments in twentieth-century physics (II); evolutionary biology, with its new insights (Monod, Prigogine, Eigen) into the creative role of the interplay of chance and law (III); the hierarchical organization of the various levels of complexity in nature and the relation between their respective sciences (IV); the scientific study of man, including the approach of sociobiology (V); ecology (VII); and scientific predictions of the future of the Earth and of the universe (VIII).

The perspectives afforded by these developments in the sciences not only provide a new context for and critique of the doctrine of creation, it is argued, but also make possible an enrichment of our understanding of God's relation to the world and to man. This enriched and expanded understanding of God's creative action in the world enables, in the last three lectures, distinctive ways to be found to express the uniqueness, for Christian faith, of the significance of Jesus the Christ (VI); to develop appropriate values for meeting the contemporary ecological challenge (VII); and to discern the basis for human hope (VIII).

It is no accident that in these lectures there are involved, often implicitly rather than explicitly, a sequence of theological themes—the ground bass, as it were, to the more evident and salient scientific motifs—that echo credal phrases (from the Book of Common Prayer): 'I believe' (I); God (the Father) as 'Maker of heaven and earth' (I, II); God (the Holy Spirit) as 'The Lord and giver of life' (III, IV, V); God (the Son) as the one 'By whom all things were made' and 'Who ... was made man' (VI); and 'the Life of the world to come' (VIII).[1] So I hope that, far removed though our world-view is from that of Canon John Bampton of Salisbury who endowed these Lectures over 200 years ago in his will of 1751, he would nevertheless have found that, even in this last quarter of the twentieth century, there could be an understanding of at least some of 'the Articles of the Christian Faith, as comprehended in the Apostles' and the Nicene Creeds' (as his last Will and Testament put it) that the Lecturer could 'confirm and establish'—even though the style of confirming and establishing a faith, in general, and the 'Christian Faith', in particular, inevitably has a very different aspect than in his own age.

The collegiate communities of our ancient Universities provide a unique and friendly forum for what is fashionably termed 'inter-disciplinary' exchange and I have benefited particularly from the comments and advice about relevant literature previously unknown to me that I have received from my colleagues at Clare College, Cambridge, especially from Lord Ashby, the Revd Professor C. F. D. Moule, and Dr M. Ruel. The lectures, as here printed, have also been enriched by comments from some of my Oxford audience whose friendly hospitality my wife and I greatly enjoyed, coming from this 'other place'.

---

[1] Phrases which have become, in the latest liturgical, revised texts, respectively, 'We believe' (in the Nicene Creed, at least), 'maker (or creator) of heaven and earth', 'the Lord, the giver of life', 'Through him all things were made', 'he ... was made man', and 'the life of the world to come'.

It was particularly fortunate that, during the academic year when these Lectures were being delivered, the Revd Professor Philip Hefner, of the Lutheran School of Theology at Chicago, was studying at Clare Hall in Cambridge. As a systematic theologian with a keen interest in the implications for Christian theology of the natural, biological, and social sciences, he proved to be a genial and acute critic of the manuscript. Discussions with him clarified my thinking on many issues as well as, from time to time, serving to mitigate, if not entirely eliminate, the endemic insularity of an English theological perspective.

Finally, I am much indebted to the Electors to the Bampton Lecturership for the stimulus and opportunity they have afforded me of concentrating my thoughts on a number of issues which have exercised me for some years, to the Delegates of the Press and their staff for their expert and informed co-operation in bringing these thoughts to print, and to Mrs Jean Pike for her impeccable typing of the manuscript.

Preface to the Paperback Edition

At the time of my delivery in Oxford in 1978 of the Bampton Lectures, the basis of this volume, there had been in the twentieth century only two previous sets of those Lectures devoted to the theme of the relation of Christian theology to the sciences. Nevertheless there had been signs in the 1950s of the dawn of a new awareness, following World War II, of the vital significance of this theme in the writings, in Britain, of C. A. Coulson, D. Lack, E. Mascall (the 1956 Bampton Lecturer), C. E. Raven, A. F. Smethhurst, E. Whittaker, J. Wren-Lewis, and G. D. Yarnold and, in Germany, *inter alia*, K. Heim.

This interaction was real but spasmodic and it was certainly true by the early 1960s, at least in Britain, that, as John Habgood[1] noted in 1963, the public and academic relation between science and theology had lapsed into a kind of 'uneasy truce'. Across the Atlantic, the dialogue appears to have been inhibited in the USA after the 1925 Scopes Trial, on the teaching of evolution in schools. The truce was even more uneasy than in Britain, it would seem, until Ralph Burhoe, at first in Boston and then in Chicago, began nurturing the debate from the early 1950s—leading to the founding of the Institute on Religion in an Age of Science and eventually the journal *Zygon*. Then, while I was writing in the later 1960s my first book in this field (published in 1970 as *Science and the Christian Experiment*), there appeared in 1966, 'out of the blue' one might say, Ian Barbour's significant *Issues in Science and Religion*. In the ensuing three decades or so there has been an almost explosive growth in interest in the interaction of the sciences with Christian and other religious beliefs, as witnessed by the formation of national and international societies devoted to the relation of science and theology, the appearance of new journals, the establishment of

---

[1] J. Habgood, 'The Uneasy Truce between Science and Religion', in *Soundings*, ed. A. R. Vidler (Cambridge University Press, Cambridge, 1963), pp. 21–41.

academic posts and centres, and the proliferation of conferences, and now websites, devoted to such issues.

All of which is a salutary and humbling milieu for at least this
author in which to look again at what he wrote in the early days
of this remarkable burgeoning of concern about the relation of
claimed knowledge of God in the Christian faith to the knowledge of the natural world that the sciences afford. For example,
in this work of 1979 I presented one of the first theological
reflections in print on the then only recently expounded
'anthropic principle'. Subsequently there has been intense discussion of this 'principle', the theological interpretation of which
is still controversial not least in the light of proposals made in the
early 2000s that there exist other universes—that we live in a
'multiverse'. Furthermore the many references in my 1979
volume to the natural emergence of complex systems, to their
anti-reductionist significance and to the thermodynamic and
kinetic processes by which systems can self-organize into more
complex regimes have proved to be but the first streamlets of a
now growing flood of work on the 'science of complexity' and its
implications for our understanding of divine creation.

These and other issues are referred to in the 'Supplementary
Notes' to this reprinting in which I have tried to give an indication of later developments with pointers to convenient sources
of the relevant literature. However, a few words are appropriate
here about certain broader features of the original edition.

In a key section of the work (Chapter IV: III, IV) I tried to work
out a model of God as Agent of the processes of the world by
making an analogy to a non-dualist understanding of the
agency of human beings with respect to their own individual
bodily actions. The analogy had its strengths but also its weaknesses—not least because God is transcendent in relation to the
world as its *Creator* which is not the case with the experienced
transcendence of human intentional thinking in relation to the
bodies in which we act. I invoked the term 'transcendence-in-
immanence' to try to express the point about God's relation to
the world. Moreover, in developing this idea I found myself
making a familiar distinction (p. 138)—by analogy with the distinction between the unconscious control of bodily activities by
the central nervous system and self-conscious, willed acts—
between the general and regular patterns of events in the world
created by God ('general providence') and those presumed to be

initiated by God for specific purposes ('special providence'). Hence, I suggested 'God's purposes would then be expected to be read more explicitly in some events and processes than in others' (p. 138). But I did not fully expound, until the first edition of my *Theology for a Scientific Age*[2] in 1990, *how* God might be coherently conceived as influencing particular patterns of events in the world to implement specific divine purposes.

Such events, or patterns of events, are what are currently referred to as the results of 'Special Divine Action' (SDA) and attempts to understand how these could occur without any divine intervention in the divinely-endowed regularities of natural processes have been the central theme of intense discussions over the last decade or so, most notably in the published volumes of the Vatican Observatory and the Center for Theology and the Natural Sciences, Berkeley, generated by the research consultations they organized (references in the Supplementary Notes). The focus has been on the possibility of interpreting SDA in the light of the indeterminacy of quantum events, of the unpredictability of the trajectories of chaotic systems and of whole-part influence, or 'top–down causation', in complex systems. There is currently no consensus on this key issue, the failure of which to be resolved in supporting 'anything like the "traditional understanding" of God's activity in the world',[3] constitutes a crisis in contemporary theology, N. Saunders goes so far as to assert.[4]

Be that as it may, I myself still see considerable potentialities[5] in developing the notion that God's interaction with the world includes a whole-part, pattern-forming influence[6] on all-that-is —so that particular patterns of events can occur at lower levels in the hierarchy of complexity (including that of human-brains-in-human-bodies) which express God's particular intentions but do not abrogate the regularities pertaining to those levels. This potentiality becomes even more coherent in a panentheistic

---

[2] *Theology for a Scientific Age: Being and Becoming—Natural and Divine* (Blackwells, Oxford, 1990), pp. 151–65. I originally proposed divine whole-part influence (top–down causation) as a model for divine agency in 1987 (see n. 1 to my paper 'God's Interaction with the World' in *Chaos and Complexity*, ed. R. J. Russell, N. Murphy, and A. R. Peacocke (Vatican Observatory and Center for Theology and the Natural Sciences, University of Notre Dame Press, Notre Dame, Ind., 1995), p. 263).

[3] In *Divine Action and Modern Science* (Cambridge University Press, Cambridge, 2003), p. 215.

[4] Loc. cit.

perspective to which reference is also made in the Supplementary Notes.

Finally *a personal comment*: Regret had frequently been expressed to me by teachers and investigators in the field of 'religion and science' that the original edition of *Creation and the World of Science* was no longer available for classes or for private usage and I can only hope that this reprinting will continue to generate some reproduction of the verve and intellectual excitement I experienced in engaging in the 1970s with those daunting issues that are still with us and the resolution of which is vital to the refreshing of religion and to its providing the sciences with a fruitful milieu for their continued advance for the enlightenment and benefit of humanity.

Arthur Peacocke
June 2003

A note on the language of the 1979 printing

A feature which may strike a third-millennium reader is that the language of the 1979 printing appears to be non-gender-inclusive. Nothing could have been further from my intentions at that time, as manifest in the strong arguments put forward in the text (pp. 141–4) for the attribution of feminine language to God to represent God's nature especially in relation to divine, creative activity. I intended this as an overt correction to the use of male language to depict God, but followed the conventions of the day in the rest of the volume until I could argue the matter more fully at the point indicated. Since that time the widespread use of neologisms such as 'Godself' has enabled one to avoid the use of male personal pronouns in referring to God in some constructions and that is my current usage—always using 'God' instead of 'He/he' for the divine, repetitive as this often turns out to be because of the limitations of the English language.

[5] As outlined for the general reader in my *Paths from Science towards God: The End of All Our Exploring* (Oneworld, Oxford, 2001), pp. 108 ff.

[6] Cf. the scientific concept of 'information' and the theological concept of the *Logos*/Word of God active in the world.

The use of the word 'man', with or without a capital M, but certainly without the definite or indefinite article, was the customary word in Britain in 1979 for referring to humanity or 'humankind': for example, the *Shorter Oxford English Dictionary* (Clarendon Press, Oxford, 1974) gives as the first meanings of 'man' the following: '**Man** . . . plural **men** . . . I.1. A human being . . . Now surviving in general or indefinite applications in the sense 'person' (e.g., with *every, any, no,* and in the plural with *all, any, some,* etc.). 2. In generic sense, without article: The human creature regarded abstractly: hence the human race or species, mankind. In *Zoology*: The human creature or race viewed as a genus of animals . . .'.

Hence my usage[7] at that time of 'man' and 'men' was fully inclusive, as I intended it to be. But times and customs have changed and I can only hope that my intentions then are not now misconstrued since it would not have been practicable in a reprinting to alter the whole text in accordance with contemporary usage.

---

[7] Cf. J. Z. Young's *An Introduction to the Study of Man* (Clarendon Press, Oxford, 1971) which is certainly as much, if not more, about female humanity as male humanity; and J. Bronowski's popular *The Ascent of Man* (BBC, London, 1973).

Acknowledgements

Grateful acknowledgement is made for permission to reproduce from the following copyright works:

COOMARASWAMY: *The Dance of Shiva*. Reprinted by permission of the publishers, Peter Owen Ltd. London.

DANTE: *The Divine Comedy: Il Paradiso*, translated by Barbara Reynolds and Dorothy Sayers (Penguin Books, 1962). Reprinted by permission of David Higham Associates.

T. S. ELIOT: *Four Quartets*, 'Little Gidding'. Copyright 1943 by T. S. Eliot; copyright 1971 by Esme Valerie Eliot. Reprinted by permission of the publishers, Faber & Faber Ltd., and Harcourt, Brace Jovanovich, Inc.

P. LAGERKVIST: *Evening Land* (Aftonland), translated by W. H. Auden and Leif Sjöberg. Reprinted by permission of the publishers, Souvenir Press Ltd., and Wayne State University Press.

J. MOLTMANN: *The Crucified God*, translated by R. A. Wilson and John Bowden. Copyright © 1974 by SCM Press Ltd. Reprinted by permission of the publishers, SCM Press Ltd., and Harper and Row, Publishers, Inc.

J. MOLTMANN: 'Creation and Redemption', in *Creation, Christ and Culture* edited by R. W. A. McKinney (T. & T. Clark Ltd., 1976). Reprinted by permission of the author.

Contents

I. THE TWO BOOKS

I. INTRODUCTION: THE TWO BOOKS   1

II. THE RELATION OF SCIENCE AND RELIGION   7

   A. The historical background   7
   B. Science and Christian faith today   14
      (i) Changes in science   15
      (ii) Changes in theology   16
      (iii) Science, theology, and the sociology of knowledge   17

III. THE RELEVANCE OF NATURAL SCIENCE TO THEOLOGY   22

IV. THE INTENTIONS OF NATURAL SCIENCE AND THEOLOGY   27

   A. The social-anthropological context   27
   B. The quest for intelligibility, explanation, and meaning: asking 'Why?'   33

V. TALK OF GOD AS CREATOR   38

   A. The need for models   38
   B. Models of creation in the Judeo-Christian tradition   41

VI. SCIENCE AND CREATION TODAY   46

II. COSMOS, MAN, AND CREATION

I. INTRODUCTION: IMMENSITY   50

II. THE TRANSFORMATION OF THE SCIENTIFIC WORLD-VIEW THROUGH TWENTIETH-CENTURY PHYSICS AND COSMOLOGY   52

   A. The twilight of the absolute gods of space, time, object, and determinism   52
   B. The scientific world-view today   55
      (i) Space, time, object, and determinism   55
      (ii) Evolution   59

(iii) A continuous, law-like nexus   60
(iv) Emergence   61
(v) Comparison of classical and contemporary
          scientific world-views   61

III. NEW PERSPECTIVES ON THE RELATION
      BETWEEN MAN AND THE UNIVERSE   63

A.   The expansion of human consciousness and its
          limitations   63
B.   A cognizing and self-cognizing universe?   65
C.   The anthropic principle   67

IV. CHANCE AND NECESSITY IN AN 'ENSEMBLE' OF
     UNIVERSES   69

V.   MAN'S EMERGENCE IN THE UNIVERSE   72

VI. THE SEARCH FOR INTELLIGIBILITY AND MEANING
     IN SCIENCE AND IN THE JUDEO-CHRISTIAN
     TRADITION   74

VII. THE DOCTRINE OF CREATION IN THE LIGHT
     OF THE SCIENTIFIC WORLD-VIEW   77

A.   Some clarifications   77
B.   'Creatio continua'   79
C.   Biblical concepts of creation   81
D.   The value of creation apart from man   84

III. CHANCE AND THE LIFE-GAME

I.   CHANCE   86

A.   'Chance' in literature   87
B.   Two meanings of 'chance'   90

II. THE LIFE-GAME   92

A.   Mutations and evolution (Monod)   92
B.   Thermodynamics of living organisms and
          dissipative systems (Prigogine)   97
C.   The origin of living molecular systems (Eigen)   101
D.   Chance-and-law as creative   103

III. CHANCE AND THE DOCTRINE OF CREATION   104

A.   Relevance of the life-game   104
B.   The music of creation   105
C.   The dance of creation   106
D.   The 'play' of God in creation   108

IV. NATURE'S HIERARCHIES—'THINGS VISIBLE AND INVISIBLE'

   I.   REDUCTIONISM   112

       A. The hierarchy of natural systems   113
       B. The hierarchy of theories   114
       C. Methodological reduction   115
       D. The hierarchy of the sciences   116
       E. Theory autonomy   117
       F. Anti-reductionism and vitalism   118

   II.   THE MENTAL AND THE MATERIAL   119

       A. 'Interfaces'   119
       B. Dualism   122
           (i) The occult and pseudo-science   122
           (ii) Demons and Christian belief   124
       C. Monism: panpsychism   125
       D. 'Materialism'   128
       E. Mind–body identity   128

   III.   MAN AS AGENT: GOD AS AGENT   131

       A. Man as agent   131
       B. God as agent   133
       C. 'Meaning' within the physical nexus 135

   IV.   MODIFICATIONS OF THE MODEL OF GOD AS AGENT   137

       A. Unconscious acts and conscious agents 137
       B. The God–world dualism   138
       C. Other models   139
           (i) Ways of God being God   139
           (ii) Process theology   140
           (iii) A spatial model (pan-en-theism) 141
           (iv) A biological model   141

   V.   CONCLUSION: A CREATOR WHO COMMUNICATES MEANING   144

V. THE 'SELFISH GENE' AND 'WHAT MEN LIVE BY'

   I.   INTRODUCTION   147

   II.   WHAT IS MAN IN THE LIGHT OF THE SCIENCES?   149

   III.   THE PROCESSES OF EVOLUTION   154
           (i) Continuity   155

  (ii) Interplay of chance and law   155
 (iii) Emergence   155
  (iv) Trends in evolution   155
   (v) Complexity   158
  (vi) Mechanism of biological evolution   160
 (vii) New life through death of the old   164
(viii) Open-ended character of evolution   167

IV. THE EMERGENCE OF MAN   169

    A. 'Evolution' becomes 'history'   169
    B. Sociobiology   170
    C. 'Memes' and survival   177

V. WHAT DO MEN LIVE BY?   179

    A. Man has biological needs   179
    B. Man needs to come to terms with his own death   179
    C. Man needs to come to terms with his finitude 181
    D. Man needs to learn how to bear suffering   182
    E. Man needs to realize his potentialities and to
        steer his path through life   182

VI. THE TENSION BETWEEN BELIEF IN GOD AS
     CREATOR AND APPRAISAL OF THE EVOLVED
     NATURE OF MAN   185

VI. EVOLVED MAN AND GOD INCARNATE

I. THE RELEVANCE OF THEOLOGY TO ANY VIEW
    OF MAN   187

II. THEOLOGICAL APPRAISALS OF MAN   188

    A. The biblical view   188
        (i) Man: a psychosomatic unity and in the
             'image of God'   189
       (ii) The 'Fall' of man   190
    B. Man's sin   192
        (i) As a 'falling short'   192
       (ii) As a failure to realize potentiality   193
    C. Man: in tension between self-centredness and
        openness   194
    D. Man: the unfulfilled paradox   195

III. THE DOCTRINE OF CREATION IN THE LIGHT OF
      THE EMERGENCE OF MAN   196

IV. OUR UNDERSTANDING OF GOD'S RELATION TO
THE WORLD IN THE LIGHT OF THE
KNOWLEDGE AFFORDED BY THE NATURAL
SCIENCES 203

A. Immanence 204
B. Transcendence 204
C. God in the world and the world in God 205
    (i) 'Logos' 205
    (ii) God as 'Spirit' 206
    (iii) The world within God: pan-en-theism 207
D. The God who unveils his meaning in the various
and distinctive levels of nature's hierarchies 208
E. God as 'exploring' and 'composing' through a
continuous, open-ended process of emergence 209
F. The possibility of God conveying meaning
through the transcendence-in-immanence of
the personal ('incarnation') 211
G. The conjecture of God as self-offering and
suffering Love active in creation 213
H. Summary 214

V. THE 'LONG SEARCH' 214

VI. WHY IS JESUS OF NAZARETH RELEVANT TO
MAN'S SEARCH FOR MEANING AND
INTELLIGIBILITY? 218

VII. WHAT IS THE SIGNIFICANCE OF THE LIFE,
DEATH, AND RESURRECTION OF JESUS FOR
MAN (in his search today for God's
meaning in a creation described by the
natural sciences)? 227

    (i) Self-offering and suffering Love active in
creation 229
    (ii) God conveying meaning through the
personal: 'incarnation'? 230
    (iii) 'Non-reducible', 'open-ended', 'emergent',
'continuous' 232
    (iv) The God who unveils his meaning in various
and distinctive levels 233
    (v) The world 'within God': 'pan-en-theism' 238
    (vi) God transcendent and immanent 239

VIII. IMPLICATIONS OF THE MEANING FOR EVOLVED
MAN OF WHAT GOD WAS UNVEILING IN
JESUS THE CHRIST 244

VII.   MAN IN CREATION

    I.   INTRODUCTION   255

   II.   THE WORLD ECOSYSTEM   258

       A. Ecosystems   258
       B. Man and the ecosystems   260

  III.   PROGNOSES   265

  IV.   THEOLOGY AND ECOLOGICAL VALUES   270

       A. Are they connected?   270
       B. The Judeo-Christian doctrine of creation and
           attitudes to nature   274
          (i) The biblical doctrine of creation   274
              (a) Creation as good, ordered, and of value
                  to God   279
              (b) Nature as desacralized, revalued, and
                  historicized   279
              (c) Man's place in nature: 'dominion'   281
              (d) Man: the image and likeness of God 283
              (e) Man: in rebellion   285
         (ii) Traditional post-biblical Christian theolog
             and attitudes to nature   287

       C. Assessment of the traditional Judeo-Christian
          'models' of creation in relation to ecological
          values   291

    V.   MAN'S ROLE IN CREATION RECONSIDERED   294

       A. Man as priest of creation   295
       B. Man as vicegerent, steward, manager of creation 297
       C. Man as symbiont, with reverence for creation   298
       D. Man as interpreter, prophet, lover, trustee, and
          preserver of creation   300
       E. Man as co-creator, co-worker, and co-explorer
          with God the Creator   304
       F. 'Incarnation' and man as co-creator with God   306
       G. Man as fellow-sufferer in creation   311

  VI.   'ECOLOGICAL VALUES' AND THE DOCTRINE OF
       CREATION   312

 VII.   CONCLUSION   315

       END-NOTE   317

VIII. CREATION AND HOPE

I. INTRODUCTION 319

II. THE FUTURE—ACCORDING TO SCIENCE 320

    A. The future on the Earth 322
    B. The future of the Earth 324
    C. The future of the galaxy and of the universe 326

III. BEGINNING AND END IN THE BIBLE 330

IV. FUTURE AND HOPE IN CONTEMPORARY
THEOLOGY 333

    A. The meaning of the future 333
        (i) The theologians of hope 334
        (ii) The Teilhardian theologians 338
        (iii) The process theologians 339
    B. The future and God 342
        (i) The theologians of hope 342
        (ii) The Teilhardian theologians 345
        (iii) The process theologians 346

V. CREATION AND HOPE IN CONTEMPORARY
THEOLOGY 347

        (i) The theologians of hope 348
        (ii) The Teilhardian theologians 348
        (iii) The process theologians 349

VI. HOPE IN CREATION 350

VII. CONCLUSION 355

    CODA 358

    APPENDICES 360

    A. MODERN ATOMIC PHYSICS AND EASTERN
       MYSTICAL THOUGHT 360
    B. 'NATURE' 364
    C. REDUCTIONISM AND RELIGION-AND-
       SCIENCE: 'THE QUEEN OF THE SCIENCES'? 367

    SUPPLEMENTARY NOTES FOR THE PAPERBACK
    EDITION 372
    INDEX OF NAMES 385
    SUBJECT INDEX 391

I

The Two Books

In November 1972 in San Francisco I was startled to read in its daily paper the headline 'God versus Evolution Decision —Move over Darwin'! The report began:

The State Curriculum Commission gave up its three-year fight yesterday to keep Eden from getting equal billing with Darwin in the State's science textbooks ... The new criteria adopted by the commission, which recommends material in textbooks, would allow use of both divine creation and evolution as opposing theories in the new science textbooks scheduled to be chosen at the Board of Education's December meeting. Charles Darwin's Theory of Evolution is now offered as the sole explanation for man's origin in science textbooks throughout California, but the practice has been under attack for nearly a decade by fundamentalists ... The new guide lines would allow books to discuss the 'how' of man's origin but would prohibit them from mentioning 'ultimate causes' of life. They would have to avoid, then, naming either God or the random chemical reactions of several billion years ago that evolutionists say led to living cells.[1]

I am glad to be able to add that this report also included a statement by the Episcopal Dean of Grace Cathedral in San Francisco, who called the Board's framework 'incredible, appalling and preposterous'. Later the distinguished geneticist, Theodosius Dobzhansky, then living in California, described to me with some chagrin the turgid political background to this decision—for he had been one of the witnesses to the Curriculum Commission because of his scientific work and his links with the Orthodox Church. His remarks are scarcely repeatable in this context, but what is repeatable is a resolution

[1] *San Franciso Chronicle*, 10 Nov. 1972.

passed by the National Academy of Sciences, at its meeting in October of that year. They resolved:

WHEREAS we understand that the California State Board of Education is considering a requirement that textbooks for use in the public-schools give parallel treatment to the theory of evolution and to belief in special creation; and
WHEREAS the essential procedural foundations of science exclude appeal to supernatural causes as a concept not susceptible to validation by objective criteria; and
WHEREAS religion and science are, therefore, separate and mutually exclusive realms of human thought whose presentation in the same context leads to misunderstanding of both scientific theory and religious belief; and
WHEREAS, further, the proposed action would almost certainly impair the proper segregation of the teaching and understanding of science and religion nationwide, therefore
We, the members of the National Academy of Science, assembled at the Autumn 1972 meeting, urge that textbooks of the sciences, utilized in the public schools of the nation, be limited to the exposition of scientific matters.[2]

The view expressed in the third 'WHEREAS', that 'religion and science are ... separate and mutually exclusive realms of human thought ...', is widely held not only by scientists, but also by philosophers and, indeed, by many Christian theologians. I shall have cause later to examine, in various contexts, whether or not the 'uneasy truce between science and theology' as the present Bishop of Durham, Dr John Habgood, called it in 1962,[3] has as firm a basis as these resolutions seem to imply.

For the moment, let us merely note that the irruption of that controversy into the educational scene in the United States —and, more recently, of a similar one here in England about a certain teacher's insistence on giving a literalist interpretation of the book of Genesis to school children—shows that, for many, the understandings of the world afforded by science and Christianity are not as easily kept in watertight compartments as the National Academy of Sciences and others might wish.

[2] Quoted by W. H. Austin, *The Relevance of Natural Science to Theology* (Macmillan, London, 1976), pp. 1–2.
[3] J. Habgood, 'The Uneasy Truce between Science and Religion', in *Soundings*, ed. A. R. Vidler (Cambridge University Press, Cambridge, 1963), pp. 21–41.

In passing their resolutions the National Academy were being true to a tradition about the *modus vivendi* between science and religion which has a distinguished history. John Wallis, the Savilian Professor of Geometry in Oxford from 1649 until his death in 1703 (fifty-four years later!) wrote in the following terms in 1678, concerning the early meetings which led to the formation of the 'Royal Society of London for the improving of natural knowledge':

I take its *first Ground and Foundation* to have been in *London*, about the year 1645. (if not sooner) when the same *Dr. Wilkins* ... [*et al.*] ... with my self and some others, met weekly ... at a certain day and hour ... with certain Rules agreed upon amongst us. Where (to avoid diversion to other discourses, and for some other reasons) we barred all Discourses of Divinity, of State-Affairs and of News, (other than what concern'd our business of Philosophy) confining ourselves to Philosophical Inquiries, and such as related thereto ...[4]

We may have our suspicions about the 'some other reasons', no doubt prudent ones, for barring 'Discourses on Divinity' in 1645, but their more positive reasons, relevant to us, for keeping apart natural philosophy and divinity are quite apparent. And their origin is not hard to find. For the charter deed of natural philosophy, science, in the English-speaking world in the seventeenth century was undoubtedly Francis Bacon's *The Advancement of Learning* of 1605 where the metaphor of the two books, the Book of Scripture and the Book of Nature, has its *locus classicus*:

Let no man, upon a weak conceit of sobriety or an ill-applied modera-tion, think or maintain, that a man can search too far or be too well studied in the book of God's word or in the book of God's works; divinity or philosophy; but rather let men endeavour an endless progress or proficience in both; only let men beware that they apply both to charity, and not to swelling; to use, and not to ostentation; and again, that they do not unwisely mingle or confound these learn-ings together.[5]

As F. E. Manuel told us in his Fremantle Lectures on Newton

[4] John Wallis, *A Defence of the Royal Society, etc.* (London, 1678), quoted by D. McKie, 'The origins and foundation of the Royal Society of London', in *The Royal Society—its Origins and Founders*, ed. H. Hartley (The Royal Society, London, 1960), pp. 11–12.
[5] Francis Bacon, *The Advancement of Learning*, The First Book, i. 3 (ed. W. A. Arm-strong, Athlone Press, London, 1975), p. 55, *ll.* 30–8.

at Balliol College in 1973, 'In general, the metaphor of the
two books served a reasonable political purpose for the advancement of science—it was a *modus vivendi*'[6] and it continued to
serve to protect science from the inroads of theology, and vice
versa—as witness its adoption 300 years later in a quite different
milieu, that of European continental 'neo-orthodoxy' of the
1930s, as represented, in this instance, by Emil Brunner: 'There
is no religion in which there is not some sort of surmise of the
Creator. But men have never known Him rightly. The book of
Nature does not suffice to reveal the Creator aright to such
unintelligent and obdurate pupils as ourselves. The Creator has
therefore given us another, even more clearly written book in
which to know Him—the Bible.'[7]

Newton himself, in spite of the immense intellectual energy
which he devoted to 'divinity', when he was President of the
Royal Society banned anything related to religion, even
apologetics. His ban clearly did not arise from personal indifference to the Christian faith. Robert Boyle, in many ways
a profounder and better-equipped theologian than Newton,
also conformed with this public stance *qua* natural philosopher,
albeit he was deeply convinced, to quote his own words, that
'... there are two chief ways to arrive at the knowledge of
God's attributes; the contemplation of his works, and the study
of his word'.[8] In his own extensive theological writings, more
public than Newton's, he explicitly developed these themes,
most notably in *The Christian Virtuoso* (1690) which aims to
show that 'by being addicted to Experimental Philosophy a Man
is rather assisted than indisposed to be a good Christian'. No
doubt there is an element here of allaying the suspicions of the
more conservative critics, both religious and political, in
defence of the 'new philosophy', with its new Royal Society,
and also of weaning the *virtuosi* of the new philosophy away

---

[6] F. E. Manuel, *The Religion of Isaac Newton* (Clarendon Press, Oxford, 1974), p. 31.
[7] E. Brunner, *Our Faith* (SCM Press, London, 1941), p. 25.
[8] R. Boyle, *The High Veneration Due to God* (1685). Reproduced in *The Philosophical
Works of the Hon. Robert Boyle, Esq.*, ed. Peter Shaw, London, 1725, Vol. ii, p. 264.
Boyle goes on to say that, as these are the two chief ways of arriving at the knowledge
of God's attributes, so 'it may be doubted whether either, or both of these, will suffice
to acquaint us with all his perfections' for '... how can we be sure, but so perfect,
and exuberant a Being [as God], has excellencies not expressed in the visible world
or any of its known parts' (loc. cit., p. 265).

from any incipient tendency to atheism. Thomas Sprat, the writer of the first history of the Royal Society in 1667, went so far as to allay the fears of churchmen by affirming

That *the Church of England* will not only be safe amidst the consequences of a *Rational Age*, but amidst all the improvements of *Knowledge*, and the subversion of old *Opinions* about *Nature*, and introduction of new ways of Reasoning thereon. This will be evident, when we behold the agreement that is between the present *Design* of the *Royal Society*, and that of our *Church* in its beginning. They both may lay equal claim to the word *Reformation*; the one having compassed it in *Religion*, the other purposing it in *Philosophy*. They both have taken a like cours to bring this about; each of them passing by the *corrupt Copies*, and referring themselves to the *perfect Originals* for their instruction; the one to the Scripture, the other to the large Volume of the *Creatures*. . . . They both suppose alike, that their *Ancestors* might err; and yet retain a sufficient reverence for them. . . . ever since that time [of King Edward VI and Elizabeth I] *Experimental Learning* has still retain'd som vital heat, though it wanted the opportunities of ripening itself, which now it injoys. The *Church of England* therefore may justly be styl'd the *Mother* of this sort of *Knowledge*; and so the care of its *nourishment* and prosperity peculiarly lyes upon it.[9]

(Would that we could say the same today of the Church of England, suspicious though there is reason for us to be of Thomas Sprat's own motives and actions in the history of the times!)

Newton and Boyle were not alone in simultaneously avoiding questions of divinity in their public natural philosophizing and yet privately being intensely interested in the repercussions of that activity on their theological reflections. For many others of the founder and early members of the Royal Society earned their livelihoods in ecclesiastical positions or as university scholars in orders and they studied both books diligently, some with less of the coolness of Francis Bacon's admonitions and more of the fervour of a Thomas Browne who in his *Religio Medici* of 1643 had urged:

The World was made to be inhabited by Beasts but studied and contemplated by Man; 'tis the Debt of our Reason we owe unto God, and the homage we pay for not being Beasts . . . The Wisdom of

[9] Thomas Sprat, *The History of the Royal Society of London for the Improving of Natural Knowledge* (London, 1702, 2nd edn.), pp. 370–2.

God receives small honour from those of vulgar Heads that rudely stare about, and with a gross rusticity admire his works: those highly magnifie him, whose judicious inquiry into his Acts, and deliberate research into his Creatures, return the duty of a devout and learned admiration.[10]

This fervour did—it must be admitted—in those who followed Newton and Boyle tend to overreach itself in an especially English kind of 'physico-theology' which, in spite of the 'castigations' of Newton (in reference to William Derham's *Physico-Theology, or a Demonstration of the Being and Attributes of God from his Works of Creation*, 1713), spawned a genre of literature which had immense influence on ordinary believers. Thus the biologist John Ray's *Wisdom of God Manifested in the Works of Creation*, 1691, went through four editions in his own lifetime and seventeen more by 1850[11] and typified a growing flood of literature culminating in William Paley's *View of the Evidences of Christianity* (1749) and the famous work of 1802 which covered more thoroughly some of the same ground, namely his *Natural Theology* (or *Evidences of the Existence and Attributes of the Deity collected from the Appearances of Nature*). Both were vastly influential books and Charles Darwin still had to 'get up' the former for his BA examination in 1831. And, let it be noted lest we be inclined to scorn, that 'careful study' of both of these works (and of Paley's *Principles of Moral and Political Philosophy* (1785)), Darwin later attested in his *Autobiography* 'was the only part of the academical course which, as I then felt, and as I still believe, was of the least use to me in the education of my mind'.[12] It is one of the ironies of the history of evolutionary thought, of course, that it was Darwin's own proposal of adaptation through *natural* selection which finally demolished Paley's own 'argument from design', based on the aptness of biological adaptation. Paley's *Evidences* was, indeed, still one of the options as late as 1919 in the 'Little-go' (Previous) Examination in Cambridge—so the 'argument' had a very long lease.

[10] Thomas Browne, *Religio Medici*, i. 13, ed. G. Keynes (Faber & Gwyer, London, 1928), p. 18.

[11] G. Keynes, *J. Ray: a Bibliography* (Faber & Faber, London, 1951; repr. van Heusden, Amsterdam, 1976), pp. 91–106.

[12] C. Darwin, *Autobiography*, ed. F. Darwin (Murray, London, 1902, 2nd edn.), Ch. II, p. 18.

Perhaps Darwin can hardly be described as an 'ordinary believer'—certainly not 'ordinary' and scarcely, later on, a 'believer'—yet it was ordinary believers who absorbed not only Ray and Paley but also that great communicator to the people, John Wesley, in his own contribution of this kind, *A Survey of the Wisdom of God in Creation* (1770). There is little doubt therefore, that in practice (and wasn't it Wittgenstein who said that philosophical analysis, if properly done, 'leaves everything as it is'?) that the language 'game' of ordinary Christian believers and that of science interact, however much the sophisticated may deplore the process. Even in more intellectual circles, who can doubt that the Copernican Revolution in astronomy altered man's understanding of his relative position *ontologically* as well as spatially in the universe? Or that the development of geology as a science, with the discovery of the historical character of the Earth's processes, had an effect on man's view of himself and his own history which was dramatically compounded when, after Darwin, man found himself a natural part of the history of organic life on the earth's surface? Some of these effects of change in the scientific world-view on belief systems, Christian, religious, or otherwise, were, of course, partly psychological. But few were entirely so, and in many cases there was a genuine new theological question which had to be posed in response to a shift in the understanding of the natural world.

II. THE RELATION OF SCIENCE AND RELIGION

A. *The historical background*

Thus the contents of the Two Books which God had been presumed to set before mankind for his illumination, interacted in ways which Francis Bacon, perhaps, might not have anticipated. Unwise though it is to attempt to generalize about such a complex development, we need to look a little more closely at the history of the relation between the Two Books in order to provide the setting for understanding their present relation, especially in connection with the idea of creation, with which these lectures will be principally concerned. For there are still many voices raised today to ask, if not 'what has Athens to do with Jerusalem?', at least 'what has South Parks Road to do with (what shall we say?)—Pusey Street?'.[13] My hesitation is not inappropriate, for the relative ease of locating geographically the scientific activities in this University and the relative difficulty of so locating the theological is not without its parallel in their respective assessment by many Western intellectuals. The received wisdom is that the stream of scientific development, rising from muddy and doubtful sources, has clarified itself of all pollutions and diversions, and now flows clear and direct on into that wide ocean of yet undiscovered truth, on whose shore the great Newton conceived himself as playing like a boy diverting himself 'in now and then finding a smoother pebble and prettier shell than ordinary'; whereas, although the springs of religion *may*, some concede, have begun pure, its course was soon diverted in a confusion worse than that of the Nile's delta—its ultimate destination a stagnant pool! Historical studies, however, suggest otherwise.

Many factors seem to have contributed to the emergence of modern science in Western Christendom, in the formation, for example, of the attitudes of the founders of the Royal Society and so (it would seem) of today's National Academy of Sciences of the USA. These factors have operated in various modes— economic, cultural, practical, psychological, and theoretical, yet since the seminal article of Michael Foster in 1934[14] there has been a strong case for the proposition that the Judeo-Christian doctrine of creation[15] was of major significance in

[13] In Oxford, South Parks Road is the location of many of the scientific laboratories, and Pusey Street of Pusey House (Anglican), housing the Theology Faculty Library, and Regent's Park College (Baptist).

[14] M. B. Foster, 'The Christian Doctrine of Creation and the Rise of Modern Natural Science', *Mind*, 43 (1934), 446–68, reprinted in *Science and Religious Belief*, ed. C. A. Russell (University of London and Open University Press, London, 1973), pp. 294 ff. The case continues to receive support e.g. R. Hooykass, *Religion and the Rise of Modern Science* (Scottish Academic Press, Edinburgh, 1972).

[15] It is, of course, an over-simplification to refer to a 'Judeo-Christian' doctrine of creation, for there have been divergencies, at least of emphasis, between the Jewish and Christian doctrines The former has not, by and large, emphasised much a doctrine of 'original sin', with the problems that that can lead to; and the latter has been modified by the doctrines of the Incarnation and of the Trinity. Even so, the main features of a biblically based doctrine of creation are common to both so, with the *caveat* understood, the doctrine will continue to be called 'Judeo-Christian', for brevity.

providing a philosophy of nature validating an empirical science, long before that science had produced enough assured results to make its presuppositions reputable. The absence of an empirical element in Greek natural science is attributable, Foster argued, to the assumption, of post-Socratic philosophers at least, that objects were intelligible in so far as they embodied form, which alone was intelligible, for

... if natural objects either are artefacts (according to the theory of the divine Demiurge) or are (according to the Aristotelian theory) in this respect analogous to artefacts that they *are* nothing but an embodiment of form, then the unavoidable element of contingency which they derive from their matter is nothing but a defect of their being. It does not make them something more than an embodiment of form, but makes them only a bad embodiment of form; just as two inches more on one leg of a table does not make it more than an artefact, but only a bad artefact.[16]

Since the embodiment of form in objects was defective, correspondingly, sensation of the material afforded only an imperfection of knowledge. This accounts for the absence of an empirical element in Greek science, which was modelled on the purely intellectual operations of geometry, with its idealization of lines and figures as the subject matter of its reflection.

Foster argues from this as follows:

The absence of an empirical element in Greek natural science follows from this. But the will of the maker can be subordinated to his reason ... only so long as 'making' is identified with formation, because form alone can be the object of reason. In the creative act the will must exceed any regulations which reason can prescribe. That is to say, the 'insubordination' of will to reason ... becomes essential to his [God's] activity so soon as he is thought of as Creator. It is what constitutes him....

The *voluntary* activity of the Creator (i.e. that in his activity which exceeds determination by reason) terminates on the *contingent* being of the creature (i.e. on that element of its being which eludes determination by form, namely its matter and the characteristics which it possesses *qua* material). If such voluntary activity is essential to God, it follows that the element of contingency is essential to what he creates. So soon as nature is conceived to be created by God, the contingent becomes more than an imperfection in the embodiment

[16] Foster, op. cit. (1973 reprinting), p. 310.

of form; it is precisely what constitutes a natural object more than an embodiment, namely a creature.

But the contingent is knowable only by sensuous experience. If, therefore, the contingent is essential to nature, experience must be indispensable to the science of nature; and *not* indispensable merely as a stage through which the human scientist must pass on his way to attaining adequate knowledge by reason, but indispensable because knowledge by reason cannot be adequate to a nature which is essentially something more than an embodiment of form. This 'something more', the element in nature which depends upon the *voluntary* activity of God, is incapable of becoming an object to reason, and science therefore must depend, in regard to this element, upon the *evidence* of sensation. The reliance upon the sense for evidence, not merely for illustration, is what constitutes the empirical character peculiar to modern natural science; and the conclusion follows that only a created nature is proper object of an empirical science.[17]

I have quoted Foster at some length to discredit the legend[18] of the inevitable 'warfare' between traditional theology and nascent science, but this is not to deny the influence of many other factors that still engage historians of science. One might well ask, for example, what it was in the intellectual climate of Western Christendom, rather than Eastern, that provided the cradle for empirical natural science. Was it the dominance of rationalistic Greek philosophy in Eastern thinking, rather than its submission to biblical thought, as in the synthesis and subsequent reformation of medieval scholasticism? For the biblical understanding of creation provided significant elements in the prelude to the emergence of empirical natural philosophy —in particular it desacralized, revalued, and historicized nature. For to affirm, with the Bible, that nature is created by God and is other than God, is to assert that nature is not itself divine, not even simply the external aspect of the divine reality. 'Man did not face a world full of ambiguous and capricious gods who were alive in the objects of the natural world. He had to do with one supreme creator God whose will was steadfast. Nature was thus abruptly desacralized,

[17] Ibid., pp. 310–11.
[18] Cf. J. W. Draper, *History of the Conflict between Religion and Science* (King, London, 1875); A. D. White, *A History of the Warfare of Science with Theology in Christendom* (Appleton, New York, 1896); J. Y. Simpson, *Landmarks in the Struggle Between Science and Religion* (Hodder & Stoughton, London, 1925).

stripped of many of its arbitrary, unpredictable, and doubtless terrifying aspects.'[19]

But although nature is not divine, in the biblical tradition it nevertheless has value, derived from the fact of creation and affirmed in the reiterated 'God saw that it was good' of Genesis.[20] Furthermore, in this tradition, nature has a history for it falls within the pattern of the outworking of God's will and purposes in time, in which he acts continuously and, more immediately, in human history in the experience of the Israelites. He is the 'living God' active in shaping history in his chosen direction, in response to human waywardness and shortcomings. This historical experience of the people of Israel was carried over into their understanding of God's ever-present action in nature which was regarded as not autonomous, as not to be personalized (in contrast with animist religions) and as moving to a consummation.

All this lies in the background to the emergence of natural science and makes intelligible the adoption of the metaphor of the Two Books in which God had made himself known—those of nature[21] and of the Scriptures. I have already mentioned that as empirical natural philosophy established itself, in the decades around the turn of the seventeenth century, there developed a 'physico-theology' which attempted to read every 'jot and tittle' of the Book of Nature as redolent of divine meaning—in a way not dissimilar to that employed at that time (and, regrettably, even now in some quarters) in the interpretation of the Scriptures. It is intriguing to observe how the same kind of error in the reading of the Two Books reinforced fantasy. What we would now regard as an uncritical biblical fundamentalism was often reinforced by a credulous and naïve 'physico-theology'.

The confinement of natural theology to elaboration of the argument from design, especially as evidenced in the intricacies of biological adaptation to environment, found, as I said, its

---

[19] T. S. Derr, *Ecology and Human Liberation* (WSCF book, World Council of Churches, Geneva, 1973, Vol iii, No. 1, Serial No. 7), p. 11; republished as *Ecology and Human Need* (Westminster Press, Philadelphia, 1975).

[20] Genesis 1: 10, 12, 18, 21, 25, 31 (AV).

[21] See Appendix B to Lecture VII (pp. 364–6) for further discussion of this ambiguous term.

classic expression in Paley's *Natural Theology* of 1802 and reached its zenith in the *Bridgewater Treatises* of 1833–6, in which the benefactor enjoined the authors to write on 'The Power, Wisdom and Goodness of God as manifested in the Creation; illustrating such work by all reasonable arguments ...' and went on to list a number of suitable topics. By this time natural theology had become completely identified with the 'argument from design', which tended to be exemplified, by some, at least, of these authors, by showing how thoughtfully everything had been arranged for the comfort of the world's inhabitants, and notably for Englishmen! These scientific authors, still, let us note, all Fellows of the Royal Society and many of them in Anglican orders, wrote while the fate of their expositions was already being sealed. For Charles Darwin was already, during the period of their publication, on HMS *Beagle* making those observations which, when he had taken the measure of them, and had read Lyell and Malthus, germinated his hypothesis concerning a *natural* means of biological transformation.

Darwin returned in 1836, and his great work appeared, after long gestation and then only because of Wallace's coming to similar conclusions, firstly in a paper parallel to Wallace's presented to the Linnean Society in 1858 and then in *The Origin of Species* in 1859. The reaction to this publication; the impressing on the public mind of what eventually became an archetypical myth, namely the 1860 meeting of the British Association in the University Museum in Oxford with its encounter between T. H. Huxley and Bishop Samuel Wilberforce; the not invariably acclamatory responses of scientists; the mixed and, not uniformly critical, response of divines; all continue to be the object of historical inquiry. Any who care to examine this fascinating literature will find many surprises awaiting any preconceived notions they may cherish about this controversy and its various participants. As David Lack, the much revered Oxford ornithologist, said in his excellent little book on the subject:

There is no need to repeat here either the ill-founded attacks of churchmen on Darwinism, which have often been recalled, or the ill-founded attacks of Darwinists on the Church, which are usually forgotten. It is enough to say that, while many churchmen, both

Roman Catholic and Protestant, showed a lamentable ignorance of the findings and the principles of biology, the same could be said of various Darwinists in relation to theology. Mixed up with the truth, there were ignorant, unjustifiable, absurd and violent assertions on both sides, and it is perhaps through the spirit of the age that we remember the arrogance of the conservative theologians rather than of revolutionary Darwinists.[22]

Then, as now, the participants were basically divided into, on the one hand, the *reconcilers*, who thought Darwinism and evolution compatible with Christian belief; and, on the other hand, the *irreconcilers*, who thought them incompatible, either on behalf of an infallible religion or on behalf of an all-embracing science. On the whole, the irreconcilers, of both kinds, that is, both pro- and anti-Christian, made the most noise and so created the situation we still, by and large, inherit— of the Christian religion and natural science retreating to their respective territories, leaving a no-man's-land between, enshrouded in the numbing silence of the 'uneasy truce'.

This situation has not been without its rationalizations on both sides, in spite of the innate conviction we all have that there should be a unity of truth and that contradictions are not bearable. I have already recalled the appeal of the National Academy of Sciences, as recently as 1972, to a classic insistence on religion and science as being 'separate and mutually exclusive realms of thought', a position which certainly does not do justice to the complexities of the historical realities of the interaction of science and Christian faith. But some theologians, too, notably Karl Barth, also retreated into citadels of their own construction, and echoed similar sentiments from the other side of the no-man's-land.

For Barth, and many of his followers, the relation between the realms of nature and grace, between the sphere of the corrupt human intellect and the pure Word of God, between the created and the Creator, was simply and starkly that of a 'great gulf fixed' with no possible traffic, that man could initiate, between the two realms. The only possible move was for God to speak his Word in revelation (which meant, in practice, through Scripture) and man accepting it in faith. For

[22] D. Lack, *Evolutionary Theory and Christian Belief* (Methuen, London, 1957), p. 18.

Barth and his followers, the doctrine of creation was an article of *faith*: it was not knowledge which a man might procure for himself or which would ever be accessible to observation or logic, with respect to which man has no uncorrupted faculty or facility. To quote Barth:

The insight that man owes his existence and form, together with all the reality distinct from God, to God's creation, is achieved *only* in the reception and answer of the divine self-witness, that is, only in faith in Jesus Christ, i.e. in the knowledge of the unity of Creator and creature actualised in Him, and in the life in the present mediated by Him, under the right and in the experience of the goodness of the Creator towards His creature.[23]

It is not surprising that that doughty exponent of the British tradition in natural theology and of Anglican incarnational theology, Charles Raven, 'naturalist, historian and theologian' as his biographer[24] rightly calls him, should have opposed Barth's theology in trenchant, and sometimes acrid, terms.[25]

It was in this atmosphere of uneasy, cautious truce that my generation of scientists grew up—a truce broken only by the unforgettable voice of Charles Raven himself, by then Regius Professor of Divinity in Cambridge, and also by that of Charles Coulson, Rouse Ball Professor of Applied Mathematics and then of Theoretical Chemistry in Oxford University, who, it is interesting to learn from Dr Dillistone, owed a great debt to Raven when, as a Cambridge undergraduate, the tension between his personal faith and newly acquired scientific knowledge became acute.[26]

B. *Science and Christian faith today*

However, in the last few years, a thaw has set in in these icy relationships and tracks are beginning to be made between the icefloes. Changes have occurred in the mood of both scientists and theologians.

---

[23] K. Barth, *Church Dogmatics*, trans. J. W. Edwards. D. Bussey, and H. Knight (T. & T. Clark, Edinburgh, 1958), Vol. iii, p. 3 (my italics).

[24] F. W. Dillistone, *Charles Raven* (Hodder & Stoughton, London, 1975).

[25] For a mild version entitled, significantly enough, 'On the recent reaction in theology', see Note IX, appended to Vol. i of his Gifford Lectures, *Natural Religion and Christian Theology: Science and Religion* (Cambridge University Press, Cambridge, 1953).

[26] Dillistone, op. cit., p. 210, n. 2.

(*i*) *Changes in science.* Thus, scientists have cause today to look back with nostalgia to the palmy days of ten or more years ago when they were assigned a role by society comparable only with that of the medieval priest. They not only had sources of knowledge and power not available to the ordinary person, they were not only supposed to 'deliver the goods', but they were also listened to with respect, and even awe, when they pronounced on non-scientific matters. Even the scientist not given to such pronouncements was flattered by this adulation —and not unwillingly accepted the research grants accorded to him by a grateful society!

All that has now changed—and one day the social historians will trace the formative influences (*inter alia* of the growing realization that the connection between investment in pure research and economic growth is tenuous and fragile; of the alarm about pollution; of well-publicized cases of the unpredictable and unexpected effects of the increasing use of drugs in medical therapy; and, supremely, of the nightmare possibility of nuclear warfare and of perpetual contamination from the use of nuclear energy—the bitter fruits of one of the most creative epochs of the human intellect, the great paradigmatic shifts in the concepts of physics in the early decades of this century). Thus, whether they have liked it or not, scientists across the whole spectrum of their activity—at first the physicists, then the biologists and medical scientists, and now more recently, to their particular surprise, the chemists and the molecular biologists—have all come face to face with baffling ethical problems and the possibly dire social consequences of, at least some, of their apparently 'pure' research. Society, in becoming more aware, and more alarmed, at the impact upon it of the work of the scientists has begun asking questions about their very human activity. This has made scientists more aware of the basis of the possibility of science being pursued at all in the norms of value-judgement in society (and we have been only too conscious of individual scientists, and indeed whole categories of scientists, who have suffered, and still do so, when and where this basis does not exist). Thus it has appeared more natural, and less forced than it might for over a hundred years, for the British Association for the Advancement of Science in 1973 to explore with the British

Council of Churches and with non-Christians the many ways
in which ethical problems arise from the practice of science,
and from its application to society—and for theologians and
bishops to work together on this Study Group with agnostic
and humanist scientists.[27]

These ethical pressures have begun to impinge on even the
most protected of the denizens of laboratories but there have
also been developments in the philosophy of science which, in
the long run, should have a great effect in modifying the well-
nigh universal assumption of scientists about their objectivity
—that they are engaged in an activity yielding real truth about
an objective world. The objective spectator of classical physics
has, as we shall discuss later, become the 'impossible' spectator,
certainly with respect to the sub-atomic and in frames of
reference moving with velocities anywhere approaching the
speed of light. Working scientists have always known that their
hypotheses are pre-eminently falsifiable and their models
usually temporary but, they have always hoped, converging
representations of an inaccessible reality. They are usually less
aware of how some of the great broad theories of science are
under-determined by the facts and how their experiments themselves are shaped by their theories from the moment of their
conception. These results of the intensive examination of the
philosophical foundations of modern science have had only a
marginal impact, so far, on the way scientists conceive of their
work. Yet consideration of such analyses of scientific method is
inescapable when the presumed status of scientific knowledge
is in question, as it inevitably is when relating science to
theological inquiry.

(*ii*) *Changes in theology.* That activity—I mean, Christian
theological inquiry, which I take to be the intellectual formulation and examination of the Christian experience—has also
had to move out of its neo-Barthian stronghold under a variety
of social and intellectual pressures which, again, it will be
intriguing for the historian eventually to map. Two of these
pressures seem to me to be as follows.

First, there is an increasing awareness not only among
Christian theologians, but even more among ordinary believers

---

[27] *The Sensitive Scientist* (Report of a British Association Study Group), D. Morley
(SCM Press, London, 1978).

that, if God is in fact the all-encompassing Reality that Christian faith proclaims, then that Reality is to be experienced in and through our actual lives as biological organisms who are persons, part of nature and living in society. So knowledge of nature and of society can never be irrelevant, to say the least, to our experience of God, if God is he whom the faith affirms.

Secondly, the neo-Barthian retreat into the pure Word of God available through the Scriptures is not a viable route. It is indeed circular, for the further it takes us away from the presumed fallibilities of our natural minds to the supposed divine word in Scripture, the closer it brings us to the question 'How can we know that these scriptures, this tradition, is transmitting to us the genuine Word of God?' And there is no answer to such questions without a resort to empirical inquiries into the nature of the biblical literature and of religious experience, as well as more philosophical inquiries into what we mean by such questions and the terms they contain, notably that of 'God' itself. It is indeed not a new feature in Christian history for dogmatic, indeed Olympian, affirmations of faith to be succeeded by cooler and more radical analysis. The pendulum has again swung this way today and inevitably leads to tension and insecurity among the faithful. At least it is some consolation that such are also not absent from the scientific community! While theologians engage in radical inquiry into the empirical foundations of their work, scientists seek out the values implicit in their activities—and both are surprised at themselves and not always too happy with the enforced exercise. For Christian theology, there can certainly now be no retreat into the citadel, and science and Christian theology cannot avoid encountering each other and thinking anew what kind of interrelationship they might have today in the light of new assessments of them both as inquiries and the internal development of their respective contents.

(*iii*) *Science, theology, and the sociology of knowledge.*   The *mise-en-scène* has however changed, for a new common factor—I almost said 'foe'—has come on to the stage, namely sociology. For the acid of the sociology of knowledge is, at least superficially, as corrosive of the presumed objectivity of science as it is of the presumed validity of dogmatic faith. To my observation, the sociology of knowledge is, indeed, more discomforting to scientists (sometimes to the point of apoplexy!) than to theologians, who have recognized far longer the social conditioning of religious belief. Although the sociology of scientific institutions has been actively studied ever since the second world war, particularly under the pioneering influence of R. K. Merton,[28] it is only relatively recently that scientific activity itself has been subjected to sociological analysis. Examples of the kind of questions being asked have been given by Barry Barnes:

Basic to these controversies [concerning the relationship of science to the wider society] are opposed analyses of the nature of scientific activity itself. Is it a powerful, highly general method of investigating reality, guided by highly general norms for the evaluation of results; or is it intelligible entirely in terms of esoteric techniques, skills and theoretical structures, perfected within particular traditions of research? These alternatives imply different general formulations of the relationship of science and society. Do the sciences act as the source of a rationality increasingly pervading the wider society; or are they isolated and encapsulated sub-cultures defined and unified only by Kuhnian paradigms? Do the theories of science offer a characteristic and total world view; or are they no more than pragmatic aids to particular types of concrete problems, losing all significance when abstracted from their practical context? Does the credibility of scientific pronouncements reside in the logic of their supporting argument and their power of prediction; or simply in the institutionalised authority of science?[29]

Elsewhere, with reference to the concept of scientific progress ('the last redoubt of teleology'[30]), he writes:

... when we look at the history of science, this very term [scientific progress] forces itself upon us; quite apart from arguments. Without allowing ourselves to be seduced by such feelings, we may still take them as a guide that there is 'something there' to be understood.

---

[28] Beginning with his *Science, Technology and Society in Seventeenth Century England* (Harper & Row, New York, 1938, repr. 1970).

[29] Introduction by Barry Barnes to *Sociology of Science*, ed. B. Barnes (Penguin Books, Harmondsworth, 1972), pp. 13, 14.

[30] Barry Barnes, *Scientific Knowledge and Sociological Theory* (Routledge & Kegan Paul, London, 1974), p. 122.

We should not assume, however, that what is there is a movement of scientific culture into closer and closer correspondence with some unspecified and unspecifiable reality.... It is likely that we are responding to a much more straight-forward teleological progression, consisting in science's increasing capacity to fulfill particular aims and purposes defined by actors themselves.[31]

The philosopher Jurgen Habermas, at Frankfurt, particularly stresses the role of such 'interests'[32] and Mary Hesse at Cambridge similarly, in the context of a discussion of the under-determination of scientific theories by the facts, has argued that the criterion of success, and hence of 'truth', in natural science is success in prediction and control:

Carefully stated, I believe this conclusion [re the under-determination of scientific theories] is both inescapable, and also that it constitutes a definitive refutation of the seventeenth-century ideal of science, and hence of its concepts of empirical knowledge and truth.... There is often resistance to accepting the conclusion on the grounds that science quite clearly is in some sense a progressive and not a constantly revolutionary enterprise. After all, it is held, science *is* a system of continuously accumulating knowledge. We have learnt a great deal about the world which we exploit in scientific technology. Knowledge is power; we have learned and therefore can control. Of course this is true. But far from entailing rejection of the conclusion regarding *theoretical* science, this progressive character of science rather shows us how the peculiar kind of knowledge attainable by science should be understood and distinguished from theoretical knowledge. It is the kind of knowledge precisely appropriate to prediction and control; it is what is learned by an organism which attempts to adapt to and change its environment by gathering data in experimental situations, processing the information gained, and learning to predict successfully further developments in the environment and the subsequent effects of its own actions. It does not yield truth about the essential nature of things, the significance of its own place in the universe, or how it should conduct its life.[33]

She goes on, later in the same paper, to argue also for the role of 'interests', other than predictive truth, in scientific viewpoints upon the world:

[31] Barnes, op. cit., pp. 122–3.

[32] J. Habermas, *Knowledge and Human Interests* (Engl. edn., Heinemann, London, 1972).

[33] M. Hesse, 'Criteria of truth in science and theology', *Religious Studies*, 11 (1975), 389. See also M. Hesse, *The Structure of Scientific Inference* (Macmillan, London, 1974).

The view of the natural sciences that I have been presenting has two characteristics that are relevant in comparison with the social sciences. First, the criterion of success and hence of truth in natural science is success in prediction and control. Second, fundamental theories or conceptual frameworks cannot be interpreted as attempts at realistic description of the hidden features of the external world, but rather as particular view-points upon the world, partially determined by interests other than predictive success. Not only do the theories themselves come and go, but so do the interests they serve: in one culture they may be theological and metaphysical, in others sociological, and in others (ours) the acceptability of many physical theories can be fully understood only in terms of internal aesthetic criteria.[34]

Thus the supposed objectivity of science in discovering features of a 'real' world do not go unquestioned today. The similar questioning of religious affirmations is more familiar, though scarcely less critical of its truth claims, if we allow a functionalist-anthropological account of religion in society to be exhaustive and adequate, a view described thus by Susan Budd:

Religion has its origins not in society itself, but in the necessity for a stable society to find an answer to men's emotional needs as they realize anew 'the conflict between human plans and realities'. The most important function of religion is in creating 'valuable mental attitudes' in connection with death, for strong personal attachments are broken by death, and only an over-riding assertion of human immortality will enable the bereaved to continue living in society.... Religion is the most powerful agent of social control not because it derives from society, but because it offers men the answers and modes of conduct which they need in periods of crisis.[35]

Or consider the apparently reductionist definition of religion of M. E. Spiro: 'a cultural system consisting of culturally patterned interaction with culturally postulated super-human beings'.[36]

Unnerving though this sociological critique of knowledge is,

---

[34] Hesse, op. cit. (1975), p. 393.

[35] Susan Budd, *Sociologists and Religion* (Collier–Macmillan, London, 1973), pp. 42, 43.

[36] M. E. Spiro, 'Religion and the Irrational', in *Symposium on New Approaches to the Study of Religion*, ed. June Helin (University of Washington Press, Washington, 1964), p. 103.

especially for scientists, and significant as it undoubtedly is, and increasingly will be, for our understanding of the relations between society and both science and religion, I do not, myself, believe that it will budge the great majority of scientists (except perhaps particle physicists and cosmologists) from a sceptical and qualified realism, according to which their models and hypotheses are regarded as 'candidates for reality', that is, models of, hypotheses about, a real (but only imperfectly known) world to which the models approximate and the hypotheses genuinely refer.[37] They are committed, on the basis of past evidence and current experience, to (for example) 'believing in' electrons—that is, that they cannot organize their current observations without asserting that electrons exist. *What* they believe about electrons may well, and has in fact, undergone many changes but it is electrons to which they still refer, by long social links going back to the first occasions when they

[37] This kind of realism has been well, and approvingly, characterized thus by H. W. Putnam: 'It is beyond question that scientists use terms as if the associated criteria were not *necessary and sufficient conditions*, but rather *approximately* correct characterizations of some world of theory-independent entities, and they talk as if later theories in a mature science were, in general, *better* descriptions of the *same* entities that earlier theories referred to. In my opinion the hypothesis that this is *right* is the only hypothesis that can account for the communicability of scientific results, the closure of acceptable scientific theories under first-order logic, and many other features of the scientific method' (H. W. Putnam, 'The Meaning of "Meaning"', in his *Mind, Language and Reality*, Philosophical Papers, Vol. 2 (Cambridge University Press, Cambridge, 1975), p. 237, Putnam's italics). Putnam is here, of course, referring obliquely to an intense philosophical debate about realism which has occurred especially in the last decade. The debate has spanned much more widely than the philosophy of science, into discussions concerning the possible definitions of truth, the applicability or otherwise, of the concept of 'truth' to propositions, sentences, and statements, and much else besides. The importance of this debate for the relation of science and theology, indeed for all intellectual discourse, is immense. Nevertheless, I think progress can be made in investigating that particular relation by adopting the position outlined in the text and amplified, in relation to science at least, in the quotation above from Putnam. My presumption is that a similar attitude is possible in the theological enterprise, with appropriate qualifications (see I. Barbour, *Myths, Models and Paradigms* (SCM Press, London, 1974) and in particular the quotation below, p. 40). The philosophical debate can be pursued in the following and references therein: H. W. Putnam, op. cit., and *Mathematics, Matter and Method*, Philosophical Papers, Vol. 1 (Cambridge University Press, Cambridge, 1975); 'What is Realism?', *Proc. Arist. Soc.* 76 (1975/6), 177–94; *Meaning and the Moral Sciences*, John Locke Lectures, Oxford, 1976 (Routledge & Kegan Paul, London, 1978); M. Dummett, 'Can Truth be Defined', in *Frege: Philosophy of Language* (Duckworth, London, 1973). Ch. 13, 'Truth', *Proc. Arist. Soc.* 59 (1958/9), 141–67, 'The Reality of the Past', *Proc. Arist. Soc.* 69 (1968/9), 239–58; *Truth and Meaning*, ed. G. Evans and J. McDowell (Oxford University Press, Oxford, 1975).

were 'discovered'. So physicists are committed to 'believing in' the existence of electrons but remain hesitant to say what electrons 'are' and are always open to new ways of thinking about them that will enhance the reliability of their predictions and render their understanding more comprehensive with respect to the range of phenomena to which it is relevant. The case for such a sceptical and qualified realism, as a defensible philosophy of science, cannot be presented here, but at least it has the merit of being, I believe, the working assumption of practical scientists and will be the stance adopted in these lectures.

In a not dissimilar manner, Christians, indeed all religious believers, also regard themselves as making meaningful assertions about a reality which man can and does encounter.[38] But for them, too, the terms which describe the reality to which they are committed are not, *should* not, in my view, be regarded as fixed and irreformable with respect to their content and conceptual resources, even if their reference remains (as with the electron) unchanged. Such believers, I would argue, should, like the scientists, always be ready to expand their terms, to take in new meanings and to enrich their imaginative resources as their consciousness and experience changes and enlarges (not least with the growth of the natural sciences themselves, these lectures urge particularly).

III. THE RELEVANCE OF NATURAL SCIENCE TO THEOLOGY

The question of the relevance, or otherwise, of science to religion, in their intellectual and cognitive aspects, therefore remains a significant one and is not, in fact, reduced to nonsense when we introduce, as we must, the social dimension as a *tertium quid*—and so science itself, as it were by the back-door, in the form of the sciences of man and human society and behaviour. For it is the case that, too often in the past, the theology–science debate, when engaged at all in this century, has been conducted in an intellectual vacuum, so that philosophers and sociologists have neither been involved nor

[38] See I. Barbour, op. cit., for the case for such a realism, which he calls a 'critical realism', in both science and religion.

themselves been alerted to the intellectual seriousness of the issues. These lectures are principally concerned with the inter-relation of the natural sciences and the Christian doctrine of creation, that is of God's relation to the world and to man-in-the-world. The anthropological and social context of this rela-tion will concern us in due course, but, first some comments on the more purely intellectual question, namely, what kind of relation between our scientific knowledge of the natural world, including man, and theological affirmation is approp-riate? Since 'natural theology'[39] has been the attempt, however misguided in some of its historical forms, to derive some of the latter from features of the former, this amounts to asking if natural theology is possible or, even, desirable.

The case for the relevance of natural science to theology has been cogently and, I think, successfully argued recently by W. H. Austin[40] when, to be more precise, he presents rather the case *against* the *irrelevance* of science to theology. It is worth looking briefly at his arguments, for although they do not go far in showing how the dialogue between natural science and Christian theology might be fruitful, he does clear some very thick air and allow us to see that that dialogue is feasible. Thus, he establishes that even a purely instrumentalist view of science, which allows its theories and models no direct bearing on theology, can concede an indirect relevance through the influence of these theories and models on the choice between putative metaphysical systems which might be conceptual schemes for expression, *inter alia*, of theological doctrines. (An example would be the adoption by 'process theologians'[41] of Whitehead's metaphysics which claimed to be based on the scientific account of the world.) This instrumentalist account of science is not now widely held, although it does seem to be the basis of some of the more sociological accounts of science (see above, J. Habermas and M. Hesse).

There are also purely instrumentalist accounts of religious

[39] 'Natural theology', in the sense given, must be distinguished from a 'theology of nature' which concerns the theological significance of nature in any schema com-prising both man and God—and, of course, from 'natural religion' which was an eighteenth-century conceit, a religion which could be derived directly from a con-sideration of the given 'nature' of man and the world, and so 'natural' in that sense.

[40] Austin, loc. cit. (p. 2 n. 2 above).

[41] See, e.g., John Cobb, *A Christian Natural Theology* (Lutterworth, London, 1961).

doctrines, to the effect that religious myths and stories are either simply aids in the pursuit of policies of life by capturing the imagination and strengthening the mind;[42] or are able to evoke mystical experiences which (on this view) are valuable in themselves and are the main object of the religious quest. Although the first of these instrumentalist views is, on Austin's view, and I concur, unsatisfactory as an account of religion, it still allows an indirect impact of science on theology by shaping and selecting those 'stories' that are to be 'entertained' (Braithwaite's term) to lead to a life manifesting Christian love (an 'agapeistic way of life', as he calls it). The mystical-instrumentalist account of religion is hardly adequate, leaving out, as it seems to do, most of the experiences of ordinary religious believers and seems, in the end, to be a form of the 'two-realm' argument to which we shall shortly come. Even if religions were concerned only with states of consciousness, as this second 'instrumentalist' view suggests, it would, nevertheless, still be sensitive, indeed vulnerable, to the sciences of consciousness (e.g. brain physiology and psychology)—one thinks of the apparently 'religious' effects of some hallucinogenic drugs.

This mystical account of religion is one form of a more general view that reality consists of two orders, or two realms, with the first of which science is concerned and the second theology: the natural/the supernatural; the spatio-temporal/ the eternal; the natural (or physical)/the historical; the physical-and-biological/mind-and-spirit. Such a dualistic ontology is not only (as I shall discuss in the fourth lecture) inadequate to the hierarchical complexity of structures in the natural world, and no defence against reductionism, but it is also inconsistent with the Christian doctrine of creation according to which God not only creates all but is related to all that is other than himself so that every 'realm' has a theological significance. (The only theologically defensible dualism, I would hold, is that between God and the world, everything else that is—not a dualism within that which is *not* God.) The two-realm ontologies lead to a God-of-the-gaps concept of God's relation to the world and are incompatible with incarna-

[42] The position of R. B. Braithwaite, 'An Empiricist's View of the Nature of Religious Belief', reprinted in *Christian Ethics and Contemporary Philosophy*, ed. I. T. Ramsey (SCM Press, London, 1956).

tional expressions of the doctrines of creation and redemption, doctrines central, in some form or other, to the Christian faith. Moreover, as Austin argues:

> Theological statements about the relation between God and nature could be preserved, without reinterpretation and without danger of conflict with science, if they could be shown to be logically independent of our beliefs about nature itself. But it is hard to see how this could be done without rendering either the statements or the relations vacuous. Moreover, this proposal can be combined with the view that theological statements are about one realm, scientific ones about another, only at the price of the peculiar consequence that statements about the relation between the two realms belong to the discipline (theology) that deals with one of the realms, and not to the discipline (science) that deals with the other.[43]

He goes on[43] to show how unsatisfactory are the often highly metaphorical terms of various authors who try to introduce a two-realm ontology into all features of the universe, as for example, in talk: of 'mutually exclusive realms of thought' (e.g. the National Academy of Sciences who distinguish nature/supernature, verifiable/not-verifiable (so it seems)); of division within the structure or 'faculties' of the human mind (Schleiermacher); of dimensions (e.g. of 'depth' (P. Tillich and W. T. Stace)); of 'spaces' (e.g. the 'space' of spatio-temporal objectivity and the 'supra-polar' space of God's omnipresence (K. Heim)); and of 'complementarity' transposed from Bohr's use in physics to describe the relationships between two kinds of descriptions (D. M. MacKay). Such two-realm ontologies seem to be difficult to uphold and, if rejected, the door is at least kept open for passage between science and theology though what will pass is yet to be elaborated.

The assignment of science and religion to two distinct 'language games' or 'forms of life' in the late-Wittgensteinian manner (for example, by D. Z. Phillips, W. D. Hudson, and P. Winch)—although it is in fact disputed if Wittgenstein really meant these terms to apply to such broad enterprises[44]—would license little or no communications between them, so another argument runs,[45] for each would then have logical preconditions

[43] Austin, op. cit., pp. 57 ff.
[44] R. H. Bell, 'Wittgenstein and Descriptive Theology', *Religious Studies*, V (1969), 5 ff.
[45] P. Winch, *The Idea of a Social Science* (Routledge & Kegan Paul, London, 1958).

of use such that the one could have no bearing on the other. It soon appears that this cannot actually be proved without importing reasons based on other than purely linguistic considerations—especi ally if, presumably in order to avoid confusion, one is attempting to extricate that sub-game within the 'language game' of Christianity which has, in fact, for centuries been concerned with the relation of religious belief to science, as we have seen in our brief survey of the history of the concept of the Two Books and of 'natural theology'. As Austin argues:

But then we are faced with a vast intricate job of disentanglement. Religious discourse as empirically available to us comprises, we are supposing, a confused intertwining of genuinely religious elements with others. How are we to extract and reconstruct from this the genuine religious language-game? It seems that we would need at least a partial theory of what religion is and what it is about—enough of a theory, at least, to show why it has nothing to do with science. And we would need some justification for the theory. *But to develop and defend such a theory is also to develop an argument, independent of the notion of language-games, for the irrelevance of science to theology.* The games being once entangled, we cannot separate them unless we have an independent basis on which to make the separation; and if we have that thesis, we don't need the language-games argument.[46]

Another way in which the irrelevance of natural science to theology might be argued is on the grounds that religious belief involves personal involvement and commitment whereas scientific activity requires objectivity and logical neutrality. But this is an over-drawn and over-simplified distinction, as evidenced by the role, on the one hand, of purely intellectual considerations in the history of Christian theology and, on the other, of the now widely accepted role of personal involvement and commitment in the process of scientific discovery.[47]

Thus, the arguments for the supposed irrelevance of natural science to religion, in general, and to Christian theology in particular, prove to be ill founded, and there seem to be good reasons for at least some kind of relevance. But of what kind?

[46] Austin, op. cit., p. 90.
[47] M. Polanyi, *Personal Knowledge* (Routledge & Kegan Paul, London, 1958); P. B. Medawar, 'Hypothesis and imagination', in *The Art of the Soluble* (Methuen, London, 1967); A. Koestler, *The Act of Creation* (Hutchinson, London, 1964).

How direct is the relation? How is a defensible and fruitful relation between natural science and Christian theology to be conceived? These are not questions readily answered and indeed this series of lectures may be regarded as empirical evidence of whether or not they *are* answerable!

My next moves in this present lecture will be to examine to what extent similarities of *intention* (and this will bring in again a sociological and anthropological critique) may be discerned between natural science and theology (§IV). Then the actual *content* of the Judeo-Christian tradition with respect to its understanding of God's relation to the world, virtually the doctrine of creation, will be recalled (§V), preparatory to outlining the form of the exercise to be undertaken in these lectures.

IV. THE INTENTIONS OF NATURAL SCIENCE AND THEOLOGY

A. *The social-anthropological context*

Much light is cast on the intentions of the scientific and theological enterprises by setting them in their social and historical, or, rather, their social-anthropological, context. It comes as something of a shock to the Western scientifically educated inquirer to find that, in the anthropological and, to some extent, the sociological literature,[48] too, the scientific perspective on the world is often included among today's 'myths' and 'rituals' —those narratives and actions which societies relate and perform in relation to the natural world in order to meet real existential needs. These narratives and actions are often closely interwoven so that the rehearsing of a narrative of creation itself makes creation become real again and thereby the individual-in-community relates himself again to the natural world whose 'origin' is being recounted. These narratives and actions are, in the anthropological literature, usually referred to, respectively, as 'myth' and 'ritual', though I would have preferred to have avoided the former term, at least, if only because of the making of definitions of 'myth' there is no end

---

[48] See, e.g., Conference of the American Academy of Arts and Sciences on 'Myth and Mythmaking', *Daedulus*, Spring 1959; *Evolution and Man's Progress*, ed. H. Hoagland and R. W. Burhoe (Columbia University Press, New York, 1962).

and the confusions resulting from its use are a weariness of the flesh. For 'myth' has, through the popular notion of objective science as exorcizing magic and hidden forces from nature, come (irreversibly and ineradicably, in my view) to refer in ordinary speech to stories and ideas about the unreal, unhistorical, and untrue (in spite of valiant efforts to rehabilitate the term in discussion of theological issues[49]).

Hence it is somewhat startling, for a scientist, to find the 'scientific myth' included, along with the Mayan, Babylonian, and Hebrew, to name but a few of the most developed, in an admittedly popular presentation of the 'myths of creation' which have been operative in various societies.[50] As we have already seen, many sociologists, and quite a number of philosophers of science, today regard scientific knowledge primarily in instrumental terms and as characterized principally by having the prediction and control of nature as criteria of its success. To recall Mary Hesse: 'fundamental theories or conceptual frameworks [of the natural sciences] cannot be interpreted as attempts at realistic descriptions of the hidden features of the external, but rather as particular view-points upon the world, partially determined by interests other than predictive success.'[51]

This functionalist account of science parallels rather closely the functionalist account of 'religious' myth which has been an important anthropological interpretative principle ever since Malinowski: 'What really matters about such a story [a myth of origin] is its social function. It conveys, expresses and strengthens the fundamental fact of the local unity and of the kinship unity of the group of people descendent from a common ancestress.'[52] In this approach, it is the role, rather than the reality, historicity, or truth, of the reference of a mythical story which is the primary concern.

This more narrowly functionalist account of myth has given

---

[49] M. Wiles, 'Myth in theology', in *The Myth of God Incarnate*, ed. J. Hick (SCM Press, London, 1977), p. 148.

[50] In, e.g., D. MacLagan, *Creation Myths* (Thames & Hudson, London, 1977).

[51] Op. cit. (1975), p. 393.

[52] B. Malinowski in *Myth in Primitive Psychology*, (1926) reprinted in *Magic, Science and Religion*, intro. by R. Redfield (Anchor Books, Doubleday, Garden City, 1954), p. 116. See also the essay from which this reprinted collection takes its title.

way, following the lead of Lévi-Strauss, to a 'structuralist'
account[53] which recognizes that

the life of myths consists in reorganizing traditional components in
the face of new circumstances or correlatively, in reorganizing new,
imported components in the light of tradition. More generally, the
mythic process is a learning device in which the unintelligible—
randomness—is reduced to the intelligible—a pattern: 'Myth may
be more uniform than history' [quoting E. B. Tylor, *Primitive Culture*
(Murray, London, 1871), p. 282].[54]

So the analysis of myths aims in this approach at discovering
the rules that govern the operations which reduce the alien to
familiar structures within a given range of possible variations.
Thus myths solve problems or declare them unsolvable and in
Lévi-Strauss's words: 'The kind of logic in mythical thought
is as rigorous as that of moden science, and ... the difference
lies, not in the quality of the intellectual process, but in the
nature of the things to which it is applied.'[55]

This parallel between scientific and mythological thinking
has been even more strongly drawn by R. Horton who has
argued that many aspects of theoretical thinking in the natural
sciences have their counterparts in traditional religious thought,
in particular in African traditional thought, with respect to
which he has worked out the parallel in some detail.[56] Horton
sets out a number of general propositions[57] which he claims

[53] See, e.g., *The Structural Study of Myth and Totemism*, ed. E. Leach (Tavistock
Publications, London, 1967), especially the article by Mary Douglas on 'The Meaning
of Myth, with special reference to "La Geste d' Asdiwal"', pp. 49–69.
[54] P. Maranda in the introduction to *Mythology*, ed. P. Maranda (Penguin Modern
Sociology Readings, Penguin Books, Harmondsworth, 1972), p. 8.
[55] C. Lévi-Strauss, *Structural Anthropology*, trans. C. Jacobson and B. Schoepf (Basic
Books, New York and London, 1964), p. 230.
[56] Robin Horton, 'African Traditional Thought and Western Science', in *Rationality*,
ed. Bryan R. Wilson (Blackwell, Oxford, 1970), pp. 131–71.
[57] These general propositions of Horton, op. cit., which are derived, he says, from
his own training in biology, chemistry, and philosophy of science, and which are
also relevant to traditional African religious thinking, are as follows. (1) The quest for
explanatory theory is basically the quest for unity underlying apparent diversity; for
simplicity underlying apparent complexity; for order underlying apparent disorder;
for regularity underlying apparent anomaly. (2) Theory places things in a causal
context wider that that provided by common sense. (3) Common sense and theory have
complementary roles in everyday life. (4) Level of theory varies with context. (5) All
theory breaks up the unitary objects of common sense into aspects, then places the
resulting elements in a wider causal context. That is, it first abstracts and analyses,

characterize theoretical thinking in Western science and then shows how these characteristics are to be found in traditional African religious thinking. For example, with respect to his proposition (2), he produces evidence that

> Given the basic process of theory-making, and an environmental stability which gives theory plenty of time to adjust to experience, a people's belief system may come, even in the absence of scientific method, to grasp at least some significant causal connexions which lie beyond the range of common sense. It is because traditional African religious beliefs demonstrate the truth of this that it seems apt to extend to them the label 'empirical'.[58]

The major difference between traditional African religious thinking and Western science Horton pin-points as being that in the former there is no developed awareness of alternatives to the established body of theoretical tenets (they are 'closed'); whereas in the latter, such an awareness is highly developed (they are 'open').[59] This difference itself engenders other significant ones, which he elaborates.[60]

So there is, it seems, an increasing convergence in the roles and in the theoretical structure assigned both to science in Western societies and to religious cosmological myths in all human societies. For these religious cosmologies are symbolic narratives which purport to describe an, otherwise indescribable and inaccessible, transcendent order. As P. Hefner puts it:

> By *myth* I mean that these [religious] cosmologies are symbolic narratives that purport to be rooted in a transcendent order and to

---

then reintegrates. (6) In evolving a theoretical scheme, the human mind seems constrained to draw inspiration from analogy between the puzzling observations to be explained and certain already familiar phenomena. (7) Where theory is founded on analogy between puzzling observations and familiar phenomena, it is generally only a limited aspect of such phenomena that is incorporated into the resulting model. (8) A theoretical model, once built, is developed in ways which sometimes obscure the analogy on which it was founded.

[58] Horton, op. cit., p. 140.

[59] Horton, op. cit., p. 153.

[60] Horton, op. cit., pp. 155 ff. His headings are : (a) Magical versus non-magical attitudes to words. (b) Ideas-bound-to-occasions versus ideas-bound-to-ideas. (c) Unreflective versus reflective thinking. (d) Mixed versus segregated motives. (e) Protective versus destructive attitude towards established theory and (f) to the category system. (g) The passage of time: [is it] good or bad?

describe the 'way things really are', i.e., they claim to describe an objective transcendent order, even as they imply an imperative as to how we should comport ourselves in order to be in harmony with that objective, transcendent order ... Myth is a special type of rendering; it is a testimony concerning what human beings have learned from their concourse with their world about 'what things are really like,' and what human response is called for in the light of 'how things really are.' ... Myth is necessary for human beings, because their encounter with the world is so serious in its actuality that they cannot refrain from bearing their testimony to what that encounter unveils to them and means for them in their living.[61]

There is indeed a prima-facie case based on their respective developments for attributing a similarity in intention to religious and scientific cosmologies (and one could reasonably extend this to the scientific perspective as a whole). Both attempt to take into account as much of the 'data' of the observed universe as possible and both use criteria of simplicity, comprehensiveness, elegance, and plausibility. (What constitutes the 'data' of observations for the scientist is, of course, its specific differentia, and indeed, its often urged claim to greater authenticity, but it is only with *intentions* that I am now concerned.) Both direct themselves to the 'way things are' not only by developing cosmogonies, accounts of the origin of the universe, but also in relation to nearer-at-hand experience of biological and inorganic nature.

What has altered the situation in recent decades is that the understanding of the nature and role of narrative myths in society has been radically transformed since the 'rationalistically biased' accounts of Tylor and Frazer.[62] For narrative myths are now regarded as profound expressions of human existence and are increasingly understood as symbols expressing human reality in history. This now renders somewhat misguided the radically 'de-mythologizing' programme of Bultmann and followers in relation to the New Testament and has given a new

[61] P. Hefner, 'Basic Christian Assumptions about the Cosmos', in *Cosmology, History and Theology*, ed. W. Yourgrau and A. D. Breck (Plenum Press, New York and London, 1977), pp. 248–9.
[62] See C. H. Long, *Alpha: The Myths of Creation* (George Brasilier, New York, 1963); For an interesting collection, see C. Blacker and M. Loewe (eds.), *Ancient Cosmologies* (Allen & Unwin, London, 1975).

dimension to the understanding of the Old Testament narratives of creation:

The newly acquired understanding of myth has altered the situation. It was realized that myth had been misunderstood by setting it in opposition to history, that myth belonged originally to the context of survival, an expression therefore of one's understanding of existence, of one's understanding of the existence of the threatened-self.... Reflection on Creation meant to rehearse (i.e., to repeat by narrative), in the present world and in man's dangerous situation, the beginning, when what now is came to be. Relationship with the beginning meant relationship with the basis of the world, and the repeated making present of what had happened at the beginning meant a reiteration of the reality by virtue of which the world continues to exist.... The way is then cleared for an understanding of the biblical account of the origins, of the biblical reflection on the Creator-Creation. And one can understand why the Bible knows no doctrine about Creator-Creation, but only tells stories about it. Only in the narrative, only in the rehearsing, can Creation be repeatedly made present. Only in the narrating can Creation become real again.... So the biblical reflection on Creator-Creation takes on a new meaning. The mythical stage is succeeded by one that is characterized by the ever-inquiring intellect. Out of the questioning of threatened man in a threatened world arose the question about the beginning and the end, about coming into existence and ceasing to exist. Limited man asks about and beyond his limitations, about his own and the world's coming into being. But this intellectual inquiry preserves within it the original inquiry of threatened man in his threatened existence, as he asks after the beginning as ground and support of his continuing in the present. The original inquiry about the ground and support of his existence is common to all mankind; it occurs in all races, civilizations, and religions; it belongs to man's being.[63]

This extract from Westermann's important contribution to understanding creation in the Bible brings to the surface a distinction between religious and scientific ways of constructing reality, which I take to be what 'myths' are doing. In religious cosmologies the primary focus is 'on describing the cosmos from the point of view of what assumptions are necessary if human beings are to live optimally in the world'[64] and so includes a

[63] C. Westermann, *Creation* (SPCK, London, 1974), pp. 12–14.
[64] P. Hefner, op. cit. (above, p. 31 n. 61) p. 350.

value judgement about what 'living optimally' is. However, the physical and biological scientific enterprise is principally directed to describing and making models of or hypotheses about nature, and so empirical reference and feedback are its main aim; it does not place human concerns at the centre of its attention and intention, for such scientists have, as yet, hardly taken any cognizance of the interests-oriented account of science (where 'interests' refers not only to sociological and ideological motives but also to innate determining structures of the mind). However, the social sciences, including anthropology, have pursued the scientific quest into the realm of human behaviour itself and have found an inherent corollary of this extension the need to be self-critical of their own scientific pre-suppositions and methodologies in a way not experienced in the physical and biological sciences. A fortiori, the survival-interest, on the other hand, appears to be essential for understanding religious mythic cosmologies and the case has recently been strongly argued for a positively selective role for religion in the survival and development of human society.[65]

B.   The quest for intelligibility, explanation, and meaning: asking 'Why?'

This excursus into a social anthropological viewpoint, brief though it has been, has, I hope, served to make explicit an intention which is common to both the religious and scientific enterprises and which can still be discerned today even in their present sophisticated forms—namely, their search for *intelligibility*, for what makes the most coherent sense of the experimental data with which they are each concerned. What proves to be intelligible is applied in science to prediction and control (if we concur with Habermas[66] and Hesse[67]); in theology, to provide moral purpose and personal meaning;

[65] D. T. Campbell, 'On the conflicts between biological and social evolution and between psychology and moral tradition', *American Psychologist*, 30 (1975), 1103–26. Reprinted in *Zygon*, 11, No. 3, which is devoted to Campbell's thesis and the ensuing controversy on the role of religion in the context of genetic and socio-cultural evolution. See also, R. W. Burhoe, 'The Human Prospect and the "Lord of History"', *Zygon*, 10 (1973), 299–375.
[66] Above, p. 19 n. 32.
[67] Above, p. 19 n. 33.

and in both (if we concur with Burhoe and Campbell[68]) to social survival. Even so, the primary objective of both enterprises is to go on pressing the question 'Why?' to its intelligible limits. Science directs this question to the causal nexus of the natural world. Very frequently it can provide answers to the question 'Why?' which are, if not verifiable, at least falsifiable. Nevertheless, a scientific hypothesis of better explanatory power than hitherto is sometimes adopted even when no empirical tests can be devised which would directly falsify it, as T. S. Kuhn's account[69] of certain historical turning-points in physics makes abundantly clear, even if it cannot be generalized to all the sciences (certainly it is hard to see the history of chemistry and biochemistry in this light). For example, such a broad generalization as the Second Law of Thermodynamics, which is a pillar of modern physical and chemical theory, derives its importance from its ability to render intelligible and coherent some otherwise widely disparate observations and in itself is not readily falsifiable *in sensu stricto* on account of its being so broad and being based on statistical probabilities. The General Theory of Relativity would be another such example.

The religious quest, or rather, the theological enterprise, as I would prefer to call it (in order to stress that we are, for the moment at least, concerned with the intellectual aspects of religion), equally presses the question 'Why?' until, as J. J. Shepherd puts it, 'to press it further is plain silly'.[70] The problem is, as Shepherd says, that 'what appears silly to one person may seem perfectly legitimate to another'[71] and this has certainly been the situation with respect to what is often regarded as a paradigm of religious questions, namely the one concerning what has been called (perhaps unfortunately) the 'mystery of existence'. I refer to such questions as 'Why is there anything at all?', 'Why does the world exist?', 'Is there a reason for the existence of the world?' Many philosophers, perhaps most in recent years, have regarded such questions as meaningless, and have argued that to ask them is already to assume the

[68] Above, p. 33 n. 65.
[69] T. S. Kuhn, *The Structure of Scientific Revolutions* (University of Chicago Press, Chicago and London, 1962).
[70] J. J. Shepherd, *Experience, Inference and God* (Macmillan, London, 1975), p. 76.
[71] Shepherd, loc. cit.

existence of (a) necessary being. At least one philosopher has found such questions in the form 'Is-there-a-reason-for-the-existence-of-the-world?' meaningful, though unanswerable by known rational methods[72] and yet others do not entirely reject it as a question, but do not know what sort of question it is.[73]

There do, indeed, seem to be good reasons for suspecting such questions if the answers to them are sought as 'explanations' conceived as effective in the same way as explanations of events within the natural-causal nexus. There also do seem to be great difficulties on purely philosophical grounds in postulating one ultimate explanation *of* the universe in the same sense in which we 'explain' individual events *within* the universe.[74] Such 'explanations' are too restricted to be the answers to the mystery-of-existence kind of 'Why?' question and to many others which men insist on pressing to their limits and which evoke religious responses and so theological inquiry (e.g. in addition to those given: 'What is the purpose of existence?'; 'What purpose is there in the universe?'; 'Why should the universe be of this particular kind, evolving men with moral purposes and aware of beauty?'; and so on). But why restrict 'explanation' only to *causal* explanations ('causal' in the sense in which the natural world is a causal nexus)? It might be more useful to equate 'explanation' with 'that which renders intelligible', and in this sense, as Keith Ward says,

For the Christian, God, as the power making for intelligibility, beauty and righteousness, may be said to explain the universe in that he gives it meaning and intelligibility, provides purpose and significance, and so sets all things within an overall context. The typical theistic religious affirmation is that everything in the world has a place in an overall pattern which, in its general design, is valuable in itself. Thus, the theist may claim to 'see the point' of the world's existence, or to 'make sense of' human life. There are three main elements involved here; first, that the world as a whole has intrinsic value, that it is good that it exists just as it does; second, that there is a rational pattern and purpose in the universe, that is not just a chance collection

---

[72] M. K. Munitz, *The Mystery of Existence* (Appleton–Century–Crofts, New York, 1965).

[73] J. C. C. Smart, 'The Existence of God', in *New Essays in Philosophical Theology*, ed. A. Flew and A. MacIntyre (SCM Press, London, 1955), p. 46.

[74] See, *inter alia*, K. Ward, *The Concept of God* (Blackwell, Oxford, 1974), Ch. 8.

of random events; and third, that there is a non-physical ground or cause of the universe, which ensures the realisation and the intrinsic value of the various purposes in the universe. To explain the world theologically is to interpret it in terms of a moral purposiveness; and God is the ground of value and of an ultimately purposive causal intelligibility.[75]

... when explaining events by reference to God's purpose, one connects them into one overall pattern, uniting parts into a purposive whole. In this case, of course, one does not refer to a familiar general action-pattern, since there is only one divine purpose. But one does refer to a pattern which is believed to exhibit intrinsic value, and to be governed by general laws, forming a unitary whole. The pattern must be accepted as the ultimate model for theological explanation; and, as in the case of explanations of human acts, it is compatible with, and may well be held to entail, denial of any explanation in terms of sufficient causality. One may thus find a basic, essentially mysterious spontaneity at the core of the world, a dynamism underlying a real history. There is a theistic form of explanation; but it has its limits; and these limits allow for a creative mystery which accords well with the Biblical notion of an unfathomable creator God.[76]

The theistic explanation only forces itself upon one as and when the sacred discloses itself in and through these general features [change, causality, order and contingency] of the universe, and as one discerns the sacred in the necessity and intelligibility of the processes of nature. Theistic explanation is not ultimate, in the way that many theologians have desired; the existence of such an ultimate explanation would undermine the creative freedom and mystery of God's being. Yet it does license talk of God as the creative cause of the universe, the one who brings it into being and shapes it in accordance with rational principles.[77]

It is in this sense of 'explanation', that of positing a cosmos-explaining-being as a kind of 'non-natural explanatory terminus'[78] to a succession of 'Why?' questions which begin at our contingent existence, that creation by God may be said to 'explain' the existence of all that is, although perhaps, by now, 'explanation' has become too misleading to denote an *ex*

---

[75] K. Ward, op. cit., pp. 148–9.
[76] K. Ward, op. cit., p. 151.
[77] K. Ward, op. cit., pp. 152, 153.
[78] Shepherd, op. cit., p. 72.

hypothesi unique relation—that between God and the world.
Note that it is our contingent world that provides the 'launch-
ing pad', as it were, for the Judeo-Christian doctrine of creation.
This has important results, as P. Hefner has stressed:

As a consequence, the Hebrew (Jewish) and Christian religions stand
under an excruciating burden to find meaning and value in the
worldly realm that is not surpassed, or even matched, by any other
religion or philosophy of life ... There is no time before creation that
is of any significance to Jews and Christians, and therefore this created
order, which includes the entire universe, must have meaning and
value, else the belief-system and the life of faith are shipwrecked.[79]

In their historical experiences of dependence on a transcendent Reality the people of Israel were led also to an awareness
of the dependence of nature, of all that is, on the same Reality.
Thus the 'Lord God of Abraham, of Isaac and of Jacob' became
identified with God whose creative action is variously described,
notably in the early chapters of Genesis, the Book of Job, and
the Psalms, that is, in literature of wide historical provenance.
Of course, the theological doctrine of God as Creator is but
the intellectual abstraction (some might say, desiccation) of the
awareness man has of the mystery of his own individual
existence, of personality, of birth, growth, and death, and of
the realization that there is nothing necessary about our
existence. We are contingent; we might not *be* at all. Concomitantly man becomes aware of the contingent character of
all that surrounds him and extends this sense of contingency to
the universe as a whole. In the individual this generates a
search for meaning: he must make sense of his own being in
relation to the world he experiences and observes. That the
Christian idea of creation is a response to the intellectual and
personal question of *meaning* has been very well elaborated by
Langdon Gilkey:

... there is another kind of question that involves the issue of 'origins'.
This is a much more burning, personal sort of question than the
scientific or metaphysical ones, which are rightly motivated by a
serene curiosity about the universe we live in. Here we ask an ultimate
question with a distinctly personal reference. We are raising the

---

[79] Hefner, op. cit. (p. 31 n. 61 above), p. 358.

question of 'origins' because we are asking about the ultimate security, the meaning and destiny of our own existence.[80]

Whenever, therefore, we become conscious of the essential contingency of our life and its fulfillment, and when the forces that we cannot control seem to thwart our every hope, then in desperation we ask 'what possible meaning can this dependent existence of mine have?' The problem of meaning springs initially from the contingency and so insecurity of man as a finite creature, crucially subject to external forces beyond his power that determine his weal or woe.[81]

The Christian doctrine of God as Creator is, then, an intellectual and rational attempt to provide a suitable answer to questions such as 'What possible meaning can this dependent existence of mine have?', that is, to satisfy the desire for meaning. The doctrine of creation also stems from a recognition of the natural human response to, and attraction for, the awesome and mysterious in both numinous and aesthetic experience. This response and attraction find their most satisfying focus, at least for the theist, in an Other who beckons as well as dazzles us. These aesthetic and mystical elements in Christian theism have provided the fertile soil of an integrating and culturally creative experience in art, architecture, painting, music, and poetry which has enriched mankind. But in the present context, we shall have to confine ourselves to the more purely intellectual features of the doctrine of creation which we have been describing as the search for answers to 'Why?' questions directed to the boundaries which mark the givenness of our existence.

V.   TALK OF GOD AS CREATOR

A.   The need for models

What *kind* of 'answer' is it possible to give to questions like those concerning the so-called mystery of existence and others which constitute the theological enterprise? Even if we agree to postulate a 'cosmos-explaining-being', or even God as creator, what are the resources of language with which the results of these inquiries may be elaborated? We have already

[80] L. Gilkey, *Maker of Heaven and Earth* (Anchor Books, Doubleday, New York, 1965), p. 19.
[81] Gilkey, op. cit., p. 169.

had to qualify and hedge rather carefully what we are to mean by 'explanation' in the theological quest for intelligibility in our existence in all its aspects, so it is not surprising that we should use models, metaphor, and analogies and all kinds of images to express what *ex hypothesi* transcends and is other than everything that exists. This is the problem of 'talk about God' to which many philosophers of religion have addressed themselves.[82] Although 'verification' and 'falsification' are not possible for talk about God in the same sense as they are for scientific talk, yet it has been argued (I think convincingly) that there are, nevertheless, adequate criteria by which the former is tested. Suggested criteria include, for example, those of internal coherence, comprehensiveness, fruitfulness, and 'convincingness' (the possession by a belief of a certain captivating quality).[83]

Talk about God's relation to the world has frequently been expressed through the over-arching and archetypal image of God as Creator and it is to such talk that criteria like the above have to be applied. The theological enterprise has always involved much unpacking and elaborating of this image and in so doing is operating in a way not unlike science. The theological enterprise, like the scientific, is concerned not so much to frame literal and universal propositions about some 'essences' which lie behind the visible manifestations of this world as to report the results of its quest for meaning. The search for such 'essences' has been abandoned in science, thereby manifesting its own kind of *via negativa*, long known to the seeker after God. In both the scientific and the theological enterprises we have to be satisfied with models which are 'candidates for reality', which are reformable and which are as close as we can approach to the reality with our given experimental limitations and conceptual resources. The similarities and contrasts between the way science and theology test and obtain consensus about their respective models of the realities with which they

---

[82] See, e.g. I. T. Ramsey, *Religious Language* (SCM Press, London, 1957); *Talk of God*, Royal Institute of Philosophy Lectures, Vol. 2, 1967/8 (Macmillan, London, 1969); J. Macquarrie, *God-Talk* (SCM Press, London, 1967); and references therein.

[83] B. Mitchell, *The Justification of Religious Belief* (Macmillan, London, 1973); D. Pailin, 'Can the theologian legitimately try to answer the question: is the Christian faith true?,' *Expository Times*, 84 (1973), 321–9.

are concerned, and which are not directly observable, have been much investigated.[84] I. Barbour summarizes his comparison in the following terms:

There are ... several *similarities* between religious models and theoretical models in science, which can be summarized as follows. First, they share the characteristics outlined previously: they are analogical in origin, extensible to new situations, and comprehensible as units. Second, they have a similar status. Neither is a literal picture of reality, yet neither should be treated as a useful fiction. Models are partial and inadequate ways of imagining what is not observable. They are symbolic representations, for particular purposes, of aspects of reality which are not directly accessible to us. They are taken seriously but not literally. Third, the use of scientific models to order observations has some parallels in the use of religious models to order the experience of individuals and communities. Organizing images help us to structure and interpret patterns of events in personal life and in the world.

There are also important *differences* between religious and scientific models. First, religious models serve non-cognitive functions which have no parallel in science. Sometimes religious models seem to survive primarily because they serve these functions effectively. Second, religious models elicit more total personal involvement than scientific models. Religious language is indeed self-involving ... Religion asks about the objects of man's trust and loyalty, the character of his ultimate concern, the final justification for his values. The call to decision and commitment ... is present throughout religious language. Third ... religious models appear to be more influential than the formal beliefs and doctrines derived from them, whereas scientific models are subservient to theories, even though a model may outlast a series of theories developed from it. Theories are the instrument for specifying positive and negative analogy, and for correlating observations. Religious images have a more direct relationship to experience, especially in worship, ethics, and the life of the religious community.[85]

The viewpoint adopted in these lectures is that in both the scientific and theological enterprises the basic stance, the working assumption, is that of a sceptical and qualified realism—the belief that they are processes of finding out the 'way things are'. This belief is justified, in the case of science, by its success in

[84] I. Barbour, op. cit. (above p. 21 n. 37); I. T. Ramsey, *Models and Mystery* (Oxford University Press, London, 1964), and op. cit. p. 39 n. 82; A. R. Peacocke, *Science and the Christian Experiment* (Oxford University Press, London, 1971).

[85] Barbour, op. cit., p. 69.

prediction and control. In the case of theology, it is justified by providing resources which give moral purpose, meaning and intelligibility to the individual plotting his path through life[86] and also, so it has been well argued, by contributing to the survival of society.[87] What then are these resources? What, in fact, is the *content* of the Judeo-Christian tradition concerning the relation between God and the world?

B. Models of creation in the Judeo-Christian tradition

God's creative activity has been depicted in a variety of models and images in the Judeo-Christian tradition. Before these are recalled, it must be stressed that it was not from speculation concerning the nature and origin of the world and the role of God, or the gods, that the biblical doctrine of creation arose. It arose from the interpreted historical experience of the ancient Hebrews of flight, exodus, and establishment in a new land and a subsequent association of the God, Yahweh, whom they had encountered in this experience, with the creator of all that is. As a result of their historical experience of radical insecurity they came to worship only one god who was indeed God and this led to a recognition of his ascendancy over all other gods who might claim authority and, in particular, over those gods of natural forces followed by the surrounding peoples. Thus was generated, according to the consensus of many leading Old Testament scholars, an explicit doctrine of creation with Yahweh as the only God, the Creator of all there is, with no other beside him. This was expressed in many ways, some of which are only now being unravelled by scholarship, but most notably it is affirmed in the magnificent first chapter of Genesis, which is properly regarded by modern Christians not as a literal record of what happened but as a way of expressing a present situation, an ever-present truth, by telling a story, a 'religious myth'. The Genesis story is in opposition to rival cosmogonic myths, for example, of Babylon,[88] which postulated something other than God (or the gods) out of which he (or they) shaped the world, and also gave accounts of the birth of the gods

---

[86] J. Bowker, 'Information Process, Systems Behaviour and the Study of Religion', *Zygon*, 11 (1976), 361–74; *The Sense of God* (Clarendon Press, Oxford, 1973).

[87] Above, p. 33 n. 65.

[88] C. F. von Weizäcker, *The Relevance of Science* (Collins, London, 1964), Chs. 2, 3.

themselves. In Genesis 1: 2 there is just possibly a hint (though this is disputed) of a possible 'chaos' (see Lecture II) 'in the beginning' but it is nevertheless quite clear that the reiterated emphasis is on the world existing entirely by the *fiat*, the word, of God: 'And God said, Let there be . . .' This is re-echoed in the opening verses of the Fourth Gospel in the New Testament: 'When all things began the Word already was. The Word dwelt with God, and what God was, the Word was. The Word, then, was with God at the beginning, and through him all things came to be; no single thing was created without him.'[89] The myths of, for example, Genesis, and indeed the whole tradition, assert that nothing comes into being but by the one God and the prime emphasis is on the dependence on God's will for the existence of everything that is. This conviction runs through the whole of the Bible as far as the ascription to God in the Revelation: '. . . thou didst create all things; by thy will they were created, and have their being!'[90]

The Hebrews did not think in abstract terms but in concrete images and also expressed themselves in the Name, 'Yahweh', they used for God himself, which, the scholars tell us, can be read as meaning 'He causes to be (or creates) what comes into existence' or 'He causes to be, creates'.[91] Moreover 'Yahweh was understood as referring not only to his work of creation, but also to His preservation and providential control' i.e. to his actions past, present, and future, according to W. H. Brownlee, who has recently made a case[92] for the Name to mean 'He who makes things happen', which moves the term from a simple reference to the Creator to depiction of his role in salvation history, two ideas which we have already seen are genetically linked. Jurgen Moltmann has summarized this aspect of the recent understanding of the biblical view of creation in the following terms:

Thus it follows [from recent Biblical exegesis] that theology must speak of creation not only at the beginning but also in history, at

[89] John 1: 1–3 (NEB).
[90] Revelation 4: 11 (NEB).
[91] F. Albright, *From Stone Age to Christianity* (Doubleday, New York, 1957), pp. 16, 259 ff.
[92] W. H. Brownlee, 'The ineffable Name of God', *Bull. Amer. Schools Oriental Res.* 226 (1977), 42 (whole article: pp. 39–46).

the end and in relation to the totality of divine creative activity. 'Creation' as the epitome of God's creative activity embraces creation at the beginning, creative activity within history and the eschatological consummation. By limiting the concept of creation to 'at the beginning' the traditions have separated either 'creation from redemption', or 'nature from supernature' or 'the first from the second creation'. As a consequence of this the continuity and unity of the divine creative activity has been brought into question. Only through an understanding of the process of creation as coherent and eschatologically oriented can the concepts of both the unity of God and of the unity of meaning within his creative activity be maintained. ... If theology wants to offer a comprehensive outline of the creative activity of God, then it must focus upon the creation as that reality which is still open and in the process of being created.[93]

Unravelling the consequences and implications of the biblical ideas on creation has proceeded throughout Christian history and still continues, as we shall see. It early became clear that the word 'creator' and its implied analogy to 'maker' was ambiguous and needed very careful handling. (For example, in the extensive debates on Arianism, Athanasius[94] had to insist that the term 'creator' was not literally meant when it referred to God 'creating' the Word in a much disputed passage, Proverbs 8: 22.) The way in which a special Hebrew word for 'create' was predicated of God in Genesis 1: 1 was reflected in the subsequently developed assertion[95] that creation was *ex nihilo*, 'out of nothing' (not explicitly stated until 2 Macc. 7: 28), which thereby denied pantheism, dualism, Manichaeism, and, of course, atheism. This assertion may at first appear to be logically absurd, for only nothing can be made out of nothing, as has frequently been pointed out. In the more philosophical development, the phrase emphasizes that 'creation' itself is not an act at a point in time, but an analogical word representing God's relation to the cosmos now, a relation of absolute

[93] J. Moltmann, 'Creation and Redemption', in *Creation, Christ and Culture*, ed. R. W. A. McKinney (T. & T. Clark, Edinburgh, 1976), p. 123.

[94] Athanasius, *Orat.* ii. 18–22.

[95] For an account of the relative balance at different times between creation as initiating event and creation as sustaining and preserving, see J. Pelikan, 'Creation and causality in the history of Christian thought', in *Evolution after Darwin*, ed. S. Tax and C. Callender (University of Chicago Press, Chicago, 1960), Vol. iii, *Issues in Evolution*, pp. 29–40.

dependence of the cosmos on God's will for its very being.[96]
In Moltmann's words:

The expression *creatio ex nihilo* . . . is meant to convey both the freedom
of the Creator and the contingent character of everything that exists;
this contingent character refers not just to the origin but to the
ongoing fundamental nature of everything that is. The question 'why
is there anything rather than nothing?' cannot be answered by
referring either to some prior necessity or to pure chance. *Creatio ex
nihilo* expresses negatively the positive basis for the creation, namely,
the good pleasure of God.[97]

Christians have affirmed, in concord with Hebraic tradition,
that the whole cosmos is other than God, but dependent on
him and that, more metaphysically, the cosmos has derived
being whereas only God has underived being, that is, an
existence not dependent on any other entity. The classical
expression of this belief is to be found in the phrases of the
Nicene Creed which attribute creativity to God: God the Father
is believed in as 'Maker of heaven and earth, and of all things
visible and invisible'; God the Son as he 'by whom all things
were made'; and God the Holy Spirit as 'the Lord, the giver
of Life'. Without going into Trinitarian doctrine, it is notable
that in this Creed all three modes of being of the one Triune
God are explicitly involved in creation. These modes of being
were originally denoted by *persona* and *hupostasis* which have
been ambiguously translated into English as 'person'. In its
developed form, the Christian doctrine of creation became an
assertion that the world was created with time, along with
matter and energy and space. The cosmos continues to exist
at all times by the sustaining creative will of God without which
it would simply not be at all. Within the Christian tradition,
there has been a rich variety of ways in which has been
depicted this asymmetrical relation subsisting between God and
the world.

A number of complementary and reinforcing models have
been necessary to avoid the extremes of a completely transcendent God (which merges into deism) and of a completely
immanent God (which merges into pantheism). In deism God

[96] Ibid.
[97] Moltmann, op. cit., p. 124.

has no effective continuous interaction with the world; and in pantheism God tends to be identified with the world: the Christian concept of creation holds to neither extreme. The models which have been used in the past have been elaborated by contemporary theologians[98] and range from those ('monarchical' models) stressing transcendence and the distance between Creator and creation (such as God as Maker, closely related to God as King and Sovereign) to those ('organic' models) stressing the close and immanent relation between creation and Creator (e.g. the relation of breath to a body, or parts of a living organism to the whole). Some modern authors have furthermore seen relevant analogies in the relation of an artist to his work and the process-theologians, as we shall see, have espoused the term 'panentheism' to denote a doctrine which attempts to combine transcendence and immanence by asserting that the world is 'in' God, but that his being is not exhausted by the world. Biblical images have included the thought of creation as like a garment worn by God; as like the work of a potter; as a kind of emanation of God's life-giving energy, or spirit; as the manifestation of God's Wisdom (*Sophia*) or Word (*Logos*), which are hypostatized so that they represent the outgoing of the being and action of God in creation from within his own inner, and ineffable, nature. This nature is believed, within Christian thought, to have been unveiled in the person of Jesus and thereby to have been revealed essentially as Love, in so far as man can understand God's being at all. Thus creation is regarded as proceeding from the inner life of God as Love, and his creating and sustaining beings other than himself as an outreach of that more-than-personal inner life. This working 'outwards' of God in his creative action was assigned to the 'energies' of God rather than to his 'essence' by the Greek Fathers, who reflected therein the dynamic, rather than static, images of the Hebrew scriptures.[99]

---

[98] e.g. J. Macquarrie, *Principles of Christian Theology* (SCM Press, London, 1966), pp. 200 ff.; and 'God and the World', *Theology*, 75 (1972), 394–403, followed (p. 403) by a comment by B. Hebblethwaite.

[99] P. Evdokimov, 'Nature', *Scottish J. Theol.*, 18, No. 1 (1965), pp. 8 ff.

VI. SCIENCE AND CREATION TODAY

These models of creation which constitute our Judeo-Christian heritage have been shaped by imaginative and intellectual reflection primarily on man's experience of God, but they have never been entirely divorced from such knowledge of the natural world as he has possessed, as we saw in our earlier survey of the metaphor of the Two Books and their inter-relation. But what of creation and the world of *science*, as we know it?

Today, after more than 300 years of the scientific revolution in man's understanding of the natural world, including himself, it seems to me proper to inquire what effects this un-paralleled expansion of man's knowledge and extension of his consciousness should have on his way of modelling, of making images, of the relation of God, the ineffable, to the world as so known. We cannot expect today to develop a 'natural theology' whereby we can hope to 'read off', as it were, the 'nature and attributes of the deity' (as was hoped in the eighteenth century) from the world of nature. Nevertheless, our understanding of God's relation to the world, the doctrine of creation, cannot remain unaffected by our new-found knowledge. For that understanding and that doctrine were developed in response to both the intellectual and existential questions concerning intelligibility and personal (and social) meaning for man in the world in which he finds himself—and today the world to which such questions refer is pre-eminently a world described in the terms of the natural sciences as the best-authenticated knowledge available of what it contains and what its processes are.

Thus, any affirmations about God's relation to the world, any doctrine of creation, if it is not to become vacuous and sterile, must be about the relation of God to, the creation by God of, the world which the natural sciences describe. It seems to me that this is not a situation where Christian, or indeed any, theology has any choice—or, indeed, ought to expect to have any. For the scientific perspective on the world affords the most reliable available answers to questions men have always asked about it: What is there? What goes on? How does it change? Why does it change? Can we tell what has happened in the past and will happen in the future by looking at it now?

Any theological account of God's relation to the world is operating in an intellectual vacuum, not to say cultural ghetto, if it fails to relate its affirmations to the answers to these questions the natural sciences have been able to develop. It is true that theology, the intellectual ordering of the religious experience, is concerned with wider and deeper questions of overall intelligibility and personal and social meaning than the natural sciences as such. But *these* fundamental questions, with the daunting implications of their possible answers, cannot be asked at all without directing them to the world as we best know and understand it, that is, through the sciences.

In these lectures we shall consider certain features of that scientific perspective and then ask again what implications that perspective has for our models of God's relation to the world: which ways of thinking about God, the world, and their interrelation are, in the light of these perspectives, going to be most appropriate, most intellectually viable, and most fertile for our imaginative life.

It would be unwise, in advance, to prescribe what kind of relation between the theological reassessment and scientific knowledge might emerge. Indeed, I would like this whole exercise to be regarded as an empirical one—of looking at developments in the sciences, some quite new, others having a longer history, and then thinking about any possible implications they might have for Christian theology. Whether or not any generalizations about a new 'natural theology' then become possible may still have to be left as an open question. We shall in fact be engaged, in practice, in what the old 'natural theologians' were doing—relating their best knowledge of the natural world to these wider issues of intelligibility and meaning which they formulated in Christian terms, but we shall (I hope) be doing this in a much more open-ended way, with no presumption concerning the results.

For too long now, Christian theology has isolated itself from formulating its basic affirmations in ways which might commend themselves to a scientifically educated public and it seems vital to me to initiate the exercise I have outlined, whatever its repercussions on received notions. For I would suggest that much of the sheer implausibility to modern men of traditional Christian formulations—of the nature of man, of his relation to nature, why he needs 'salvation', in what salvation might consist, and where mankind and individuals are heading —arises not from any basic inadequacy in their analysis of man's predicament or from any mistaking of the reality of God's word to man, but through the traditional static images not really relating at all to the world of dynamic process that the sciences now show it to be. As a distinguished earlier Bampton lecturer, Austin Farrer, urged in a notable series, we need a 'rebirth of images'—and today the 'glass of vision', through which we might discern, however obscurely, new images, cannot but be that ground and polished by science.

It may also not only be the Christian theologian who, by such reconsideration of the interaction between science and theology, might find himself 'strangely moved'. For science itself, as a social activity has, as I pointed out earlier, its own need to be located meaningfully in the total pattern of human activity and concern. It is true that many scientists have testified how their work, as a personal activity, is motivated by and serves to enhance their respect for and sensitivity to the order and beauty of nature,[100] but this is far from being widely appreciated.

Man as investigator, user, and denizen of nature needs to regain a new sense of wholeness in which his deepest aspirations (hitherto channelled, in this country at least, through the Christian faith) can be integrated with the practical concerns of life in a natural world described by, and utilisable through, the knowledge the natural sciences provide. We need to regain this sense of wholeness for we seem to be so constituted that we seek to hold together in a coherent way, in a unified vision which can integrate our existence, all our models of reality— whether from the sciences or from religion. Why we are so constituted as to require this intellectual and personal integration is hidden, no doubt, deep in the wisdom of the evolutionary processes through which the Wisdom of God has chosen to create us. It may be, indeed, that such a unified vision is rapidly becoming one of the conditions for man's survival and,

[100] Cf. the interviews with leading scientists reported in *The God of Science* by F. E. Trinklein (W. B. Eerdmans Publ. Co., Grand Rapids, Michigan, 1971).

as I have indicated, there are those, with no particular religious (or indeed any) axe to grind, who are sensitive to man's global predicaments and who therefore seek a new vision and ethic stemming from a new understanding of God's relation to nature, including man.[101]

Perhaps we should not set our sights so high but I hope at least that we may have the same reward in our endeavours as the Hon. Robert Boyle desired for the young Royal Society to whom he bequeathed his collection of specimens and ores while —'Wishing them also a happy success in their laudable attempts to discover the true nature of the works of God, and praying that they, and all other searchers into physical truths, may cordially refer their attainments to the glory of the great Author of Nature, and to the comfort of mankind.'

---

[101] See Lecture VII.

II

Cosmos, Man, and Creation

I. INTRODUCTION: IMMENSITY

FROM time to time in the history of thought there emerges from the laboratory a scientist who, throwing aside the conventional detachment of his kind from the affairs of the world, throws down a gauntlet at the feet of the believer in God—and does so with especial vehemence if that believer is a Christian. Such a one, in his day, was Thomas Henry Huxley, 'Darwin's bulldog', who espoused Darwin's theory of natural selection as much for its use as a stick with which to beat the Christianity of his time as for the scientific evidence in favour of it. Reviewing *On the Origin of Species* he wrote gleefully:

Extinguished theologians lie about the cradle of every science as the strangled snakes beside that of Hercules; and history records that whenever science and orthodoxy have been fairly opposed, the latter has been forced to retire from the lists, bleeding and crushed if not annihilated; scotched, if not slain. But orthodoxy is the Bourbon of the world of thought. It learns not, neither can it forget; and though, at present, bewildered and afraid to move, it is as willing as ever to insist that the first chapter of Genesis contains the beginning and end of sound science; and to visit, with such petty thunderbolts as its half-paralysed hands can hurl, those who refuse to degrade Nature to the level of primitive Judaism.[1]

Such a one, in our own times, was Jacques Monod, the molecular biologist, whose book *Chance and Necessity*, delineating what he perceived to be the philosophical and theological consequences of molecular biology, was widely read in Europe and America and whose lectures in Oxford and Cambridge could be relied on to draw large audiences of students. Monod

---

[1] T. H. Huxley, *Westminster Review*, 17 (1860), 541–70; reprinted in *Darwin*, A Norton Critical Edition, ed. P. Appleman (Norton, New York, 1970), pp. 435–6.

urged that the random nature of mutations in the genetic material at the molecular level implied that the existence and development of life were 'due to chance' in a sense which renders human existence meaningless. His approach may be epitomized by some of the concluding sentences of his book: 'The ancient covenant is in pieces; man at last knows that he is alone in the unfeeling immensity of the universe out of which he emerged only by chance.'[2] The 'ancient covenant' which he claimed had been ruptured was that established between man and nature by man's projection into inanimate nature of his own self-awareness. He was not the first of his countrymen to experience the 'unfeeling immensity of the universe' but Pascal, at least, consoled himself with the well-known reflection that 'All bodies, the firmament, the stars, the earth and its kingdoms, are not equal to the lowest mind; for mind knows all these and itself; and these bodies nothing'[3]—and this reflection is not far removed from Monod's concluding existentialist, indeed apocalyptic, plea that for man 'Neither his destiny nor his duty have been written down. The Kingdom above or the darkness below: it is for him to choose.'[4] This is a noble response to the 'unfeeling immensity of the universe' whose processes are governed, to use his phrase, 'only by chance'. It is intriguing to note that Sir Bernard Lovell made a similar allusion when he entitled his 1975 Presidential Address to the British Association,[5] 'In the centre of immensities', quoting Thomas Carlyle who, 'in *Sartor Resartus* ... enquired, What is Man? who "sees and fashions for himself a Universe, with starry spaces and long thousands of years ... Stands he not thereby in the centre of Immensities, in the conflux of Eternities?"'

I shall later examine more closely the role of so-called chance and its implications. Here I consider some of the questions about the 'unfeeling immensity of the universe' and about man's place in it which are evoked by modern physics and cosmology. I shall relate these questions to a parallel exploration in search

[2] J. Monod, *Chance and Necessity* (Collins, London, 1972), p. 167.
[3] B. Pascal, *Pensées*, 1670 (p. 235 of Everyman edn., 1931).
[4] Loc. cit.
[5] Sir Bernard Lovell, 'In the Centre of Immensities', *Advancement of Science*, NS 1 (1975), 2.

of intelligibility and meaning, namely that represented by the Judeo-Christian tradition with its doctrine of God as Creator of the universe, including man, and the questions raised in the course of such an exploration about the immensity of the universe and man's place in it—as classically expressed by the psalmist's:

For I will consider thy heavens, even the works of thy fingers, the moon and the stars, which thou hast ordained.
What is man that thou art mindful of him: and the son of man, that thou visitest him?[6]

We inquire first, then, into the world-view of physics and cosmology and find ourselves having to adjust to a radical transformation of that world-view during the last century.

II. THE TRANSFORMATION OF THE SCIENTIFIC WORLD-VIEW THROUGH TWENTIETH-CENTURY PHYSICS AND COSMOLOGY

A. *The twilight of the absolute gods of space, time, object, and determinism*

It is a commonplace that the 'immensities' of space and time which confront man in the universe have been magnified since Galileo by orders of such magnitude that they daunt the imagination. It is less widely appreciated than it should be that twentieth-century physics has necessitated a transformation of our commonsense view of the world, a transformation fundamentally far more radical than any mere multiplication, however enormous, of the scale of Euclidean space and Newtonian time. For that extension of scale tends to be envisaged in ways which are derived directly from our apprehension of space and time through our senses, with the aid of instruments and clocks. This presupposition of our common sense was shared, up to the end of the nineteenth century, with classical physics which, although sophisticated mathematically, and although not in any sense a naïve duplication of our sensory experience, nevertheless still assigned a certain epistemological priority to the visual and the tactile. For matter was still regarded as essentially

---

[6] Psalm 8: 3, 4 (AV).

inpenetrable and solid, and particles of matter were imagined to possess a certain bulk, shape, and position, which could vary with time. This classical corpuscular-kinetic view of matter, although it involved a modification of our immediate sense perception of matter, did not, nevertheless, transcend the limits of our sensory imagination. It could still fulfil the requirement of John Tyndall (1872) for a satisfactory scientific theory: 'Ask your imagination if it will accept it'—and what was acceptable involved some kind of mental picture or model located in an absolute three-dimensional Euclidean space, and in an absolute time which Newton had long since established in the general scientific imagination as being that 'Absolute, true and mathematical time', which 'of itself, and from its own nature, flows equably without relation to anything external, and by another name is called duration.'[7]

Besides absolute *space* and *time*, there were other gods in the pantheon of classical physics. Underlying the corpuscular-kinetic view of matter are the ideas of the absolute *object*, that there is an objective entity of a determinate structure independent of observer and experiment; and the idea of absolute *determinism*, that the distribution of these objects changes continuously according to the immutable laws of mechanics. In its weaker form, still widely accepted today, this determinism can simply refer to the assumption of scientists that, in nature, certain events appear to be connected and their presumption that there is a generative mechanism which can make these interconnections intelligible. But in its stronger form it can be an iron law of 'necessity' (a word much used by Monod in this connection), a 'principle of determinism', meaning that everything that happens occurs of necessity as if it were fixed in advance. This notion, of course, has its origins, like those of chance and chaos, in antiquity but the predictive power of Newtonian mechanics undoubtedly gave it a tremendous fillip. Its implications were finely, indeed notoriously, expressed by Laplace in the following well-known passage:

Consider an intelligence which, at any instant, could have a knowledge of all forces controlling nature together with the momentary

---

[7] Isaac Newton, *Principia*, Scholium to Definition VIII, 1; reprinted in H. G. Alexander, *The Leibniz–Clarke Correspondence* (Manchester University Press, Manchester, 1956, 1965), p. 152.

conditions of all the entities of which nature consists. If this intelligence were powerful enough to submit all this data to analysis it would be able to embrace in a single formula the movements of the largest bodies in the universe and those of the lightest atoms; for it nothing would be uncertain; the future and the past would be equally present to its eyes.[8]

So expressed, this kind of determinism has close links with the theological notion of predestination and both indeed may be regarded as rooted in the concept of an ultra-transcendent Creator who, after one act of creation in time, left his universe to follow its course controlled by unalterable laws. Historically, of course, what happened in eighteenth-century England was that the support given to physical determinism by Newtonian mechanics led many to adopt such a deist view of the Creator.

By the end of the nineteenth century the absolutes of space, time, object, and determinism were apparently securely enthroned in an unmysterious, mechanically determined world, basically simple in structure at the atomic level and, statistically at least, unchanging in form—for even geological and biological transformations operated under fixed laws. Physicists were astonishingly confident, as witness the now somewhat notorious claim of the catalogue of the University of Chicago for 1898-9 that

While it is never safe to affirm that the future of Physical Science has no marvels in store even more astonishing than those of the past, it seems probable that most of the grand underlying principles have been firmly established and that further advances are to be sought chiefly in the rigorous application of these principles to all the phenomena which come under our notice.[9]

Within a few decades, under the pressure of experimental facts

[8] P. S. de Laplace, *Essai philosophique sur les probabilités* (Bachelier, Paris, 5th French edn. 1825), pp. 3, 4. More fully, as Laplace wrote it: 'Nous devons donc envisager l'etat présent de l'univers, comme l'effet de son état antérieur, et comme la cause de celui qui va suivre. Une intelligence qui pour un instant donné, connaîtrait toutes les forces dont la nature est animée, et la situation respective des êtres qui la composent, si d'ailleurs elle était assez vaste pour soumettre ces données à l'analyse, embrasserait dans la même formule les mouvemens des plus grands corps de l'univers et ceux du plus léger atome: rien ne serait incertain pour elle, et l'avenir comme le passé, serait présent à ses yeux. L'esprit humain offre, dans la perfection qu'il a su donner à l'Astronomie, une faible esquisse de cette intelligence.'

[9] Quoted by R. S. Mulliken in 'Spectroscopy, Quantum Chemistry and Molecular Physics', *Physics Today* (April 1968), p. 56.

and the bold and convincing analyses of Planck and Einstein, there was, as Karl Heim[10] puts it, a 'twilight of the gods' of absolute space, time, object, and determinism—a Wagnerian *Götterdämmerung* in which the golden prize of absolute intellectual ascendancy over nature's laws which these gods had attempted to seize was finally interred in the inscrutable depths of nature's intrinsic realities from which it had been so roughly alienated, while the Valhalla of the world those gods had constructed around them was consumed by the new fires of quantum and relativity theory. Although most of us, including physicists, still move in that old world, and there is sense in this, considering the scale of our sensory apparatus, yet these gods really have been eclipsed and their world gone beyond recall.

B.   *The scientific world-view today*

(*i*) *Space, time, object, and determinism.* What is the new world-view then, that we rise to face on our side of the curtain fall, with those final, but not unhopeful, strains of this *Götterdämmerung* fading in our ears? Within a few decades, the development of quantum and relativity theory began to have an impact on the philosophical world-view—if not, scarcely even yet, on the theological. Absolute *space* and *time* had been relativized by Einstein in showing that all frameworks of reference were relative and in unveiling the intricate relation between space, time, and the velocity of light, the fastest signal that can be transmitted through the universe. Moreover, in his later Theory of General Relativity, the four-dimensional continuum of space–time was related, through an appropriate geometry, to gravitation, hitherto regarded as dependent on mass, which itself in the Special Theory of Relativity had already been shown to be interchangeable with energy. Thus from the ashes of absolute space and absolute time arose the phoenix of a new deep-seated relation between space, time, matter, and energy, as well as a new relativization of all of them considered separately.

Furthermore, under the impact of the need to adopt wave–particle complementarity for small particles and the acceptance

---

[10] K. Heim, *The Transformation of the Scientific World-view* (SCM Press, London, 1953), p. 24. See also A. R. Peacocke, 'The theory of relativity and our world-view' in *Einstein: the first hundred years*, ed. M. Goldsmith, A. Mackay and J. Woudhuysen (Pergamon Press, Oxford, 1979).

of the Heisenberg Uncertainty Principle, the ideal of classical physics, of the *objective observer* who rationally describes the properties of the world as they exist independently of his observations, had become untenable. As the physicist Richard Schlegel puts it:

We have learned that man cannot describe the physical world as if his own investigations had no effect upon it. The classical physicist who could sit, as it were, on one side of a translucent screen with his thoughts and experiences, viewing the world he studied on the other, is now the impossible spectator. For much of physics the dividing screen is lost, and cannot be replaced. Especially on the level of individual atomic processes the scientist now finds that he in fact has a role in the creation of the world that he is describing. It is not ... that his emotions bias his results, but rather that his act of observation participates in forming the natural world.

... even in so traditionally a model of an objective science as physics the completely uninvolved spectator has been shown to be an impossibility.[11]

There are alternative potentialities in a system at any moment and only some are realized according to their subsequent encounters, for example, with an observer. Man cannot describe the physical world as if his own investigations had no effect on it; especially at the level of the individual atomic processes, the scientific observer has a role in creating the world he is describing by his mere act of observation. 'We are both onlookers and actors in the great drama of existence', as Niels Bohr put it.[12] This is not to resort to subjectivism, still less to solipsism, for it is still possible to confirm observations intersubjectively. As Schlegel says: 'The quantum concepts are not to be regarded, then, as perturbations applying only to a highly limited part of nature. Rather we must think of quantum theory as telling us what we find the natural world to be when we penetrate to its micro-structure.'[13]

The other major feature of the world-view which incorporated classical physics was that of absolute *determinism* with its corollary of *predictability*. Today, in the light of

[11] R. Schlegel, 'The Impossible Spectator', 6th Centennial Review Lecture at Michigan State University, 12 May 1975, *The Centennial Review*, pp. 218, 230.

[12] N. Bohr, *Atomic Theory and Description of Nature* (Cambridge University Press, Cambridge, 1934), p. 119.

[13] Schlegel, op. cit., p. 223.

twentieth-century physics, this is no longer tenable in its old Laplacian form. For

> After such radical transformation of the basic classical concepts of space, time, matter, and motion, very little is left of the traditional corpuscular-kinetic scheme of nature. It is natural that classical determinism of the Laplacian type is threatened when the scheme on which it was based is disintegrating.... Not a single constituent concept of this Laplacian model of the universe remains unaffected; what has been left intact by the relativity theory was challenged by the theory of quanta or wave mechanics. Relativistically speaking, there is no such thing as a 'state of the world at an instant'; there is no such thing as an instantaneous configuration of particles [both of which determinism also assumes]. Moreover the concept of immutable and permanent particle, identifiable through space and time, is as obsolete as the concept of durationless instant.[14]

Moreover it is now realized more clearly that there is no logical necessity in believing determinism in the sense that 'if a state A of any sufficiently isolated system is followed by state B, the same state A will always be followed by B in the finest detail.'[15] It appears much more to be a postulate, an assumption, and an injunction to continue to look for causes, for generative mechanisms, connecting state A and state B. The notion of determinism in its strong form is closely linked with that of predictability. But we now know that there are certain systems at the sub-atomic level of which we shall never be able to say precisely what new state will be consequent upon any particular state at any earlier instant. As already mentioned, we know only the probability of a number of alternative states succeeding the initial one. So Born, at least, claimed that quantum theory does not deny causality, although it does deny absolute determinism: 'Causality ... is the postulate that one physical situation depends on the other, and causal research means the discovery of such dependence. This is still true in quantum physics, though the objects of observation for which a dependence is claimed are different: they are the probabilities of elementary events, not the single events themselves.'[16]

---

[14] M. Capek, *The Philosophical Impact of Contemporary Physics* (van Nostrand, Princeton, 1961), p. 392.

[15] K. Denbigh, *An Inventive Universe* (Hutchinson, London, 1975), p. 122.

[16] M. Born, *Natural Philosophy of Cause and Chance* (Clarendon Press, Oxford, 1949), p. 102.

The complexity of biological systems is also relevant to the question of predictability. Two individuals of the same biological species are often distinguishable through having individual attributes of their own, with respect to behaviour (in the case of larger organisms) or with respect to the specific molecular patterns and distribution in cells. This variability of their material, which is the lot of the experimental biologists, makes it inevitable that most biological laws are statistical. Only average properties can be related, so that, for example, the concept of evolution applies only to populations of organisms and not to individual organisms. Though this limits predictability, it does not mean that there are no causes in biology. There *are* intelligible interconnections between events, or patterns of events, with associated statistical reproducibility in prediction, in many cases.

In cases intermediate between sub-atomic particles and living organisms, that is, macroscopic bodies which are not living (the range covered by much classical mechanics, physics, and chemistry), we appear to be able to make predictions of a kind which satisfies the strong determinist view. But even here, in the case of molecular assemblies, knowledge is again usually statistical because law-like behaviour at the *macro*-level often rests on a statistical analysis at the *micro*-level, cf. the interpretations of statistical thermodynamics and of Boyle's law, relating pressure, volume and temperature of a gas. As Denbigh says: 'Physics displays many examples of processes where there are discontinuities at the atomic level but which can still be expressed at the macroscopic level by means of laws which effectively conceal these discontinuities (e.g., the laws of heat conduction and of diffusion).'[17] Even in this intermediate range between the world of fundamental particles and that of living organisms, the possibility of convergence towards perfectly precise prediction seems to be unattainable, because (see Denbigh[18]) at any particular stage there may be phenomena which remain to be discovered and which have a bearing on the prediction in question, because there are likely to be external influences which give rise to uncontrollable disturbances and,

---

[17] Denbigh, op. cit., pp. 121, 122.
[18] Denbigh, op. cit., Ch. 4.

finally, because not all relevant physical parameters can be accurately known to the degree of accuracy to make prediction possible over a long enough period to be of use (cf. the problems in predicting the weather or cloud formation).

Thus it is that the twentieth-century developments in physics and our new statistical awareness and understanding of the complexity of many natural phenomena have combined to modify drastically Laplacian determinism and predictability without denying causality. This implies an 'openness' in the texture of the nexus of natural events which was not generally appreciated before the revolution in physics which began in the first decade of this century.

(*ii*) *Evolution.* Perhaps the most distinctive feature of the modern scientific world-view is the converging perspective of a number of quite different sciences on the world as being in *process of evolution.* Historically it was geologists who first discovered time as the matrix of intelligible change in the eighteenth century, followed by biologists in the nineteenth century (as elaborated magnificently by molecular biologists in recent decades) and now the astro-physicists and astronomers have provided the evidence on which to base a scientific cosmology—the account of the evolution in time of the universe, of its galaxies, of the solar system, and of the planet Earth. These insights of cosmology have now been coupled with speculation and knowledge about the origin and evolution of life on the Earth to yield a perspective which is of a beauty and an all-embracing scope that, when fully apprehended, dazzles the mind and heightens the sensibilities. Only a latter twentieth-century Dante could do justice to the splendour of this panorama. But let me more modestly, and briefly, just remind you of some of its salient features.

The cosmologists and astro-physicists have shown us how, from a time of the order of ten billion (10^{10}) years ago, a primeval unimaginably condensed mass of fundamental particles could have been transformed, at the same time expanding, into the present observable universe in which these particles have undergone various transformations and condensations to give rise to the matter we now observe through our telescopes and spectroscopes in the universe. The nuclear physicists and chemists have unravelled how, in the nuclear furnaces of some very hot stars, the heavy elements formed. This evidence, combined with that of astronomers and the geophysicists, has shown how it is that, through super-novae explosions which distributed these heavy elements to a 'second generation' of stars, planets such as our own Earth came into existence. The chemists have demonstrated how, on the surface of this planet as it cooled, the simpler molecules, both large and small, which can form the building blocks of living systems, could have arisen by purely chemical processes. The molecular biologists, the biochemists, the geneticists, have given us the basis for inferring how from this 'primeval soup' might well have emerged complex organizations of matter which could become self-reproducing. The biologists have elaborated how, once given these primeval living forms, the processes of natural selection operating upon genetic mutations, that is of changes in the information and instructions transmitted from one generation to another, could have given rise to the vast variety of living forms that have existed, and many of which still do exist, on the surface of the Earth. The psychologists and linguists and anthropologists are beginning to tell us how the emergent self-conscious man acquired language, and society, and culture—a culture which has engendered a desire to ask questions such as those to which we now address ourselves.

(*iii*) *A continuous, law-like nexus.* A notable aspect of this picture is the seamless character of the web which has been spun on the loom of time: the process is continuous from beginning to end and at no point does the modern natural scientist have to invoke any non-natural causes to explain what he observes or infers about the past. His explanations are usually in terms of concepts, theories, and mechanisms which he can confirm by, or infer from, present-day experiments, or reasonably infer by extrapolating from fundamental principles which themselves are confirmable by experiment. In brief, the natural scientist would say the evolution of the cosmos is according to 'natural laws', that is, by processes built in as natural potentialities of the stuff of the world, of matter–energy–space–time. The scientist's confidence is sufficiently well based that it would be extremely unwise for any proponent of theism to attempt to find any gaps to be closed by the intervention of some non-natural agent, such as a god.

(*iv*) *Emergence*.   Another outstanding feature of this process of evolution is its *emergent* character. K. Denbigh, who is a well-known thermodynamicist, describes it thus:

> What *can* be said with a considerable degree of confidence is that cosmic evolution has been attended by a great increase in *the richness and diversity of forms*. No doubt such an 'increase' would be difficult to define in precise scientific terms, but even so the evolutionary sequence which has been outlined is consistent with the idea that diversity has made its appearance out of homogeneity, and also that many of the significant events in the sequence may have occurred non-deterministically in some of their details. If so, this is an inventive process and is one that is still continuing.[19]

As matter has coalesced into more and more complex forms, new and very different kinds of behaviour and properties have come into existence and these require special methods of investigation, special interpretative principles and concepts, and indeed often generate an entirely new language for describing them at their own particular new level. The extent to which these new emergent features of the universe can be explained, 'reduced', to descriptions relevant to less complex levels in the natural hierarchy will be a question to which we must return.[20] For the moment we notice the nature of the development and observe that time has been given new meaning as the 'carrier or locus of innovative change',[21] a role scarcely envisaged as a possibility within that Newtonian absolute time which flowed 'equably without relation to anything external'.

(*v*) *Comparison of classical and contemporary scientific world-views*. Looking back, we now see that the beginning of the twentieth century initiated a series of fundamental changes in the scientific perspective of the world. Let us summarize some of the

---

[19] Denbigh, op. cit., p. 156. Note that Denbigh assumes (p. 153), in a way I myself would not, that an essential condition for a process to be inventive, and so to result in the production of something novel, is the absence of necessity, that is, not to be fully determined, which is (in his treatment) not to be fully predictable.

[20] See Lecture IV.

[21] H. K. Schilling, *The New Consciousness in Science and Religion* (SCM Press, London, 1973), p. 126.

contrasts between the scientific world-view of the half-century terminating at 1900, the classical 'then', and that of today.

Then, nature was regarded as simple in structure, basically substantive and reducible to a pattern of combination of relatively few entities: *now* we know it is enormously complex, of multitudinous variety, basically relational, consisting of a hierarchy of levels of organization, which are not always conceptually reducible[22] and which span from the baffling *micro*-world of the sub-atomic through the *macro*-world, which includes the biosphere and is within the range of our sense perceptions, to the *mega*-world of inter-galactic distances, of cosmological processes unfolding over billions of years and of the gravitational fields of 'black holes'.

Then, as we saw earlier, the natural world was regarded as mechanically determined and predictable, à la Laplace, from any given state by means of laws of all-embracing scope: *now* the world is regarded rather as the scene of the interplay[23] of chance and of statistical, as well as causal, uniformity in which there is indeterminacy at the *micro*-level and unpredictability because of the complexity of causal chains at the *macro*-level, especially that of the biological.

Then, in spite of Darwinism, the natural world was still largely regarded as static in form, exhibiting little novelty, essentially complete, unchanging and closed: *now* it is discovered to be dynamic—always in process—a nexus of evolving forms, essentially incomplete, inexhaustible in its potential for change and open to the future.

Then, the world seemed to be decomposable into readily intelligible sub-units and to have accessible foundations: *now* a sense of mystery at the quality of the known and the quantity of the unknown has been engendered by the depths of reality encountered at the edges of experimental and theoretical inquiry—there seems to be no 'ground' level of simplicity, no accessible bed-rock on which to build the structure of the universe. Physicists have become aware of the 'infinite complexity that can be fitted into a finite domain'[24] both with

[22] See Lecture IV.
[23] See Lecture III.
[24] C. W. Misner, 'Cosmology and Theology', in *Cosmology, History and Theology*, ed. W. Yourgrau and A. D. Breck (Plenum Press, New York and London, 1977), p. 90.

respect to the sub-atomic domain of space and the new world of 'entities' discovered therein, and to the unimaginably small, but finite, intervals of time immediately on 'our' side of that singularity in cosmic history from which the present universe expanded roughly 10^{10} years ago—

... as we understand better and better the very early Universe, we may learn that complexities are to be found at every smaller and smaller level in the remote past. This need not mean that each underlying or previous level is a scale model of the adjacent one (as in the simple models that can be presented explicitly)—it may ultimately prove novel and interesting in various ways—but the infinite regress should be a part of our picture of the cosmological singularity.[25]

III. NEW PERSPECTIVES ON THE RELATION BETWEEN MAN AND THE UNIVERSE

A. The expansion of human consciousness and its limitations

From these contrasts between the scientific perspective on the world of the *then* of 1900 and the *now* of the second half of the twentieth century, it becomes clear that we have in our times witnessed an unparalleled saltation in the expansion of human consciousness of the world which is its ambience. This expansion has, curiously and significantly, been coupled with a new awareness of the fragility of human knowledge consequent upon the realization, on the one hand, of its ambiguity, on account of the loss of the 'impossible' objective spectator through the Uncertainty Principle and relativity; and also consequent upon, on the other hand, the physical limitations which constitute 'horizons' beyond which we are unable to explore the universe. For parts of the universe are always, it seems, causally out of contact with some other parts at any given point in space–time,[26] and there are limitations at the other end of the spatial scale which ensure that there is a lower limit, which we are far from approaching yet, to the smallest distance we can dis-

---

The situation is superbly illustrated in a computer-animated film displaying the infinite degree of tortuosity nested within tortuosity of a curve that snakes its way about sufficiently to cover every point on a square (N. Max, *Space Filling Curves*, (1974), 16 mm film, Educational Development Center, 39 Chapel St., Newton, Mass.).

[25] Misner, op. cit., p. 91.
[26] Misner, op. cit., pp. 81–2.

criminate by virtue of the upper limit to the energy available to man and so to the lower limit of wavelength of any energized investigating 'particle'. In such a context, it is then not surprising that Sir Bernard Lovell entitled his BA address 'In the centre of immensities', and that the physicist V. Weisskopf reminds us that 'Our knowledge is an island in the infinite ocean of the unknown.'[27]

It is not surprising, too, that the intellectual beauty, coherence, and all-embracing scope of the present scientific perspective on the universe that the physical (let alone the biological) sciences have vouchsafed us in the last few decades provokes even in quite hard-headed scientists a response of awe, almost of a sense of the 'mysterium tremendum et fascinans'[28] beloved of theologians. Many of the former would indeed, all rhetoric apart, echo the remarks with which Hoyle concluded his broadcast lectures on the nature of the universe in 1950: 'When by patient enquiry we learn the answer to any problem, we always find, both as a whole and in detail, that the answer thus revealed is finer in concept and design than anything we could ever have arrived at by a random guess.'[29] And the wonder in our expanded consciousness of the universe continues nearly thirty years later with no diminution in intensity.[30] If the world were a closed system we would

---

[27] V. Weisskopf, *Knowledge and Wonder* (Doubleday, Garden City, N.Y., 1962), p. 100.

[28] R. Otto, *The Idea of the Holy* (Oxford University Press, London, 1923).

[29] F. Hoyle, *The Nature of the Universe* (Blackwell, Oxford, 1960 edn.), p. 103.

[30] In his day, too, Kant had to admit that whatever he made of the 'physico-theological proof' of the existence of God, nevertheless: 'This world presents to us so immeasurable a stage of variety, order, purposiveness, and beauty, as displayed alike in its infinite extent and in the unlimited divisibility of its parts, that even with such knowledge as our weak understanding can acquire of it, we are brought face to face with so many marvels immeasurably great, that all speech loses its force, all numbers their power to measure, our thoughts themselves all definiteness, and that our judgement of the whole resolves itself into an amazement which is speechless, and only the more eloquent on that account. Everywhere we see a chain of effects and causes, of ends and means, a regularity in origination and dissolution. Nothing has of itself come into the condition in which we find it to exist, but always points to something else as its cause, while this in turn commits us to repetition of the same enquiry. The whole universe must thus sink into the abyss of nothingness, unless, over and above this infinite chain of contingencies, we assume something to support it—something which is original and independently self-subsistent, and which as the cause of the origin of the universe secures also at the same time its continuance. What magnitude are we to ascribe to this supreme cause—admitting that it is supreme in respect of all things in the world? We are not acquainted with the whole content of the world,

expect an ultimate convergence in our knowledge as it accumu-
lates, but nothing like this seems to be happening. Our awareness of our ignorance grows in parallel with, indeed faster
than, the growth in our knowledge.

B. A cognizing and self-cognizing universe?

Perhaps the limitations on the human intellect to fathom these
depths should cause no surprise. For the human brain which
generates this inquiring activity is itself made up of the same
matter–energy in space–time as the world it is investigating
and has evolved as a particular form of organization of that
world-stuff. Man may well wonder, with Darwin, 'But then
arises the doubt, can the mind of man, which has, as I fully
believe, been developed from a mind as low as that possessed
by the lowest animals, be trusted when it draws such grand
conclusions?'[31] Yet this has never inhibited man from seeking
the evidence for 'grand conclusions' and, like Darwin himself,
drawing them when need be. Our unity with the rest of the
biological world should hardly need emphasizing in these days
of ecological concern, yet even the most hardened molecular
biologist may find his imagination quickened by the extraordinary unity of the biochemical metabolic mechanisms which
man shares with other organisms, as lowly as bacteria, and by
the common genetic code which translates the genetic information of the nucleotide sequences in DNA into amino-acid
sequences of working proteins, a translation code which might
have been otherwise, chemically speaking, and whose universality points to a common origin for all living organisms.
Even more striking is the thought that the very existence of
the atoms, heavier than hydrogen, which make life possible
(C, N, O, P, Fe, etc.) is the result of nuclear-formation processes
in some remote super-novae explosions. But for those explosions
we would have, for example, no iron to carry the oxygen in

---

still less do we know how to estimate its magnitude by comparison with all that is
possible. But since we cannot, as regards causality, dispense with an ultimate and
supreme being, what is there to prevent us ascribing to it a degree of perfection that
sets it *above everything else that is possible*?' (I. Kant, *Critique of Pure Reason*, translated
by N. Kemp Smith (Macmillan Press, London, edition of 1933 reprinted 1976), p. 519.)
   [31] C. Darwin, *Autobiography*, 1876, in *The Life and Letters of Charles Darwin*, ed.
F. Darwin (Murray, London, 1887), i. 313.

the haemoglobin of our blood stream, and so maintain our brains in an active state to communicate with each other.

Indeed our dependence and involvement in the cosmic processes can be pushed back further. The values of the fundamental constants (velocity of light, gravitational constant, electronic charge, mass of the proton, Planck's constant, etc.) determine the kind of physical world in which we live and are the basis of physicists' calculations. If, for example, the proton–proton interaction were only slightly different, then all of the protons in the universe (which were the raw material of heavier atoms in the subsequent 'nuclear furnaces') would have turned into the more inert helium in the early stages of expansion of the galaxies. As Sir Bernard Lovell put it: 'No galaxies, no stars, no life would have emerged. It would be a universe forever unknowable by living creatures. The existence of a remarkable and intimate relationship between man, the fundamental constants of nature and the initial moments of space and time, seems to be an inescapable condition of our presence here . . .'[32] And a similar thought is echoed by the physicist J. Wheeler, who has been quoted as saying that

No theory of physics that deals only with physics will ever explain physics. I believe that as we go on trying to understand the universe, we are at the same time trying to understand man. . . . Only as we recognise that tie will we be able to make headway into some of the most difficult issues that confront us. . . . Man, the start of the analysis, man the end of the analysis—because the physical world is in some deep sense tied to the human being.[33]

The material units of the universe—the sub-atomic particles, the atoms and the molecules they can form—are the fundamental entities constituted in their matter–energy–space–time relationships, and are such that they have built in, as it were, the potentiality of becoming organized in that special kind of complex system we call living and, in particular, in the system of the human brain in the human body which displays conscious activity. In man, the stuff of the universe has become cognizing and self-cognizing. How this potentiality has become actualized in living forms and the role of 'chance' in this process

[32] Lovell, op. cit., p. 6.
[33] Quoted by F. Helitzer, 'The Princeton Galaxy', *Intellectual Digest*, June 1973, p. 32.

will concern us later, but we must now consider some fascinating speculations which arise from the intimacy of our relation with the nature of the universe. One, long entertained, is the possibility of conscious life elsewhere in this universe. But new ones have recently emerged.

C. The anthropic principle

The first is that of the 'anthropic principle', as it has been called[34] by Carter, who has proposed this principle to try to make intelligible certain 'large number coincidences' which have often been noted—these include: (i) the equality, to within a few powers of ten (the actual number is $\sim 10^{-60}$) between the Hubble fractional expansion rate of the universe and the reciprocal of the number of baryons in most stars (from red giants to white dwarfs); and (ii) Eddington's famous relation that the 'number of particles in the visible universe' is the inverse square of the gravitational coupling constant. Carter argues that these, and some other, large number coincidences can be seen to be consistent with current ('General Relativistic Big Bang') physics and cosmology if one evokes an '*anthropic principle* to the effect that what we expect to observe must be restricted to the conditions necessary for our presence as observers'.[35] In its 'weak' form he enunciates this principle as: '... we must be prepared to take account of the fact that our location in the universe is *necessarily* privileged to the extent of being compatible with our existence as observers.'[36] So that, for example, for life to have evolved at all, the time for which the present universe has existed (which is the reciprocal of the Hubble constant, H, the ratio of the recessional speed and distance of the galaxies) must be such that there are stars in it which have existed long enough for life to have evolved upon them—and so to generate man, as observer. (If the life of the universe were much greater than the life of a typical star, there would be too few energy-producing stars for any chance of

---

[34] B. Carter, 'Large number coincidences and the anthropic principle in cosmology', in *Confrontation of Cosmological Theories with Observational Data*, ed. M. S. Longair (IAU, 1974), pp. 291–8.

[35] Carter, op. cit., p. 291.

[36] Carter, op. cit., p. 293.

life surviving now; if it were much less, there would have been insufficient time for the formation of the heavy atoms on which life depends.) This 'weak anthropic' restriction implies, he claims, certain large number coincidences (such as (i) above), and others (such as (ii)) are indicated by a 'strong' form of the same principle, which Carter states as: '... that the Universe (and hence the fundamental parameters on which it depends) must be such as to admit the creation of observers within it at some stage.'[37] He develops this further:

It is of course always philosophically possible ... to promote a *prediction* based on the strong anthropic principle to the status of an *explanation* by thinking in terms of a 'world ensemble'. By this I mean an ensemble of universes characterised by all conceivable combinations of initial conditions and fundamental constants (the distinction between these concepts, which is not clear cut, being that the former refer essentially to local and the latter to global features). The existence of any organism describable as an observer will only be possible for certain restricted combinations of the parameters, which distinguish within the world-ensemble an exceptional *cognizable* subset.[38]

Briefly, because we have evolved to observe it, our universe is a *cognizable* one and this, he suggests, places restrictions on the kind of universe it could be out of an 'ensemble of universes' (to quote Carter's phrase). This seems to express in a new way the old assertion that the universe in which we exist is contingent.

To summarize: we now observe that our looking out on to the great vistas of space and our peering back into aeons of unimaginably distant time to the earliest stages of the formation of the universe have curiously turned full circle and we find ourselves reflecting on our own presence in the universe and our cognitive role as observers of it. Far from man's presence in the universe being a curious and inexplicable surd, we find we are remarkably and intimately related to it on the basis of this contemporary scientific evidence which is 'indicative of a far greater degree of man's total involvement with the universe'[39] than ever before envisaged.

---

[37] Carter, op. cit., p. 294.
[38] Carter, op. cit., pp. 295–6.
[39] Lovell, op. cit., p. 6.

IV. CHANCE AND NECESSITY IN AN 'ENSEMBLE' OF UNIVERSES

Carter's reference to an 'ensemble of universes' serves to introduce us to another major speculation of cosmologists. It is clear that, in tracing the history of the universe back to the point c. 10 billion years ago when all its mass is postulated as having been concentrated into a relatively small space (of the size of an average laboratory), there comes a point beyond which the laws of physics as we know, test, or extrapolate them, cannot be applied. Even so, this does not exclude the possibility that there is another side from us beyond the 'hot big bang'. Beyond this point, when the 'universe is squeezed through a knot hole',[40] all physical constants might be different—even though all such extrapolation is speculative and hazardous. So that the nuclear- and electronic-energy levels of the atoms of carbon, nitrogen, hydrogen, oxygen, and phosphorus on which living matter, as we know it, is so utterly dependent, would be different. Indeed these atoms, or even atoms as such, might not be constituent units of the universe on the 'other' side of the condensed gravitational mass from which our present observable universe expanded. So we have to envisage the possibility that our universe (the one which has allowed the emergence of life, and so of man) is but one amongst a, possibly infinite, cycle of universes. Our universe would then just happen to be one in which the physical constants (and even the physical laws) are such that living matter, and thus man, could, in time, appear within it—man who could then argue about cosmology and the existence of God! A small change in the physical constants could result in an uninhabitable universe and, if there were various possible sets of values of these constants, perhaps with different physical laws, there could be a run of universes of which a number, possibly the great majority, would not produce forms of living and eventually, conscious beings. In other words, our present universe may well be the only 'cognizable' universe which is possible according to the physical laws we know; that is, it might be the only one which could, by generating life, be observed at all from within itself.

[40] C. W. Misner, K. S. Thorne, and J. A. Wheeler, *Gravitation* (W. H. Freeman, San Francisco, 1973), Ch. 44.

If we are to take this suggestion seriously, and I believe we must, and if we are to look upon the role of 'chance' as the means whereby all the potentialities of the universe are explored, then we have to extend both the time-scale and the ontological range over which 'chance' is thought to operate. Chance must now be regarded as, not only operating (as we shall see in Lecture III) to elicit the potentialities of matter–energy–space–time over the spatial and temporal scale of our present universe, but also over the ensemble of possible universes, in most of which matter–energy–space–time might be replaced by new entities consistent with other values of the physical constants and acting, presumably, according to quite different physical laws than those we can ascertain in principle in this universe. Even so, the point is that over the extension of space–time (or whatever replaces it) the potentialities of the ensemble of universes, as well as of this particular universe, are being or have been run through, or 'explored', and it is this which transforms 'chance' and randomness into creative agents. If we see 'chance' in this context, we need not be daunted by the fact that the existence of life and, indeed, of our actual universe, is the result of its operation; we no longer have to apotheosize 'chance' (*pace* Monod) as a metaphysical principle destructive of any attribution of significance and meaning to the universe. For however long it may have taken on the time-scale of our universe, or however many universes may have preceded (and might follow) it, the fact is that matter–energy has in space–time, in *this* universe, acquired the ability to adopt self-replicating living structures which have acquired self-consciousness and the ability to know that they exist and have even now found ways of discovering how they have come to be.

So it is that we came to stress the particularity of our universe. For in this universe there are certain basic given features—the fundamental constants, the nature of the fundamental particles (and so of atoms, and so of molecules, and so of complex organizations of molecules), the physical laws of the interrelation of matter, energy, space, and time—which limit what can eventually be realized through its dynamic, evolutionary processes. Even though these limitations are not 'necessary' in the sense of being features of all worlds that may have existed, or will do so, yet for us they constitute the givenness of our existence, its 'necessity', in this sense. The givenness of these limitations appear to us as part of the 'necessity' of our existence—as boundary conditions which will never be otherwise. But this now appears as a limited kind of 'necessity' for these apparently given features of our universe are not 'necessary' in the sense of being features of all possible actual worlds, in the light of the foregoing speculations. Man's existence is non-necessary, that is, is contingent, in the sense of his not being present in all possible actual worlds, whose existence he can infer, and the same could also be affirmed of any other self-conscious being composed of particles of the kind which make up this universe.

Although the potentialities of our given universe may not be unlimited, their actualization nevertheless remains quite open from the vantage-point of the twentieth-century scientific perspective. The givenness of the parameters of our universe, its 'necessity', does not 'crib, cabin, or confine' the open future in a universe in which dynamic processes have led, and still do lead, all the time to the emergence of new complex entities of distinctive qualities and activities which include not only biological life, but the whole historical, social, and personal life of man. What constitutes these qualities and this distinctiveness, especially the human, we shall need to think about again, but it is worth noting that it is the very givenness of the parameters of the milieu of human life—the parameters of the fundamental constants, fundamental particles, and the laws of matter–energy–space–time—which make human freedom and human perception possible. Only in a universe with this kind of ordered givenness is there the stable matrix within which freedom can be genuinely exercised and which makes perception and conceptualization possible. In other words, the emergence of human consciousness, with its characteristics of freedom and perception, is only possible in a cosmos which exerts certain constraints. A chaos in which no entity existed long enough to be stable and perceivable would be simply nothing at all in relation to conscious action or perception. So in this more metaphysical sense too, the cosmic order is a necessary prerequisite of conscious personal existence as we know it in human beings. The *way* in which such personal existences have emerged in the universe will concern us later: for the moment we now see that it was always possible and the question of whether or not it was 'likely', or even 'inevitable', will have to be deferred until the next lecture. My present point is that the emergence of conscious life has indeed happened in this universe and it is the *fact* of this which now raises certain questions.

V. MAN'S EMERGENCE IN THE UNIVERSE

One of the outstanding features of the processes of development in the cosmos is, then, that in time new forms of organization of matter emerge with new qualities and behaviour, and man is one such emergent entity. Even allowing for our natural anthropocentrism, there are purely biological criteria[41] whereby man may be seen to constitute a point of development in which many tendencies have reached a pre-eminently high level. Yet a full description of the 'man' who has emerged in the universe goes beyond his purely biological features. One's assessment of the nature of man has a determinative influence at this point and the challenge of the presence of man in the universe as the outcome of evolution evokes various responses among scientists—not surprisingly, because evaluation is involved. To some, like Monod, it is a stark fact but in itself not significant for the nature of the cosmos. But to others such as Eccles, Dobzhansky, Hardy, Hinshelwood, and Thorpe (to name a few) 'It is the height of intellectual perversion to renounce, in the name of scientific objectivity, our position as the highest form of life on earth, and our own advent by a process of evolution as the most important problem of evolution.'[42] For to take seriously, as scientists ought, the presence of man as the outcome of the evolution of matter–energy in space–time, in this cosmos, or in the ensemble of cosmoses, is to open up many questions of evaluation which go far beyond the applicable range of languages, concepts, and modes of investigation developed by the natural sciences for describing and examining the less developed and less complex forms of matter which preceded the emergence of man. For if the

---

[41] See G. G. Simpson, *The Meaning of Evolution* (Yale University Press, New Haven, 1949, and Bantam Books, New York, 1971); A. R. Peacocke, *Science and the Christian Experiment* (Oxford University Press, London, 1971), Ch. 3.
[42] M. Polanyi, *The Tacit Dimension* (Routledge & Kegan Paul, London, 1967), p. 47.

stuff of the world, the primeval concourse of protons, neutrinos, photons, etc. has, as a matter of fact and not conjecture, become man—man who possesses not only a social life and biological organization but also an 'inner', self-conscious life in relation to others, which makes him creative and personal—then how are we properly to interpret the cosmological development (or the development of the cosmoses) if, after aeons of time, the fundamental particles have become human beings, have evidenced that quality of life we call 'personal'?

Moreover, paradoxically and significantly, knowledge of the process by which they have arrived in the world seems to be confined to human beings. We alone reflect on our atomic and simpler forebears and we alone adjust our behaviour in the light of this perspective. To ignore the glory, the predicament, and the possibilities of man in assessing the trend and meaning of the cosmic development would be as unscientific as the former pre-Copernican account of the universe, based as it was on the contrary prejudice.

En passant, let us note that, in order to raise such questions we do not have to be tied specifically to any particular cosmological theory, whether of the 'hot big bang' kind, to which I have been principally referring, or of a cold early universe,[43] or of an oscillating universe.[44] For it is salutary to remember that most cosmological theories are under-determined by the facts and greatly influenced by mathematical considerations, from which quasi-aesthetic criteria are not entirely absent.[45] Nevertheless, all models include the empirically observed feature of continuity of the universe with its past, i.e. the continuance of the operation of physical laws as we now know them (even if under an almost unimaginable extremity of conditions) and converge on the history of the solar system and, more particularly, on the Earth as the scene of the origin of life and of organic evolution to man. So questions of explanation and of meaning are raised in response to quite general

[43] K. Tomita, 'On a Chaotic Early Universe', in *Cosmology, History and Theology*, in Yourgrau and Breck (eds.), op. cit. (above, p. 62 n. 24), p. 133.

[44] J. Heidemann, 'The Expansion of the Universe in the Frame of Conventional General Relativity', in Yourgrau and Breck (eds.), op. cit., pp. 48 ff.; Paul Davies, *The Runaway Universe* (Dent & Sons, London, 1977), pp. 162 ff.; and Lecture VIII.

[45] Cf. M. Hesse, 'Criteria of truth in science and theology', *Religious Studies*, 11 (1975), 389; and *The Structure of Scientific Inference* (Macmillan, London, 1974).

features of the scientific perspective of the universe (even though these general features have become apparent only on the basis of a vast programme of detailed work) and are not specifically tied to any one model. Nevertheless I have found it convenient to develop my points in relation to the best current available model, that of the 'hot big bang', which happens, not only to be particularly dramatic, but also to locate at a point in time an apparent beginning to the universe as we can observe it.

VI.   THE SEARCH FOR INTELLIGIBILITY AND MEANING IN SCIENCE AND IN THE JUDEO-CHRISTIAN TRADITION

In the previous lecture, I spoke of two kinds of search in which men are engaged in relation to the world in which they live. One, primarily intellectual, is the search for intelligibility, for explanation, and, though not without existential urgency, arises from the asking of questions such as 'Why is there anything at all?', 'Why does the world exist?', 'Is there a reason for the existence of the world?', and, somewhat differently, 'Why are things the way they are?' Such questions, even if logically unanswerable, add impetus to the other search—that for personal meaning in human existence, in general, and our own in particular.

What has happened, it seems to me, is that the twentieth-century scientific perspective of a developing cosmos which generates persons now ties together, in a stronger bond than ever before, our search for intelligibility, our questions about the fact of existence, and our search for personal meaning. For it now appears that the universe is of such a kind that we are generated within it out of its very stuff by its own natural processes; then, having arrived, we seek intelligibility and meaning in that universe and in that process. Indeed we cannot avoid, in the light of the scientific perspective, merging into one the problems of intelligibility of the universe and of personal meaning—by urging our questions about the cosmos in forms which include ourselves and therefore, implicitly, also include both our own search for meaning and the fact of our presence in the universe. We cannot help asking a question something like this: 'What is the intelligible meaning of a cosmos in which the primeval assembly of fundamental particles has eventually manifested the potentiality of becoming organized in forms which are conscious and self-conscious, that is, are human and personal and in their very thinking transcend that out of which they have emerged?' Or: 'If we continue to press for "explanation" and to search for "meaning", does not the very continuity of the universe, with its gradual elaboration of its potentialities, from its dispersal *c.* 10^{10} years ago as an expanding mass of particles to the emergence of persons on the surface of the planet Earth (perhaps elsewhere too), imply that any categories of "explanation" and "meaning" must at least *include* the personal?' That is, any 'explanation' and 'meaning' will be satisfactory only if that which serves as source of explanation and content of meaning includes, and is not subsumed by, both physical and personal categories to the extent required for it actually to be explanation and to provide meaning. But this is nothing else than to assert that the source and meaning of all-that-is is other than the world, transcends the word and is least misleadingly described in supra-personal terms. In English, the concept of 'God' has served to name this transcendent source and meaning—that is, the doctrine of creation is a response to both searches.

It is important to see what moves we have been making here. I am suggesting that the perspective of the world that science has in our age engendered raises acutely questions about the world and our relation to it which by their very nature cannot be answered from within the realm of discourse of science alone. That is why we have, willy-nilly, found ourselves moving into theological language and using terms such as 'God', 'Creator', and 'transcendent'. For the questions raised by the character of the physical universe, and by man's presence and emergence within it, are not questions of the kind which the tools of science have been developed to answer. For, ironically, the scientific perspective has given a new urgency and point to the search for intelligibility and meaning, both by showing how man is an intimate part of the universe and also by the very success of the scientific enterprise itself exemplifying how man stands over against the world as subject (even if not in the absolute sense of 'classical' physics). Man who seeks intelligibility and meaning *in* the world himself transcends that world through his personal consciousness. Thus in the perspective of science, the emergence of human consciousness is both a problem and a clue. It is a *problem* because why should the universe self-generate structures composed of its basic units that should seek intelligibility and meaning? And it is a *clue* afforded by the emergence, within the cosmic process, of self-conscious beings which (who) constitute a mode of self-integration which is transcendent with respect to (stands as subject over) the units of which it is composed.

It is at this point, with science at the end of its tether, that perhaps late-twentieth-century scientific man might come to listen again, and more attentively, to another resource at his disposal—the resource afforded by that parallel search for intelligibility and meaning which characterizes all religious quests, but which has been particularly and explicitly developed within the very Judeo-Christian tradition that provided the fertile seedbed of empirical science itself. The appetite for intelligibility and meaning which the scientific perspective both induces and sharpens is one which the Judeo-Christian understanding of God as Creator seeks to satisfy. We therefore have an obligation to examine the riches offered by this resource in our culture for satisfying our search for intelligibility and meaning in the world.

Such an examination involves a dialectic and a dialogue, for it is *to* the world described by science that our questions inevitably refer, and it is *in* the world so described that we seek meaning—for that world-view has been forged by a science which is the most reliable intellectual tool man has devised for understanding the structure and nature of the cosmos into which he is born. So we should expect the language (images, metaphors, and models) that constitute the Judeo-Christian understanding of God as Creator not to remain unaffected by the perspective on the world that science now affords. The drift of the argument up to this point has been well expressed in a statement which a group of us drew up in the report of a World Council of Churches' consultation in 1975:

The middle half of the 20th century has changed all this [Newtonian world-view] in two fundamental ways. The universe as a whole and everything within it is now seen to have a history. Everything is born, develops, and ultimately must die. Nothing is self-explanatory or eternal. Our particular cosmos emerged in the beginning equipped with three spatial dimensions, time, and a particular form of matter governed by particular and contingent physical laws together with at least three fundamental constants whose numerical values seem to have been arbitrarily chosen. During the first few hours of its history, this original matter formed itself into atoms of hydrogen and helium, and this was all there was for a long time thereafter. Much later the hydrogen and helium separated under gravity into large masses which became galaxies. Long after this birth of galaxies, stars were formed within them and the evolution of atoms began. In time all the atoms beyond helium were formed within stars. Then much later, on our earth nucleic acids and proteins were produced out of methane, ammonia, and water in its atmosphere. From these, living cells were constituted, and finally the human race was produced. But people die, the sun and the earth must finally die, and ultimately all atoms, galaxies, and the universe itself must die. Nothing—not even space, time, matter, or the laws of physics—is self-explanatory. This is the most radical contingency imaginable. Why and for what purpose was this particular cosmos brought into existence in the first place? What accounts for the fact that the design of its atoms and the laws governing their behaviour made it possible finally to produce the human being within it? The cosmos did not have to be at all, and it certainly did not have to be designed in such a way as to make humanity a possibility. Such questions have no answers within science, and their contemplation leads to some sort of theological inquiry.[46]

So it is we come to consider again—

VII. THE DOCTRINE OF CREATION IN THE LIGHT OF THE SCIENTIFIC WORLD-VIEW

A. *Some clarifications*

Certain clarifications are required from the outset. In saying that God is, and that God is Creator, we do not affirm that he/ she (rather than it, for personal pronouns are now clearly less misleading than impersonal ones) is any ordinary 'cause' in the physical nexus of the universe itself—otherwise God would be

[46] Report of a World Council of Churches' Consultation in Mexico City, 1975, on 'The Christian faith and the changing face of science and technology', published in *Anticipation*, May 1976, No. 22 (for Church & Society, World Council of Churches, 150 Route de Ferney, 1211, Geneva, 20).

neither explanation nor possible meaning. He[47] cannot be the old 'God of the gaps'—but we shall have to explore, in the light of the scientific account of the world, what images are best now employed to unfold the relation of the all-embracing reality of God to that world to which he stands as Creator. For, *ex hypothesi*, God's uniqueness and distinction from the world ensures that nothing in the world itself can ever be a totally satisfactory and true image of his all-embracing Reality. Furthermore, the principal stress in the Judeo-Christian doctrine of creation, as mentioned in Lecture I, is on the dependence and contingency of all entities, and events, other than God himself: it is about a perennial relationship between God and the world and not about the beginning of the Earth, or the whole universe at a point in time. The phrase 'the whole universe' is notoriously ambiguous since it seems to imply a boundary or limit 'beyond' or outside which, in some sense, God exists—and this will not do at all for God would then be in a 'beyond' or 'outside' which would be but an extension of the same framework of reference as that in which the 'whole universe' is conceived to exist. The doctrine of creation avoids this conceptual impasse by affirming that any particular event or entity would not happen or would not be at all were it not for the sustaining creative will and activity of God. By the time of Darwin, in spite of Schleiermacher, as recounted by J. Pelikan in his valuable article[48] establishing this point, the doctrine of creation as generally propounded in Christian theology had come to lay its stress on 'original' creation, the primal initiating act of God, rather than on God's continuing creative work in sustaining and preserving—with the theological repercussions we have briefly referred to in the first lecture. But, as Pelikan shows,[49] this emphasis of the eighteenth- and nineteenth-century doctrine of creation was, by then, an unbalanced version of both the biblical understanding (the God in whom 'we live, and move, and have our being' of Acts 17: 28)

---

[47] Dropping the female personal pronoun only for brevity. We shall have cause later to recall this omission—and to regret the limitation it implies.

[48] J. Pelikan, 'Creation and causality in the history of Christian thought', in *Evolution after Darwin*, ed. Sol Tax and C. Callender (University of Chicago Press, Chicago, 1960), Vol. iii, *Issues in Evolution*, pp. 29–40.

[49] Ibid.

and that of some of the early Fathers, such as Justin Martyr. Pelikan argues that even *creatio ex nihilo* was apparently first expounded by Theophilus of Antioch as a corollary to the biblical understanding, in order to stress that what God sustains, namely matter, he himself originated. So the world was dependent on God in both respects.

Time, in modern relativistic physics, as we have seen, is an integral and basic constituent of nature; hence, on any theistic view, time itself has to be regarded as owing its existence to God,[50] as Augustine perceived (in the 11th chapter of the *Confessions*). It is this 'owing its existence to God' which is the essential core of the idea of creation.

Scientific cosmology, in investigating and making theoretical deductions about the remote history of our universe cannot, in principle, be doing anything which can contradict such a concept of creation. From our radio-telescopes and other analyses of the nature of the universe at great distances of space and time we may, or may not, be able to infer that there was a point (the 'hot big bang') in space–time when the universe, as we can observe it, began and, perhaps, what happened on the other side of that critical point. But, whatever we eventually do infer, the central characteristic core of the doctrine of creation itself would not be affected, since that concerns the relationship of all the created order, including time itself, to their Creator—their Sustainer and Preserver.

B. 'Creatio continua'

Nevertheless, there is an important feature which the scientific perspective inevitably reintroduces into this idea of creation. It is the realization, now made explicit, that the cosmos which is sustained and held in being by God (this sustaining and holding itself constituting 'creation') is a cosmos which has always been in process of producing new emergent forms of matter— it is a *creatio continua*, as it has long been called in Christian theology (with, however, no suggestion of pantheism).[51] Molt-

---

[50] A. R. Peacocke, 'Cosmos and Creation', in Yourgrau and Breck (eds.), op. cit., pp. 365–81.

[51] Cf. E. Brunner, *The Christian Doctrine of Creation and Redemption*, Eng. trans. O. Wyon (Lutterworth Press, London, 1952), Vol. ii, pp. 33 f.

mann has expressed the relation between the 'beginning' and 'now' of creation as follows:

Creation at the beginning is simultaneously the creation of time; therefore it must be understood as *creatio mutabilis*. It is not perfect, but perfectible, in that it is open both to the history of damnation and salvation as well as to destruction and consummation. If we understand creation, in its individual parts as well as in its totality, as an *open system*, then the conditions for both its history and its consummation are established simultaneous with its beginning. *Creation at the beginning establishes the conditions for the possibilities emergent in the history of creation.* It defines the experimental area for both constructive and destructive possibilities. It is open to time and to its own alteration within time. We can see in it not the unvarying nature of history but, rather, the beginning of the history of nature. Creation at the beginning is not a balanced or fulfilled reality.[52]

The world is still being made and, on the surface of the Earth, at least, man has emerged from biological life and his history is still developing. Any static conception of the way in which God sustains and holds the cosmos in being is therefore precluded, for the cosmos is in a dynamic state and, in the corner which man can observe, it has evolved conscious and self-conscious minds, who shape their environment and choose between ends. The scientific perspective of a cosmos in development introduces a dynamic element into our understanding of God's relation to the cosmos which was, even if obscured, always implicit in the Hebrew conception of a 'living God', dynamic in action. If time itself is part of the created cosmos, there seems at first to be no more difficulty in regarding God as having an innovative relationship to the cosmos at all times than in postulating such a relationship only at some posited 'zero' time. Indeed there is less difficulty, for why should God have a relation to one point in time which is different from his relation to any other point, if his mode of being is not within the temporal process?[53]

[52] J. Moltmann, 'Creation and Redemption', in *Creation, Christ and Culture*, ed. R. W. A. McKinney (T. & T. Clark, Edinburgh, 1976), pp. 124–5 (last italics mine).

[53] But if God's mode of being is not within the temporal process, does this not mean that God is 'timeless'? This is a particular form of the problem of the relation between transcendence and immanence which always arises in any discussion of the various models of the activity and nature of God as Creator. How can God be thought to act *in* time and yet be the creator *of* time? Recent analyses of this question show

C. Biblical concepts of creation

I have referred *en passant* to the Hebrew conception of the 'living God', dynamic in action in the created world and in the historical experience of Israel. As P. Evdokimov summarizes it: 'The Bible shows creation in genesis, a surge of unforeseeable novelties.'[54] It is this understanding of God which underpins and develops with the Christian conception of God the Holy Spirit, God as active and personally immanent in creation, in man and in the Christian community. Furthermore, some of the hidden treasures of the resource of the traditions of ancient Israel have recently been brought to light by Old Testament scholars and, in being unveiled for what they are, they reinforce remarkably certain implications of the scientific perspective concerning the way in which we must understand God's relation to the world he is creating.

Although it continues to be debatable[55] whether the Priestly account of creation in Genesis 1 does or does not imply a *creatio ex nihilo*, there does seem to be a consensus that the principal emphasis in ancient Israel's understanding of creation was that Yahweh created order, a cosmos, out of chaos, so

---

that a number of important traditional attributes of God (e.g. his personhood,[a,b] his ability to act in the cosmos,[b] his ability to know the world as temporal and changing[a,c]) lose coherence and meaning if God is regarded as 'timeless' in the sense of being 'outside' time altogether in a way which means time cannot be said to enter his nature at all, so that he can have no temporal succession in his experience. But similar remarks pertain in relation to space in relation to God: how can God be thought to act *in* space, and to be the creator *of* space, and yet to be non-spatial, to have no spatial location? We appear to have less difficulty with space in relation to God than with time, presumably because the content of mental life includes the sense of temporal succession. We must therefore posit *both* that God transcends space and time, for they owe their being to him, he is their Creator; *and* that space and time can exist 'within' God in such a way that he is not precluded from being present at all points in space and time, a way of speaking of the world's relation to God we shall have cause to employ again. (*a* J. R. Lucas, *A Treatise on Time and Space* (Methuen, London, 1973), §§ 55, 56; *b*. Nelson Pike, *God and Timelessness* (Routledge & Kegan Paul, London, 1970); *c*. P. T. Geach on 'The Future', *New Blackfriars*, 54 (1973), 208.)

[54] P. Evdokimov, 'Nature', *Scottish J. Theol.*, 18, No. 1 (1965), p. 8.

[55] See W. Eichrodt, 'In the beginning', in *Israel's Prophetic Heritage*, ed. B. W. Anderson and W. Harrelson (Harper, New York, 1962) as well as the authors quoted in the text following.

that thereby man is given the possibility of life. L. R. Fisher[56] calls this creation of the 'Baal type' and gives reason for believing it is to be found in certain Ugaritic texts. The Baal conquers Yamm, the god of the sea, is then proclaimed king, establishes order, and a temple is built in seven days, which is a microcosm symbolic of the whole cosmos. This cosmos is ordered by Baal from his temple from which he can send forth gifts to mankind. After the temple building there is a great banquet. The term 'Baal' and 'King' became synonymous with the term 'creator'.

The people of Israel incorporated these ideas from this and other sources and for them '... this creation of the Baal type (with modifications) was very usable not only when speaking of the cosmos but also for formulating the event of creating a people of God.'[57] Fisher claims to show that the early Hebrews used the creation of the Baal type in the Exodus–Sinai tradition to speak of the greatness of Yahweh who, as 'man-of-war' and as 'King', created them as a people and that it then begins to make sense why they would use the same type of creation in speaking of the ordering of the cosmos. Moreover the alternative creation of the El type (or *creatio ex nihilo* for that matter) was not a real possibility. For them 'Yahweh is not only to be identified with the God of the Patriarchs but also with the one who creates cosmos and the possibility of life. Creation in this sense is redemption. Chaos and death still threaten (as is seen in the flood story), but Yahweh lives and can control the waters or chaos.'[58] This is also the understanding of Deutero–Isaiah and his disciples:

The viewpoint which is expressed here [Isaiah 54] is that the flood was a return to chaos, but that once again, Yahweh was able to control chaos and to create the possibility for life ... only the one who controls the floods can make covenant (54.10). A relationship is created which is limiting, but at the same time it provides the frame-

[56] L. R. Fisher, 'From Chaos to Cosmos', in *Encounter* (Butler University School of Religion, Indianapolis), 26 (1965), 183–97. (See also L. R. Fisher, 'Creation at Ugarit and in the Old Testament', *Vetus Testamentum*, 15 (1965), 313–24.) I am indebted to Dr G. Brooke, of Salisbury and Wells Theological College, for drawing my attention to these papers.

[57] Fisher, op. cit., p. 187.

[58] Fisher, op. cit., p. 191.

work for freedom which is a relationship (Bonhoeffer). The opposite of freedom is wandering and boundlessness, chaos and death.[59]

W. R. Lane, who thinks that although there is no *creatio ex nihilo* in Genesis 1: 1–3, writes even so: 'To the Priestly writer, God is in complete control of the universe. He brought it under his control in creation. It was this act that brought order out of chaos, made life possible, and gave meaning and purpose to all that does exist. To him this was the thing of importance; this was all that needed to be known about creation.'[60] G. von Rad, in commenting on Genesis 1: 1, 2, and taking a different view from Lane with respect to the *creatio ex nihilo*, nevertheless makes a similar point:

Verse 2 [of Genesis 1] teaches one to understand the marvel of creation, therefore, from the viewpoint of its negation; thus it speaks first of the formless and the abysmal out of which God's will lifted creation and above which it holds it unceasingly. For the cosmos stands permanently in need of this supporting Creator's will. We see here that the theological thought of ch. 1 moves not so much between the poles of nothingness and creation as between the poles of chaos and cosmos.[61]

The biblical understanding of reality, according to B. S. Childs,[62] is of three stages: (i) a state of non-being, pictured in the Old Testament as chaos, which is overcome by (ii) God's gracious act of creation which brought world reality into being which is (iii) threatened by man's disobedience which is a perversion of reality. The Old Testament recounts this struggle between reality and its perversion.

These and other investigators, in keeping purely to the insights of the authors and editors of the biblical literature, have shown us that there is a balance and judicious wisdom in the attitude of the ancient people of Israel to creation. The scientific perspective of modern cosmology has enhanced our sense of awe and contingency at our presence in the world, and has generated questions about the significance of that presence.

[59] Fisher, op. cit., p. 193.

[60] W. R. Lane, 'The initiation of creation', *Vetus Testamentum*, 13 (1963), 63–73.

[61] G. von Rad, *Genesis—a Commentary*, Eng. trans. J. H. Marks (SCM Press, London, 1951), p. 49.

[62] B. S. Childs, *Myth and Reality in the Old Testament*, Studies in Biblical Theology, No. 27 (SCM Press, London, 1961), Ch. 4.

This is very much in tune with the sense of these ancient people that they lived in an ordered world which allowed the possibility of human life, but that that life was a gift of the Creator and not to be assumed as so built into the structure of things that the disordered nothingness of chaos could never return to overwhelm man and his affairs—as *we* would say, in some future contraction of the universe, or, more proximately, in the absorption of the Earth back into an expanding Sun.

D.   The value of creation apart from man

I have, for the most part, been stressing the significance of man's presence in this universe for man's own search for meaning within it. But man has long recognized how much of the universe seems to proceed apparently without any reference to him. Now the expanding scale of cosmology even embraces the possibility that this universe we observe might be but one of a 'run' of possible universes and demonstrates convincingly that vast tracks of matter–energy–space–time have, and probably will, exist without any man to observe them and with no apparent reference or relation to man (unless it is to provide a reservoir of potentiality vast enough to allow to emerge that improbable coalescence of matter we call man). The excessively anthropocentric cosmic outlook of medieval, and even of Newtonian, man is thereby healthily restored to that more sober assessment which characterizes the Old Testament —especially the Psalms[63] and the 'Wisdom' literature,[64] but also some of the prophets.[65] The Book of Job, supremely, urges emphatically that man's whole attitude to the created order is wrongheadedly egoistic and anthropocentric, for it is clear, the writer says in effect, that the greater part of creation is of no relevance to man at all. When, in the 38th chapter, God finally answers Job it is not to justify his actions with respect to him, or even with respect to mankind in general, but simply to point to the whole range of the created order and to ask Job if he as man took any part in non-human processes of creation, both past and present. As John Baker has put it:

[63] e.g. Psalm 8: 3, 4 (quoted above, p. 52); 19: 1–6; 65: 9–13; 104; 136; 1–9; 148.
[64] Job, Proverbs, Ecclesiastes, and, in the Apocrypha, the Wisdom of Solomon and Ecclesiasticus.
[65] e.g. Jeremiah 8: 7.

... nature [in the O.T.] is not to be evaluated simply in terms of man's needs and interests; and to think that it is, is merely a mark of folly. God created the greater part of the world for its own sake; and wisdom consists in recognising this, and the limitations which this imposes on us, so that the truly 'wise' man will never imagine that he knows what God was 'at' in creation.[66]

God asks Job out of the whirlwind:

Who is this whose ignorant words
cloud my design in darkness?
Brace yourself and stand up like a man;
I will ask questions, and you will answer.
Where were you when I laid the earth's foundations?
Tell me, if you know and understand.[67]

Today, even with our modern knowledge of cosmology, with all the exhilarating panorama that science now unfolds in the dimensions of space and time, and other dimensions too, we can only, and certainly anyone who presumes to expound such high themes must, respond with Job:

I know that thou canst do all things
and that no purpose is beyond thee.
But I have spoken of great things which I have not understood,
things too wonderful for me to know.[68]

---

[66] J. Baker, 'Biblical Attitudes to Nature', an appendix to *Man and Nature*, ed. H. Montefiore (Collins, London, 1975), a report of a sub-group of the Doctrine Commission of the Church of England, 1974, pp. 101, 102.

[67] Job 38: 2–4, NEB.

[68] Job 42: 2, 3, NEB.

III

Chance and the Life-Game

I. CHANCE

IN the preceding lecture I referred frequently to the element
of 'necessity' in the universe—the givenness, from our point of
view, of certain of its basic features: the fundamental constants,
the nature of the fundamental particles (and so of atoms, and so
of molecules and so of complex organizations of molecules), the
physical laws of the interrelation of matter, energy, space, and
time. We were in the position, as it were, of the audience before
the pianist begins his extemporizations—there is the instrument,
there is the range of available notes, but what tune is to be
played and on what principle and in what forms is it to be
developed? Given the limiting features which constitute our
'necessity', how are the potentialities of the universe going to
be made manifest? Monod's answer was that it is by 'chance',
indeed man's emergence in the 'unfeeling immensity of the
universe' was said to be '*only* by chance'.[1] So the question to
which we now turn is that of the roles of chance and necessity
or 'law'[2] in the evolutionary process, in particular in the origin
and development of living forms, and of the implications of
this balance and interplay for discourse about belief in God as
Creator. It will transpire that, by and large, I agree that

[1] My italics.
[2] 'Necessity' was the word used by Monod in his *Chance and Necessity* (Collins,
London, 1972) to denote the deterministic aspect of natural processes. But we need
also to refer to the basic 'givenness' of the features of the universe mentioned in the
first sentence of this Lecture (i.e. the fundamental physical constants, the fundamental
particles, as well as the physical laws of the interrelation of matter, energy, space, and
time, and of other physical features of the universe). Because of this wider reference,
I shall usually use the word 'law', rather than 'necessity', to refer to these 'given'
aspects of the universe that include the statistical, apparently deterministic laws
governing the behaviour of matter, at least above the sub-atomic level. These natural
'laws' provide the rules according to which the life-game is played.

'chance', appropriately defined, is the means whereby the potentialities of the universe are actualized, but that I shall draw from this conclusions different from those of Monod.

A. 'Chance' in literature

'Chance' has often been apotheosized into a metaphysical principle threatening the very possibility of finding meaning in human life, as recognized in the bitter comment of the author of Ecclesiastes: 'Time and Chance govern all ...'[3] In the ancient Greek myths, Chance reigned in Chaos, that state of affairs which preceded the Cosmos we now inhabit, to which we adverted briefly in Lecture II. Thus Milton, in this, as ever, as much classical pagan as Christian poet:

> Chaos umpire sits,
> And by decision more embroils the fray,
> By which he reigns; next him high arbiter
> Chance governs all.[4]

Chaos was the mythical state of affairs which preceded the emergence of the world order, of Cosmos, which was thought to manifest itself in the totality of natural phenomena. Chaos was apparently a transitional stage and in one of the myths was represented as a dark and windy chasm. It is into this chasm that many of Darwin's contemporaries peered and it was the fearfulness of this vision of a universe, no more ordered than the roulette tables of a Monte Carlo saloon, which induced the anguish Tennyson expressed in *In Memoriam*—published in 1850 and written between 1833 (after the death of his friend Arthur Hallam) and 1849, that is, well before the publication of the *Origin of Species*. For the spectre of a Nature ringing its changes of chance and death regardless of human welfare and aspirations had been conjured long before Darwin by the lengthening, through geology, of the time-scale of the Earth, with all its vicissitudes and apparent catastrophes, and by the growing conviction that species came into existence, flourished and died.

---

[3] Ecclesiastes 9: 11.
[4] John Milton, *Paradise Lost*, Book II. ll. 907–9.

The wish, that of the living whole
  No life may fail beyond the grave,
  Derives it not from what we have
The likest God within the soul?

Are God and Nature then at strife,
  That Nature lends such evil dreams?
  So careful of the type she seems,
So careless of the single life;

That I, considering everywhere
  Her secret meaning in her deeds,
  And finding that of fifty seeds
She often brings but one to bear,

I falter where I firmly trod,
  And falling with my weight of cares
  Upon the great world's altar-stairs
That slope thro' darkness up to God,

I stretch lame hands of faith, and grope
  And gather dust and chaff, and call
  To what I feel is Lord of all,
And faintly trust the larger hope.

  .   .   .   .

'So careful of the type?' but no.
  From scarped cliff and quarried stone
  She cries, 'A thousand types are gone:
I care for nothing, all shall go.

'Thou makest thine appeal to me:
  I bring to life, I bring to death:
  The spirit does but mean the breath:
I know no more.' And he, shall he,

Man, her last work, who seem'd so fair,
  Such splendid purpose in his eyes,
  Who roll'd the psalm to wintry skies,
Who built him fanes of fruitless prayer,

Who trusted God was love indeed
  And love Creation's final law—
  Tho' Nature, red in tooth and claw
With ravine, shriek'd against his creed—

Who loved, who suffer'd countless ills,
    Who battled for the True, the Just,
    Be blown about the desert dust,
Or seal'd within the iron hills?

No more? A monster then, a dream,
    A discord. Dragons of the prime,
    That tare each other in their slime,
Were mellow music match'd with him.

O life as futile, then, as frail!
    O for thy voice to soothe and bless!
    What hope of answer, or redress?
Behind the veil, behind the veil.[5]

So—even before Darwin—men were disturbed by this ancient fear of Chaos ruled by chance, and Tennyson echoed this— being, as Carlyle described him:[6] 'a man solitary and sad, as certain men are, dwelling in an element of gloom,—carrying a bit of Chaos about him, in short, which he is manufacturing into a Cosmos'. The publication of Darwin's ideas gave an impetus to the anguish of those already despairing of finding meaning or purpose in the universe. It was this mood and judgement which provoked the Bertrand Russell of the 1920s to his famous peroration:

That Man is the product of causes which had no prevision of the end they were achieving; that his origin, his growth, his hopes and fears, his loves and beliefs, are but the outcome of accidental collocations of atoms; that no fire, no heroism, no intensity of thought and feeling, can preserve an individual life beyond the grave; that all the labours of the ages, all the devotion, all the inspiration, all the noonday brightness of human genius, are destined to extinction in the vast death of the solar system, and that the whole temple of Man's achieve- ment must inevitably be buried beneath the debris of a universe in ruins—all these things, if not quite beyond dispute, are yet so nearly certain that no philosophy which rejects them can hope to stand. Only within the scaffolding of these truths, only on the firm founda-

---

[5] A. Tennyson, *In Memoriam*, LV, LVI.
[6] *Correspondence of Emerson and Carlyle*, ed. J. Slater (Columbia University Press, New York and London, 1964), p. 363. Carlyle to Emerson 5 Aug. 1844.

tion of unyielding despair, can the soul's habitation henceforth be safely built.[7]

Clearly to attribute the processes of the universe to 'chance' can trigger off in sensitive men a profound sense of despair at the meaninglessness of all life, and of human life in particular. Such an emotive word warrants closer analysis for there are more precise meanings which may be given to it in the context of the sciences. It is, of course, to these uses that Monod refers but such a reference inevitably sets ringing much more emotional bells.

B. Two meanings of 'chance'

For our present purposes we can usefully distinguish two meanings of 'chance'.

(i) When we toss a coin, we say that the chances of it coming down heads or tails are even. We mean that, in any long run of tossings of coins, 50 per cent will come down 'heads' and 50 per cent 'tails' to a proportional accuracy which increases with the number of throws we make. But we also know that, had we sufficient knowledge of the exact values of the relevant parameters, the laws of mechanics would in fact enable us to say in any particular toss which way the coin would fall. In practice we cannot have all the information needed to analyse these multiple causes and all we *can* know is that their net effect is equally likely to produce 'heads' as 'tails', after any individual tossing. So to apply 'chance' in this context is simply to recognize our ignorance of the multiple parameters involved. It is a confession of our partial ignorance, 'partial' because we *do* know enough from the symmetry of the problem to say that, in any long run of such tossings, there will be an equal number of heads and tails uppermost at the end of the process. The use of the word 'chance' in this context does *not* imply a denial of causality in the sequence of events.

(ii) A second use of the word 'chance' is that of the intersection of two otherwise unrelated causal chains. Suppose that when you leave the building in which you are reading these pages, as you step on to the pavement you are struck on the

[7] B. Russell, 'A Free Man's Worship' (1903) in *Mysticism and Logic, and other essays* (Allen & Unwin, London, 1963 edn.), p. 41.

head by a hammer dropped by a man repairing the roof. From this accidental collision many consequences might follow for your mental life and for the welfare of your families. In ordinary parlance we would say it was due to 'pure chance'. The two trains of events—your leaving the building at the time you did, and the dropping of the hammer—are each within themselves explicable as causal chains. Yet there is no connection between these two causal chains except their point of intersection and *when* the hammer hits you on the head could not have been predicted from within the terms of reference of either chain taken by itself. In this case, causality is again not denied, but because there is no cross connection between the two causal chains we could not, unlike the previous case of the tossing of a coin, make any accurate prediction of the chance of it happening. (The second instance is sometimes more properly called 'accident' and some authors distinguish between chance and accident in this sense.)

Much more needs to be said (and indeed *is* said in the vast literature on the mathematical theory of probability) but at least this initial simple analysis serves to show that when, in ordinary parlance, some event is said to be 'due to chance' this phrase is really not giving an explanation of the event in question or saying what its cause is, but is simply acting as a stop card. It is saying in effect 'the event in question has many multiple causes, or seems to have been the result of the intersection of unrelated causal chains, so that we cannot attribute any *particular* cause to it.' It is therefore a phrase to be avoided in our discussions. No doubt the phrase 'due to chance' has acquired currency because many of the laws in natural science are statistical in character. They do not take the form of statements to the effect that event or situation A will be followed by event or situation B, but rather of the form that A will be followed by B′, B″, and B‴ with different respective probabilities. Whether this incomplete knowledge of the consequence of A arises from a fundamental absence of causality in the old sense or is the consequence of the incompleteness of our knowledge of the operative multiple causes (as in the coin tossing example) will depend on the particular situation. The first of these two alternatives, a fundamental absence of causality, is sometimes called 'pure chance' but any event whose cause has not yet been discovered may be viewed either as a pure chance event that possesses no cause, or as a complex event of cause as yet unknown.[8] Indeed the very notion of 'pure chance', of *un*caused events, in the sense of absolutely unqualified disorder, is self-contradictory, as well as running counter to a basic assumption of scientists in their, not unsuccessful, work.

II. THE LIFE-GAME

Until the recent past, chance and law have often been regarded as alternatives for interpreting the natural world. But I hope enough has now been said to show that, at many levels (from those of fundamental particles up to living organisms, and indeed in the processes of coalescence that occur in cloud and in galaxy formation), the interplay between these principles is more subtle and complex than the simple dichotomies of the past would allow. For any particular state of a system, we have to weigh carefully what the evidence is about their respective roles in determining its present behaviour and for interpreting its past. The origin and development of living organisms is no exception and we must now consider some interpretations of the life-game which have emerged from scientific work of the last three decades—I refer to the ideas of Monod, Prigogine, and Eigen, and their colleagues.

A.   Mutations and evolution (Monod)

Jacques Monod, in the widely read book to which I have already referred,[9] contrasts the 'chance' processes which bring about mutations in the genetic material of an organism and the 'necessity' of their consequences in the well-ordered, replicative, interlocking mechanisms which constitute that organism's continuity as a living form. He pointed out, as has been well known in principle for many years, though the detailed chemical account has been forthcoming only in the last few decades, that mutations in the genetic material, or DNA, are the results of chemical or physical events and their locations in the molecular apparatus carrying the genetic information are entirely random with respect to the biological needs of the organism.

[8] Cf. E. Nagel, *The Structure of Science* (Routledge & Kegan Paul, London, 1961), Ch. 10.
[9] Above, p. 86 n. 2.

Thus, one causal chain is a chain of events, which may be the chemical modification of one of the nucleotide bases in DNA or its disintegration through absorption of a quantum of ultra-violet or cosmic radiation. These changes in the nucleotide bases, and so in the information which the DNA is carrying, are incorporated into the genetic apparatus of the organisms (the 'genome'—a system of transmissible genes of the organisms constituted by its DNA) only if they are not lethal and if, on interacting with its environment, they have a higher rate of reproduction than before. This sequence represents a second causal chain—the interplay between the genetic constitution, and behaviour, of a living organism and the pressures to which it is subjected by the environment that includes, not only physical features, but also the biological pressures of food resources and predators. These two causal chains are entirely independent and it is in the second sense (ii) of 'chance' that Monod is correct in saying that evolution depends on chance. It also qualifies for this description, in the other sense (i) of chance, since in most cases we are not now in a position to specify all the factors which led to the mutated organisms being selected and, even less, the mechanism by which mutation was induced in the first place. (Indeed this latter is at the sub-molecular level at which quantum considerations begin to operate and is probably fundamentally precluded from any *exactly* predictive operation.)

The molecular biology of recent years has thus been able to give a much more detailed picture of the process of interplay between mutation and environment: however it does not really add anything new *in principle* to the debates of the last hundred years. For the essential crux in these debates was, and is, that the mechanism of variation was causally entirely independent of the processes of selection, so that mutations were regarded as purely random with respect to the selective needs of the organism long before the molecular mechanisms of transmission, and alteration, of genetic information were unravelled in the last two decades. This is the basis on which Monod stresses the role of chance:

Pure chance, absolutely free but blind, at the very root of the stupendous edifice of evolution: this central concept of modern biology is no longer one among other possible or even conceivable hypotheses. It is today the *sole* conceivable hypothesis, the only one compatible with observation and tested fact. And nothing warrants the supposition (or the hope) that conceptions about this should, or ever could, be revised.[10]

As mentioned earlier, Monod goes on to draw the conclusion that man, and so all the works of his mind and culture, are the products of pure chance and therefore without any cosmic significance. The universe must be seen not as a directionally ordered whole (a cosmos) but as a giant Monte Carlo saloon in which the dice have happened to fall out in a way which produced man. There is no general purpose in the universe and in the existence of life, and so none in the universe as a whole. It need not, it might not, have existed—nor might man.

However *pace* Monod, I see no reason why this randomness of molecular event in relation to biological consequence, that Monod rightly emphasizes, has to be raised to the level of a metaphysical principle interpreting the universe. For, as we have already seen, in the behaviour of matter on a larger scale many regularities, which have been raised to the level of being describable as 'laws', arise from the combined effect of random microscopic events that constitute the macroscopic. So the involvement of chance at the level of mutations does not, of itself, preclude these events manifesting a law-like behaviour at the level of populations of organisms and indeed of populations of bio-systems that may be presumed to exist on the many planets throughout the universe which might support life. Instead of being daunted by the role of chance in genetic mutations as being the manifestation of irrationality in the universe, it would be more consistent with the observations to assert that the full gamut of the potentialities of living matter could be explored only through the agency of the rapid and frequent randomization which is possible at the molecular level of the DNA. In other words, the designation 'chance' in this context refers to the multiple effects whereby the (very large) number of mutations is elicited that constitute the 'noise' which, via an independent causal chain, the environment then selects for viability. This role of chance is what one would

[10] Monod, op. cit., p. 110.

expect if the universe were so constituted as to be able to explore all the potential forms of organizations of matter (both living and non-living) which it contains. Moreover, even if the present biological world *is* only one out of an already large number of possibilities, it must be the case that the potentiality of forming such a world is present in the fundamental constitution of matter as it exists in our universe. The original primeval cloud of fundamental particles must have had the potentiality of being able to develop into the complex molecular forms we call modern biological life. It is this that I find significant about the emergence of life in the universe and the role of chance, in both its forms (i) and (ii), seems to me neither repulsive nor attractive, but simply what is required if all the potentialities of the universe, especially for life, were going to be elicited effectively. Furthermore if we propose that the world owes its being to a Creator God then I see no reason why God should not allow the potentialities of his universe to be developed in all their ramifications through the operation of random events; indeed, in principle, this is the only way in which all potentialities might eventually, given enough time and space, be actualized. Or, to change the metaphor, it is as if chance is the search radar of God, sweeping through all the possible targets available to its probing.

To this extent I agree with W. G. Pollard when he says 'To Einstein's famous question expressing his abhorrence of quantum mechanics, "Does God throw dice?", the Judeo-Christian answer is not, as so many have wrongly supposed, a denial, but a very positive affirmative.'[11] The judgement expressed in this last sentence of Pollard is based on his view of 'Providence' as the expression of God's will and purpose in the particularities of events in history. As he says, history, including biological history, is 'a maze, a fabric of turning points, open at every step to new choices and new direction'.[12] For Pollard, God expresses his will for the universe in those particular events, selected from amongst all the alternatives at any instant, which have in fact occurred and which then give rise to a succession of new particular events, each providing a turning-point. I agree with Pollard about the statistical character of many

---

[11] W. G. Pollard, *Chance and Providence* (Faber, London, 1958), p. 97.
[12] Pollard, op. cit., p. 72.

scientific laws, the fact that alternative possibilities follow any particular event with varying probabilities attributed to each. But, apart from events at the level of the fundamental sub-atomic particles, these probabilities represent simply our ignorance of all the factors contributing to the situation—they do not imply any lack of causality in the situation itself (and presumably any lack of knowledge of the outcome of the events in the mind of God), at least in so far as we are discussing systems below the level of that of consciousness and human self-consciousness. The assertion that any given situation or event can be followed only by a number of alternative situations or events each with their own probability is a statement about our inability to predict the outcome of these situations, in view of our own ignorance of many multiple causes or (in the case of genetic mutations) of intersecting independent causal chains. It is not an assertion of a basic non-causality in the situation or event. Since Pollard denies that he means that God alters the natural probability of a pattern of events to achieve his purposes, I find it hard to find any other meaning in 'Providence', as he uses the term, than as a label or description of the particularity of the single, unique, events which constitute history—and so, it seems to me, it is not capable of carrying the theological weight, in relationship to the biblical tradition, which he places on it.

Oddly enough Monod and Pollard have this in common—both regard the emergence and development of life as an improbable 'surd' in a universe otherwise governed by the iron law of 'necessity'. The response of Monod is to accept the 'Absurd' in the spirit of French existentialism, and to plead eloquently for the autonomy and validity of human values in themselves, more particularly those that are derived from the method of scientific objectivity. Pollard, on the other hand, recognizing equally the unique character of the turning-points in history, and in particular in biological evolution,[13] attributes the uniqueness of the historical and biological sequence so constructed to 'Providence'. This enables him to welcome the specific and distinctive character of any event, as only one amongst several alternatives, and at the same time to worship

<hr />

[13] W. G. Pollard, *Soundings* (Winter 1973), pp. 433–55.

God for it. The danger of this move is that this worship has to be evoked whatever the event and one may be inclined to select those events which are worthy of divine providence, on the basis of criteria derived from some other source, and reject those which are inconsistent with one's concept of God. The concept of the role of chance in biological evolution as eliciting the potentialities inherent in the created order seems to me not to require Monod's conclusion nor to lead to the contradictions about the role of God in the universe which Pollard's entails.

Since Monod and Pollard made their contributions, there have been developments in theoretical biology which cast new light on the interrelation of chance and law in the origin and evolution of life. In these developments it is possible to see more clearly than Monod was able to analyse, in his consideration of the mutations of the genetic material and their consequences for natural selection, the way in which chance processes can operate in a law-regulated system to produce new forms of organized and information-carrying systems of the kind which life requires. To these more recent ideas we must now turn.[14]

B. Thermodynamics of living organisms and dissipative systems (Prigogine)

Ilya Prigogine and his colleagues at Brussels, who were already well known for their development and extension of the theories of thermodynamics to irreversible processes not previously covered by the classical approaches, have increasingly turned their attention to the analysis of living systems. The underlying problem here is one which emerged in full force in the nineteenth century: in biology we observe, in the course of geological time, increases in organization with the emergence of structures of greater and greater functional and structural complexity. But in the general course of natural events there is an increase in *dis*order with time; in the more precise terminology of thermodynamics and statistical mechanics,

[14] For a brief account, see A. R. Peacocke, 'Chance and necessity in the life-game', *Trends in Biochemical Sciences*, 2 (1977), 99–100; and for a more thorough exposition, A. R. Peacocke, 'The Nature and Evolution of Biological Hierarchies', in *New Approaches to Genetics*, ed. P. W. Kent (Oriel Press, Routledge & Kegan Paul, London, 1978), pp. 245–304.

there is an irreversible increase in entropy (which is related logarithmically to a measure of disorder) of any isolated system such that it will more and more tend to a state of equilibrium and maximum disorder. How can biological systems swim, as it were, against the entropic stream, always enhancing their structural order at the expense of their surroundings? Formally, this question may be answered by pointing out that biological organisms maintain their structure and order at the expense of the free energy of compounds which they consume and, by returning heat to their environment, in fact eventually produce a greater increase in entropy than the decrease that occurs in the living organisms themselves. So the laws of thermodynamics are not contravened by active, living, biological systems.

However, this still does not answer the question of how it was that such highly ordered systems as living organisms could ever have come into existence in a world in which irreversible processes always tend to lead to an increase in entropy, in disorder. We know that, in systems near to equilibrium, any fluctuations away from that state will be damped down and the system will tend to revert to its equilibrium state. What Prigogine and his colleagues have been able to show is that there exists a class of steady-state systems, 'dissipative structures', which by taking in matter and energy can maintain themselves in an ordered, steady state far from equilibrium. In such states there can occur, under the right conditions, fluctuations which are no longer damped and which are amplified so that the system changes its whole structure to a *new* ordered state in which it can again become steady and imbibe energy and matter from the outside and maintain its new structured form. This instability of dissipative structures has been studied by these workers who have set out more precisely the thermodynamic conditions for a dissipative structure to move from one state to a new state which is more ordered than previously. It turns out that these conditions are not so restrictive that no systems can ever possibly obey them. Indeed a very large number of systems, such as those of the first living forms of matter which must have involved complex networks of chemical reactions, are very likely to do so, since they are non-linear in the relationship between the forces and fluxes involved (which is one of the necessary conditions for these fluctuations to be amplified).

Many model systems could be cited. I shall confine myself to two, one purely physical and one more chemical. The physical situation is that which simply arises when one heats a fluid layer from the bottom so that there is a gradation of temperature from a high temperature at the bottom of the heated vessel to a lower temperature at the top. At first, when the temperature gradient is small, heat is transferred simply by conduction and the fluid as a whole remains at rest. But, at a critical value of the temperature gradient, internal convective motion appears spontaneously and groups of molecules start moving together in concert. Indeed the co-operativity of motion between these molecules is extremely high and a regular pattern of hexagonal 'cells' can be found within the moving fluid. This seems quite contrary to the Boltzmann principle and to the randomization of the movements of molecules which seems inherent to the second law. The point is, this system is a long way from equilibrium and it can be shown that at certain conditions of viscosity, and so on, which themselves depend on temperature, the system ceases to be linear and 'order-through-fluctuations' may occur with the production of a new structure resulting from an instability.

Even more striking is the observation of order-through-fluctuations in chemical systems. Chemical networks can be of a very high degree of complexity through incorporating one or more autocatalytic steps and they are often non-linear (in the sense above) when not close to equilibrium. Then various kinds of oscillating reactions and other features can occur. One of the most striking of these is the so called Zhabotinsky reaction (the oxidation of malonic acid by bromate in the presence of cerium ions in solution). With the right combination of solution conditions, and at constant temperature, one observes the transformation of an original homogeneous reaction mixture into a series of pulsing waves of concentration of cerium ions, moving up and down the tube, until eventually a steady state is reached. In this, there are static, banded layers of alternating high and low concentrations of ceric ions. From an originally homogeneous system, a highly ordered structure has appeared through the fluctuations that are possible in a non-linear system far removed from equilibrium. What has happened is that fluctuations in such a system have been amplified and, through the ordinary laws of chemical kinetics, a new structure has appeared which is ordered, at first in time and then finally in space—a new kind of alliance of chance and law. Under the conditions of this reaction the structural formation has a probability of unity provided the initial fluctuation arises from within the system and the causal chain leading to this fluctuation, although it cannot be discerned by ourselves, must itself be the result of law-like processes occurring at the micro-level. Because of the discovery of these dissipative systems, and of the possibility of 'order-through fluctuations', it is now possible, on the basis of these physico-chemical considerations, to regard as highly probable the emergence of those ordered and articulated molecular structures which are living. Instead of them having only an inconceivably small chance of emerging in the 'primeval soup' on the suface of the earth before life appeared, we now see that ordered dissipative structures of some kind will appear in due course. To this extent, the emergence of life was inevitable, but the form it was to take remained entirely open and unpredictable, at least to us. Prigogine and Nicolis go further:

We ... begin to understand, in quantitative terms, the role of the statistical element in the description of a [dissipative] system ... we are led to a first parallelism between dissipative structure formation and certain features occurring in the early stages of biogenesis and the subsequent evolution to higher forms. The analogy would even become closer if the model we discuss has further critical points of unstable transition. One would then obtain a hierarchy of dissipative structures, each one enriched further by the information content of the previous models through the 'memory' of the initial fluctuations which created them successively.[15]

But how can a molecular population have information content and how can it store a 'memory'? It is to problems of this kind that Eigen and his colleagues at Göttingen have directed their attention.

---

[15] I. Prigogine and G. Nicolis, *Quart. Rev. Biophysics* 4 (1971), 132.

C.   The origin of living molecular systems (Eigen)

The work of Eigen, which first appeared in a magnificent paper published in 1971,[16] has now been developed in a wider context, and in a most attractive form, as *Das Spiel*, a book at present available only in its German edition.[17] In these studies, Eigen and his colleagues examine the changes in time of a population of a system of replicating biological macromolecules, each capable of carrying the information required to make a copy of itself (as can DNA). The virtue of these investigations is that they show how the determinism of the physico-chemical laws of kinetics can be linked with the random, time-dependent ('stochastic') processes which must be evoked when one is concerned with only a finite number of *kinds* of macromolecule. In the first stage of their study, the application of the laws of chemical kinetics by themselves gives a deterministic account, which shows how any population of such macromolecules must inevitably move to the situation in which a particular macromolecule with the highest 'selective value' (which Eigen is able to define precisely and independently in physical terms) dominates the population. However this deterministic account of the selection process gives only mean values and applies only to great numbers of macromolecules. In fact there are two processes occurring which are inherently subject to chance, namely: the occurrence of a specific mutant is an elementary event subject to quantum-mechanical uncertainty; and the growth in numbers of a particular molecular species is subject to statistical fluctuations—for if the last remaining representative of one kind of informational macromolecule decomposed before being copied, it would become extinct.

This is nicely illustrated by a model 'selection game' in which one starts with a box containing ten balls of ten different colours and a separate supply of balls of all these same ten

[16] M. Eigen, 'The Self-Organization of Matter and the Evolution of Biological Macromolecules', *Naturwissenschaften*, 58 (1971), 465–523. Since then: M. Eigen and P. Schuster, 'The Hypercycle—A Principle of Natural Self-Organization': 'Part A: Emergence of a Hypercycle', *Naturwissenschaften*, 64 (1977), 541–65; 'Part B: The Abstract Hypercycle', ibid. 65 (1978), 7–41.

[17] R. Winkler and M. Eigen, *Das Spiel* (R. Piper & Co. Verlag, Munich and Zürich, 1975).

colours. Then alternate the following moves: (A) pick a ball at random from the box and return it to the box together with another ball of the *same* colour (net numerical effect: $+1$); (B) take out a ball, again at random, and discard it (net numerical effect: -1). The total *number* of balls in the box remains at ten after any number of repetitions of A + B ($= +1 - 1$), but the range of *colours* narrows down surprisingly rapidly. For once the last representative of a given colour is irrevocably removed by B it can never again be built up by A. So although the chances of the number of a given colour being increased or decreased remain equal, the time course of the operation of chance is such that one colour eventually predominates in the box.

The treatment of Eigen and his colleagues is highly mathematical and is based on the theory of games and of stochastic processes, but he has been able also to illustrate the principles involved by inventing actual games which the novice can play (with, for example, octahedral dice!). They have been able to delineate fairly precisely what kind of combination of chance and law (the rules of the game) will allow such a population of information-carrying macromolecules both to develop into one 'dominant species', as it were, and at the same time to maintain enough inherent flexibility to evolve into new forms if conditions change.

They have carried these investigations further to see what kind of self-organizing cycles of macromolecules would most likely be able to be viable and self-reproducing given the known properties of proteins and nucleic acids, and have been able to devise a suitable 'hypercycle' which involves both kinds of macromolecule in an autocatalytic cyclic sequence. Although it may not represent exactly the way in which such self-reproducing systems emerged, this 'hypercycle' shows that at least it is possible in principle for it to happen with quite a high degree of probability. Their treatment demonstrates that natural selection of the fittest, at the macromolecular level at least, is no tautology, it is *not* a question simply of affirming the 'survival of the survivor', as some have gibed at Darwinism. (There are inherent molecular properties which will enable a certain macromolecule to be the fittest to survive.) He concludes that:

the evolution of life, if it is based on a derivable physical principle must be considered an *inevitable* process despite its indeterminate course . . . The models treated . . . and the experiments discussed earlier in the article indicate that it is not only inevitable 'in principle' but also sufficiently probable within a realistic span of time. It requires appropriate environmental conditions (which are not fulfilled everywhere) and their maintenance. These conditions have existed on Earth and must still exist on many planets in the universe. There is no temporal restriction to the continuation of the evolutionary process, as long as energy can be supplied.[18]

According to this analysis, although the emergence of living systems may be 'inevitable', it is nevertheless 'indeterminate'. For it is impossible to trace back the precise historical route or to predict the exact course of the future development, beyond certain time limits, as a consequence of the involvement of fluctuation, i.e. of random processes, in the development of the population of informational macromolecules.

D. *Chance-and-law as creative*

From the interaction of genetic mutations and natural selection, from the role of so-called 'chance' events, in the emergence and development of life, many (as we saw) who have reflected on the processes of biological evolution have concluded that they are 'due to chance' and therefore of no significance for man's understanding of the universe and of his place in it. But the work of Prigogine and Eigen and their collaborators now shows how subtle can be the interplay of chance and law, of randomness and determinism, in the processes which lead to the emergence of living structures. These studies demonstrate that the mutual interplay of chance and law is in fact creative, for it is the combination of the two which allows new forms to emerge and evolve. Furthermore, the character of this interplay of chance and law appears now to be of a kind which makes it 'inevitable' both that living structures should emerge and that they should evolve—given the physical and chemical properties of the atomic units (and presumably, therefore, of sub-atomic particles) in the universe we actually have. One obtains the impression that the universe has potentialities which

[18] Eigen, op. cit., ref. 16 (1971) p. 519.

are becoming actualized by the joint operation, in time, of chance and law, of random time-dependent processes in a framework of law-like determined properties—and that these potentialities include the possibility of biological, and so of human, life.

III.   CHANCE AND THE DOCTRINE OF CREATION

A.   *Relevance of the life-game*

I have tried to give a fair account of one aspect—the inter-play of chance and law in the life-game—of our present scientific perspective on the world and to draw out its general implications, so far without much reference to a theism which conceives of a Creator God. I have, negatively, tried to show that the deduction (of Monod for example) from this picture, that the quest for meaning for man in the cosmos is hopeless, is not warranted by the role of chance in evolution— both as Monod conceived it and, even more clearly, in the form the more thermodynamic and kinetic work of Prigogine and Eigen has indicated.

However, man does not stop his questioning as soon as the latest brick has been definitively added to the edifice of science. He never stops asking questions about himself and the cosmos and its *meaning* to him. The questions he asks are perennial, going back to the dawn of human self-consciousness, but the context to which the answers are now referred cannot but be that of the world-view created by the sciences. So we are inevitably involved in thinking again what the assertion that there is a God who is Creator really can mean in this new context. What kind of images are going to be appropriate to any continued theistic affirmation?

We have earlier (Lecture I) considered some of the complementary and reinforcing analogical models which have developed in the Judeo-Christian intellectual tradition to explicate God's relation to the world as Creator, models that avoid an excessive stress on transcendence, which becomes deism, or an excessive stress on immanence, which merges into pantheism. How does the scientific picture of the interplay of chance and law that I have outlined bear upon these models?

Clearly, many authors, including myself, have stressed the continuity and unity of the created order, and that God is *semper Creator*—he is creating at every moment of the world's existence in and through the self-perpetuating creativity of the very stuff of the world. Indeed it is possible to see the Logos, the creative out-going Word of God (see Lecture VI), as most distinctively discerned in the creative self-transformation which occurs in all events and most particularly in man's personal response to the created order, to other men and, John Cobb has argued,[19] to God in Christ.

Be that as it may, the new evidence about the roles of chance and law in the life-game encourages us to add a further dimension, or set of metaphors, to our images and models of God's continuous activity in creation. For we now see more clearly than ever before the role in the eliciting of life, and so of man, of the interplay of random chance micro-events with the 'necessity' which arises from the stuff of this world having their particular given properties—that is, having one set of potentialities and not another (Lecture II). These potentialities are written into creation by the Creator himself and they are unveiled by chance exploring their gamut. 'Gamut' is a musical term which has come to mean 'the whole scale, range or compass of a thing',[20] and perhaps I may be allowed to press the musical analogy further.

B. *The music of creation*

God as Creator we now see as, perhaps, somewhat like a bell-ringer, ringing all the possible changes, all the possible permutations and combinations he can out of a given set of harmonious bells—though it is God who creates the 'bells' too. Or, perhaps better, he is more like a composer who, beginning with an arrangement of notes in an apparently simple tune, elaborates and expands it into a fugue by a variety of devices of fragmentation and reassociation; of turning it upside down and back to front; by overlapping these and other variations of it in a range of tonalities; by a profusion of patterns of sequences in time, with always the consequent interplay of sound flowing in an orderly way from the chosen initiating ploy (that is, more

---

[19] John Cobb, *Christ in a Pluralistic Age* (Westminster Press, Philadelphia, 1975).
[20] *Oxford English Dictionary*.

technically, by inversion, stretto, and canon, etc.). Thus does a
J. S. Bach create a complex and interlocking harmonious fusion
of his seminal material, both through time and at any particular instant, which, beautiful in its elaboration, only reaches
its consummation when all the threads have been drawn into
the return to the home key of the last few bars—the key of
the initial melody whose potential elaboration was conceived
from the moment it was first expounded. In this kind of way
might the Creator be imagined to unfold the potentialities of
the univèrse which he himself has given it. He appears to do
this by a process in which the creative possibilities, inherent, by
his own creative intention, within the fundamental entities of
that universe and their interrelations, become actualized within
a temporal development shaped and determined by those self-
same inherent potentialities that he conceived from the very
first note. One cannot help recalling how, when the Lord
answers Job out of the whirlwind, he averred that at creation
'the morning stars sang together, and all the sons of God
shouted for joy'.[21]

C.   The dance of creation

The music in creation has been a constant theme of the religions
of India, in particular.[22] It was, indeed, a correct and shrewd
instinct on the part of Glansdorff and Prigogine to depict on
the dust-cover of their major work, expounding with much
rigour the ideas of the Brussels school which I have briefly
outlined,[23] the South Indian representation, in bronze, of Shiva,
the Creator–Destroyer, as Lord of the Dance of creation.
Within a fiery circle representing the action of material energy
and matter in nature, Shiva Nataraja (as 'he' is called in this
aspect of his being) dances the dance of wisdom and enlightenment to maintain the life of the cosmos and to give release to

[21] Job 38: 7. Cf. Kepler, for whom the cosmos was a spiritual harmony ('concertus
intellectualis') which 'pure spirits and in a certain way even God sense with no less
enjoyment and pleasure than man experiences when listening to musical chords',
quoted by Max Caspar, *Kepler*, trans. and ed. C. Doris Hellman (Abelard–Schumann,
London and New York, 1959), p. 95.

[22] For a much wider treatment of Eastern thought and mysticism in relation to
modern physics in particular, see F. Capra's *The Tao of Physics*, discussed in Appendix A.

[23] A. Glansdorff and I. Prigogine, *Thermodynamic theory of structure, stability and
fluctuations* (Wiley–Interscience, New York, 1971).

those who seek him. In one of his two right hands, he holds a drum which touches the fiery circle and by its pulsating waves of sound awakens matter to join in the dance; his other right hand is raised in a protecting gesture of hope, 'do not fear'—while one of the left hands brings destructive fire to the encircling nature, and this fire, by erasing old forms, allows new ones to be evoked in the dance. These bronze images are one of the profoundest representations in art of the 'five activities of God' in overlooking, creating, evolving; in preservation and support; in destruction; in embodiment, illusion, and giving of rest; and in release, salvation, and grace.[24] Shiva is the Presence contained within Nature—the universal omnipresent Spirit dancing within and touching the whole arch of matter–nature with head, hands, and feet.

> His form is everywhere: all-pervading in his Shiva-Shakti
> Chidabaram [the centre of the universe] is everywhere,
>   everywhere His dance:
> As Shiva is all and omnipresent,
> Everywhere is Shiva's gracious dance made manifest.
> His five-fold dances are temporal and timeless.
> His five-fold dances are His Five Activities . . .[25]

Coomaraswamy emphasizes

the grandeur of this conception itself as a synthesis of science, religion and art ... No artist of today, however great, could more exactly or more wisely create an image of that Energy which science must postulate behind all phenomena. If we would reconcile Time with Eternity, we can scarcely do so otherwise than by the conception of alternations of phase extending over vast regions of space and great tracts of time. Especially significant, then, is the phase alternation implied by the drum, and the fire which 'changes' not destroys. These are but visual symbols of the theory of the day and night of Brahma.

In the night of Brahma, Nature is inert, and cannot dance till Shiva wills it: He rises from His rapture, and dancing sends through inert matter pulsing waves of awakening sound, and lo! matter also dances appearing as a glory round about Him. Dancing, He sustains its manifold phenomena. In the fulness of time, still dancing, he

[24] A. K. Coomaraswamy, *The Dance of Shiva* (Peter Owen, London, 1958), p. 70.
[25] 'The Vision of the Sacred Dance' of Tirumular's *Tirumantrum*, quoted by Coomaraswamy, op. cit., p. 71.

destroys all forms and names by fire and gives new rest. This is poetry; but none the less, science.[26]

The idea of the dance of creation is not absent from Western culture either—for example, in the ancient Cornish carol, the 'General Dance', and in the well-known setting by Gustav Holst of the carol 'Tomorrow shall be my dancing day', often sung in English parish churches and cathedrals in the Christmas season. The idea is reflected, too, in a sixteenth-century poem by Sir John Davies, entitled 'Orchestra, or, a Poem of Dancing' in which one of the suitors of Penelope, long bereft of Ulysses' presence, is depicted as trying to persuade her to dance:

> Dancing, bright lady, then began to be
> When the first seeds whereof the world did spring,
> The fire air earth and water, did agree
> By Love's persuasion, nature's mighty king,
> To leave their first discorded combating
> And in a dance such measure to observe
> And all the world their motion should preserve.
>
> Since when they still are carried in a round,
> And changing come one in another's place;
> Yet do they neither mingle nor confound,
> But every one doth keep the bounded space
> Wherein the dance doth bid it turn or trace.
> This wondrous miracle doth Love devise,
> For dancing is love's proper exercise.
>
> Or if this all, which round about we see,
> As idle Morpheus some sick brains hath taught,
> Of individual notes compacted be,
> How was this goodly architecture wrought?
> Or by what means were they together brought?
> They err that say they did concur by chance;
> Love made them meet in a well-ordered dance![27]

D. The 'play' of God in creation

Dancing involves play and joy and the conception of the world process as the Lord Shiva's play is a prominent theme in the

---

[26] Coomaraswamy, op. cit., pp. 77, 78.

[27] Sir John Davies (1569–1626), 'Orchestra, or, a Poem on Dancing' in *Silver Poets of the 16th Century*, ed. G. Bullett, (Everyman's Library, Dent, London, 1947), pp. 320 f., I am indebted to Mrs Jane Brooke, Salisbury, for drawing my attention to this poem.

Hindu scriptures—'The perpetual dance is His play.'[28] Indeed both of our images, of the writing of a fugue and of the execution of a dance, express the idea of God enjoying, of playing in, creation. Nor is this an idea new to Christian thought. The Greek fathers, so Harvey Cox argues, contended that the creation of the world was a form of play. 'God did it they insisted out of freedom, not because he had to, spontaneously and not in obedience to some inexorable law of necessity. He did it, so to speak, "just for the hell of it".'[29] J. Moltmann calls this play the 'theological play of the good will of God'[30] which he later elaborates:

... God created the world neither out of his own essence nor by caprice. It did not have to be, but creation suits his deepest nature or else he would not enjoy it.... when we say that the creative God is playing, we are talking about a playing that differs from that of man. The creative God plays with his own possibilities and creates out of nothing that which pleases him.[31]

No wonder that Dante could liken, in an unforgettable phrase, the angelic praises of the Trinity in paradise to the 'laughter of the universe' ('un riso dell' universo').[32]

This understanding of why God should create the world at all finds an echo in the concept of *līla* in some aspects of Indian thought.[33] According to this tradition of the *Vedanta Sutra*, the creative activity of God is his sport or play, *līlā*; the worlds are created by and for the enjoyment of God. In later devotional Hinduism, nature is the *līla*, the cosmic play or dance, of the Lord: 'the perfect devotee does not suffer; for he can both visualize and experience life and the universe as the revelation of that Supreme Divine Force (*sakti*) with which he is in love, the

[28] Tirumular, quoted by Coomaraswamy, op. cit., p. 74.

[29] Harvey Cox, *The Feast of Fools* (Harvard University Press, Cambridge, Mass., 1969), p. 151.

[30] J. Moltmann, *Theology and Joy* (SCM Press, London, 1973), p. 38.

[31] Moltmann, op. cit., pp. 40–1. Again cf. Kepler: 'As God the Creator played/so He also taught nature, as His image, to play/the very game/which He played before her', quoted by Caspar, op. cit., p. 185.

[32] Il Paradiso, Canto XXVII, ll. 4–5.

[33] I am much indebted to Dr J. Lipner, St. Edmund House, Cambridge, and the Revd J. S. Thekkumkal, Campion Hall, Oxford, and Dharmaram College, Bangalore, for introducing me to this concept. The latter kindly also allowed me to see a draft of the part on 'Nature in Indian thought', of his, as yet unpublished, thesis. These paragraphs owe much to his account.

all-comprehensive Divine Being in its cosmic aspect of playful aimless display (*līlā*)—which precipitates pain as well as joy, but in its bliss transcends them both'.[34] This represents the world-accepting strand in Indian religion (Tantra and popular Hinduism) in which 'The world is the unending manifestation of the dynamic aspect of the divine, and as such should not be devaluated and discarded as suffering and imperfection, but celebrated, penetrated by enlightening insight, and experienced with understanding.'[35] In the majestic sculptures, bronzes and 'expanding form' of the Indian aesthetic phenomenon, Zimmer claims, there is portrayed nature as

Prakriti herself (*natura naturans*, not the merely visible surface of things) ... with no resistance to her charm—as She gives birth to the oceans of the worlds. Individuals—mere waves, mere moments, in the rapidly flowing, unending torrent of ephemeral forms—are tangibly present; but their tangibility itself is simply a gesture, an affectionate flash of expression on the otherwise invisible countenance of the Goddess Mother whose play (līlā) is the universe of her own beauty.[36]

The world order as the expression of the creative urge (*sakti*) of God is really his/her play, *līla*, which is the motivation which prompts God to creation, preservation and destruction. According to the idea of *līla*, God is not constrained by any external agency or desire. God's creative activities are a spontaneous overflow of the fullness of his own joy and perfection—it is like that spontaneity and freedom which is experienced in human play and sport. The contemporary Indian proponent of an 'integral philosophy', Sri Aurobindo, also takes up this theme (in the account of N. A. Nikam):

In relation to ... the self-delight of the eternally self-existing being, the world, according to Sri Aurobindo, is not *maya* [in the 'pejorative sense of cunning, fraud or illusion'—a phenomenal and mutable, and so not fundamental and immutable, truth] but *līlā*,: i.e. a play, and joy of play, wherever this is found: 'the child's joy, the poet's joy, the actor's joy, the mechanician's joy ...'; the cause and purpose of play is: 'being ever busy with its own innumerable self-representations ... Himself the play, Himself the player, Himself the playground'. There

[34] H. Zimmer, *Philosophies of India*, ed. J. Campbell (Routledge & Kegan Paul, London, 1951), p. 571.
[35] Zimmer, op. cit., p. 570.
[36] Zimmer, op. cit., p. 593.

is behind all our experiences one reality, one indivisible conscious being, supporting our experiences by its inalienable delight. The delight of being is, or ought to be, therefore, our real response in all situations. The experience of pain, pleasure, and indifference, is only a superficial arrangement effected by the limited part of our selves, caused by what is uppermost in our waking consciousness. There is ... a vast bliss behind our mental being.[37]

In conclusion: the creative role of chance operating upon the lawful 'necessities' which are themselves created has led us to accept models of God's activity which express God's gratuitousness and joy in creation as a whole, and not in man alone. The created world is then seen as an expression of the overflow of the divine generosity. The model is, as we have seen, almost of God displaying the delight and sheer exuberance of play in the unceasing act of creation, as represented in the Wisdom literature by the female personification of God's Wisdom present in the creation:

When he [the Lord] set the heavens in their place I [Wisdom] was
    there,
when he girdled the ocean with the horizon,
when he fixed the canopy of clouds overhead
and set the springs of oceans firm in their place,
when he prescribed its limits for the sea
and knit together earth's foundations.
Then I was at his side each day,
his darling and delight,
playing in his presence continually,
playing on the earth, when he had finished it,
while my delight was in mankind.[38]

---

[37] N. A. Nikam, 'The Problem of Creation: Concepts of Māyā and Līlā', in *The Integral Philosophy of Sri Aurobindo*, ed. H. Chaudhuri and F. Spiegelberg (Allen & Unwin, London, 1960), p. 147. The quotations within this passage are from Sri Aurobindo, *The Life Divine* (Sri Aurobindo International University Collection, Pondicherry, 1955).

[38] Proverbs 8: 27–31, NEB.

IV

Nature's Hierarchies—'Things Visible and Invisible'

I. REDUCTIONISM

We have all, whatever our particular professional academic expertise, from time to time been irritated by those of our colleagues who, coming from another discipline, claim that our discipline X is 'nothing but' an example and application of their discipline Y. The game applies along the whole length of the pecking order of academic life. Thus X may be religion and Y the sociology of ideological functions in society; or X may be sociology itself and Y individual psychology; or X may be psychology and Y neurophysiology; or X may be neurophysiology and Y may be biochemistry; or X may be biology and Y physics and chemistry; and so the game goes on. The game is called reductionism or, more colloquially, 'nothing buttery'. It is practised by any given number of academic players and the prizes are a sense of superiority in those who would otherwise regard themselves, perhaps, as at the end of the line from the point of view of the relevance to human life of that on which they spend most of their lives; and the malicious joy at watching the apoplectic response of one's colleagues as one devastatingly demonstrates that their discipline is not only a waste of time but unworthy of the receipt of grants from limited funds! If the game were merely an exercise in *odium academicum*, which has succeeded *odium theologicum* in the ploys of academic gamesmanship, and were simply a means whereby otherwise inadequate personalities bolstered their own egos and their sense of doing something worth while, it would perhaps matter little. It would be just one of the quirks of the academic life which no doubt will, in due course, come under the microscope of the sociologists and the psychologists. However, the game is really much more serious than this, for it is a game which has been played ever since the days when Democritus and Lucretius, by their atomistic determinism, tried to reduce the whole of human life and the history of the world to a mere concatenation of colliding atoms—with obvious implications for the concepts of human mental processes and autonomy.

There are many pairs of Xs and Ys, that is, many interfaces, at which this game may be played. Although the contenders vary, it does seem to me that the game that is played at these various interfaces is the *same* game even when the nature of the arguments between the contenders at first appears very different. Thus, those of us who have tried on occasion to support theological statements find ourselves having to contend with those who, while listening to us politely, yet know—and soon tell us—that 'of course' these statement are all very interesting but what they are *really* doing is simply to express, say, the social function of religion, or the need for various kinds of psychological appetites to be satisfied. It is not, in my experience, very easy to meet these arguments without at the same time having some general view of the relations between the different kinds of knowledge of different natural systems, including the human. Only when these relations have been clarified can we have any hope of assembling the knowledge from the various natural sciences on any broad canvas upon which we may hope to locate man's existence and experience.

A. *The hierarchy of natural systems*

During this century, and with increasing acceleration in recent decades, the expansion of our knowledge of the natural world has more and more shown it to consist of a hierarchy of systems. This is particularly true of the various levels of organization to be observed in living organisms: the sequence of increasing complexity to be found in the living world (atom–molecule–macromolecule–subcellular organelle–cell–multicellular functioning organ–whole living organism–populations of organisms–ecosystem) represents a series of levels of organization of matter in which each successive member of the series is a 'whole' constituted of 'parts' preceding it in the series (for convenience only and with no other implications, we often call each member of this series 'higher' than the one preceding it in this list). The issue which arises is whether or not a higher (for example, biological) system is a unity (an 'organic unity') which can be analysed into its constituent parts in a non-additive way or whether simple additive assembly of its component units (physico-chemical in the biological case) is adequate for the comprehension of the higher system. To be more precise: the philosophical debate on this question of 'reductionism', as it is called, in relation to the sciences is centred principally on 'whether the theories and experimental laws formulated in one field of science can be shown to be special cases of theories and laws formulated in some other branch of science. If such is the case, the former branch of science is said to have been reduced to the latter.'[1] To resolve this issue it is necessary to distinguish carefully the hierarchy of *systems* from the hierarchy of the *theories* of the *sciences* concerned with the systems.

The hierarchy of natural systems has been frequently described and needs no further elaboration, especially as it is not in dispute amongst scientists. The concept of a set of hierarchically organized systems has also been thoroughly investigated from more abstract viewpoints and the conditions for a set of part–whole relations to constitute a 'perfect hierarchy' have been formulated. Thus Morton Beckner (1974) writes

The hierarchy model has historically provided a large part of the framework of discussion in the philosophy of biology. It is involved in a wide range of connected ideas: levels of organisation, sequences of boundaries ... autonomy at one level with respect to lower ones, a temporal order in the arrival of the higher levels on the cosmic scene, the emergence of higher-level entities, etc. The existence of hierarchical systems is certainly connected with the hierarchical arrangement of theories.[2]

B.   The hierarchy of theories

Beckner goes on to argue that our view of what constitutes a hierarchy of theories is influenced by the empirical fact that

[1] F. J. Ayala, in the introduction to *Studies in the Philosophy of Biology: Reduction and Related Problems*, ed. F. J. Ayala and T. Dobzhansky (Macmillan, London, 1974), p. ix. *Vide* A. R. Peacocke, 'Reductionism: a review of the epistemological issues and their relevance to biology and the problem of consciousness', *Zygon*, 11 (1976), pp. 306–34.

[2] M. Beckner, 'Reduction, Hierarchies and Organicism', in Ayala and Dobzhansky, op. cit., pp. 164–5.

there are very many hierarchically organized systems and these provide us with a way of arranging sciences (and their associated theories) on a scale so that there is a science which studies systems at any particular level and this science is comprised of theories and experimental laws characteristic *of* that particular level. Thus, the various studies of the units which comprise the hierarchy of levels in a living organism that I have just listed generate, in the same order, the respective sciences of: physics, chemistry, biochemistry and biophysics, cell physiology, cytology, cell biology, physiology, population genetics and ecology, etc. The reducibility of a theory at a higher level to a theory at a lower level has, of course, been a central concern of philosophers of science over recent decades. Examples of such pairs of higher and lower level of theories might be, respectively: (much of chemistry)–(physics); (gas laws)–(laws of molecular motion); (Mendelian genetics)–(DNA structure, coding and transcription). Conditions of reducibility of one theory to another have been widely discussed and carefully formulated in a distinctively linguistic manner, for reduction is regarded as the deduction of one set of empirically confirmable *statements* from another such set—and not the derivation of one set of phenomena from another, or of the properties of one subject matter from the properties of another.

The point here is not whether or not any particular set of criteria are in themselves adequate (whether those of Nagel, or of Feyerabend, etc.) but that it is the relation of theories, concepts, terms, and (even) observations obtained with reference to the higher level of complexity to the theories, etc., obtained with reference to the lower level which is to be analysed for reducibility.

C. *Methodological reduction*

There is, of course, also a methodological issue here which, because it is scarcely a matter of controversy, need not detain us long. The progress of the sciences has certainly been, in part, due to their successful propensity to break down, for purposes of exploration, unintelligible, complex wholes into their experimentally more manageable component units. One builds up from the micro- to the macro-level. Even the most holistic of biologists would not deny the value of the unravelling of the molecular basis of heredity in the structure and coding of DNA or the protein-structural basis of immunological response. This strategy is an inevitable consequence of the natural world consisting of a hierarchy of organized systems at multiple levels, one system (e.g. biological macromolecules and living organisms) constituting the interacting units from which more complex systems are assembled at the next level (i.e., respectively, in single living cells and in ecosystems of populations of organisms in their environment). Such relationships, which emerge empirically, necessitate an analytical strategy of a methodologically reductionist kind. So each 'science' becomes a relatively autonomous interlocking network of theories, descriptions, concepts, experimental techniques, fields of observations and (one should honestly add) also of individual scientists and *their* network of personal relationships. There is nothing wrong in this and it is widely accepted as the way in which a science progresses, even though the relationship of the hierarchy of *systems* which are studied to the hierarchy of *theories and sciences* may not be well understood and has been grist to the mill of arguments about reductionism. It must be recognized that the investigation of various levels of integration of structure and function at different levels in the hierarchy of systems necessitates methods, both experimental and intellectual, which are specific to that level. Understanding of *both* the pattern and the component units of any one level is required.

D. *The hierarchy of the sciences*

Moreover as one progresses 'upwards' through the hierarchy of the sciences, for example, along the series physics–chemistry–biology–ecology or sociology, each represents a sub-class within the possible interaction of the units of the preceding level and, as Medawar has noted, 'the sciences become richer and richer in their empirical content and new concepts emerge at each level which simply do not appear in the preceding sciences.'[3] Corresponding to each level in the hierarchy of systems, the appropriate science employs concepts which are peculiar to it and indeed have little meaning for levels lower down (or even

[3] P. Medawar, 'A Geometric Model of Reduction and Emergence', in Ayala and Dobzhansky, op. cit., p. 61.

higher up in some cases). As new forms of matter, non-living and living, emerge in the universe, new categories of description of their form and properties are necessary and these categories will be other than those of the physics and chemistry appropriate to the subnuclear, atomic, and molecular levels. Every statement which is true when applied to systems earlier (or lower) in the series is true when applied to the later (or higher), but these lower-level statements are usually not the focus of interest for the practitioners of the higher level science. Thus sociologists have insisted, recently with explosive force, on the distinctiveness of sociological concepts from biological, and biologists, for longer (and more quietly), have stressed the distinctiveness of their concepts in relation to physics and chemistry. As E. O. Wilson has put it recently, every discipline has its 'antidiscipline' at the level below and is an 'antidiscipline' for the level above.[4]

E. Theory autonomy

What practising scientists have been concerned to emphasize is the distinctiveness of the *concepts* of their own science, of which they are only too well aware when they try to communicate with scientists of other disciplines. This distinctiveness is more precisely delineated by Beckner[5] as *theory autonomy*, that autonomy of higher-level theories whereby they are not epistemologically reducible to lower-level theories. This analysis stresses *theory* autonomy as a relation between parts of scientific languages and is to be carefully distinguished from *process autonomy*, whereby a process characteristic of a 'higher' level in a hierarchy is autonomous with respect to processes in a 'lower' level if, and only if, the laws of the higher-level process are not fully determined by the laws of processes (of a different kind) at the lower level. Much confusion in the discussion of reductionism has resulted from the failure to distinguish adequately between, on the one hand, the hierarchy of *sciences* (with their associated theories, concepts, descriptions, etc. and the logical relationships between them) and, on the other hand, the hierarchy of actual *systems* and the real relations (causal,

---

[4] E. O. Wilson, 'Biology and the social sciences', *Daedalus*, 106. 4 (Autumn 1977), 127–40.
[5] Above, p. 114 n. 2.

spatial, temporal, etc.) between the events, processes, etc. occurring at each level in this hierarchy. Causal connections have to be more carefully defined and analysed for hierarchical systems than they do for pairs of systems which have no parts in common.

From this analysis it becomes clear that the irreducibility, the autonomy, of a higher-level theory with respect to a lower-level theory may be due to differences in their conceptual structure, and not to lack of determination of processes in the higher level by processes in the lower level.

F. Anti-reductionism and vitalism

This analysis also clarifies claims that complex wholes in the natural world are 'nothing but' their component parts; that, as Francis Crick has put it, in relation to biological systems, 'The ultimate aim of the modern movement in biology is in fact to explain *all* biology in terms of physics and chemistry.'[6] This apparently strongly reductionist statement is more ambiguous than first appears, being about explanation rather than ontology, i.e. about what biological organisms *are*. If it is meant to assert that the laws of physics and chemistry fully apply to all the processes occurring in biological organisms at the atomic and molecular level, then few would be found to disagree. For 'vitalism', the view that some entities or forces, other than physico-chemical ones, are present and operate in biological organisms and constitute their distinctiveness as 'living' organisms, is totally rejected by biological scientists, having been found to be a dead-end hypothesis in research and in interpretation. But to be anti-vitalist does not necessitate being reductionist, at least in the sense of opposing the autonomy of higher level—in this case, biological—theories, as the preceding analysis indicates. Biological scientists are keenly conscious that biological organization is not only a hierarchy of parts making wholes at different levels, but also that dynamic physico-chemical processes in biological organisms are themselves interlocked dynamically in space and time in a hierarchy of increasingly complex networks. They are therefore bound to

[6] F. H. C. Crick, *Of Molecules and Man* (University of Washington Press, Seattle, 1966), p. 10.

stress the special concepts they have to employ to describe and understand such complexities. There is indeed a strong case for arguing that many biological concepts and theories are distinctive of that level in the natural hierarchy of systems and that some are irreducible. (Medawar, for example, cites[7] heredity, infection, immunity, sexuality, fear, and I would add, the concept of genetic information, transmitted via DNA).

II. THE MENTAL AND THE MATERIAL

A. 'Interfaces'

What is true about the interface between biology and the physical sciences is also true of interfaces higher up in the scale of complexity of the hierarchy of natural systems. At these levels we begin to be concerned with phenomena which are particularly relevant to individual and social human life and many of the terms used in the discussions are likely to change. For it is of the very essence of the non-reducibility of a theory describing a higher level in the natural hierarchies with which we have been concerned up till now that it implies that certain phenomena are 'emergent' with respect to lower-level theories. In this context, and note that we are still dealing with theories and concepts and not with processes, 'emergence' is synonymous with 'theory autonomy' so that as we move from, say, the physico-chemical to the biochemical, or from the biochemical to the physiological, or from the physiological to the neurophysiological, or from the biological to the sociological, new phenomena characteristic of the higher level will have the character of being 'emergent'—if the theories about them are not epistemologically reducible to the lower-level theories. So that new terms, new concepts, new descriptions, new kinds of language will be used to describe and to articulate and to understand these phenomena. Already the complexities of neurophysiology require reference to systems and control theory and to the theory of computers in a way which is not necessary for the 'lower-level' study of conduction in a single nerve. It should therefore not surprise us that, at the level of description to which the terms 'conscious', 'unconscious', and 'self-

[7] Medawar, op. cit., p. 57.

conscious' apply, the description of the content of consciousness and of the unconscious should not be reducible to neuro-physiological terms. However, taking our clue from the biology/physics–chemistry interface, we would expect the understanding of consciousness and of the unconscious to be amplified and helped by detailed knowledge of neurophysiology, which will not exhaust but supplement any psychological theories of consciousness and of the unconscious. Indeed the two will interact and the knowledge of neurophysiology will provide the context to which psychological theories are relevant but psychological theories may well have an autonomy of their own and a validity of their own in their own sphere—an autonomy and validity which has to be separately established. To say this is not to deny that neurophysiological processes occur in the brain but it is to avoid statements such as 'consciousness is nothing but a physico-chemical process in the brain'. Here the 'nothing but' implies a non-existent ability to reduce the language of mental events, in this instance consciousness, to physico-chemical events (whether or not the physico-chemical events are to be regarded as identical with mental events is another question—at the moment I refer only to the 'nothing but' and its reductionist implications). If the language describing mental events is not reducible to that of cerebral physico-chemical events, a proposition widely supported by philosophers of many different views on the mind–brain relation, then mental activity and functions, 'consciousness', may be regarded as a genuinely emergent feature at that level in the hierarchy of complexity which is the human brain in the human body, and almost certainly at lower levels of evolution, too (judging from recent work on the training of higher primates in sign-languages). Thus consciousness, mental activity and function in general, is an activity which emerges when certain complex structures have evolved—an activity which is not epistemologically reducible to lower-level descriptions. The newness of the activity and function are real enough, but these are not an activity and function of some new thing or entity, the 'mind', but are a new activity and function of the all-pervasive physico-chemical units that emerge when these units have evolved a particular kind of organized complexity. According to this view, mental activity does not necessarily have to be predicated of some new entity, the 'mind', which is, as it were, added as a new kind of order of being to the neurological network of physico-chemical structures and processes which constitute the brain. To say it is would, on this view, be to make precisely the same error as the vitalists when they wished to add some vital essence (*élan vital*, entelechy, or life force) to physico-chemical structures to endow them with 'life', which we now see as a special kind of organized activity. As with vitalism, one can be anti-reductionist about mental processes and events and 'anti-mentalist', in the sense of not postulating an entity called the 'mind'.

Leaving aside, for the moment, further consideration of philosophical issues, let us recall the strength of the evidence for the intimate relation between mental activity and the physico-chemical state of the brain. It includes *inter alia*:[8] the dependence of personality states on hormone balance; the genetic determination of the human body, mental attributes and defects (and so their basis in DNA structure); the effects of drugs on mental states, and of mental states on the effects drugs can produce; personality changes in patients who have undergone frontal leucotomy or temporal lobectomy, i.e. separation of the frontal or temporal lobes, respectively, of the brain from the remainder; the studies of Sperry and his colleagues on the states of consciousness and the control abilities of patients whose two cerebral hemispheres have been severed at the *corpus callosum* and the problems these raise concerning the unity of their consciousness and of their personality; evidence that the threshold of consciousness of sensations is passed only when there has been an elaboration of the spatio-temporal patterns of impulse discharged across as many as 200 synaptic linkages between nerves,[9] each impulse activating the huge number ($\sim$ 10,000) of nerves with which it is in contact over an unimaginably complex network.

Thus all the regular, repeatable observations link mental activity and processes with the physico-chemical activity and

[8] See the 1976 Reith Lectures of C. Blakemore, *The Mechanics of the Mind* (Cambridge University Press, Cambridge, 1976).

[9] B. Libet, 'Brain stimulation and the threshold of conscious experience', in *Brain and conscious experience*, ed. J. C. Eccles (Springer, Berlin, Heidelberg, New York, 1966), pp. 165–81.

organization of the human brain in the human body. This is only to be expected from the relationships within the hierarchy of natural systems in which new activities and functions are observed as emergent features of new levels of complexity— 'emergent' both in the sense of being non-reducible and in the sense that they appeared successively at later times in the evolutionary development. It is because of the evidence for the neuro-physiological basis of mental events and because of the general character of our scientific understanding of the world, hammered out by so much hard work and analysis over the last few centuries, that scientists are naturally suspicious of certain views, widely current today—I refer to certain kinds of both dualism and monism.

B. Dualism

(*i*) *The occult and pseudo-science.*   To take dualism first. As an emotional and inevitable sociological response to the general disillusion with a scientific technology that has not ushered in Utopia, there has been a reversion in current society to an interest in, and practice of, the occult, as well as a growing adherence to a pseudo-science which dwells on individual, berserk (and usually unrepeatable) phenomena which are adduced to support the existence of a non-physical 'super-nature'. This has led *inter alia* to the spread, like a disease, of the interpretation of mental illness in terms of demon possession. Let us be clear why scientists must object to such a resurgence of pre-scientific thinking. It is not because there are not many unusual and unexplained occurrences in the world. It is not because biologists, neuro-physiologists, and psychologists think they understand all there is to know about the complexities of human mental experience, brain behaviour, and the transmission of signals between persons. On all sides, the subtlety and complexity of these and our relative ignorance of, for example, the time course of unconscious mental events, the influences upon the unconscious, the images which dwell in it, and the emergence of events in the unconscious into consciousness, are widely recognized, together with their profound and baffling character. The brain is clearly the most complex organized piece of matter in the world, of a daunting intricacy so that we lack even the conceptual models adequately to represent it. What scientists rightly object to, it seems to me, is that acceptance of the occult, demonological, 'supernaturalist' mythology would imply not just a lack of understanding of a particular phenomenon, the mental-brain processes, but also the falsity of the entire scientific understanding the world so painstakingly built up and so intellectually comprehensive and inspiring in its scope and depth. Whatever the explanations for some of the odd events described in the occult and pseudo-science literature are, they must be consistent with repeatable and established observations we already possess. Major conceptual changes (e.g. the paradigm shifts of T. S. Kuhn) and the discovery of new kinds of interactions are always possible. But in the past such new departures have been eventually accepted into scientific knowledge on account of their ability to incorporate old observations and understandings into a wider and more comprehensive framework. We must not let the occurrence of odd phenomena lead to intellectual anarchy in the name of a bogus openness to the unexpected. In the past, 'anomalies', that is odd unexplained phenomena, have had to be repeatable, public, objective phenomena to cause any 'paradigm shift'. One thinks of the anomalies of the black-body spectrum, of specific heats of solids, of the photo-electric effect which, failing to fit with 'classical' physical theory, eventually formed the experimental basis of the quantum theory that displaced the classical theories of energy; or the earlier and magnificently simple observations of Michael Faraday with wires, galvanometers, and magnets which demonstrated a connection between electricity and magnetism and uncovered new and unsuspected relationships. It is for this kind of reason that extra-sensory perception, perhaps the strongest of the 'occult' candidates for scientific recognition, still awaits acceptance by the scientific community; it is not sheer purblind prejudice which prevents this but the absence of sufficient testable, repeatable evidence and the existence of rival plausible explanations consistent with our understanding of mental processes as an activity of a physico-chemical structure, the brain. The postulate of mental activity as a kind of activity *of* the brain itself (with some provisos about its anomalousness to be discussed below) is adequate to the evidence, as the postulate of a non-physical entity, the 'mind', which causes the neurophysiological events, is not. The so-called 'psychic' explanations do not explain for they offer no understanding of how these personalized entities, of a distinctively different nature (whether 'disembodied spirits' or even 'demons'), operate upon the physical world—in particular, on the brain, for which the evidence is now strong that it is the location of consciousness.

(*ii*) *Demons and Christian belief.* Unfortunately, many churchmen have been misguided enough to jump on the accelerating bandwagon of the occult, and to bring back long-forgotten rites of 'exorcism' to expel supposedly non-physical quasi-personal entities ('demons') which are said to be possessing the 'minds' (or 'souls') of the mentally sick. So it is not surprising that many bookshops, at least in the USA, now (sadly) have a section labelled 'Religion and the Occult' instead of the old-fashioned 'Philosophy and Religion'. Of course, as has often been pointed out, but not yet sufficiently heeded by the Church, an escalation of theological errors results from postulating the existence of independently willing, entirely evil entities: did God make them?; if so, why?; if he didn't, how did they come into existence?; if he did, why is their evil unmitigated by any potentiality for good?, and if this is so, can we attribute their existence to the God whom Christians worship? It cannot be too strongly emphasized that the Christian faith is not committed to a world-view which incorporates this kind of dualism, both because of the theological impasses in which it results, as just indicated, and because it is also not committed to the dualistic view of human nature which the whole scheme presupposes. In so far as Christians adopt any particular view of the nature of man in himself, as distinct from their insight into man as alienated from God, it must be presumed to stem from the anthropology of the Bible, and in particular of the Old Testament—for the New Testament writers, by and large, inherit these, albeit often in Greek terminology. As H. Wheeler Robinson pointed out in a much quoted sentence: 'The Hebrew idea of personality is an animated body, and not an incarnated soul'[10] or as Eichrodt put it 'Man does not *have* a body and

[10] H. Wheeler Robinson, 'Hebrew Psychology' in *The People and the Book*, ed. A. S. Peake (Clarendon Press, Oxford, 1925), p. 362.

a soul, he *is* both of them at once.'[11] (Replace 'soul' by 'mind' in this statement and this would not be a bad summary of the body–mind identitist view!) The body is regarded as the medium and living form of the self; it is not, as in a more Platonic view, the temporary mortal prison of an eternal, immortal 'soul'. Within this view of man as a psychosomatic unity, there was allowed a distinctive character for the inner (we would say, in the present context, 'mental') life of man as contrasted with the external physical processes. The Hebrews, who were not prone to abstract conceptualizing, saw man as a unity with various differentiating functions, which they associated with different organs, through any one of which the person in his totality could express himself and be apprehended. Man was regarded as a personal unity, who could be addressed as 'thou', and was not subdivided into mortal and immortal parts. The complicated transformations of this concept through the early and subsequent centuries of Christian thought have been many and varied and many Christian thinkers have taken a more stratified, dichotomous, or trichotomous, view of human nature. We cannot follow these threads now but can only assert that these stratified views are not necessary to Christian belief and that the view of man as a psychosomatic unity was what characterized the biblical tradition.

C. *Monism: panpsychism*

As well as these kinds of dualism, some authors have adopted kinds of monism which, if accepted in a simplistic form, would be inconsistent with the understanding of human mental activity for which I have been arguing on the basis both of the neurophysiological evidence and of the general relation of emergent activities to the complex structures capable of manifesting them. Such a tendency is apparent in the writings of Teilhard de Chardin and of the process philosophers and theologians. They have a proper desire to emphasize that matter has the potential, at the appropriate level of complexity in the evolutionary process, of displaying mental activity. But they use a panpsychic model to elaborate this mental poten-

---

[11] W. Eichrodt, *Theology of the Old Testament*, trans. J. A. Baker (SCM Press, London, 1967), Vol. 2, p. 124.

tiality of matter, in which they appear to assert that even elementary matter *is* already, in some vestigial sense, 'mental'. For example, Teilhard de Chardin infers from the presence of consciousness in man that there must have been 'a rudimentary consciousness' that 'precedes the emergence of life'[12] which, elsewhere, he more explicitly locates in the 'stuff of the universe' which has

an inner aspect at one point of itself ... *co-extensive with their Without, there is a Within to things* ... primitive matter is something more than the particulate swarming so marvellously analysed by modern physics ... Beneath this mechanical layer we must think of a 'biological' layer that is attenuated to the uttermost, but yet is absolutely necessary to explain the cosmos in succeeding ages. The *within, consciousness,* and then *spontaneity*—three expressions for the same thing.[13]

He explains that 'consciousness' is here taken 'in its widest sense to indicate every kind of psychism, from the most rudimentary forms of interior perception imaginable to the human phenomenon of reflective thought'[14] and he asks 'have we not already come to the conclusion that they ["proteins on the level of the very big molecular accumulations"] would be incomprehensible if they did not possess already, deep down in themselves, some sort of rudimentary psyche?'[15]

'Process theologians' also postulate only one genus of actual entities which, following A. N. Whitehead, they call '(actual) occasions of experience' for 'If human experience is genuinely a part of nature, and if there be only one type of actual entity within nature ... then, since it is that part of nature one knows most intimately, it provides the best starting point for finding principles that can be generalized to all actual entities.'[16] On this basis, it is a natural move to a position not unlike Teilhard de Chardin's panpsychism, in which each 'occasion of experience' (the fundamental units of existence in process philosophy) all have both a 'physical pole', representing the

[12] Teilhard de Chardin, *The Phenomenon of Man* (Collins, London, 1959), p. 89.
[13] Teilhard de Chardin, op. cit., pp. 56, 57 (author's italics).
[14] Ibid., p. 57 n. 1.
[15] Ibid., p. 77.
[16] D. R. Griffin, 'Whitehead's philosophy and some general notions of physics and biology', in *Mind in nature: essays on the interface of science and philosophy,* ed. J. B. Cobb and D. R. Griffin (University Press of America, R. F. Publishing, Washingson, D.C., 1977), p. 124.

'physical impact of the world' upon it, and a 'mental pole', representing the 'originality of the occasion of experience which is not derivative from the thing experienced but is contributed by the experiment'.[17] Griffin even goes so far as to say 'there is at least some iota of mental functioning in all occasions'.[18]

However, according to the earlier exposition in this lecture, mental activity and functions have been shown to be best regarded as emergent, and non-reducible, only with respect to a certain level of complexity in the organization and pattern of the component physico-chemical units. So that 'mentality' is not to be thought of as an entity whose existence could be separately postulated, which seems to be Teilhard de Chardin's assumption; nor can mental activity and function be predicated of matter organized in forms much below that of the brain—though no doubt there is a gradation in what might legitimately be called consciousness among, at least, the higher mammals. So the attribution by Teilhard de Chardin and the process theologians of 'consciousness' or a 'mental pole' to *all* entities, even to sub-atomic particles, now seems to be an inadequate model, in the light of our analysis of the hierarchy of natural systems and of the reducibility, or otherwise, of higher-level theories. It is inadequate in the same sense as would be the postulating of some inherent 'wetness' in oxygen or hydrogen molecules because they can combine to form water, which itself is wet. Or, more accurately since we are dealing with genuine non-reducible emergent activities, the inadequacy of this panpsychic model seems to be of the same kind as would be entailed in attributing some attenuated information content to an individual, isolated separate deoxyribonucleotide unit because the intact DNA, that is linearly assembled *in vivo* from such units, also possesses information content *in vivo* which it transmits to the cell and to its progeny. That mental activities are genuinely emergent and not theoretically or conceptually or linguistically reducible to neurophysiological events renders unnecessary, it seems to me, such a panpsychic model for preserving an emphasis on the mental potentialities of matter.

---

[17] Using the terminology of A. N. Whitehead, recounted by J. B. Cobb, *A Christian Natural Theology* (Lutterworth, London, 1966), pp. 30, 33.

[18] Griffin, op. cit., p. 129.

D. 'Materialism'

We must now pursue further some consequences of this view that mental activity is a non-reducible emergent in a certain specific kind of complex, physico-chemical, neuro-physiological organism, the brain-in-the-body. Is this simply old-fashioned 'materialism'? It is 'materialism' only in the sense that no *thing* is there other than the atoms and molecules, but it is not 'old-fashioned' if by that one means that that is all there is to be said and the deterministic laws of physics and chemistry describe all. For it could equally be argued that we did not know of what 'matter', as described by physics and chemistry (or even biophysics and biochemistry), was capable until brains had evolved. So the mental capabilities of matter are real functions of matter which must be reckoned with, if we are ever so rash as to ask what matter is 'in itself'. No doubt we are wise to avoid that question, in the light of modern sub-nuclear studies and philosophy of science, but, at least, such considerations mean that the epithet 'materialist' need not have any necessary implications of 'reductionist'[19] and that the label 'materialism' could include more than its earlier proponents bargained for.

E. Mind–body identity

So far, we have been concerned with the neuro-physiological events of our brains in relation to the dynamic processes of consciousness and have avoided the philosophical issue: '*Are* mental events identical with neuro-physiological events?' This question has been the centre of philosophical debates in recent decades. I would not presume to enter the lists of that fearsome tiltyard from which so many, more competent and distinguished philosophically than I am, have retreated to lick their logical wounds. But from the stands, as it were, I note certain aspects of the state of play.

I note that many philosophers now accept that there is identity between mental states and brain states, but that they differ as to whether this is a contingent or a necessary identity,[20]

---

[19] As also argued, e.g., by J. A. Fodor, in *Psychological Explanation* (Random House, New York, 1968), Ch. 3.
[20] Cf. D. Wiggins, 'Identity-Statements', in *Analytical Philosophy, Second Series*, ed. R. J. Butler (Blackwell, Oxford, 1965), p. 41.

a debate which involves the possible definition and role of rigid designation,[21] and that they also differ on whether or not mental events fall under any laws, so that a single, particular mental event could be predicted or explained. D. Davidson[22] has argued for an 'anomalous monism' according to which, although mental events are identical with physical, there are no general laws correlating the mental and the physical ('psycho-physical laws'):

Anomalous monism resembles materialism in its claim that all events are physical, but rejects the thesis, usually considered essential to materialism, that mental phenomena can be given purely physical explanations.

... it is consistent with the view that mental characterisics are in some sense dependent, or supervenient, on physical characteristics.... Dependence or supervenience of this kind does not entail reducibility through law or definition.[23]

... we see that it is possible to know that a mental event is identical with some physical event without knowing which one (in the sense of being able to give it a unique physical description that brings it under the relevant law). Even if someone knew the entire physical history of the world, and every mental event were identical with a physical, it would not follow that he could predict or explain a single mental event (so described, of course).

Two features of mental events in their relation to the physical— causal dependence and nomological independence—combine, then, to dissolve what has often seemed a paradox, the efficacy of thought and purpose in the material world, and their freedom from law. When we portray events as perceivings, rememberings, decisions and actions, we necessarily locate them amid physical happenings through the relation of cause and effect; but that same mode of portrayal insulates mental events, as long as we do not change the idiom, from the strict laws that can in principle be called upon to explain and predict physical phenomena.

Mental events as a class cannot be explained by physical science;

---

[21] S. Kripke, 'Identity and Necessity', in *Identity and Individuation*, ed. M. Munitz (New York University Press, New York, 1971), pp. 135–64; and 'Naming and Necessity', in *Semantics of Natural Language*, ed. G. Harman and D. Davidson (Reidel, Dordrecht, 2nd edn. 1972), pp. 253–355.

[22] D. Davidson, 'Mental events' in *Experience and Theory*, ed. L. Foster and J. W. Swanson (University of Massachusetts Press, 1970).

[23] Davidson, op. cit., pp. 87–8.

particular mental events can when we know particular identities. But the explanations of mental events in which we are typically interested relate them to other mental events and conditions. We explain a man's free actions, for example, by appeal to his desires, habits, knowledge and perceptions. Such accounts of intentional behavior operate in a conceptual framework removed from the direct reach of physical law by describing both cause and effect, reason and action, as aspects of a portrait of a human agent. The anomalism of the mental is thus a necessary condition for viewing action as autonomous.[24]

So such 'anomalous monism', although a form of material-ism, licences discourse about human reasons, decisions, free actions—in brief, it recognizes man as an agent, albeit also an organized structure in the physical world. (Again what can we think matter 'is' if it is capable of being an agent when so organized?) Similarly, T. Nagel, in arguing for a similar 'physicalism', which is 'the thesis that a person, with all his psychological attributes, is nothing over and above his body, with all its physical attributes',[25] has stressed the psychological sense of the self, of the 'I' who is the subject who possesses mental states, who is the subject of *his* experiences, both mental and physical. He goes on to show that the self is not a substance (whether as a body or as a 'mind') and being a self is not the possessing of certain attributes by a subject.

I cite these authors to show that even apparently materialist or physicalist views of the body–mind relation have not been able to capture fully what more mentalist and less physicalist views are often designed to ensure, namely, the ability of the human brain in the human body to be a self-conscious free agent with interconnecting mental events linked in a causal nexus of a kind peculiar to themselves. These authors frankly accept this as a valid description of human beings and so

[24] Ibid., pp. 100–1. Davidson bases his arguments here on earlier moves in which he has argued that events, as much as objects, constitute a fundamental ontological category (in 'The Individuation of Events', in *Essays in Honor of Carl G. Hempel* (Reidel Publ. Co., Dordrecht, 1969), pp. 216–34); that primary reasons of an agent are causes of his actions (in 'Actions, Reasons and Causes', 1963, reprinted in *The Philosophy of Action* (Oxford University Press, Oxford, 1968), pp. 79–94); that we must distinguish firmly between causes and the features we hit on for describing them (in 'Causal Relations', *J. Phil.* 64 (1967), 691–703); and that we do not have 'to dredge up a law if we know a singular causal statement to be true: all that follows is that we know there must be a covering law' (ibid. p. 701).

[25] T. Nagel, 'Physicalism', *Phil. Review* 74 (1965), 339–56.

explicitly reject behaviourism and reductionism[26] for which there seems little support among even quite positivist philosophers. I see no reason why Christian theology should not accept a body–mind identist position which is qualified at least to the extent Davidson urges, with respect to the 'anomaly' of mental events and to their non-reducibility to the physical[27] and provided the autonomy of man as a free agent, as a 'self', is preserved, which is in fact the case with many of these 'qualified identitists'. However strong the arguments may be for any of these qualified identitist positions, the sense of the self as an agent remains a given fact of our experience of ourselves in relation to our bodies and to the world and, surd though it may be, demands incorporation into our view of our bodies and of the world—even as we recognize that the mental events which are the experience of being an 'I', an agent, are identical, under another description, with neurophysiological events in the brain.

III. MAN AS AGENT: GOD AS AGENT

A. Man as agent

The recurrent ground bass to the upper and more obvious tones of these lectures is the relation of God and the world. We have been elaborating how the sciences unveil that world as a hierarchy of levels of systems each requiring its own conceptual schemes for understanding and articulation, as well as experimental tools for investigation, and that these systems have appeared in time through the operation of the laws governing the behaviour of the units and with no discontinuity. At the extremity of one of the longest of the branches, perhaps justifiably described as the topmost point, of this hierarchical tree of systems and sciences, is to be found the evolved human being in society. He is describable individually in physical language in terms of a brain in a body but also requires the application of the non-reducible language of persons (of selfhood, self-conscious agency) and of social realities (e.g. Karl Popper's 'World 3' and Teilhard's 'noosphere') to explicate the

[26] See Fodor, op. cit., Ch. 3.
[27] Ibid. and Davidson, loc. cit.

mental activity he manifests, experiences and communicates. We encounter here a lacuna in our thinking, almost amounting to a paradox, and certainly to a problem, of how the mental events which are identical with the neuro-physical events can, nevertheless, include a sense of selfhood and of agency with respect to the very body that experiences it. I would suggest that this problem of the human sense of being an agent, of being a self, an 'I', acting in this physical causal nexus, is of the same ilk as the relation of God to the world. How can God act in a world in which every event is tied to every other by regularities which the sciences explain with increasing power and accuracy? Is it not a parallel and similar question to ask: How can I, experiencing myself mentally as an agent, initiate processes, within the causal physical nexus that is my body, which themselves *are* my intended action?

Natural science is autonomous and does not need the hypothesis of God to explain individual events and relationships, even when these are not as rigidly causal and mechanistic as in the Newtonian universe. We have had to learn that God is not in the gaps in the nexus of events but is somehow in the whole process. But how to conceive of this? What models can help? When, mentally, I have reasons and an intention to act, these reasons and intention are the cause of what follows and themselves are, if we accept the ideas just outlined, some complex state in my brain and nervous system—even though I can only describe and experience them *as* reasons and intentions, in mental-language terms. The reasons and intentions cause the neuronal network to be activated appropriately to initiate the sequence of physical events, the whole process being fully describable, in principle, if not yet in practice, in terms of the neurophysiology of muscle, eyes, tongue, etc. This sequence is at the same time the action itself. *I* am the agent of this action, say, raising my arm, acting through and moving my arm. In this action, *I* am not external to the process, for *I* am my living body in action, the very reason and intentions which are mine initiated the process by being a pattern within my brain in my body. *I* am not another cause alongside my body but simply my body in reasoned and intended action. Nevertheless in my experience of myself as an agent, I transcend any particular action or intended group of actions. I try to express myself in actions whose meaning, *as* action, can only be viewed in terms of means and ends and, usually, as part of a highly complex ramified whole. For any one physical action, for example raising my arm, can express many different intentions in various contexts, so that it is then not only differently described (e.g. salute, threat, greeting, or exercise, etc.) but also was differently intended and done for different reasons—and these make it the action it is. Moreover, because actions express meanings (they arise from intentions and reasons), I am rarely fully expressed in my actions—even when they are speech acts—and this, too, is an aspect of my transcendence over my actions. Thus in my mental experience I am a transcendent causal agent expressing myself in and through the physical structure of my body.

If we take a non-dualist view of the human person, as we have done so far, that is a more functionalist view of mental activity, then human actions can properly be described as transcendence-in-immanence, the functional intending 'I' transcends the physiological-physical sequence which yet, as it unfolds, is the same 'I' in action. Traditionally a more dualist view of man has prevailed in Western thought, and not least in many Christian circles, but we have seen that, in the light both of the hierarchy of natural systems in which man is now shown by the sciences to be placed and of philosophical analysis, this dualist view cannot be made coherent and clearly articulated.

B.   God as agent

This is not loss but gain—not only because of its consistency with the Hebraic understanding of man, but because it provides us with a familiar model to enable us to imagine how a transcendent agent *could* be immanent in a physical process. If man, when he is an agent, can experience a sense of transcendence, within his mental life, which is 'supervenient' on the physical process and 'anomalous' with respect to it (Davidson's terms[28]), so that it remains uncaptured by any general laws and talk about it is irreducible, cannot we similarly so conceive of God's transcendent relation to the whole world in which he

[28] Loc. cit.

is immanent, in the sense that it expresses his intentions within a law-like physical network? God's transcendence would be of a higher order than that of any self over his body, since he transcends the whole world process. This could still be consistent with the world being the realm of law-like relations, which the sciences show it to be—as consistent, that is, as is the mental character of the experience of being a human agent with the implementation of that human agent's intentions within his law-obeying physical body. Language about the experience (or 'life') of God himself should then be irreducible and could not improperly be extrapolations of the mental language used for human persons.

The notion of God's relation to the world as at least analogous to the relation of the human mind to the human body (God : world :: mind : body), so that God is, as it were, the 'soul of the world', has a long history. But it was earlier always based on dualist assumptions about man, which we have found reason to reject, and on interventionist assumptions about God's action in the world, which is inconsistent and incoherent with what the sciences show about the way the world actually goes and with the way God actually seems to be creating new entities in the world. Our new awareness of the hierarchy of natural systems, the putative irreducibility of at least some higher level laws and concepts, and our new knowledge of the relation between consciousness and brain processes now alter entirely the context within which such a model is propounded.

It is worth examining further, for its strengths and weaknesses, this model or analogy of God as agent in relation to what goes on in the world, for even its inadequacies may be illuminating for refining the model and suggesting others. The use of models of God's relation to the world should need no special justification for the procedure parallels in many respects the use of models (conceptual, mathematical, and mechanical) as 'candidates for reality' in the natural sciences—though the hazards are more subtle and numerous in the case of theological models which frequently enter the scene trailing non-glorious and obscuring clouds from the past. In the case of the present question of the relation of God's action to the world, indeed the relation of God to the world, the pressures on earlier models arise from our understanding of the world as a nexus of law-like events and the recognition that God is not a physical agent, propelling the planets or inflicting disease primarily on the morally depraved. Such ideas have been almost completely, and rightly, eliminated from the modern mind by science. But when we say the world is a nexus of law-like events we must not forget the difference between the twentieth-century scientific outlook and that of previous centuries. Today nature is recognized, as we have seen, as being in dynamic process, evolving new forms and as a realm where strict causality has to be modified by statistical, stochastic, and quantum-theoretical considerations. It is a system of much more change and open potentiality than was envisaged in the heyday of Newtonian science and these features must never be too far from our minds when we refer to it as a 'lawlike nexus of physical events', or some similar shorthand, as we shall in what follows.

C. 'Meaning' within the physical nexus

The meaning of an action by a human agent is not to be found by scientific analysis of the physiological, chemical, and mechanical processes going on in the agent's body (when, for example, he raises his arm), but by discovering his reasons and intentions, that is, the mental events which preceded and accompanied the action in question. Briefly, the 'physical' features of an agent's action only have meaning in terms of the associated 'mental' events of which he can usually give an account. The meaning is expressed in terms of its own language (of reason, intention, etc.) even if the meaning has to be communicated through physical signs, on paper or as sound vibrations, or whatever. (The *meaning* of the message of a telegram is in a different realm of discourse from the description of the wires which transmitted the electrical impulses or the paper on which it is finally printed out). The model therefore suggests that if God is to be regarded as, in some sense, the agent of the law-like nexus of physical events then we should look for the meaning of those events in *his* reasons and intentions, i.e. his purposes. As J. J. Compton, who has supported this model, puts it:

We can distinguish the causal development of events from the meaning of those events viewed as God's action. Scientific analysis of physical nature and of human history has no more need of God as an explanatory factor than the physiologist needs my conscious intent to explain my bodily movements. Nor does God need to find a 'gap' in nature in order to act, any more than you or I need a similar interstice in our body chemistry.... What happens is that the evolution of things is *seen* or *read* in religious life ... as part of an action, as an expression of divine purpose, in addition to its being viewed as a naturalistic process.[29]

This amounts to an explication of God's relation to the world as its Creator—for the doctrine of creation asserts that all that is, the law-like nexus of events, has its activity, and so its existence as what it is, endowed upon it by a transcendent purpose and this is indeed one of the denotata of God the Creator. The affirmation of God as Creator is an answer to the question about the meaning of the nexus of physical events which constitute the world. Such an attribution of meaning is at least licensed by the attribution of meaning in mental terms to the physical action of human agents, even if it cannot prove its applicability. Thus, according to the model, all the law-like processes in the physical world (which includes human persons), in being what they are, are expressions of his creative purposes. He is in all that goes on and acts through nature and its processes—even if, as we shall have cause to discuss, his purposes are not always fully implemented in a world which has generated free human agents within itself.

Perhaps we can develop the model a little further. The fact that we cannot net in a law-like framework the 'divine mental' acts, God's intention and purposes, in relation to the law-like nexus of physical events should no more be cause for concern than the anomalous character of the mental events occurring in human agents (see Davidson[30]). But, as with all models attempting to explicate God's action in the world, we experience a certain unease about it which arises from the unknown nature of that which forms one component in our analogy, namely God himself. However difficult we find it to understand what the self-motivating agent *is* which is 'I', we do have direct experience of our own subjectivity. Not so with

[29] J. J. Compton, 'Science and God's Action in Nature', in *Earth Might be Fair*, ed. I. Barbour (Prentice-Hall, Englewood Cliffs, N.J., 1972), p. 39.
[30] Loc. cit.

other people, and *a fortiori* not so with God—at least in the context of this discussion. This difficulty is ineradicable in any discursive talk about God and is a limitation of our knowledge of God which we have to accept and is not peculiar to this particular model. What is peculiar is that this model pivots in its application on this very lacuna, the haziness we have already observed (p. 132) in all discourse, from whatever viewpoint including that of the indentitists, about the sense of self of a human agent and the transmission of that agency into a constellation of physical processes, in the brain-in-the-body (for no doubt the senses contribute to this awareness of self-identity). Puzzling though this is, affronting as it does our subjective sense that at times we appear to be free from bodily conditions, yet we know physiological events cannot but have (neuro-) physiological causes. Little though we can understand it, our sense of being a self and of being *self*-regulating must have a basis in the functional systems of our bodies for the control by the self to be bodily effective. So having to endure this puzzle, this lacuna, in describing our actions which we *do* know, we should not let it count against applying the model to God's actions.

IV. MODIFICATIONS OF THE MODEL OF GOD AS AGENT

However, there are other inadequacies in the model which are basically theological and will lead us into both modifying it and suggesting other complementary models—as, we earlier hinted, is likely to be the case with any useful theological model.

A. *Unconscious acts and conscious agents*

We note, firstly, that many individual events in our bodies, and many regular patterns of events, occur without any conscious control by the self—all the regular processes that maintain us alive—digestion, control of breathing, body temperature, balance, and many others, including all reflex actions (roughly, functions controlled by the central nervous system). Much of the nervous system, whose evolutionary history can be traced for it persists far down the evolutionary scale, is of this kind. It is only certain complex supervening spatial and temporal patterns of physical events in our bodies which are initiated by mental events we associate with *self*-consciousness and which we have used, so far, to constitute our model for God's actions in the world. This suggests that perhaps the model should recognize that there are such events of the body which are not, for most of the time, consciously controlled by self-conscious mental events. So the model might still then be applicable both to those patterns of events in the world initiated by the purposes of God and to those many other individual events and some regular patterns which cannot be regarded as initiated by a *specific* purpose of God—even though what they are and what regular patterns they adopt are what they are because God created them so. So God's purposes would then be expected to be read more explicitly in some events and processes than in others. Moreover, since human persons themselves are, at least partially, free agents in the world, we have to infer that God as Creator has chosen to fulfil his own purposes in the world by devolving freedom upon them and, in so doing, has rendered these divine purposes more opaque and less discernible in the sphere of human action.

B. *The God–world dualism*

The qualifiers of the model point to another of its inadequacies which is indeed true of any model for God's relation to the world based on natural situations we know. God is *ex hypothesi* unique in being the Creator of all that is; so that degree of differentiation of God from the world must be retained which guards this essential feature of any doctrine of creation, namely the dependence on God of the world process of physical events (some of which are identical with human mental events, on the functional view) and God's fundamental independence of, and therefore transcendence over, the world. In the past, this differentiation has often been so great and this essential dualism of God and the world was so sharply defined that it has become almost inconceivable how God could be related to the world and the absentee god of deism results—which readily becomes tantamount to practical atheism. The model we are discussing runs into the opposite danger of making God identical with the world if the model is taken from that interpretation of the relation between mental and physical events which postulates identity.[31] Even if some qualified form of the identity of mental events is adopted, as we have provisionally suggested, the model cannot be pressed that far. For however much we may regard God as immanent in and expressing himself as agent through the world process, he is, after all, beyond all such descriptions and experiencing of him, the perpetual Creator of that process, and never ceases to be such. The model of human action is a model for transcendence-in-immanence, but the transcendence of God with respect to his actions in the world is that of Creator, a transcendence that is immanent (as I suggested earlier, pp. 133, 134, on account of it being the whole world process over which God is transcendent) but of a higher order of transcendence than that of the human agent over his own actions. Perhaps one should say it is of a higher power (in the mathematical sense) of transcendence. There is therefore an ineradicable asymmetry in the God–world relation which resides in the distinction between the Creator and what he has created (creatures) whereas the only distinction (apart from subjective experience itself) between the mental and physical which some identitists can allow[32] is with respect to their predictability and obedience to ascertainable general laws (anomalous monism).

C.   Other models

(i) *Ways of God being God.* The model has been helpful in enabling us to conceive how there could be transcendence-in-immanence but we have seen that we have to reckon with an ineradicable transcendence of God as Creator, over and beyond his immanence. One way of developing the concept of God is then to say that in one aspect, or mode, of his being God is transcendent Creator but in another aspect he is transcendence-

---

[31] One is reminded of the two quantum-mechanical theories of the covalent bond in, say, the hydrogen molecule: one, the valence-bond theory, overestimates inter-electronic repulsion; the other, the molecular orbital theory, underestimates these repulsions. The situation arises because both are approximations employing too few parameters to deal with a complex multi-particle situation. Both accounts are 'improved' by modifications which introduce the parameters each most notably lack until, less elegant and simple though they then appear, the theories both correspond closer to the actual situation—and are remarkably successful at calculating *ab initio* the energy of the hydrogen molecule.

[32] Cf. Davidson, loc. cit.

in-immanence and in this mode he acts within the physical world, including human brains-in-bodies, and is Agent with respect to the whole physical causal nexus. If we say that this is 'all the time' (noting that time itself is a feature of the created order) true of God's being, then we here come very close to features of classical trinitarian doctrine—the mode of being of God as transcendent and as immanent, usually more personalized (though, of course, in a notoriously special sense of 'person' (or rather *persona*)) as God the Father and God the Holy Spirit.

(*ii*) *Process theology*. If we make a distinction between the relation to time of these two modes of being of God the Creator, we come close to the concept of process theologians of God as having two 'poles' or aspects: a primordial nature and a consequent nature (A. N. Whitehead); or God's abstract essence and God's concrete actuality (C. Hartshorne). The process theologians have taken more seriously than most others in the twentieth century the problem of God's action in a world in which all is describable in terms of law-like processes. I cannot now do justice to their thought, which I find the more rich and stimulating the more it can be divorced from its much too specific dependence on a metaphysic, that of A. N. Whitehead, which is no longer of currency even in an intellectual and philosophical climate deeply influenced by science. In process thought, God in his primordial nature (or abstract essence) is regarded as providing 'aims' for all actual occasions, the ideals which they are striving to become, and in this aspect God is the envisager and fund of universals—he is eternal, absolute, independent, unchangeable, and is properly described as Creative Love; in his consequent nature (concrete actuality) he is Responsive Love and is temporal, relative, dependent, and constantly changing in response to new unforeseen happenings. This contrast of the process theologians is a starker one than I think is conceptually necessary, and one which was avoided by the classical doctrines of 'coinherence' within the Trinity. For the distinction between the 'primordial' and 'consequent' pole of God is a much stronger one, namely the distinction between an abstraction from actuality and the actuality itself. Moreover in process theology God does not create occasions (or events) but each actual occasion is its own creator and God only influences them—there is no *creatio ex nihilo*; nor does God create the 'eternal objects' (approximately universals) which God is striving to bring into fulfilment in each occasion.[33] This certainly seems at variance with the notion of God as the Creator of actuality which most Christian thought, including these lectures, has been concerned to affirm.

These brief remarks do scant justice to the stimulating ideas of process theology, but indicate some of my grounds of discomfort with it—though it must be reckoned as the most systematic attempt to date to understand God's action in the world in relation to the scientific picture of that world.

(*iii*) *Spatial model* (*pan-en-theism*). In order to bring together the conception of creative transcendence and transcendence-in-immanence, one could perhaps resort to spatial metaphors, referring to the 'space' of different kinds of distinction, as in a Venn diagram. Because there is no part of the world where God is not active and present in the events and processes themselves (he is immanent in it), and because God's being is more than, and other than, the world (he transcends it), we could say that the world is 'in' God: there is nothing in the world not in God, a view often called 'pan*en*theism'. Process theologians include this idea in their schema, for example: 'For the panentheist everything which is not itself divine is yet believed to be "in" God, in the sense that he is regarded as the circumambient reality operative in and through, while also more than, all that is not himself; or conversely, all which is not God has its existence within his operation and nature.'[34]

Pan*en*theism must be distinguished from pantheism which identifies the entirety of God's being with the world. We say God is 'greater' and 'larger' than the world and it is hard to avoid spatial metaphors when we wish to stress that God's being is not entirely encompassed by his immanence in, his relation to, the world—and so is not accessible to us, without revelation.

(*iv*) *A biological model*. The spatial metaphor can be

---

[33] Cobb, op. cit., pp. 205 ff. See also *Process Theology* by J. B. Cobb and D. R. Griffin (Christian Journals Ltd., Belfast, 1976).

[34] N. Pittenger, *Process thought and Christian Faith* (Nisbet. London, 1968), p. 40.

developed into what I think is a more fruitful biological model based on human pro-creation (*mot juste*, as we shall see!). The concept of God as Creator has, in the past, been too much dominated by a stress on the externality of God's creative acts—he is regarded as creating something external to himself, just as the male fertilizes the womb from outside. But mammalian females, at least, create within themselves and the growing embryo resides within the female body and this is a proper corrective to the masculine picture—it is an analogy of God creating the world within herself, we would have to say. This is yet another of the prices we pay, in the West at least, for having in the past been more ready to attribute to God the active, powerful, external adjectives popularly associated with masculinity rather than the more passive, responsive, internal adjectives popularly associated with femininity. God creates a world that is, in principle and in origin, other than him/herself but creates it, the world, within him/herself.

Although this seems, at first sight, to be alien to the obvious emphasis of the biblical tradition on the male aspects of Yahweh, the god of the people of Israel, yet there do exist 'enough indications that ancient Israel and Judah have worshipped motherly aspects of their God', according to P. A. H. de Boer and, he continues: 'The Gospels bear witness to the continuity of this form of ancient piety, "O Jerusalem, Jerusalem, killing the prophets and stoning who are sent to you: How often would I have gathered your children together as a hen gathers her brood under her wings, and you would not (Matt. 23 v. 37, cf. Luke 13 v. 34)"'[35] Furthermore, and more relevantly to our present point, he brings forward reasons for interpreting the 'us' in Genesis 1:26, 'And God said, let us make man in our image, after our likeness ... (R.V.)', as referring to God as joint sovereign, a God-and-Goddess, reigning in a court and he renders this verse as 'We shall make people in the form of *our* image, looking like *us*':[36]

All these reasons point at a God and a Goddess as subject of 'We shall make people'. God, pictured as a king with a court, making heaven

[35] P. A. H. de Boer, *Fatherhood and Motherhood in Israelite and Judean Piety* (F. J. Brill, Leiden, 1974), p. 37.
[36] de Boer, op. cit., p. 46.

and earth through creative royal strength, makes man. The ancient believer recognised man's fertility and power as a gift of his God who 'himself' [our inverted commas] is male and female. Only if man is conscious of holiness in his being man and woman he might be able to understand that a conception of God: Father and Mother, guarantee of life and existence, is no blasphemy but expression of true faith.[37]

In his translation, Genesis 1: 26 and 27 read thus (omitting, for brevity, the phrases describing man's rule over creation): 'And God said: We shall make people in the form of our image, looking like us ... Then God fashioned man. In the shape of his image, in the shape of a divine image, he fashioned him. Male and female he fashioned them.'[38] He concludes, on a more personal note:

Praying to God, 'Our Father who art in heaven' and forgetting the Mother of all living, is inadequate. Praying to 'Our Mother who art in earth' and forgetting the fatherly authority, is likewise inadequate. Due to what became visible of divine Fatherhood and Motherhood in ancient Israelite and Judean piety we ought, I think, to pray to God's totality, respectfully desiring to belong to his family. The most adequate prayer will be a silent prayer for *when we are silent we are one, when we speak we are two.*[39]

In the Wisdom literature, the wisdom of God is personified as a woman who is God's creative agent and companion in creation[40]—a personification of a divine attribute but spoken of as having a separate existence. There is a genetic link between this concept and that of the creative Word of God[41] which reappears in the prologue to St. John's Gospel and later becomes subsumed into the second 'persona' (another feminine noun) of the Trinity. So there is reason to believe that, in proposing this bi-sexual model for God's action in the world, in order to satisfy our preoccupation with God's immanence, we may be being less out of line with the human sense of the divine, as expressed in many cultures, including the Judeo-Christian, than our local Protestant culture would incline us to

[37] de Boer, op. cit., pp. 46–7.
[38] de Boer, op. cit., p. 50.
[39] de Boer, op. cit., p. 53 (de Boer's italics).
[40] e.g. Proverbs 8, Wisdom 9.
[41] Wisdom 9: 1.

think.[42] But perhaps enough has been said to facilitate serious consideration of this particular model.

V. CONCLUSION: A CREATOR WHO COMMUNICATES MEANING

Even with these powerful models of God's action in the world—whether of God as agent, of the world being in God, of the masculine and feminine aspects of procreation—I find myself still left with a sense of unease about some vital feature which is missing. We have been using the model of human agency, of the self, the 'I' whose intentions are implemented in and through the physical body, in order to take serious account of our scientific understanding of the unity of the world as a hierarchy of complex systems of physical units. We have recognized the lacuna that comes in our talk of the sense of selfhood which our brains-in-our-bodies possess. What I have omitted so far is, as developmental psychology and studies on the use of language make abundantly clear, that the sense of self, of being a person, arises only in so far as we interact and communicate with *other* persons. Our selfhood seems only to be able to be constituted if we are in personal contact with the others—and this is a deep-seated need throughout our lives. Thus any model or analogy between ourselves as the agents of our bodies to God as the agent of the world suggests that the selfhood of God must be a *communicating* selfhood. Now we express our actions through our bodies, which include our brains and speech organs, and many other modes of communication. We have said that this model also suggests that God's purposes provide the meaning of the world process. *Our* meanings are discerned, if we are fortunate (and we mostly are) by other personal agents, but who discerns God's meanings and how are they discerned? It seems that man is, above all, the one created being who seeks to discern, even to create, meaning in the structures of his existence—natural, personal, and social. We have found ourselves having to stress that God's meanings are to be found within the very texture of the net-

---

[42] For a short account of this and of the feminine aspects of God in other religious situations, see J. E. Bruns, *God as Woman, Woman as God* (Paulist Press, New York, 1973), where references to the literature are given.

work of causal physical processes which constitute the world. But within that network, there has emerged those intricately ramified and interlaced structures we call human brains, the very processes of which so operate that they can discern meanings in the physical world process and in their own processes. It is as if the Creator has endowed matter–space–time–energy, the stuff of existence, with a propensity, now actualized in man, of tuning in, as it were, to discern that meaning in the cosmic process which its Creator has written into it. In man, the stuff of the world has become persons, who are aware of their selfhood and whose intentions and reasons, those of their physical processes which are also mental, become causes in their bodies and in the societies they form. They are self-conscious free agents, that have been generated by natural processes within the natural order, immanent in which is the transcendent Creator. No wonder the ancient writer said that 'God created man in his own image, in the image of God created he him: male and female created he them.'[43] For, in man, physicality has become capable of reading those meanings in existence which are the immanence of the transcendent God in the whole cosmic process. The way in which God has made himself heard and understood is by endowing the stuff of the world with the ability to acquire discernment of his meanings and to listen to his word in creation. The psalmist truly said that 'By the *word* of God were the heavens made.'[44] Creation is an expression of the purpose and intention of God and these purposes have expressed themselves in and through a cosmic evolutionary process which has generated within the physical fabric of the cosmos, beings (ourselves) who can *listen* and *discern*. The stuff of the world in becoming self-reflective in ourselves has found it can hear the word conveying God's purposes through our very neurophysiological brain processes themselves. We have almost reached the paradox[45] that the only theology is *natural* theology! If God is indeed the communicating active agent expressing his purposes in the cosmos, it seems not at all impossible, indeed it would be consistent with our understanding of him that we have developed, that

[43] Genesis 1: 27.
[44] Psalm 33: 6.
[45] But see pp. 357, 358.

he should be deliberately communicating his meaning through his world to those who can listen to and discern it—those who have the apparatus to tune in, to use the terminology of what are significantly called the media. Then we should not be surprised, indeed we should expect, that such a transcendent Creator, immanent in the physical nexus which is his self-expression, should make his meanings known to those forms of existence which, in time, emerge with the capacity to discern them. These meanings, these communications he addresses to the man who emerges with this capacity, cannot but be patterns of meaning within the world of nature and within that part of nature, man, in which transcendence is manifest in immanence. God's meaning is, then, to be sought where we are in this world, and what he communicates is Himself.

When all things began, the Word already was. The Word dwelt with God, and what God was, the Word was ... through him all things came to be. All that came to be was alive with his life, and that life was the light of man.[46]

[46] From John 1: 1, 2, 3 (NEB).

V

The 'Selfish Gene' and 'What Men Live By'

I. INTRODUCTION

IN the previous lectures, after an examination of the historical relation of science and theology, as represented in the metaphor of the 'Two Books', I have given reasons for thinking that we might be entering into a more fruitful phase of this relation, in which the results and methods of the two enterprises might be regarded as complementary in that quest for intelligibility and personal meaning in which we are all engaged—even now, perhaps especially now, in this age of burgeoning technology and uniquely energetic and fecund science. At any rate, after a brief account (Lecture I) of the Judeo-Christian models of God as Creator, we have been exploring various aspects of the scientific perspective of the world and how these, in inevitably shaping the context with reference to which men ask their questions about intelligibility and meaning, affect the plausibility and character of models of creation, of God's relation to the world. We found (Lecture II) that there was, in fact, such a close connection between the fundamental parameters of the physical universe and the emergence of life (and so of man) that we had to recognize that the potentiality of life (and so of man) was inherent in it from the beginning—and that therefore the emergence of self-conscious man, with his unique existence as a 'person', out of insentient matter sharpened the questions of intelligibility and of personal meaning. These questions, I suggested, could be reasonably and coherently answered in terms of a doctrine of creation, that is by the affirmation that the world had its being and is derived from and dependent upon One who transcends matter, energy, space, and time and is more-than-personal, who calls into being a cosmos, a purposively ordered existence. *Ex hypothesi,* the nature of this Creator 'God' could not be expressed in terms derived from language developed to describe what is other than that Creator, but nevertheless models of the Creator's relation to the world could be usefully developed and modified in the light of new scientific knowledge of the world which shows it to be a system more open for both constructive and destructive potentialities than previously envisaged. Thus, the creative interplay of random chance events embedded in contexts which were under the constraints of law-like necessities encouraged us to develop (Lecture III) the metaphor of God's joy and gratuitousness in creation, and of the dance of creation—in which chance rings the changes on law, in which the Creator God unfolds the fugue and variations which he draws out of his own chosen notes. In the last lecture (IV), we noted that the natural world displays a hierarchical structure of interlocking systems, with new properties and behaviour emerging at each level, and that the theories and concepts applicable to any particular level were frequently not reducible to those pertinent to lower levels in these hierarchies. In particular, the autonomy of language about human self-consciousness and personal agency coupled with the recognition that the constituent units of a human being are as atomic and molecular as those of other structures in the world, enabled us both to stress the need for the use of mental and personal terms with respect to man and to reject various kinds of dualism and panpsychism. We were then free to use man's personal agency in the action of the physico-chemical causal nexus of his body as a model for God's action in the world, for his immanence in its continuously creative processes. Furthermore, we found cause to prefer speaking of the world and its processes as being 'in God' (pan-en-theism) and this led us to reflect on the excessively male character of most traditional imagery of God and to stress the appropriateness of the female, with its implications of 'creation within'. We concluded the last lecture (IV) by noting that if God can be appropriately regarded as an agent expressing meaning in the natural, created and creative world, then he (we could not avoid using one of the personal pronouns) must also be regarded as a communicating selfhood. 'God's meaning', I said, 'is to be sought where we are in this world and what he communicates is himself.'

But to whom does he communicate? We noted that man who has evolved within the created order, through its natural processes, seems to be uniquely capable of reading God's meanings and of listening to his 'word' in creation, even as we recognized, with the Book of Job, that God has purposes with other creatures which will always be opaque to us.

In this lecture we focus more sharply on that particular product of the cosmic development of most interest to us, namely man, whom we have already seen reason for regarding as a psychosomatic unity, a person whose brain-in-his-body displays mental activity and in whom certain tendencies in evolution reach a pre-eminently high level.[1] We shall first take a closer look at man from a static viewpoint, in terms of the different levels of description afforded by the various sciences. Then we shall look more closely both at the character of the processes through which life has evolved and at particular features of the emergence of man as a social being into history and culture. For if God is creating all the time through the processes we shall outline and these have in any sense culminated in man, then this must be an important clue to us for modelling God's relation to the world as Creator.

II. WHAT IS MAN IN THE LIGHT OF THE SCIENCES?

What, then, is man? In the light of the sciences, is he 'nothing but' a bipedal terrestrial mammal, a featherless biped, a tool-making naked ape, an aggressive carnivore, a gene machine programmed to ensure the preservation of its selfish genes, a homeostatic mechanism equipped with a language-programmed computer, or a self-programmed centre of conscious activity? Clearly, these epigrams represent only an absurdly small proportion of the accounts of man which science now provides and which are admirably described in a work as comprehensive as that of J. Z. Young[2] which, I note, he nevertheless called an 'Introduction' to the study of man. Its 700 or so pages contain many expressions of caution and humility—and indeed judicious agnosticism—about the limitations of the scientific understanding of man, while properly urging the

[1] See Lecture II for an earlier brief reference to this.
[2] J. Z. Young, *An Introduction to the Study of Man* (Clarendon Press, Oxford, 1971).

contributions that science can make, e.g. in brain research, to our understanding of our consciousness as persons. I cannot hope, within the straitjacket of these lectures, to emulate Professor Young's achievement, but one can obtain some perception of the complexion of these studies by looking at man through, as it were, the spectacles of various kinds of scientist.

The *cosmologist and astrophysicist* see man as a particular configuration of atoms, and so of more fundamental particles, existing on a planet circulating a star, the Sun, which is only one of 10^{11} such in our galaxy, which itself is one in 10^9 such galaxies. They see our Sun is about half way through its life of energy emission—so that the Earth and the material configuration we call man have a *terminus ad quem* as structures.[3] They note that, as we mentioned earlier, the molecular organization of man depends on the presence of certain heavier atoms than hydrogen, which is the 'basic material out of which the Universe is built'[4] and that these heavier atoms are present on the Earth as a result of high-temperature nuclear reactions and super-novae explosions occurring millions of years before the Earth and Sun condensed into the revolving solar system of the last *c.* 5,000 million years.

The *physicist and physical chemist* can give an account of the structure of the atoms comprising a man and can quantify the extent and rates of many of the exchanges of energy (mechanical, chemical, electromagnetic, electrochemical) and interchange of atoms in chemical reactions that go on within him. As Sir Cyril Hinshelwood once put it, a physical chemist 'might in very general terms regard a mass of living matter as a macromolecular, polyfunctional free radical system, of low entropy in virtue of its order, with low activation energy for various reactions in virtue of its centres, and possessing a high degree of permanence in virtue of a relatively rigid structure.'[5]

The *chemist* analyses a human being as containing, out of the 100 or so kinds of atoms there are, those of the sixteen elements (O, C, H, N, Ca, P, K, S, Cl, Na, Mg, Fe, Cu, Mn, Zn, I,

---

[3] See Lecture VIII.
[4] F. Hoyle, *The Nature of the Universe* (Blackwell, Oxford, 1960), p. 42.
[5] C. N. Hinshelwood, *The Structure of Physical Chemistry* (Clarendon Press, Oxford, 1951), p. 449.

in decreasing order of relative quantity) found in all living organisms, and in proportions differing markedly from those in the atmosphere or lithosphere. This common composition of all human beings would bring to one level all sorts and condition of men and women—Mother Teresa, Richard Nixon, and the Archbishop of Canterbury!

The *biochemist* sees in man a collection of smaller organic molecules common to all living organisms (according to G. Wald[6] and H. J. Morowitz:[7] 18 vitamins, co-enzymes and pre-cursors, 21 amino-acids, 16 sugars and derivatives, 4 lipids and pre-cursors, 5 purines and pyrimidines and derivatives, and 9 other molecules) and also the common interlocking cycles of chemical reactions (the glycolytic pathway, the citric acid cycle, membrane mechanisms, etc.) on which the maintenance and reproduction of all living organisms depend.

The *molecular biologist* sees that the genetic material, DNA, which carries the genetic information from human parents to their children, has the same structure and operates with the same genetic code, for translating its stored information into other (protein) structures and their consequent activities, as all other living organisms from bacteria to whales. Indeed, the biochemist is aware of a sense in which all human beings are at the earliest stage of their growth 'nothing but' DNA molecules derived from their parents.

The *cell biologist* sees how, given this common basis of transmission of genetic information in DNA, nevertheless each human being (apart from the case of identical twins) has a unique genetic constitution through the mechanisms of mitosis and meiosis which reassort the parental genes. Each individual human being has a unique, unrepeatable contingent inherited endowment.

The *anatomist* sees the similarities of *homo sapiens* to other primates but notes important differences on account of man's upright stance and (two to three times) relatively heavier brain—more forward and far greater sweep of vision, hands freed for use of tools, more difficult childbirth, etc. But the anatomist cannot discriminate more finely between the intrinsic structure of the brain of a genius and that of the average

---

[6] G. Wald, *Proc. Nat. Acad. Sci., USA* 52 (1964), 596–611.
[7] H. J. Morowitz, *Energy Flow in Biology* (Academic Press, New York, 1968).

man, and he is aware that the human brain has not changed in size or structure for the last 200,000 years.

The *physiologist* sees the interrelationships between the biochemical processes of different organs and focuses *inter alia* on the role of chemical messengers ('hormones') between them. He is aware of the complex effects of the balance of these hormones on human personality, with respect to initiative, aggressiveness, mental retardation, sexual behaviour, and much else, even including moral turpitude.

The *neurophysiologist* sees especially the extraordinary complexity of the human brain with its *c.* 10^{10} long nerve cells each of which on the average makes contact with 10,000 other such cells through special interfaces under the control of chemical messengers. Even the brain of a rat or an octopus far exceeds in complexity any human artefact, and the human brain seems to be one of the most complex pieces of matter in the universe—a complexity never better described than in Sir Charles Sherrington's famous description of the waking brain as an 'enchanted loom where millions of flashing shuttles weave a dissolving pattern, always a meaningful pattern though never an abiding one; a shifting harmony of sub-patterns'.[8] The role of the frontal and temporal lobes, elucidated by studying the effects of their isolation, excision, or degeneration on behaviour and personality, the interplay of the two hemispheres and the areas involved in speech control have been and still are the subject of intensive research which is already illuminating our understanding of consciousness.[9] A close intimacy between brain event, amenable to neurophysiological description, and the content of conscious life is increasingly substantiated, for example by work on split brains and on the effect of drugs on mental states, and by other studies on the genetic bases of human personality and mental attributes.[10] In spite of the different levels of description of the individual as seen through the spectacles of different kinds of scientist, man is a unity of

[8] Charles Sherrington, *Man on his Nature*, 1937–8 Gifford Lectures (Pelican Books, 1955), p. 187—the whole passage beginning on p. 185 is a masterpiece of imaginative scientific prose.

[9] For a recent excellent exposition for the layman, see Colin Blakemore's Reith Lectures, *Mechanics of the Mind* (Cambridge University Press, Cambridge, 1977).

[10] Ibid.

these various levels, including the last-mentioned, brain and mental event. He is a psychosomatic unity, but this does not mean that psychology is necessarily to be reduced to neurophysiology, for the reasons we have already given.[11]

Up to this point, we have been speaking of scientific knowledge relevant to the individual human being. But the *biologist*, and in particular those who study animal behaviour, the *ethologists*, are concerned with the development and behaviour of populations and groups of living organisms in their habitats. Some of the established, and some of the controversial, features of these sciences will concern us in a moment but it is worth emphasizing at this point how much of what has hitherto been regarded as features of human consciousness alone now appear to have their correlate, even if in a weaker and more rudimentary form, in animals earlier in the evolutionary tree than ourselves—I refer, *inter alia*, to the evidence in such animals of emotional (affective) and of learned behaviour, of 'insight-learning', of 'proto-aesthetic' impulses, of arithmetical sense, of perception and of communicating language systems.[12]

There clearly is continuity between man and the rest of the living world, especially the higher primates, the social insects, and (it seems increasingly) the dolphins. The studies of man in his societies and of the history of his culture, such as social psychology, social anthropology, sociology, economics, and history itself, have developed separately from that of biology and ethology. In such studies we leave the areas of human inquiry (the 'natural sciences') which can plausibly claim to make value-free judgements—even if this plausibility has less warrant than at first might appear. With the studies of society, culture, and history we are well into the sphere of the human and it is there that discontinuities between man and the animal world have to be recognized, and often the discontinuities are differences of degree so marked that they emerge as differences in kind. Of the making of lists of distinctively human attributes there seems to be no end, but, at least, there is now a wide recognition amongst scientists of both the continuities *and* the discontinuities between man and the rest of the animal world.

[11] Lecture IV.

[12] Surveyed by W. H. Thorpe, 1969–71 Gifford Lectures, *Animal Nature and Human Nature* (Methuen, London, 1974).

Any such list[13] would include the following, and no doubt more besides: the exceptional level of man's intelligence, which is manifested in his capacity for abstract thought—itself related to an exceptional ability to use both verbal and visual symbols for communication,[14] to his exceptionally avid curiosity in the exploration of his environment, to his unusual flexibility and adaptability, and to his capacity for handling and storing wide ranges of information; man's self-consciousness, which includes the ability to transcend the environment in thought and to survey it as subject; the use of 'I' which seems thereby to constitute a new kind of entity, a 'person', which makes each one a bearer of rights and unique, so that we can imagine ourselves changing places; the ability to act rationally, to make moral choices and set long-term ends; man's aesthetic sense and creativity in the arts, literature, science, and in play; the ability to worship and pray, that is, man's openness to God (what has traditionally been called his 'spirit')—and so each of us could go on with his own personal list. What is clear is that, even though the various distinctive components that constitute the human often have some correlate in other biological life, they are intensified and enhanced, often to the point of qualitative difference, and combined in a distinctive and unique unity.

III. THE PROCESSES OF EVOLUTION

The broad features of the processes of cosmic and biological

---

[13] Some *distinctive* attributes of man are mentioned, but this by no means exhausts his *essential* attributes, those which might be regarded as innate. G. E. Pugh (in *The Biological Origin of Human Values*, Basic Books Inc., New York, 1977) has provisionally identified the following 'values' (i.e. aims which the human decision system seeks to fulfil) as built in by evolution and so as innate, or primary (i.e. fundamental and unalterable by human beings themselves):

A. Selfish 'values'. Hunger, thirst, fear, rocking urge, sucking urge, anger, itch, excretion urge. *B. Social 'values'.* Desire for dominance (rivalry), for approval, for social acceptance, gregariousness, enjoyment of conversation (both talking and listening), desire for bodily exercise and exploitation of one's physical skills, enjoyment of humour, social preferences, desire to work with others, desire to make or build, desire to contribute or do something meaningful for society. *C. Intellectual 'values'.* Curiosity, humour, truth, simplicity, comprehensiveness, elegance, aesthetic values.

A are entirely shared with the higher primates, *B* only partly so, and *C* almost (but not entirely, e.g. curiosity) are distinctively human.

[14] See W. H. Thorpe, *Biology and the Nature of Man* (Oxford University Press, London, 1962), pp. 42–3.

evolution, as described by the sciences, have been partly out-lined in earlier lectures. Three features were then pointed out.

(*i*) The *continuity* of these processes—that, although many questions still remain (in particular concerning the origin of life), the present gamut of the natural sciences can make reason-able postulates, and sometimes well-substantiated inferences, about the temporal sequence of natural events which range from the initial moments of the 'hot big bang' to the arrival of man on the Earth.

(*ii*) The *interplay of chance and law*, of time-dependent random (stochastic) occurrences operating within a framework of 'natural laws' and of given physical parameters.

(*iii*) The *emergence* in time within these natural processes, through this interplay, of new forms of the organization of matter with properties and behaviour that are often only capable of elucidation by concepts that are not reducible to those applicable to less organized, and frequently earlier, struc-tures (i.e. the world process is 'inventive'[15] and 'innova-tive'[16]).

When we consider man as a relatively recent product of this process, further questions arise and some other features become relevant to our putative understanding of God's relation to the world and these must now be elaborated.

(*iv*) We are bound to ask if there are any *trends* discernible in the processes of the cosmic development and, in particular, of biological evolution. This is, of course, a notoriously loaded question which men (cf. the Book of Job) are only too ready to answer on the basis of their own significance in the universe grounded on their own importance to themselves! Yet enough has been said to establish the distinctiveness of man—and his uniqueness in being alone, of all living creatures, capable of distancing himself from himself and asking questions of the kind to which we are here addressing ourselves.[17]

But, setting aside this unique feature of man, which is tanta-mount to not reflecting on our current process of reflection,

[15] K. Denbigh, *An Inventive Universe* (Methuen, London, 1975).
[16] H. K. Schilling, *The New Consciousness in Science and Religion* (SCM Press, London, 1973), p. 126.
[17] Cf. Pascal, cit. above, p. 51.

is there any objective, non-anthropocentrically biased, evidence for directions or, at least, trends in evolution? Biologists have frequently asked themselves this question. They are, of course, only too well aware of the complexity of the interlocking lines of development of the myriads of species both living and extinct and of the staggering variety, and 'ingenuity', if one may dare call it that, of the ways in which organisms manage to live in their particular biological niches. They are cautious, therefore, about postulating 'progress' in evolution, for the criteria of progress are often already chosen with man's special exemplification of them in mind, deliberately or otherwise (cf. Julian Huxley's definition of progress as involving increased complexity, control over the environment, independence from the environment, individualization, capacity for acquiring and organizing knowledge, for experiencing emotion, for exerting purpose, and for appreciating values[18]). As G. G. Simpson says,

Within the framework of the evolutionary history of life there have been not one but many different sorts of progress. Each sort appears not with one single line or even with one central but branching line throughout the course of evolution, but separately in many different lines. These phenomena seem fully consistent with, and indeed readily explained by, the naturalistic theory of evolution....[19]

It is therefore more rewarding to discern any trends in evolution which reach their maximum expression in man. Because he is innocent of any desire to support any Christian view it is worth quoting in full Simpson's judgement on man's place in nature.

Man has certain basic diagnostic features which set him off most sharply from any other animal and which have involved other developments not only increasing this sharp distinction but also making it an absolute difference in kind and not only a relative difference of degree. In the basic diagnosis of *Homo sapiens* the most important features are probably interrelated factors of intelligence, flexibility, individualization, and socialization. All four of these are features that occur rather widely in the animal kingdom as progressive developments, and all define different, but related, sorts of

---

[18] J. Huxley, *New Bottles for New Wine* (Harper Bros., New York, 1957).
[19] G. G. Simpson, *The Meaning of Evolution* (Bantam Books, Yale University Press, New Haven, 1971 edn.), p. 236.

evolutionary progress. In man all four are carried to a degree incomparably greater than in any other sort of animal. All have as their requisite and basis the still more fundamental evolutionary progress 'in the direction of increase in the range and variety of adjustments of the organism to its environment' [C. J. Herrick, 'Progressive Evolution', *Science*, 104 (1946), 469], which involves increased and improved means of perception of the environment and, particularly, of integrating, coordinating, and reacting flexibly to these perceptions.

In other respects, too, man represents an unusual or unique degree and direction of progress in evolution ... He embodies an unusually large bulk of life substance and carries on a large share of the earth's vital metabolism. He is one of the dominant current forms of life, the latest to arise and now the only one within the particular dominance sequence to which he belongs. He has successfully replaced any competing type and has occupied a sphere of life or great adaptive zone which was, historically, the most recent to be entered by animals. His particular sort of progress has not, to this point, been self-limiting and leads to no obvious future blind end. He is, on the whole, the most adaptable of animals. He is about as independent of environment as any animal, or, as it may more accurately be put, is able to get along in about as wide an environmental range as any. He is almost the only animal that really exerts any significant degree of control over the environment. His reproductive efficiency is the highest in the animal kingdom, with prenatal protection at least as high as in any other animal and post-natal care decidedly higher.

Even when viewed within the framework of the animal kingdom and judged by criteria of progress applicable to that kingdom as a whole and not peculiar to man, man is thus the highest animal.[20]

Man is, then, the 'highest animal' from a purely biological viewpoint but he also possesses those unique differentia of which I gave my personal list earlier.[21] One can see a trend if one follows the branching lines that terminate in man—it is a distinctive line characterized by the features mentioned in the above quotation from Simpson and which culminates in man who exemplifies these characteristics to the extent of starting an entirely new phase in cosmic development—human culture and its history, as we shall shortly see. But this is only one, no doubt golden, thread to be drawn out of the tangled skein

[20] Simpson, op. cit., pp. 258-9.
[21] p. 154.

of evolutionary history. Again we recall those Israelite writings which responded to the rich fecundity, variety, and non-anthropocentric autonomous value to God of the world and all life apart from man, and we recognize again that God's creativity within the world has objects and foci of joy other than man. This is not to demote man but to value the world and frees us to face, without any taint of anthropocentrism, the questions raised by the presence of man in the world and the questions he himself raises about the world.

(v) *Complexity*.   There is one broad feature which seems to be common to both the cosmic and biological development and, indeed, to human social and cultural history. It is the tendency for more and more complex structures to emerge in the world. Attempts to find a suitable measure of the complexity of structures, inorganic and biological, by means of information theory, have not been as fruitful as was earlier hoped in spite of its apparently obvious pertinence to the genetic function of DNA in transmitting 'information' from one generation to another of a living organism.[22] More fruitful may be a sugges-tion of K. Denbigh[23] who has pointed out that, although we have concepts of orderliness, or order, and of disorder (related to thermodynamic entropy by the Boltzmann relation), we do not have any satisfactory measure of *organization*. He has there-for proposed as a measure of complexity, a quantity he calls integrality (ϕ), which he defines, for any given structure, as proportional to the product of the number (c) of connections which facilitate the functions of the whole and the number (n) of different *kinds* of parts. $\phi = f(x)cn$, where $f(x)$ represents other variables. Integrality, so defined, is applicable to structures and is clearly related to our intuitive sense of complexity. It is not identical with 'information', nor with entropy, and it can increase in a closed system (e.g. when an egg develops into (say) a chick). Moreover, the total value of integrality over the earth's ecosystem has increased since life began. This affords only a start to finding a measure of complexity, but it is worth

[22] See *Symposium on Information Theory in Biology*, ed. H. P. Yockey, R. L. Platzman, and H. Quastler (Pergamon, London, 1958), and the earlier *Information Theory in Biology*, ed. H. Quastler (University of Illinois Press, Urbana, 1953).
[23] Denbigh, op. cit., pp. 98 ff.

mentioning to show that the task is not necessarily insuperable.[24]

Thus, one day, it may be possible to give sharper content to the impression that in evolution there has been an increase in 'complexity' as one goes out along the branches of at least some of the evolutionary trees. I surmise that, eventually, not only static structure, but also the function and behaviour of living organisms, will have to enter any satisfactory definition of any measure of 'complexity', in which case the branches leading to man would evidence very markedly an increase in such an all-inclusive quantity. The need for clarity here is provoked especially by the proposal that there is a connection between 'complexity' and consciousness. This has been strongly urged and gained wide currency through the writings of Teilhard de Chardin, who calls this his 'law of complexity-consciousness'.[25] This 'law' has been summarized by B. Towers[26] as: (1) Throughout time there has been a tendency in evolution for matter to become increasingly complex in its organization, and (2) with increase in material complexity there is a corresponding rise in the consciousness of the matter (or organism as it eventually becomes). The first part of this 'law' is certainly an impression, though an imprecise one (what *kind* of complexity is to be correlated with consciousness?), that is given by the broad sweep of evolution; but the unwarranted panpsychic assumptions of its second part (actually quite explicit in Teilhard's writings—as we noted in Lecture IV when we gave reasons for rejecting such a view) give cause for doubting such a generalization. Certainly the human brain is one of the most, perhaps *the* most, complex structure we know in the world, certainly more complex (as well as larger) than that of other primates and animals and there is no doubt that human consciousness exceeds in intensity that of other animals. But until more is known about *their* consciousness and until we can quantify 'complexity' better it is unwise to promote this

[24] For further discussion, see A. R. Peacocke, 'The Nature and Evolution of Biological Hierarchies', in *New Approaches to Genetics*, ed. P. W. Kent (Oriel Press (Routledge & Kegan Paul), Stocksfield, England, 1978), pp. 245–304.

[25] Teilhard de Chardin, *The Phenomenon of Man* (Collins, London, 1959), pp. 300–2, discussed further in the present author's *Science and the Christian Experiment* (Oxford University Press, London, 1971), pp. 95–7.

[26] B. Towers, *Teilhard de Chardin* (Carey Kingsgate Press, London, 1966), p. 32.

intuition into a 'law' that can tempt one to apply it to the complexity of intra- and inter-communicating human societies. Undoubtedly a system of consciousnesses functions differently from a single consciousness and, because of *its* kind of complexity, will display new emergent features, often loosely and collectively denoted as 'corporate consciousness', though it is a moot point whether the word 'consciousness' is appropriate here. Teilhard de Chardin invents the neologism 'noosphere' for this new emergent, but I suspect he regards this as a universalization and socialization of the panpsychic component that he attributes to all the stuff of the world.

(*vi*) The *mechanism of biological evolution* has been outlined earlier[27] when, in discussing Monod's views, a brief account was given of the 'synthetic theory' of evolution, of 'neo-Darwinism'—the combination of genetics with Darwin's mechanism of 'natural' selection through the impact of the environment. This synthesis was given greater rigour and cutting edge in the subsequent development of mathematical population genetics and, in recent decades, it has been underpinned by the knowledge of the structure of and processes involving DNA, the information carrier at the molecular level. This 'modern synthesis' commands almost total support from biologists, though the subtleties of the interactions between the environment and the individual, whether or not a carrier of genetic mutants in its DNA, have become increasingly appreciated. For 'natural selection' comprises a variety of modes of interaction between individuals, sub-groups within populations, the total population and the environment (which includes other living organisms as well as the physical world)—there even seem to be genes which *dispose* an organism to become modified in response to a particular environmental change (C. H. Waddington's 'genetic assimilation'; see his very readable *The Nature of Life*.)[28]

In the last few years, this area of biology has witnessed sharp controversy which has emanated from the confrontation of the theory, until then widely accepted by biologists, of 'group selection' by the theory of 'individual, or gene, selection'. The

[27] Lecture II.
[28] C. H. Waddington, *The Nature of Life* (Unwin Books, London, 1963), pp. 88 ff.

controversy was associated with different interpretations of altruistic behaviour which, for these purposes, may be defined as behaviour by an individual organism of a kind that increases the chances of survival of another like individual, with increased risk to its own survival. 'Survival' is taken here in its Darwinian sense, namely, 'survival in order to reproduce' and it is now well established that quite small increments in the chance of survival, in this sense, lead surprisingly rapidly to the dominance in biological populations of individuals possessing the genetic factors responsible for this increment. On the 'group selection' theory, altruism was explained on the supposition that a group (e.g. a species, or a population within a species) whose individual members were altruistic was less likely to become extinct than one whose members were non-altruistic, i.e. selfish.[29]

But there was a paradox here—for altruistic behaviour reduces the chance of an organism surviving (to reproduce) and so, eventually, organisms which behave thus should disappear from the group, or species. In recent years, a very active group of biologists have resuscitated Darwin's own emphasis on 'individual selection' and now represent altruistic behaviour as *genetic* selfishness. On this theory, what we call altruistic behaviour on the part of an individual, apparently on behalf of other organisms in the group, is simply behaviour which enhances the chance of survival (and so of the reappearance in the next generation) of genes in those other organisms which they also share with the 'altruistic' individual. So those on behalf of whom the sacrifice is made must be genetically kin to the altruistic individual. The 'altruism' of, for example, a bird emitting a warning cry to the rest of its kin-group of the approach of a predator, thereby attracting the attack to itself, is simply, on this view, a mechanism for enhancing the chances of survival of genes which are like its own but are carried by those other, related, individuals. (J. B. S. Haldane once affirmed that he would lay down his life for two brothers or eight cousins![30]) No special 'motivation', or 'purpose', or any special awareness of the group, needs to be

[29] V. C. Wynne-Edwards, *Animal Dispersion in Relation to Social Behaviour* (Oliver & Boyd, Edinburgh, 1962); R. Ardrey, *The Social Contract* (Collins, London, 1970).
[30] J. B. S. Haldane, 'Population genetics', *New Biology*, 18 (1955), 34–51.

attributed to the organism—the selection processes, the associated statistics, ensure this result (the increased chance of reproduction of the genes which the 'altruistic' individual shares with the rest of the group)—and to introduce teleological or group language is simply a *post ipso facto* gloss on what is actually going on. These ideas have been powerfully argued in Edward Wilson's monumental work, *Sociobiology*[31] and, more recently, expounded in Richard Dawkins's *The Selfish Gene*.[32]

The argument for individual, or gene, selection as the appropriate interpretative category of behaviour rests on the assumption that one can properly speak of a gene[33] for a particular kind of behaviour, even if we have no knowledge of the actual causal chains linking genes and behaviour. Thus a 'gene for altruistic behaviour' would be one that transmits information which affects the development of the organism's nervous system so as to make them more likely to behave altruistically—and so might have its effect at a number of levels.

For purposes of argument it will be necessary to speculate about genes 'for' doing all sorts of improbable things. If I speak, for example, of a hypothetical gene 'for saving companions from drowning', and you find such a concept incredible, remember the story of the hygienic bees [a reference to the work of W. C. Rothenbuhler (*Amer. Zool.* 4 (1964), 111–23) who found evidence for the genetic control of the behaviour of bees who put into operation (or did not do so, or did so only partially) procedures for removing diseased grubs from their hive]. Recall that we are not talking about the gene as the sole antecedent cause of all the complex muscular contractions, sensory integrations, and even conscious decisions, which are involved in saving somebody from drowning. We are saying nothing about the question of whether learning, experience, or environmental influences enter into the development of the behaviour. All you have to concede is that it is possible for a single gene, other things being equal and lots of other essential genes and environmental factors being

---

[31] E. O. Wilson, *Sociobiology—The New Synthesis* (Belknap Press, Harvard University Press, Cambridge, Mass., 1975).

[32] Richard Dawkins, *The Selfish Gene* (Oxford University Press, Oxford, 1976).

[33] Though, on any reckoning, it would have to be a *system* of concomitantly acting, linked genes, i.e. inheritance of behavioural characteristics is likely to be polygenic. So in the text, as in the Dawkins quotation, take the singular 'gene' to refer to such a system.

present, to make a body more likely to save somebody from drowning than its allele would.[34]

This way of regarding the role of the 'selfish' gene has been applied to interpreting a wide range of behaviour, other than altruistic, e.g. aggression, the 'battle of the sexes', parental policies, feeding habits, the relation between old and young, etc. The application involves employing the theory of games to work out what is the most evolutionarily stable strategy, that is, the behavioural policy which, if adopted by most members of a population, cannot be bettered, from the viewpoint of gene *and* population survival, by any other strategy.[35] It is interesting to note the not dissimilar application of games theory by M. Eigen[36] to the problem of competing, reproducing macromolecules, 'replicators'[37], under pre-biotic conditions: these early replicators are the direct ancesters of the genes of DNA in present living organisms—and may well also have been some kind of nucleic acid.

Dawkins summarizes this way of looking at biological evolution and the behaviour of living organisms thus:

Replicators began not merely to exist, but to construct for themselves containers, vehicles for continued existence. The replicators which survived were the ones which built *survival machines* for themselves to live in. The first survival machines probably consisted of nothing more than a protective coat. But making a living got steadily harder as new arrivals arose with better and more effective survival machines. Survival machines got bigger and more elaborate, and the process was cumulative and progressive.

Was there to be any end to the gradual improvement in the techniques and artifices used by the replicators to ensure their own continuance in the world? There would be plenty of time for improvement. What weird engines of self-preservation would the millennia bring forth? Four thousand million years on, what was to be the fate of the ancient replicators? They did not die out, for they are past masters of the survival arts. But do not look for them floating loose in the sea; they gave up that cavalier freedom long ago. Now they swarm in huge colonies, safe inside gigantic lumbering robots, sealed off from the outside world, communicating with it by tortuous

---

[34] Dawkins, op. cit., p. 66.
[35] Dawkins, op. cit., pp. 74 ff.
[36] See Lecture II.
[37] Dawkins, op. cit., Ch. 2.

indirect routes, manipulating it by remote control. They are in you and in me; they created us, body and mind; and their preservation is the ultimate rationale for our existence. They have come a long way, those replicators. Now they go by the name of genes, and we are their survival machines ...

We are survival machines, but 'we' does not mean just people, it embraces all animals, plants, bacteria, and viruses.[38]

This passage already has overtones of some of the wider significance that sociobiologists have attributed to their ideas and already gives some foretaste of the controverises this has provoked. This will emerge later but it is clear that at the level of interpretation of biological behaviour these new concepts are fruitful and illuminating and open to refutation or confirmation by observation (one of their important virtues). To the question 'What is man for?' the sociobiological answer appears to be: he is a gene machine, a robot vehicle, blindly programmed to preserve its selfish genes. The human brain-in-the-human body with all its special characteristics would then be reduced to this function. But let us not anticipate and continue with our account of the features of the evolutionary process. There are two remaining aspects of these processes of which any account of God's relation to the world is bound to take cognisance

(*vii*) The processes by which new species appear is a process of *new life through death of the old* and involves a degree of competition and struggle in nature which has often offended man's moral and aesthetic sensibilities. But we recall that the epithet of nature as 'red in tooth and claw' was written by Tennyson long before Darwin proposed his theory with its apparent emphasis on the 'struggle for existence'. It has taken modern biologists to restore the balance in our view of the organic world by reminding us, as Simpson puts it:

To generalize ... that natural selection is over-all and even in a figurative sense the outcome of struggle is quite unjustified under the modern understanding of the process ... Struggle is sometimes involved, but it usually is not, and when it is, it may even work against rather than toward natural selection. Advantage in differential reproduction is usually a peaceful process in which the concept of

[38] Dawkins, op. cit., pp. 21, 22.

struggle is really irrelevant. It more often involves such things as better integration into the ecological situation, maintenance of a balance of nature, more efficient utilization of available food, better care of the young, elimination of intragroup discords (struggles) that might hamper reproduction, exploitation of environmental possibilities that are not the objects of competition or are less effectively exploited by others.[39]

The death of old organisms is a prerequisite for the appearance of new ones. For the death of individuals is essential for release of food resources for new arrivals and the death of species for creating biological 'niches' for new species (in practice, over a period of time the new, better adapted, simply oust the older by the processes we have described). Moreover, more complex structures can only have a finite chance of both coming into existence and of surviving if they are not assembled *de novo*, as it were, from their atomic components, but emerge through accumulation of changes in a simpler form[40] and, in the case of living organisms, can also survive by building preformed chemical structures into their own fabric through imbibing the materials of other living organisms. There is indeed a kind of 'structural logic' about all this, for we cannot conceive, in a lawful, non-magical universe, of any way whereby new structural complexity might appear, except by utilizing structures already existing, either by way of modification (as in the evolutionary process) or of incorporation (as in feeding).

Thus the law of 'new life through death of the old' (the 'sublime law of sacrifice' of J. H. Fabre which C. Raven so often quoted)[41] is inevitable in a world composed of common 'building blocks' (atoms etc.). But in biological evolution the creation of the new does not happen without pain and suffering and both seem unavoidable. Biologically, pain is a warning signal of danger from external sources or internal injury or disease and is essential to survival. It is mediated through nervous systems which have developed because they are needed for

[39] Simpson, op. cit., p. 201.

[40] H. A. Simon, 'The Architecture of Complexity', *Proc. Amer Philosophical Soc.* 106 (1962), 467–82; see also A. R. Peacocke, loc. cit. (above, p. 159 n. 24), for further discussion of the evolution of complex structures.

[41] e.g. in C. E. Raven, *Natural Religion and Christian Theology*, 1951 Gifford Lectures, Series 1, *Science and Religion* (Cambridge University Press, Cambridge, 1953), p. 15.

delicate sensing of the environment to obtain a wide range of information necessary for the organism to survive. This feature reaches its apogee of complexity and sensitivity in man's brain and nervous system. But this sensitivity to signals from the environment entails a certain softness of outer structure, to be tactually sensitive to other objects when in contact, and this again involves fragility and vulnerability to impersonal forces and structures in the non-living environment. Thus it is not easy, given the world of the atomic etc. constitution we actually have, readily to envisage how mobile, exploring, sensitive aware creatures could have come into existence which did not experience pain and were not fragile and vulnerable.

So it appears that new life through death of the old, pain, fragility, and vulnerability are all inevitably aspects of living structures that can evolve in a universe of material units—and such units can only exist in a cosmos if they have regular and definite properties. Otherwise we have not a cosmos but a chaos, which is indistinguishable from nothingness (as we discussed earlier). That there should be parameters (such as the fundamental physical constants) which characterize this (or any) universe is necessary for any distinct entities to exist at all and is the prerequisite of the existence of matter itself, out of which self-reproducing structures aware of themselves and the rest of the world might then evolve. Thus death, pain, and the risk of suffering are intimately connected with the possibilities of new life, in general, and of the emergence of conscious, and especially human, life, in particular. Moreover, only in a world of ordered regularity can a free creature make decisions with predictable consequences. So the very order and impersonality of the physical cosmos which makes pain and suffering inevitable for conscious and self-conscious creatures is, at the same time, also the prerequisite of their exercise of freedom as persons. In exercising their freedom they are bound to encounter the opposition of the random elements in the world process, which come to man as 'natural evil'—those same elements of chance whose creative interplay with law have been the means of their own emergence in the universe. Again, it seems hard to avoid the paradox that 'natural evil' is a necessary prerequisite for the the emergence of free, self-conscious beings.

I make these remarks only to hint at the paradox of the boundaries of our existence, boundaries which appear, at the minimum irksome, and at the worst overwhelmingly tragic. The paradox resides in the close relation to these same boundary conditions of our very presence in the cosmos at all as free, aware persons.

(*viii*) *Open-ended character of evolution.* The emergence of persons making free decisions within the context of a cosmos characterized by, at least, statistical regularities, is but the most obvious and maximal manifestation of the last feature of the evolutionary process that I wish to refer to. In retrospect, each innovation, each emergence of new forms of the organization of both inorganic and living matter, is, in principle, intelligible to us now as the lawful consequences (usually at a higher level of complexity) of a concatenation of random events (often at a lower level). As we have seen, in the process of cosmic and biological evolution there has been involved this element of randomness, of contingency, of 'chance'—in, for example, the events of nucleation within the galactic clouds which gave rise to the stars and their planets, and the continuation of the mutational chemical events in DNA with the sifting of their survival value by the actual environment of the organism in which they occur. This involvement of randomness means that, although in retrospect the development is intelligible (at least in principle) to modern science, yet in prospect the development would not have been strictly predictable. The development of the world has not unfolded a predetermined sequence of events, like the development of an oak from the acorn or of a mammalian embryo from the fertilized ovum. The whole process cannot be fore-ordained in detail since it actualizes only a minute fraction of the vast potentialities at any stage. The view that biological evolution, in particular, is predetermined, in the same way as the development of the biological individual is predetermined by its DNA, is called 'orthogenesis': one of its stricter forms is 'finalist' in positing that all evolution occurred for the express purpose of producing man and that it was guided to this end by some external, superimposed, spiritual, or other, forces. We have already given reasons for rejecting such 'vitalism', not least when, I believe mistakenly, it purports to express the mode of God's creative activity in evolution. We have to recognize that the processes of evolution, both cosmic and biological, do not appear as directional and as directed, as would be required by such a view, whether a theistically 'vitalist' or theistically creationist. The processes of evolution, in fact, are sufficiently open-ended and involve such an element of 'trial and error', that Teilhard's description of them as 'groping' ('tatonnement') seems far more appropriate. As T. Dobzhansky puts it: 'The chief characteristic, or at any rate one of the characteristics, of progressive evolution, is its open-endedness. Conquest of new environments and acquisition of new ways of life create opportunities for further evolutionary developments.'[42]

Earlier, I used the word 'exploration' to express this feature of the processes in which the gamut of potentialities is explored. As one goes up the scale of biological evolution, increasingly the innovations which are established, the organisms that actually emerge, result from a subtle interplay of random mutation and interaction with the selecting environment, which includes the purposeful behaviour of the organism itself. At these levels, where mobile creatures explore their environment and imitate any successful ploys of the same members of their species, the involvement of consciousness and some rudimentary form of decision-taking cannot be denied to them. (This aspect of the role of the *behaviour* of the organisms in evolution has been particularly strongly urged by Sir Alister Hardy in his Gifford Lectures.[43]) That is, the open-ended character, unpredictability, and creativity of the process becomes more and more focused in the activity of the biological individual. It was this feature of the process that, as I implied just now, reaches its apogee in man's creativity and his sense of freedom in taking responsibility for his decisions. Again, as Dobzhansky puts it,

The concepts of creativity and freedom are not directly applicable below the human level. It may nevertheless be argued that the rigid determinism [not so rigid according to the arguments of these Lectures] is becoming gradually relaxed as the evolution of life progresses.

[42] T. Dobzhansky, *The Biology of Ultimate Concern* (New American Library, New York, 1967), p. 129.

[43] A. Hardy, *The Living Stream* (Collins, London, 1965), pp. 161 ff., 189 ff.

The elements of creativity are more perceptible in the evolution of higher than in that of lower organisms.[44]

This perspective on evolution still therefore attributes a special significance to man's emergence in and from the material universe but recognizes he has arrived by means of an open-ended, trial-and-error, exploration of possibilities—an exploration devoid neither of false trails and dead ends nor, as consciousness emerges, of pain, suffering, and struggle.

IV. THE EMERGENCE OF MAN

A. 'Evolution' becomes 'history'

Man has emerged as a natural product of this process but with his advent 'evolution', hitherto effected by the processes I have been describing, takes on a new form. As Simpson says,

> It is still false to conclude that man is *nothing but* the highest animal, or the most progressive product of organic evolution. He is also a fundamentally new sort of animal and one in which, although organic evolution continues on its way, a fundamentally new sort of evolution has also appeared. The basis of this new sort of evolution is a new sort of heredity, the inheritance of learning. This sort of heredity appears modestly in other animals and even lower in the animal kingdom, but in man it has incomparably fuller development and it combines with man's other characteristics unique in degree with a result that cannot be considered unique only in degree but must also be considered unique in kind.[45]

This 'new sort of evolution' occurs notably at the social level at which man develops variegated cultures of many kinds, so that Julian Huxley has called it psychosocial evolution to include both learning and culture: '. . . the evolutionary process, as now embodied in man, has for the first time become aware of itself, is studying the laws of its own unfolding, and has a dawning realization of the possibilities of its own future guidance or control. In other words, evolution is on the verge of becoming internalized, conscious and self-directing.'[46]

[44] Dobzhansky, op. cit., p. 125; see also his *Mankind Evolving* (Yale University Press, New Haven, 1963).

[45] Simpson, op. cit., p. 260.

[46] J. Huxley, 'The Evolutionary Process' in *Evolution as a Process*, ed. J. Huxley, A. C. Hardy, E. B. Ford (George Allen & Unwin, London, 1954), p. 13.

However, if man is also the first animal who, by consciously shaping and choosing his own environment, has stepped outside the process of evolution by natural selection operating on genetic mutations, the use of the word 'evolution' is scarcely permissible if this is taken to imply that man evolves only by this neo-Darwinian mechanism. For man alters himself by himself altering his own environment through the impact of his social organization and applied science, which depend on his ability to formulate and transmit knowledge from one generation to another. This 'Lamarckian' inheritance of acquired knowledge is transmitted through what Karl Popper[47] has called 'World 3', the world of knowledge in the objective sense of what is recorded in books, music, tapes, films, computers, diagrams, etc., contained in special institutions designed for their preservation and transmission (libraries, museums; universities and institutes of learning and research). Perhaps it would be best simply to say that with man 'evolution' has become 'history'. Whatever terms we employ, the point is that a unique transition has occurred at the emergence of man with his cultures possessing a history. Man's activities and development display distinctive characteristics which, as with other emergent forms at other levels, require new modes of discourse and concepts to delineate and new methods of inquiry to discriminate and understand. We should not, *ab initio*, expect these modes of inquiry and discourse that are appropriate for all the various levels of the phenomenon of man to be entirely reducible (in the sense of Lecture IV, i.e. of not being theory-autonomous) to the terms and concepts of lower levels.

B. *Sociobiology*

We have already seen[48] the sense in which biology is not 'nothing but' physics and chemistry—at the same time affirming that the component units of biological organisms obey the laws of physics and chemistry. Similarly the sociologist and anthropologist would claim that society and cultures exhibit

---

[47] K. Popper, 'Epistemology without a knowing subject', in *Logic, Methodology and Philosophy of Science* iii, ed. B. van Rootselaar and J. F. Staal (North Holland Publ. Co., Amsterdam, 1968); and see the exposition of J. Eccles, *Facing Reality* (Springer-Verlag, New York, 1970), pp. 163 ff.

[48] Lecture IV.

emergent properties over and beyond those exhibited by individual human beings.

When people relate together they do so in such a way that the group they are in exhibits certain properties which are not reducible to the individuals themselves. That is to say that certain actions become possible and certain constraints are imposed by the organisation of the group. A group of three people interacting have certain potentialities not available to two (for example, you can have a variety of alliances or a situation of divide and rule) which lead to the possession or loss of power for particular individuals. When one comes to large scale organisations where interaction is impersonal and often mediated along predefined communication networks, the range of possibilities and constraints that emerge for the groups as a whole are legion.[49]

However, in recent years, in an accelerating trend initiated by the publication of Edward Wilson's *Sociobiology* in 1975, some biologists, after rebutting the attempts of recent decades to reduce their discipline to the molecular sciences, have taken upon themselves the role of the unjust steward and have appeared to be attempting to reduce sociology, anthropology, and the sciences of human behaviour to biology. Perhaps this assertiveness should not be taken as an attempt at outright reduction of these sciences to biology, for Wilson has, since the publication of *Sociobiology*, argued[50] for the value to any discipline of its *antidiscipline* (referring to the special, creative, adversary relation that exists initially between the studies of adjacent levels of organization)—with biology as the anti-discipline to the social sciences. Moreover, in the same article[51] he explicitly repudiates any reductionist ambitions of biology with respect to the social sciences which he recognizes as 'potentially far richer in content' than biology. For Wilson is quite aware that the properties of societies are emergent and hence deserving of 'a special language and treatment'[52] but he, nevertheless, wishes to give a prime and determinative role to the biological basis of human social behaviour and patterns:

---

[49] Eileen Barker, 'Value systems generated by biologists', *Contact*, 55. 4 (1976), 12.
[50] E. O. Wilson, 'Biology and the Social Sciences', *Daedalus*, 106. 4 (Autumn 1977), 127–40.
[51] Wilson, op. cit. (1977), p. 138.
[52] Wilson, op. cit. (see above, p. 162 n. 31), p. 7.

Sociobiology is defined as the systematic study of the biological basis of all social behavior. For the present it focuses on animal societies, their population structure, castes, and communication, together with all the physiology underlying the social adaptations. But the discipline is also concerned with the social behavior of early man and the adaptive features of organization in the more primitive contemporary human societies. Sociology *sensu stricto*, the study of human societies at all levels of complexity, still stands apart from sociobiology because of its largely structuralist and nongenetic approach. It attempts to explain human behavior primarily by empirical description of the outermost pheno-types and by unaided intuition, without reference to evolutionary explanations in the true genetic sense. It is most successful, in the way descriptive taxonomy and ecology have been most successful, when it provides a detailed description of particular phenomena and demonstrates first-order correlations with features of the environment. Taxonomy and ecology, however, have been re-shaped entirely during the past forty years by integration into the neo-Darwinist evolutionary theory—the 'Modern Synthesis', as it is often called—in which each phenomenon is weighed for its adaptive significance and then related to the basic principles of population genetics. It may not be too much to say that sociology and the other social sciences, as well as the humanities, are the last branches of biology waiting to be included in the Modern Synthesis. One of the functions of sociobiology, then, is to reformulate the foundations of the social sciences in a way that draws these subjects into the Modern Synthesis. Whether the social sciences can be truly biologicized in this fashion remains to be seen.[53]

The genuflexion towards scientific objectivity in the last sentence has not served to mollify adequately the assertiveness of what precedes it and, needless to say, such apparent intellectual imperialism has provoked strong reactions from the native denizens of anthropology and sociology—not to mention political opposition which sees sociobiologists as reincarnated nineteenth-century social Darwinists. What is clearly correct in the claim of sociobiologists, as expounded by Wilson, is that there are significant biological patterns of behaviour which must have formed the starting-point, at least, of the development of human culture. The argument turns on the extent to which these biological patterns have persisted and still are factors shaping human social behaviour within even early forms

[53] Wilson, op. cit. (1975), p. 4.

of 'primitive' human societies, let alone the complex technological civilization of Western man. It is clear that many neo-
Darwinian biologists have found the concept of the 'selfish gene'
(i.e. of individual selection) more illuminating in interpreting
behaviour in groups of living organisms than earlier theories
of 'group selection'. It may well be that this way of analysing
the social behaviour of living organisms will go on being useful
but the fact that it has not hitherto been much applied to
human behaviour does not immediately warrant its validity in
that sphere. (The 'behaviour' in question here includes *inter
alia* such key areas of human life as: altruism and ethics;
aggressiveness; relations between the sexes, parent and child, the
old and the young, the strong and the weak.) Neglect is not
in itself the guarantee that a new touchstone of truth in interpreting human culture has been unearthed. Similar reflections
could well have been prompted by an earlier attempt, that of
C. D. Darlington,[54] to subsume human history under the
history of the genetic mixing of populations. Then, as now
with sociobiology, attention was drawn to biological parameters in the situation that had certainly been neglected, both
because of inadequate recognition of the existence of such
factors and because of lack of evidence to determine their
influence.

So, even though we may be sceptical, for reasons already
developed in protecting biology itself from being reduced to the
molecular sciences, of some sociobiologists' apparently reductionist ambitions, it would be a mistake to dismiss any new
insights it can bring to bear on the complexities of human
existence. The weightiest attack on sociobiology so far published from within one of the 'threatened' sciences is that of
Marshall Sahlins, an anthropologist. To Wilson's question,
quoted above, of 'whether the social sciences can be truly
biologicized in this fashion [of sociobiology]', Sahlins responds:
'The answer I suggest here is that they cannot, because biology,
while it is an absolutely necessary condition for culture, is
equally and absolutely insufficient: it is completely unable to

---

[54] C. D. Darlington, *The Evolution of Man and Society* (George Allen & Unwin,
London, 1969).

specify the cultural properies of human behavior or their variations from one human group to another.'[55] For, he argues,

... the central intellectual problem does come down to the autonomy
of culture and of the study of culture. *Sociobiology* [E. Wilson's book]
challenges the integrity of culture as a thing-in-itself, as a distinctive
and symbolic human creation. In place of a social constitution of
meanings, it offers a biological determination of human interactions
with a source primarily in the general evolutionary propensity of
individual genotypes to maximize their reproductive success.[56]

Scientific sociobiologists (e.g. E. O. Wilson, R. L. Trivers,
W. D. Hamilton, R. Alexander, M. West-Eberhard) who
attempt to place social behaviour on sound evolutionary principles (notably the self-maximization of the individual genotype) do so, Sahlins suggests, by assuming as premiss the
proposition of a more 'vulgar' sociobiology that human social
behaviour can be explained as the expression of those needs and
drives of the human organism which have been imprinted by
biological evolution.[57] So in scientific sociobiology, Sahlins
says,

The chain of biological causation is accordingly lengthened: from
genes through phenotypical dispositions to characteristic social interactions. But the idea of a necessary correspondence between the last
two, between human emotions or needs and human social relations,
remains indispensable to the scientific analysis ... The interactions
of organisms will inscribe these organic tendencies [aggressiveness,
altruism, male 'bonding', sexuality, etc.] in their social relations.
Accordingly there is a one-to-one parallel between the character of
human biological propensities and the properties of human social
systems ... For him [E. O. Wilson], any Durkheimian notion of
the independent existence and persistence of the social fact is a lapse
into mysticism. Social organization is rather, and nothing more than,
the behavioral outcome of the interaction of organisms having biologically fixed inclinations. There is nothing in society that was not
first in the organisms.[58]

[55] M. Sahlins, *The Use and Abuse of Biology* (University of Michigan Press, Ann Arbor, 1976), p. xi.
[56] Sahlins, op. cit., p. x.
[57] Cf. the biological determinism of such authors as R. Ardrey (above, p. 161 n. 29); K. Lorenz, *On Aggression* (Methuen, London, 1966); D. Morris, *The Naked Ape* (Jonathan Cape, London, 1967; Corgi Books, London, 1968).
[58] Sahlins, op. cit., pp. 4–5.

But this position does not correspond to the results of anthropological study. For

the problem is that there is no necessary relation between the phenomenal form of a human social institution and the individual motivations that may be realized or satisfied therein. The idea of a fixed correspondence between innate human dispositions and human social forms constitutes a weak link, a rupture in fact, in the chain of sociobiological reasoning.[59]

As evidence of this he cites the absence of any relation between war and individual human aggressiveness. The latter may be mobilized to pursue a war but its existence does not in itself explain the existence of war, in general, and the causes of any particular war—'Aggression does not regulate social conflict, but social conflict does regulate aggression.'[60]

Many sociobiologists (Wilson, Trivers, et al.) argue that kin selection—an essentially cost–benefit analysis of an individual's behaviour towards genetic relatives, the 'selfish gene' model—is the deep structure of human social patterns and behaviour. Sahlins, by ranging over the actual arrangements in a number of carefully studied cultures, shows[61] clearly that (i) no system of human kinship relations is organized in accord with the genetic coefficients of relationship as known to sociobiologists; (ii) the *culturally constituted* kinship relations, which govern production, property, mutual aid, and marital exchange, have an entirely different calculus from that predicted by genetic kin selection; (iii) kinship is a unique characteristic of human societies, distinguishable precisely by its freedom from natural (genetic) relationships; (iv) human beings reproduce not as physical or biological beings but as *social* beings, i.e. human reproduction is engaged as the means for the persistence of co-operative social orders not vice versa, and so, finally, (v) culture is the indispensable condition of systems of human organization and reproduction. For 'Human society is cultural, unique in virtue of its construction by symbolic means'[62] and

[59] Sahlins, op. cit., p. 7.
[60] Sahlins, op. cit., p. 9; cf. the similar conclusion of M. Csikszentmihalyi, 'Socio-cultural speciation and human aggression', *Zygon*, 8 (1973), 96–112.
[61] Sahlins, op. cit., Ch. II.
[62] Sahlins, op. cit., p. 61.

'Culture is biology plus the symbolic faculty'[63], where the importance of the symbolic is to generate meaning not merely to convey information, as Wilson would have.

It seems to me that Sahlins has demonstrated what he set out to do, namely, that 'sociobiological reasoning from evolutionary phylogeny to social morphology is interrupted by culture',[64] so that any claims for sociobiology to be the key to all the human sciences, and indeed to all the humanities, are exaggerated (and indeed in his 1977 article[65] Wilson, whatever impression his *Sociobiology* may have given, demurs from any such claim).

But, this is not to dismiss the real insights biology can afford into the *constraints* which man's biological nature place upon him. That this is the way biology can help in the understanding of man in society has become apparent from the extensive discussions, which began in the nineteenth century, about whether our knowledge of the evolutionary process could generate ethical norms. The conclusion of most philosophers of ethics[66] that it cannot do so, being guilty of the 'naturalistic fallacy' of deducing what ought to be the case from what is, has not deterred a succession of biologists, such as Julian Huxley and C. H. Waddington, from urging not merely the relevance of, but the decisiveness of biology for ethics.[67] Without going so far, it is nevertheless clear that the new biological work on 'altruism' and 'selfishness', in the restricted *biological* sense we described earlier (note the anthropomorphism of these biological terms), must now be weighed as possible factors in or better, constraints upon or natural limits to, the development of ethical norms in human cultures. But Sahlins' evidence and arguments show that too much must not be expected from this and the biological analysis may, in the end, be restricted to accounting chiefly for the emotional colouring which accompanies much human behaviour (as urged by Wilson himself in

---

[63] Sahlins, op. cit., p. 65.
[64] Sahlins, op. cit., p. 11.
[65] Above, p. 171 n. 50.
[66] See, e.g., A. M. Quinton, 'Ethics and the Theory of Evolution', in *Biology and Personality*, ed. I. T. Ramsey (Blackwell, Oxford, 1975), pp. 107 ff.; A. G. N. Flew, *Evolutionary Ethics* (Macmillan, London, 1967).
[67] Cf. above, p. 171, n. 49.

the opening section[68] of his book, where he says that ethics and ethical philosophers should be 'explained' by the 'pursuit', at all depths, of the biological statement that the hypothalamus and limbic systems, which flood our consciousness with emotions, were evolved by natural selection).

C. 'Memes' and survival

Richard Dawkins concludes his account of *The Selfish Gene* by working out an analogy. He recognizes the rapidity of human cultural 'evolution' (he calls it that, rather than 'history') and the inadequacy of Darwinism, even in its modern form, to account for it. He points out that if we are to look for a unit of replication, having the same relation to cultural evolution as the gene has to biological, then we must look for it in a unit of *imitation*, which he calls a 'meme', a unit of cultural transmission. Memes can be tunes, ideas, catch-phrases, fashions in clothes, or ways of doing things and they propagate by being passed from one human brain to another, in a process of imitation. Not all memes are successful in replicating for they are in competition for limited storage time and space in human brains (and in general in the objects of 'World 3' of K. Popper). Groups of memes can be co-adapted, as when the god-meme (the 'idea-meme' that is the idea of God) is associated with other memes of architecture, ritual, and literature.

In biology, the genes are 'selfish', at least in the exposition of Dawkins and the sociobiologists, by virtue of the automatic ensurance of their survival in organisms which compete to produce progeny, that is, to replicate the gene in another organism. 'Survival', in the case of the meme, means being reproduced ('imitated') in the brain of another human being. But what renders one *idea*-meme more likely to be reproduced in a brain than another meme—i.e. what operates on the memes to discriminate between their chances of 'surviving' in the same way that premature death before producing progeny acts differentially on organisms containing different genes? This is, of course, a very biological kind of question which is being asked about cultural 'evolution', and it implies that 'a cultural trait may have evolved in the way that it has, simply because

[68] Wilson, op. cit. (1975), p. 3.

it is *advantageous to itself*.[69] Accepting for the moment these terms of reference, it is a fair question: 'What qualities make for high survival value among idea-memes?' Clearly, as with genes, a meme has a better chance of surviving if it is fecund, that is, can spread rapidly amongst brains, and if it displays copying-fidelity.[70] (Dawkins also mentions longevity as having survival value for a meme but that seems too tautologous.) Copying-fidelity of an idea-meme will itself depend on many factors (can the idea be broken into simpler units, and are the units then transmissible by actual existing structures, components of 'World 3'?) but the analysis is worth pursuing with respect to *fecundity*, the ability of an idea-meme to spread to other brains. This depends on how acceptable the idea is and, at least in relation to the god-meme (the replicating idea of God), Dawkins suggests that 'great psychological appeal'[71] is what gives the meme 'stability and penetrance in the cultural environment'.

The meme suggestion is admittedly only an analogy but it is developed with the use of biological terms so that we may think it is explaining cultural evolution and the content of human brains, in a way which is, in principle, reducible to biology. So we have to press our questions further. What, when referred to idea-memes (i.e. ideas as replicating units), does 'being acceptable to', or 'having a great psychological appeal for', a brain really mean? At this point the flood-gates burst, and a biology tending to be reductionist can no longer stem the torrent of questions which are directed to it from levels higher in the hierarchy of reality (not to say complexity) than that of the purely biological.

For to ask what is acceptable and what has psychological appeal is to ask what do men really want, what quality of life do they seek, what will satisfy their needs, what will fulfil their aspirations—it is, to use the haunting title of a famous story of Tolstoy, to ask 'What do men live by?'

---

[69] Dawkins, op. cit., p. 214.
[70] Dawkins, op. cit., pp. 208-9.
[71] Dawkins, op. cit., p. 207.

V.   WHAT DO MEN LIVE BY?

It is significant that, as far as we can tell, this question is asked by only one evolved living organism, man, who alone seems to be able to distance himself from both himself and the world in which he has emerged and then to reflect upon his existence there. It seems to be one of the distinctive features of his being a person, of being able to say 'I' of himself. In asking this question, and those of the last paragraph, we are trying to unravel man's needs. I would distinguish the following needs of man—the compilation is not meant to be exhaustive and the needs interlock and overlap, and no doubt each of us will have his own list.

A.   Man has biological needs[72]

Like any other terrestrial mammalian vertebrate human beings need food, rest, shelter, sex, an environment in which pro-creation and care of the young is possible, and to understand the eco-system of which he is a part and his role and niche in that system. The way in which all such needs are satisfied varies with the evolutionary history of the animal in question and, no doubt, there are built-in constraints, even now, to the ways in which modern man may satisfy these needs. The pursuit of their satisfaction has shaped human history but even when these basic needs have been met man is not necessarily happy. He has a restlessness which stems from his failure to satisfy other needs, which he seems not to share with other animals.

B.   Man needs to come to terms with his own death

In the animal world fear operates as part of a safety mechanism when danger to life threatens and it diminishes as the threat recedes. Such a mechanism, with its attendant physiological changes, still operates in man but in him it is 'sicklied o'er with the pale cast of thought', so that his self-awareness makes him more continuously conscious, even in the absence of immediate dangers, of the terminus to his biological life. 'Man is burdened with death-awareness. A being who knows that he will die

---

[72] See also the more comprehensive list of G. E. Pugh (p. 154 n. 13) above.

arose from ancestors who did not know'.[73] Such death-awareness is not obviously adaptive and may even be biologically
detrimental; but it is a concomitant of self-awareness that
clearly does have adaptive significance, serving as it does to
integrate man's physical and mental capacities in relation to
his environment.[74] Although some of the social insects remove
their dead from their colonies as a hygienic measure, no other
living creatures bury their dead with ritual—even Neanderthal
man did so and late Palaeolithic, Mesolithic, and Neolithic
burial sites are numerous. These rituals, varied though they
are, all testify to man's questioning concern with death. Only
man, it seems, is affronted by death. The sciences, in so far as
they show how what we are has evolved out of the matter of the
world and how we are one of the individual hierarchies of
complexity of that matter, have sharpened the question of death
by rendering all ontological dualisms less plausible.[75] There is
no doubt that at a given moment in time the material organization which is 'I' will disintegrate in structure while its components will undergo chemical transformations. Then the 'I' which
is that body in its most integrated and directed mode of being
will cease to be, according to anything that we can discover
through our science about the way things are. I have spoken in
the first person because it is our use of 'I' which is distinctive
of persons. It is not generalizations of the kind 'man is mortal'
but the fact that nothing is true about 'man' which is not
true of 'me' (and of you) with which we need to come to terms.
As Ivan Ilyich recalls in another story of Tolstoy (*The Death of
Iván Ilých*): 'Caius is a man, men are mortal, therefore Caius
is mortal', but with a shock he [Ivan] realizes '... That Caius—
man in the abstract—was mortal, was perfectly correct, but
he was not Caius, not an abstract man, but a creature, quite,
quite separate from all others ... It cannot be that I ought to
die. That would be too terrible.'[76] Every man will in the end
be identified with materiality and it appears as though the
universe will go on its way as though he had never been born.
Or will it? That is the question to which man needs an answer.

[73] Dobzhansky, op. cit. (p. 168 n. 42), p. 69.
[74] Dobzhansky, op. cit., pp. 73 ff.
[75] See Lecture IV.
[76] Leo Tolstoy, *The Death of Iván Ilých, and other stories* (The World's Classics, Oxford University Press, London, 1971, transl. L. and A. Maude), pp. 44, 45.

C. Man needs to come to terms with his finitude

The awareness of death is but the most intense of a number of other experiences of finitude: experiences of man's physical limitation, in encounter with material objects and, more recently, in his encounter with the extent of space and time in the observed universe;[77] experiences of organic limitations, in illness, exhaustion, failure, etc.; experiences of personal limitations, in clashes with the wills of other persons, in decisions etc; and in experiences of normative constraints, expressed in the making of distinctions such as true/false, right/wrong, and ugly/beautiful.[78] Realism accepts these limitations, but frequently these experiences of finitude themselves push one to a sense of our ultimate limit which acts as a medium through which is challenged the very way in which we regard our own personal identity (and, for some, another dynamic Reality meets them within this process of deepening self-knowledge, though that is not our immediate point here). This awareness of his finitude is an incongruity between man and his niche in the world not accountable by and not satisfied within the biological as such—an incongruity eloquently expressed by that great nineteenth-century Presbyterian preacher and divine, Thomas Chalmers, in the first Bridgwater Treatise, in phrases which echo the Augustine who stands behind his tradition:

There is in man, a restlessness of ambition; an interminable longing after nobler and higher things, which nought but immortality and the greatness of immortality can satiate, a dissatisfaction with the present, which never is appeased by all that the world has to offer; an impatience and distaste with the felt littleness of all that he finds, and an unsated appetency for something larger and better, which he fancies in the perspective before him—to all which there is nothing like among any of the inferior animals, with whom there is a certain squareness of adjustment, if we may so term it, between each desire and its corresponding gratification. The one is evenly met by the other; and there is a fulness and definiteness of enjoyment, up to the

[77] See Lecture II.
[78] Following the analysis of G. D. Kaufman, 'On the Meaning of "God": Transcendence without Mythology', in *New Theology*, ed. M. E. Marty and D. G. Pearman (Macmillan, New York, 1967).

capacity of enjoyment. Not so with man, who, both from the vastness of his propensities and the vastness of his powers, feels himself straitened and beset in a field too narrow for him. He alone labours under the discomfort of an incongruity between his circumstances and his powers; and, unless there be new circumstances awaiting him in a more advanced state of being, he, the noblest of Nature's products here below, would turn out to be the greatest of her failures.[79]

D.   *Man needs to learn how to bear suffering*

We have already discussed briefly suffering in the non-human world and that caused to human beings by natural events. Again, our self-awareness has as a concomitant the rendering almost intolerable of our experience of suffering, whether in ourselves or in other people, and even in the non-human world. The sciences, by increasing our intellectual self-confidence, incline us to think superficially that we would have been able to order things better than, say, a creator God has managed. However, we have seen reasons for thinking that the emergence of self-conscious beings in a cosmos regular enough in its properties to include existing distinct entities does entail many of those features of our existence which give rise to 'natural evil'. Biological science makes more intelligible the roles of pain and suffering and death in order both preserve and to create new forms of life. But although this may mollify us intellectually, we nevertheless wonder whether the pain, suffering, and death which we see in biological life, in general, and man in particular, can be justified in any way that satisfies our moral sense. Moreover, the advent of applied science in the form of medicine, more and more softens our experience of pain and thereby lowers our threshold of tolerance to and acceptance of it.

E.   *Man needs to realize his potentialities and to steer his path through life*

At every stage in evolution, cosmic and biological, there were potentialities for development of which only a few were actualized, as a result of the sifting of the effects of 'chance'

---

[79] T. Chalmers, 'The Power, Wisdom and Goodness of God, as manifested in the Adaptation of external nature to the moral and intellectual constitution of man', 1st Bridgewater Treatise, vol. III, 3rd edn. (William Pickering, London, 1834), p. 308.

occurrences within a milieu which is controlled by 'law'. The entities which had these developmental possibilities had no choice in the matter. But increasingly with the emergence of consciousness in animals[80] the self-directed behaviour of the organism plays a part in determining what possibilities can be selected. Man is an organism whose choices affect his environment, and so his own evolution, and who is increasingly aware, through his intellectual inquiries, of the potentialities of the future. Man has always been aware of the potentialities for achievement and fulfilment of his individual life and only too well aware of his inability to attain to his highest aspirations. This is a commonplace of all tragic literature—and also the underlying theme of comedy.

Increasingly he has become aware of his social inadequacies; always he seeks to bring in a better order in society only to find unexpected inadequacies in the new making him regretfully think the old was better. This awareness of social inadequacy is now intensified by our knowledge of the power we have acquired over the natural world and its future. So, again, our scientific knowledge renders more acute our need to have guide-lines for the direction we should take, to have principles on which to base decisions. We are tragically aware, as all men have been, of our failure to become what we might be and what we ought to be—and today we realize more acutely than ever how much higher the stakes are through our enhanced power. Man is to himself an unfulfilled paradox. We ask as urgently as ever 'What should men be striving to become?', that is, 'What is man for?' and yet the resources of the sciences do not seem to be adequate in themselves for helping man to steer their way between birth and death, through the limitations which circumscribe their projected activities.[81]

This exercise in discerning the needs of man when we ask 'What do men live by?' could be extended indefinitely—each one of us has his own insights and priorities. No doubt the Marxist would emphasize the need for man to break down alienation and the existentialist his quest for authentic existence.

[80] See above, p. 168.
[81] Cf. J. Bowker, *The Sense of God* (Clarendon Press, Oxford, 1973).

But the point is the same—it is that what men live by, what they most need, can only be provided at personal and social levels on which the sciences, as such, can cast little light. What the sciences *do* do, in unveiling the manner and method of evolution and in analysing man at various levels, is to sharpen and make more urgent the questions that man raises about himself. They have this effect both by revealing new aspects of man's complex nature and, through the applied sciences, by intensifying the effects man produces on himself and on his environment (and thereby, reflexively, on himself). What he chooses depends on what he thinks is worth maintaining or innovating. 'Man does not have absolute, certain control of his evolution, but he cannot avoid deliberate, rational intervention in that evolution.'[82] Man is unique among living organisms in having the ability to choose the direction in which society should develop and what kind of life man should have—and thereby also to determine the environment of other living organisms. But it is at this very point that man is an enigma to himself—never better expressed than by St. Paul when, in a famous outburst, he expresses the moral ambiguities of even the most God-directed lives.

I discover this principle, then: that when I want to do the right, only the wrong is within my reach. In my inmost self I delight in the law of God, but I perceive that there is in my bodily members a different law, fighting against the law that my reason approves and making me a prisoner under the law that is my members, the law of sin. Miserable creature that I am, who is there to rescue me out of this body doomed to death?[83]

He expressed, perhaps better than he realized, the apparent paradox that man as we know him has evolved through the creative acts of God. So, to conclude this lecture, even if it is to anticipate somewhat, we must experience again the stress of this tension and adumbrate how it might be resolved.

---

[82] A. W. Ravin, 'On Natural and Human Selection; or Saving Religion', *Zygon*, 12 (1977), 27–41.

[83] Romans 7: 21–4 (NEB).

VI. THE TENSION BETWEEN BELIEF IN GOD AS CREATOR AND APPRAISAL OF THE EVOLVED NATURE OF MAN

With man's arrival, there appears an apparently irresolvable tension between, on the one hand, man's freedom in his own self-determination, to work against, as well as with, God's action immanent in his creative processes and, on the other hand, God's overall and ultimately transcendent and not-to-be-set-aside intentions in creation. It is, to use the musical analogy which I used earlier for God's creative activity,[84] as if the great cosmic fugue which the Creator is writing has now moved to a distant key, vastly remote from its original, to which there now seems little hope of a successful return, and that the harmony has become so entangled and discordant that it appears incapable of resolution. How can God's general purposes for his creation, and, in particular, for man, the self-determining person and paradox whom he has elicited within it, be consummated and yet not belie, or be self-contradictory of, the laws of the immanent creative processes which *are* themselves God's own mode of action in the world? It is at this point that we have to step back, as it were, from the strongly immanentist viewpoint that is engendered by our emphasis on God's action in the natural world to remind ourselves that God *is* Creator, that the initiative for creation came from him and that he transcends all. We must let God be God, for it is only by a movement from God towards, and also within, his creation that the tension and paradox we have been all along concerned with may be resolved. Only if God as Creator makes an explicit move towards man would it seem now that man could become what God intended. This move, whatever form it takes, must be within the very fabric of the created order itself, indeed within *man* the paradox himself, if God is to be the Creator God whose intentions are not, in the end, to be frustrated.

We are now concerned not with an intellectual problem in abstract theologizing or philosophizing; it is the dilemma and anguish of the tragic that lurks in all human lives as a consequence of the frustration of those deep-seated needs we have discerned—the seemingly unbridgeable gap between what we are and what we would be. Is indeed the whole splendid cosmic, biological, and human development to fizzle out, is it after all, now, in man, 'played out'—to end 'not with a bang but a whimper'?   'Up to the present', we do indeed know, with Paul, only too well, 'the whole created universe groans in all its part as if in the pangs of childbirth.' Paul goes on to affirm[85] that, while recognizing that we are still 'groaning inwardly', yet there is indeed hope that we may be made whole, and become so much in accord with what God intends for human nature that we can be called God's 'sons'. How could Paul possibly have such confidence? How can we? The only possible grounds would be if we had reasons to believe that there had indeed been an explicit movement from God towards man to resolve the tensions and paradoxes of man's existence—and thereby to make it at least possible for man to attain the glory God intended for him. Our reasons for thinking that God has so stretched out towards man will be the concern of the next lecture (VI). That it *might* be so (and we shall have to see) rests on our apprehension that the world only becomes intelligible to our minds and meaningful in our experience when it is seen as the realm of the immanent creative agency of the One 'in whom we live and move and have our being', who suffers in it, with it and for it and thereby can bring out of it new, hazardous, and unimaginable possibilities.

---

[85] Romans 8: 22 ff. (N.E.B.)

VI

Evolved Man and God Incarnate

I. THE RELEVANCE OF THEOLOGY TO ANY VIEW OF MAN

So far we have been examining how various features of the scientific landscape modify and enlarge, or should do so, the way we may conceive of God's relation to the world, that is, the doctrine of creation. In the last lecture, in examining the scientific analyses of man at various levels, we stressed the non-reducible level of the human person who has a history which succeeds, indeed supersedes, biological evolution. Man is evolved out of and in the physical stuff of the universe and, although biologically adapted and one of the most (if not *the* most) successful of species, to judge by his proliferation, nevertheless in his personal being he searches to fill the gap between reality and his unfulfilled aspirations. He seeks that by which to live—that which, going beyond the satisfaction of his purely biological needs, will enable him to come to terms with his awareness of death and with his finitude; to bear suffering; to realize his own potentialities and to steer his path through life. We saw that there seemed to be little hope of satisfying, from within scientific discourse and knowledge, those needs that are discerned on asking what men live by and that they are, if anything, sharpened rather than satisfied by the enlargement of man's consciousness by the world of science.

Moreover, we now have to recognize that this paradox which is man is that part of the natural world which consciously asks about and attempts to move towards, or away from, God. Our assessment of man and of the relation of God to the world, i.e. of the doctrine of creation, mutually interact and modify each other. In this lecture we shall have to reconsider the doctrine of creation in the light of the emergence of man and then the specifically Christian claim that through what a particular person in history himself did and was, man's possibilities and his relation to God have, potentially at least, undergone a transformation which is to be understood in the context of the relation of God to the world which we have been developing.

But first we inquire how man might appear when he is assessed from a viewpoint other than that of science, namely from the theological perspective of a doctrine of creation which regards him as having been brought into existence by the immanent activity of a transcendent and supra-personal Reality to whom purposes might reasonably be attributed. To some this may appear to be simply a typically obscurantist ploy on behalf of religion in what has hitherto been (I trust) a reasonably objective account of the state of the science of man and of man's needs. But religious assessments of man have had a profound influence on the course, and indeed the possibility, of human civilization, as we shall have cause to recall again.[1] So, if for no other reason, we must examine some understandings of man which have been propounded from within the theological perspective, both ancient and modern, that is most familiar and communicable to us, namely, the Judeo-Christian.

II.   THEOLOGICAL APPRAISALS OF MAN

A.   The biblical view

Man's nature, predicament and hope have always been, it need hardly be said, central in the articulation of the Judeo-Christian experience of God's action towards him.[2] Out of the rich kaleidoscope of this experience and its intellectual formulation, I can pick only a few pieces here and there which refract light of such colour and direction that they may illuminate those facets of the nature and needs of evolved man upon which we have already focused. These few are selected primarily to illustrate the relevance of this tradition and its contemporary

---

[1] Lecture VII.

[2] For excellent and succinct surveys of the understanding of 'Man: His Nature, Predicament and Hope' in the Old and New Testaments see the articles under this title, by J. A. Baker and J. L. Houlden, respectively, in *Man: Fallen and Free*, ed. E. W. Kemp (Hodder & Stoughton, London, 1969), Chs. 5, 6.

developments to man's problem of survival, of what men must
live by.

(*i*) *Man: a psychosomatic unity and in the 'image of God'*. The per-
ceptiveness and realism of the biblical literature can be quite
refreshing when its, sometimes scattered, allusions are system-
atically assembled. For example, it tacitly assumes, rather than
stating explicitly, that man is a psychosomatic personal unity.[3]
It does not take a Hellenistic dichotomous, or trichotomous,
view of man—not even St. Paul whose use of Greek words about
man has to be tied back to Hebraic usage.[4] This biblical view
of man, summarized in Eichrodt's 'Man does not *have* a body
and a soul, he *is* both of them at once'[5] is more consistent with
the understanding of man which these lectures have been
developing, from the perspective of the sciences, than the
dichotomous view that many Christians have later adopted,
under the influence of essentially Greek concepts of man as a
mortal body, temporarily united to an immortal 'soul'. In the
Bible, it should be noted, man is created from 'the dust of the
ground', according to the older of the two accounts in Genesis[6],
but nevertheless, according to the later one, he is *also* created
'in the image of God'. In what respect he is created in God's
'image' has been much debated,[7] and we shall later[8] describe
the assessments of Westermann[9] and Barr[10] of the meaning of
this term in relation to the concept of the 'dominion' over
nature apparently attributed to man in Genesis 1. For the
moment, the judgement of W. Eichrodt may be quoted as
in accord with these assessments: '[On man] personhood is

[3] For references, see A. R. Peacocke, *Science and the Christian Experiment* (Oxford
University Press, London, 1971), pp. 148 ff.; see also Lecture IV, above.
[4] Peacocke, op. cit., pp. 151 ff.
[5] W. Eichrodt, *Theology of the Old Testament*, trans. J. A. Baker (SCM Press,
London, 1967), Vol. 2, p. 124.
[6] Genesis 2: 6.
[7] e.g. D. Cairns, *The Image of God in Man* (SCM Press, London, 1953); V. Lossky,
'The Theology of the Image', in *In the Image and Likeness of God*, trans. A. M. Allchin
(Mowbrays, London & Oxford, 1974), pp. 125 ff.; C. F. D. Moule, *Man and Nature
in the New Testament* (University of London, Athlone Press, 1964; Facet Books, Fortress
Press, Philadelphia, 1967); J. Y. Campbell, 'Image', in *A Theological Word Book of the
Bible*, ed. A. Richardson (SCM Press, London, 1957); and references therein.
[8] Lecture VII: §IV B (i) (d), pp. 283 ff.
[9] C. Westermann, *Creation*, trans. J. J. Scullion (SPCK, London, 1971), pp. 55 ff.
[10] J. Barr, 'The Image of God in the Book of Genesis—A Study of Terminology',
Bull. J. Rylands Lib., 51 (1968–9), 11–26.

bestowed as the definitive characteristic of his nature. He has a share in the personhood of God; and as a being capable of self-awareness and self-determination he is open to the divine address and capable of responsible conduct.'[11]

In the New Testament the image of God in man is regarded by St. Paul as having been defaced, or at least as being incomplete, for he claims that Christians are those who 'have discarded the old nature with its deeds and have put on the new nature, which is constantly being renewed in the image of its Creator and brought to know God.'[12] Elsewhere, he describes man as the 'image of God and the mirror of his glory'[13] (even though, in the context, he is making distinctions between man and woman). This Pauline link, between restoration of the image of God in man and man's glory as coming to know God, is undoubtedly echoed centuries later in the Westminster Catechisms of 1647 where the question 'What is the chief (and highest) end of man?' receives the pungent reply 'Man's chief (and highest) end is to glorifie God and (fully) to enjoy Him for ever.'[14]

(*ii*) *The 'Fall' of man.*   Such image as man is of God is clearly a distorted one and for centuries the Genesis stories were taken literally as giving a historical account of what came to be known as the 'Fall' of the two supposed individual ancestors of the human race, and this 'Fall' was regarded as constituting the cause and source of all men's 'original sin', which was often (e.g. by Augustine) regarded as being transmitted to succeeding generations in a quasi-hereditary manner of an almost biological kind (no doubt Dawkins would call it a sin-gene or even a sin-meme). Such an interpretation did not take account of the mythical character of the biblical literature ('Adam', of course, means simply 'man', individually and collectively) and appeared to be based on the doubtful proposition that all mankind has originated from one pair of individuals. This latter is a proposition to which it is hard to attribute any real meaning in the light of the complex interplay of genetic con-

[11] Eichrodt, op. cit., Vol. 2, p. 126.
[12] Col. 3: 9, 10 (NEB).
[13] 1 Cor. 1: 7 (NEB).
[14] The bracketed words occur in the 'Longer' as distinct from the 'Shorter' Catechism.

stitution and environment over a long period of time that characterize the early stages of the emergence of all species, and for which there is little concrete evidence in view of the diversity of human origins. This view was insensitive to the character of myth and shallow with respect to its analysis of human experience. As Alan Richardson put it:

The doctrine of Original Sin is not so much an *a priori* theory as an empirical description of human nature; we all of us tend at every moment to put ourselves in the place of God by setting ourselves in the centre of the universe.... The time element in the myths of Creation and Fall (as in all the biblical myths) must be discounted; it is not that *once* (in 4004 BC—or a hundred thousand years ago) God created man perfect and then he fell from grace. God is eternally Creator; he is eternally making man and holding him in being and seeing that his handiwork is good (Gen.1.31). And just as creation is an eternal activity, so the 'Fall' is an ingredient of every moment of human life; man is at every moment 'falling', putting himself in the centre, rebelling against the will of God. Adam is Everyman.[15]

So interpreted this ancient myth becomes for us a shrewd analysis of man's state as the possessor of a self-consciousness, which by enabling him to be a 'subject' over against the 'objects' of nature, *ipso facto* renders him out of harmony with nature, with his fellow man and with himself—thereby thwarting the divine purposes. Yet, in spite of the wisdom of biblical scholars distilled in the above quotations, Christian theology is still deeply tinctured with the assumption of an 'original righteousness' which man lost at a point in time, of an original innocent state, from which man 'fell', and which it was the role of God in Jesus the Christ to 'restore'. Such ways of thinking are no longer plausible in the light of what we now know about man's evolution, and indeed, to be more accurate, one should note that it is *Western* theology which is so coloured:

For Eastern anthropology and cosmology, nature has kept something of its initial norm. The Fall has not touched the image of God in man; it has only reduced it to ontological silence by destroying the likeness, the actualisation of the image. St. Antony ... declares that 'our nature

---

[15] A. Richardson, on 'Adam, Man', in *A Theological Word Book of the Bible*, ed. A. Richardson (SCM Press, London, 1957), p. 14.

is essentially good' and, according to St. John of Damascus, asceticism re-establishes the balance which is 'the return of what is contrary to nature towards what is proper to it.'[16]

What geology, palaeontology, biology, and anthropology show man to be is, on the contrary, a creature who has emerged into a self-consciousness which has enhanced his adaptational flexibility and power over his environment, and so his biological survival ability. The religious and moral experience of mankind, on which theological interpretation rests, is that this evolved self-consciousness, by its very character as *self*-consciousness, has made man paradoxically aware of what he might become—and of his failure to fulfil his potentialities and to satisfy his finest aspirations. Moreover this characteristic of the *individual*, as a succession of Christian thinkers from Schleiermacher to Tillich has elaborated, is activated by and perpetuates itself by a transmission, within the *culture* into which individuals are born, of a social bias that thwarts the divine purposes. Thus 'sin' is not only individual but also cultural and corporate and, in this sense, is 'original', i.e. consequent upon origins. These modern interpretations of the 'Fall' and of 'original sin' seem to me to be highly persuasive both in their realistic account of actual human experience and in their consistency with man's evolutionary history.

B.   Man's sin

(*i*) *As a 'falling short'*.   In the perspective of evolution, then, man's 'sin' is not only a 'falling short' (itself a biblical phrase) from his aspirations for himself and for his societies, but it is, more profoundly and comprehensively in the light of a doctrine of creation, a perennial failure to become what God intends him to be. This is the 'original sin' which is so monotonously repeated in all of us that it might less inaccurately be better described as our very unoriginal sin. Man's failure to become what God intends him to be is freely willed and stems from the setting of himself at the centre of his individual and social life, and this constitutes his 'sin' ('... you will be like gods

---

[16] P. Evdokimov, 'Nature', *Scottish J. Theol.*, 18, No. 1 (1965) p. 11.

knowing both good and evil', said the Tempter).[17] As soon as a creature, man, became self-conscious and able to choose—and there must have been a real period of time, however imprecise, during which this transition occurred[18]—then it became possible for action and events to occur in the universe contrary to God's creative purpose. For men are able to act in a way contrary to what they discern, however obscurely, of God's creative purpose for them. Thus 'sin' became possible and, indeed actual, *pari passu* with the emergence of man's self-awareness.[19] So man alone of all creatures has, through the freedom of action his self-awareness allows him, the power not to choose what God intends for him.

(*ii*) *As a failure to realize potentiality.* Not to choose what God intends is, for man, a failure to realize potentiality,[20] to attain the divine image. This has, for some time, seemed to me to be the only way in which the shrewd biblical diagnosis of the nature of man and his actions can be understood and be brought to bear upon man viewed, as he must be, as the latest and, in many senses, the highest product of evolution[21]—indeed the potentiality of man, not yet fully realized, seems to me to be accurately identifiable with what traditional theology long called 'original righteousness' supposedly lost at a past historical 'Fall'. Recognition of the mythical character of the biblical story and its reinterpretation in existential terms directed to present experience and future hope recovers, for our times, the profundity of the biblical analysis of man's predicament. It was encouraging, therefore, to find a similar view propounded by Jürgen Moltmann:

... it follows ... that man was created with open potentialities. He is destined, certainly, for justice and not for sin, for glory and not

[17] Genesis 2: 5.

[18] To this extent and to this extent only, may the 'Fall' be associated with a presumed period of historical time.

[19] P. J. Tillich speaks of the Fall as a 'symbol for the human situation universally' and not as the story of an event that happened 'once upon a time' (*Systematic Theology*, Vol. 2 (Nisbet, London, 1957), p. 33).

[20] What these potentialities are we may rightly inquire, but at this point we postpone this question. 'Adam before the Fall' and 'nature before the curse', Tillich (op. cit., p. 46) describes as 'states of potentiality'.

[21] A. R. Peacocke, op. cit. (p. 189 n. 3 above), and 'The nature and purpose of man in science and Christian theology', *Zygon*, 8 (1973), 373–94.

for death. He can, however, fail to achieve his appointed destiny. Such failure cannot be described, in ontological terms, as 'the impossible possibility' (Barth) but is better described, in ethical terms, as a potentiality which may not be realised.[22]

C. Man: in tension between self-centredness and openness

The emphasis of Wolfhart Pannenberg[23] on human life as being carried on in 'the tension between self-centeredness and openness to the world'[24] leads him to a similar position as regards man's failure to attain his 'destiny', *Bestimmung*. This word, *Bestimmung*, also has the sense of 'definition' and Pannenberg uses it to refer to man's destiny which defines or gives content to what man is as man—it expresses what God intends man to be, which is accomplished only through the course of history.[25] He expresses his understanding of man thus:

Since on his own man cannot live in God's truth, he provisionally remains caught in the conflict between openness to the world and selfhood. Man remains imprisoned in his selfhood. He secures himself through what has been attained, or he insists on his plans. In any case, to the extent that he is able, he fits what is new into what was already in his mind. In this way not only does he readily damage his destiny to be open to the world; he also closes himself off from the God who summons him to his destiny. The selfhood that is closed up within itself is sin.... Self-love prevents us from turning to other men for their own sake, and, not least, it hinders us in loving God for his own sake.... Where man does not live by trust in God, anxiety appears, namely, anxiety about himself.... It is through anxiety that the sinner remains related to his infinite destiny. In despair, however, man separates himself from his destiny, whether it be that he gives up hope for it or, on the contrary, that he wants to achieve it on his own and only wants to be indebted to himself. Both anxiety and despair reveal the emptiness of the ego that revolves about itself.... In and of itself, selfhood is not sin, any more than control over the world—with which the ego asserts itself and prevails—is sin; God has commissioned men to such control. To that extent, man's selfhood also belongs to God's good creation; however, it is sin insofar as it

---

[22] J. Moltmann, 'Creation and Redemption', in *Creation, Christ and Culture*, ed. R. W. A. McKinney (T. & T. Clark, Edinburgh, 1976), p. 125.

[23] W. Pannenberg, *What is Man?*, trans. D. A. Priebe (Fortress Press, Philadelphia, 1970).

[24] Pannenberg, op. cit., p. 56.

[25] Pannenberg, op. cit., Preface, p. vii.

falls into conflict with man's infinite destiny. This happens when the ego adheres to itself instead of letting itself be inserted into a higher unity of life.[26]

D. Man: the unfulfilled paradox

Elsewhere we have had reason to emphasize the openness of the creative process, the almost sheer spontaneity of its fecundity and inventiveness: both Moltmann and Pannenberg also stress this in relation to man's own freedom and creativity by virtue of which he might unite with God's creative activity. Man's self-centredness continually makes him close up on himself, and so close himself off from his own potentialities which are attainable only if he is open to that which transcends both himself and the world, the two spheres which fill his consciousness. That which so transcends is the divine Creator, the Eternal, and it is with and in that that man's destiny is attained. It is towards this 'God' who transcends the world and stands over against him that man's perennial restlessness is directed (so Pannenberg). This understanding of man as an 'unfulfilled paradox',[27] as having potentiality always falling short of his divinely intended actualization, also accords with the way in which V. Lossky has developed his understanding of man in the context of his treatment of man as the image of God. Lossky wants to support, he says,

a dynamic concept of human nature, rich in possibilities, poised ... between likeness [to God] and possible unlikeness; this would presuppose ... another conception of the image, closely linked with the condition of personhood—and which would extend to the whole human make-up.... Man created 'in the image' is the person capable of manifesting God to the extent to which his nature allows itself to be penetrated by deifying grace.[28]

These penetrating theological analyses of man's nature and destiny cannot now be expounded more fully, but I hope enough has been said to show that current theological inquiry is, in these quarters at least, extraordinarily relevant to those questions about man which were provoked by our looking at his evolutionary history.

[26] Pannenberg, op. cit., pp. 63–5.
[27] Peacocke, op. cit. (p. 189 n. 3 above), Ch. 6.
[28] Lossky, op. cit. (p. 189 n. 7 above), p. 139.

In giving this brief indication of some recent theological diagnoses I have perhaps too glibly implied a potential destiny for man which is related to the intention of the Creator for him. We are thus led to ask what these intentions might be in the light of what we have been able so far to discern of God's relation to the world. Even a superficial glance at the history of the twentieth century, with its extraordinary peaks of human achievement and abysses of human crime, degradation, and folly lead to no optimistic assessment of man or his future. If God *is*, indeed, doing a great work in creation, man, at least, is clearly not yet what he intended. But since our assessment of man, together with the processes through the operation of which he has emerged, and our understanding of God's relation to the world interact mutually and dialectically, we need to clarify this latter before reconsidering the former.

III. THE DOCTRINE OF CREATION IN THE LIGHT OF THE EMERGENCE OF MAN

So we ask, how does the foregoing account of the nature of man and of the processes leading to his emergence affect our models of Creation, the concept that all that is comes into being as an expression of the purpose and as a result of the action of a transcendent, yet immanent, Creator God? We recall that this concept was formulated to render the fact of existence intelligible and that the models appropriate for God's creative action have (in these lectures) been devised and elaborated (or so I have intended) in the light of what the sciences have shown is in the world and how it has come to be there. So, now, as we reflect on the nature both of man and of the processes leading to his emergence, we are bound to ask that any conclusions we draw from such reflection be coherent with the intelligibility which, I have claimed, is provided by the affirmation of the world as created, that is, of God as Creator. Can this putative intelligibility survive scrutiny under the light of the known nature of man and of the processes leading to his arrival in the world? Earlier,[29] I argued that the questions evoked by matter being able to evolve into persons were given answers of greater intelligibility in terms of a doctrine of creation

[29] Lectures I, II.

than otherwise. But this intelligibility is in danger of collapsing in view of the enigmatic and paradoxical nature of man, the person who has been so evolved. To put it more directly, what does God think he is up to in evolving man, this 'glory, jest and riddle of the world'[30] with his enormous potentiality both for creative good and for degradation and evil, destructive both to himself and the rest of the created world? What are God's purposes, what is the meaning he is expressing in creating man?

What has happened in biological evolution is that matter has, through the consequences of the interplay of random micro-events and law-like necessities, become more and more elaborated as complex self-reproducing systems capable of receiving information from their environment and of reacting upon that environment, that is, capable of consciousness. In man that 'environment' which is so sensed includes man's own consciousness itself: he is *self*-conscious. The sequence from the inanimate to the conscious, and then to the self-conscious is concomitant with an increasing independence of and freedom over against the environment. This independence and freedom in man attains the critical point where it can attempt an independence of, and freedom from, the intentions of the Creator—and this independence and freedom are an inevitable consequence of that very self-consciousness which has emerged through the evolutionary processes, with no break in the operation of natural 'laws', in God's regular way of making effectual his creative intentions. We must conclude that God intended that out of matter persons should evolve who had this freedom, and thereby allowed the possibility that they might challenge his purposes and depart from his intentions. To be consistent, we must go on to assume that God had some overarching intention which made this risk worth taking, that there was and is some fundamental way of God being God which allows God's relationship with freely responding persons to be valued by God over that with other forms of matter, which have no option but to be what they are created to be in their relation to God. This is not meant to be at all dismissive of the significance of the non-human creation. For at every level

[30] A. Pope, *An Essay on Man*, Epistle ii, 1.28.

in the operation of the creative process, something is reflected in its own measure of the divine purpose. As Charles Raven put it, 'from atom and molecule to mammal and man each by its appropriate order and function expresses the design inherent in it and contributes, so far as it can by failure or success, to the fulfilment of the common purpose.'[31] And in man this ability to express God becomes personal and capable of responding freely *to* God: it is this we must suppose God intended.

In thus purporting to lift the veil of God's intentions, one speaks, with St. Paul, 'as a fool'. But at least such a purpose of God in creating the freely willing unfulfilled paradox which is man is not entirely unintelligible. The basic point is that, since to be free to respond to God, man must be genuinely free also *not* so to respond, it follows that in evolving man through his creative action within the processes of the universe, God was *taking a risk*, the risk that God's own ability to effect his purposes would be frustrated by the actions of another personal existence, namely man. But because we also have to infer that God has higher purposes for man by giving him this hazardous yet potentially creative ability to be free, we have then to conclude that there was a cost to God in his giving man this gift. Yet God did not refrain from giving man the gift of potentiality to become more than he is now through the exercise of his (man's) freedom. Furthermore it does not derogate from the divine nature than man should be other than an automaton. In other words, God in freely creating man was acting with supreme magnanimity on behalf of the good of another existent, namely man, *qua* person. There is always *pathos* in persons creating something which then has independent, if derived, existence and such *pathos* can be properly predicated of God as Creator.

In human life, action by one person in which that person takes risks entirely on behalf of another's ultimate good is regarded as an expression of love. So, if we may be allowed to extrapolate such terms to the more-than-personal being of the Creator, it is meaningful to say that God's acts of creation

[31] C. E. Raven, *Natural Religion and Christian Theology*, Gifford Lectures, 1952, 2nd Series, *Experience and Interpretation* (Cambridge University Press, Cambridge, 1953), Vol. ii, p. 157.

—the interplay of risky chance and law-like necessity in the creative processes of the cosmos, in relation to which God stands as agent—are an expression of 'love', an outgoing of his inner being on behalf of another, albeit created, person. God the Creator is, then, the One that is the 'love that moves the sun and the other stars' of Dante and he of whom the First Epistle of John[32] says bluntly, 'God is love'. Yet, in thus creating persons, God remains free. Indeed, the depths and boundlessness of God's freedom are supremely manifested in the derived freedom he accords *to* man and in the response God makes to the free response *of* man.

Furthermore, if we take seriously this way of speaking of God's act of creation, as putting God's purpose at risk and so as an act of costly love on behalf of the created, is it not reasonable to go further and to conclude that the creative loving action which operates in the universe, eventually bringing forth man, is not incorrectly described as that of a *suffering* Creator? For love that takes risks on behalf of another who remains free always entails suffering in the human experience of love. Our 'words strain, crack and sometimes break, under the burden'[33] of trying to speak in the least misleading way possible about the divine nature, but we seem bound to talk of God as suffering in the expression of the creative love that elicits man. It is moreover consistent with the processes of creation through evolution themselves being characterized by eliciting new life[34] through suffering, pain, and death (the 'sublime law of sacrifice'). So our 'model' of God as the personal agent of the creative process now has to be amplified to include a recognition of him as the Creator who suffers in, with and through his creation as it brings into existence new and hazardous possibilities—most of all those implicit in the creation of man, the self-determining person. Creation is thus seen as a self-emptying by God, a risk which he incurs lovingly and willingly for the opportunity of the greater good of freely responsive man coming to be within the created world. Love and self-sacrifice are, from this perspective, seen as inherent to the divine nature. Perhaps this is what the author of the

[32] 1 John 4: 9, 16.
[33] T. S. Eliot, *Burnt Norton*.
[34] pp. 164–167.

Revelation is hinting at when he did not shrink from describing Christ, whom he saw as now present within God, as 'the Lamb slain *from the foundation of the world*'.[35]

In recent times, there has been a recovery of this sense of God as suffering as Creator in and with the creation and a rejection of the concept of God as distant, transcendent, and entirely impassible. This rejection, together with a positive sense of God as a suffering Creator, was a characteristic of A. N. Whitehead's philosophy ('God is the great companion—the fellow-sufferer who understands'[36]) and C. Hartshorne, who has been very influential in this regard in American theology, also strongly argued for the passibility of God.[37] Both these writers have been major formative agents in the rise of process theology and we find writers of this school on both sides of the Atlantic with this same emphasis on God as suffering in creation.[38] Process theology has developed as a result of taking seriously the dynamic evolutionary character of the processes through which the world has come, and continues to come, into being. This stress is entirely consonant with the approach of these lectures which, however, try not to tie themselves to any particular metaphysical system, in the way that process theology depends on that of Whitehead.

Any serious consideration of the creative action of God as dynamic and evolutionary is inexorably led to face the fact of death, pain, and suffering in that process and so come to an understanding of God as the suffering Creator. This movement of thought has occurred principally in the USA and in Britain (going back to Charles Raven and, indeed, to J. R. Illingworth, one of the contributors to *Lux Mundi*[39] of 1889),

[35] Revelation 13: 8 (AV); cf. the discussion in Peacocke, op. cit. (p. 189 n. 3 above), pp. 135 ff.

[36] A. N. Whitehead, *Process and Reality* (Cambridge University Press, Cambridge, 1929), p. 497.

[37] C. Hartshorne, *The Divine Relativity* (Yale University Press, New Haven, 1948).

[38] See, e.g., *Process Theology*, by J. B. Cobb and D. R. Griffin (Christian Journals Ltd., Belfast, 1977) for a useful account and a guide to the literature; P. N. Hamilton, *The Living God and the Modern World* (Hodder & Stoughton, London, 1967); N. Pittenger, *God in Process* (SCM Press, London, 1967)—an appendix provides a useful account of process thought up to 1967; and N. Pittenger, *Process Thought and Christian Faith* (Nisbet, Welwyn, 1968).

[39] J. R. Illingworth, 'The Incarnation and Development', in *Lux Mundi*, ed. C. Gore (John Murray, London, 12th edn., 1891), pp. 132–57.

where the encounter of theology with evolutionary ideas and 'natural theology' has had a long history. It was, of course, reinforced by the publication in the 1950s and 1960s, long after they were written, of the works of the Frenchman Teilhard de Chardin. More recently, and with characteristic depth, German theology has also moved in this direction: I refer particularly to the profound work of Jürgen Moltmann.[40] We shall have cause to advert to some of his major themes again but, in the present context, it is fascinating to see him making similar affirmations to the process theologians about the suffering Creator, but on the basis of a full acceptance of orthodox Christian beliefs, of Jesus Christ as God Incarnate and of God as a Trinity in Unity, and by pursuing the far-reaching implications of Jesus' death and cry of dereliction on the cross. Moltmann, starting from very different presuppositions and with a quite different theological method, arrives at the concept of the suffering Creator which has been developed as a response to the nature of the evolutionary process by process theologians, and also, in their own way, in these lectures. Moltmann also notes a similar development within Judaism in A. Heschel's description of the Israelite prophets' proclamation of God as 'pathetic theology'—that is, the history of the divine *pathos*, suffering, is embedded in the history of his people—God suffers with his people.[41]

I have been speaking, analogically, of suffering *within* God, this suffering being an identification with, and participation in, the suffering of the world. We have already had reason for talking in panentheistic terms of the world being 'within God', and also for using female, as well as male, metaphors for the relation of God and the world. Now the dimension of suffering which we are here incorporating into our understanding of this relation gives an enhanced significance to this 'female' pan-en-theistic model. Moreover it gives a new, and poignant, pertinence to the poetic vision of St. Paul of creation as being in the pangs of childbirth:

For the created universe waits with eager expectation for God's sons

[40] J. Moltmann, *The Crucified God*, trans. R. A. Wilson and J. Bowden (SCM Press, London, 1974).

[41] A. Heschel, *The Prophets* (New York, 1962) as expounded by Moltmann, op. cit., pp. 270 ff.

to be revealed. It was made the victim of frustration, not by its own choice, but because of him who made it so; yet always there was hope, because the universe itself is to be freed from the shackles of mortality and enter upon the liberty and splendour of the children of God. Up to the present, we know, the whole created universe groans in all its parts as if in the pangs of childbirth.[42]

Paul here rightly juxtaposes the paradox of man and the enigma of suffering in creation, for these combine to intensify the questions which we have already posed: of what God was up to in evolving man, with his potentialities for good and evil, of what the meaning of the processes can be whereby man has evolved and of the suffering this entailed, and entails.

Here it is pertinent to recall our earlier stress on the models of the Creator as being supra-*personal*, for it is of the essence of persons to communicate their meanings from the self outwards. G. D. Kaufman has pointed out[43] how this provides us with a model of transcendence which affords intelligibility for talk of the transcendence of God. He reminds us that knowledge of other persons derives from their acts of revealing and unveiling themselves to us when they communicate with us and so such knowledge is radically different from the knowledge of objects which is obtained from what *we* do to them. Knowledge of persons depends on what *they* do in relation to us; it derives from complex interpersonal processes which involve, but go beyond, the reach and observation of our senses. Interpersonal knowledge depends on the other's acts, on something intrinsically inaccessible to oneself, a reality beyond our reach, known only if the other reveals himself and dispels the mystery about him. Thus it was that, at the end of Lecture IV, when we were developing the concept of God as agent in relation to the world, we voiced the hope, indeed gave grounds for believing, that we might well expect such a Creator to reach out to man to express his meanings explicitly to the one creature that has developed in the cosmos who can read them and elucidate his intentions—in brief, who can listen to the Creator and hear his word. So we might well, with hopeful anticipation, look and hope for an outreach, a communicating expression in act,

[42] Romans 8: 19–23 (NEB).

[43] G. D. Kaufman, 'Two models of transcendence: an inquiry into the problem of theological meaning', in *The Heritage of Christian Thought*, eds. R. F. Cughman and E. Grislis (Harper & Row, New York, Evanston and London, 1965), pp. 182, 196.

or in a series of acts (i.e. in a process), from God to man that would express to man the meaning God is intending in his creative processes. Man needs such an initiating movement, of communication of meaning from God *to* man, within the actual created world and, in particular, within the life of man in order so to resolve the paradoxes of his existence, to relieve its tensions and to fulfil his unachieved potentialities that he might become that which God intends man to be. The 'meaning' of God, the communication of which man needs, is by definition that which God means, i.e. intends, proposes, purposes, within his creation. So this 'meaning' can be discerned only through attending to what God is doing in the world, that is to what goes on in the world—expecting, from our model of God as agent, that some features of the world, some sequences in its processes, some points in man's history may well be more revelatory of meaning than others, just as some acts, gestures, tones of voice are more expressive of our inner selves than are others. So in order to discern any such particularly meaningful aspects of, or episodes in, creation, we must again first remind ourselves of some of the main features of our understanding of God's relation to the world that we have developed so far in these lectures in the light of the natural sciences of the world.

IV. OUR UNDERSTANDING OF GOD'S RELATION TO THE WORLD IN THE LIGHT OF THE KNOWLEDGE AFFORDED BY THE NATURAL SCIENCES

Before we proceed, it is important to be clear about the picture of the world and God's relation to it that we are rejecting because it is inconsistent with both our scientific perspective on the world and with theological insights. This is the picture of the world as a closèd mechanism, operating according to laws and within boundary conditions both prescribed 'at the beginning' and identified with a temporal act of creation by God. Although time is a parameter of such a universe, the model is basically *static* rather than *dynamic*, for it does not allow space–time to be, to use the phrase of H. K. Schilling,[44] the 'locus of innovative change'. The God who is the creator

---

[44] H. K. Schilling, *The New Consciousness in Science and Religion* (SCM Press, London, 1973), p. 126.

of a static world readily becomes, in philosophical reflection if not in religious experience, a deistic clock-maker God, who, having wound up his universe, as it were, leaves it to tick away for all eternity. This model is inconsistent both with the present scientific understanding of the world and with Judeo-Christian experience of and belief in the dynamic 'living God' of their scriptures.

A.   Immanence

From the continuity and creativity (the emergence of the new and non-reducible) of the processes of the natural world we inferred that God's creative relation to the world must be conceived of as a continuous, sustaining creative action within these natural processes, everywhere and all the time. God is in all the creative processes of his creation and they are all equally 'acts of God', for he is everywhere and all the time present and active in them as their agent. They *are* his acts and he cannot be more or less present in some acts rather than in others, for he is not, as it were, a substance diffused through the cosmos more concentrated at one point or time than at another. All this is what we meant by saying that the Creator is *immanent* in his creation, and that is why we look for his 'meanings' (his intentions, proposals, and purposes) *within* the world of which we are part.

B.   Transcendence

The natural processes of the world have led to the emergence within it of living organisms that are conscious and of human beings who possess a self-consciousness which transcends their own bodies and environment sufficiently to seek for meaning and intelligibility and to ask 'the meaning of existence' kind of question. The posing of such questions and experience of man's finitude, and of the limitations of his transcendence, led us to an awareness of the world as dependent and contingent: it is and need not have been at all, or could have been otherwise. The generation within the world of that sense of partial transcendence which is man's served to sharpen the quest for One who transcends all and who made it 'out of nothing', whose existence is underived. Thus we come to postulate God the Creator as *transcendent*. But this talk of transcendence was

always an extrapolation beyond the limits of the characteristic-
ally human transcendence, and we attempted to express this
by describing God as 'supra-personal', which implies both that
the 'meaning' of God's actions in the world are most suitably
expressed in personal, rather than (say) mechanical, categories;
and that in God there is an intensification of the personal
beyond that of any individual human personality we have ever
encountered.

C. God in the world and the world in God

However, the concept of God the Creator as both immanent
and transcendent, analogous though it might be to the human
sense of transcendent self-conscious agency with respect to one's
own body which expresses immanently our conscious intentions, is not entirely satisfactory when applied to One who is
the Creator of that in which he is immanent. I have developed
talk of the transcendent being and immanent activity of God
from within the perspective on the world described by science,
because this seems to me to be where I, and many of us, have
to begin. But the relation of the transcendence to the immanence of God has been a perennial paradox of religious experience and affirmation, frequently resolved by stressing one at
the expense of the other—compare only the broad differences
between Islam and Buddhism. The Judeo-Christian tradition
has always attempted to maintain, however uneasily and in
a variety of ways, the sense of God as *both* transcendent being
and immanent activity. Of outstanding historical importance
are two models which I cannot fail to mention, with absurd
brevity, because of their subsequent significance for the theme
of this lecture.

(*i*) *'Logos'*.   The first is the 'logos' concept, implanted firmly
and deeply within Christian thought by the Prologue to the
Fourth Gospel. In this prologue, the 'logos', the 'Word' about
whom, it is affirmed—'When all things began, the Word
already was. The Word dwelt with God, and what God was, the
Word was. The Word, then, was with God at the beginning,
and through him all things come to be'[45]—is a profoundly
fruitful conflation of at least two concepts. One is the Old

[45] John 1: 1, 2, 3 (NEB).

Testament usage of the 'word of the Lord' for the will of God expressed in utterance, to the prophets ('The word of the Lord came unto ...') and in creative activity.[46] This concept of the 'word of God', it has frequently been demonstrated, has close affinities with the concept in Hellenistic Judaism of the Wisdom (*Sophia*) of God as the hypostatized thought of God projected in creation and remaining as an immanent power within the world and in man. Thus some degree of hypostatization of the 'word of God' also occurred, justifying the capital letter for 'Word' in the English translations of the Prologue to the Fourth Gospel.[47] The other sense attributed to 'logos' is that which arose within Hellenistic Judaism as expressed by Philo. He is usually taken to echo the development within Judaism of Stoic thought, for which the Divine Logos, the principle of rationality, is especially apparent in the human 'logos' or reason. According to C. H. Dodd,

His [Philo's] *logos* is not simply the uttered word or command of God; it is the meaning, plan or purpose of the universe, conceived as transcendent as well as immanent, as the thought of God, formed within the eternal Mind and projected into objectivity ... as Philo puts it, all that man can know of ultimate Deity is ... the fact that He is; beyond that, we know Him only in His *logos*, His thought which is the principle of reality in the universe. This thought however is not merely a meaning or plan visible in the universe; it is also the creative power by which the universe came into being and is sustained.[48]

Scholars differ concerning the weight given to these two backgrounds in the mind of the author of the Fourth Gospel, but clearly both would be involved in the response of many of his readers, no doubt to varying degrees.

(*ii*) *God as 'Spirit'*.   The second significant 'model', in the Judeo-Christian tradition, which strives to hold together God's immanence and transcendence, is that of God as Spirit. There is no need for me now to elaborate this model since it was the

---

[46] Genesis 1: 3, 6, 9, 14, 20, 24—the 'six words of creation': 'God said, Let there be ... and there was'; and also 'The Lord's word made the heavens ... For he spoke, and it was' of Psalm 33: 6, 9 (NEB).

[47] See C. H. Dodd, *The Interpretation of the Fouth Gospel* (Cambridge University Press, Cambridge, 1953), Ch. 12.

[48] Dodd, op. cit., p. 277.

subject of the distinguished Bampton Lectures which preceded the present series.[49] Professor Lampe argued that '"the Spirit of God" is to be understood, not as referring to a divine hypostasis distinct from God the Father and God the Son or Word, but as indicating God himself as active towards and in his human creation. We are speaking of God disclosed and experienced as Spirit: that is, in his personal outreach,'[50] and that 'in scriptural usage, especially in the Wisdom literature, "Spirit" denotes an immanent divine presence, in the cosmos and in man, which is at the same time not other than transcendent deity.'[51] Elsewhere he put it thus: 'God's Spirit, being God, is transcendent and free, "blowing", like the wind, "where it wills", but it does not enter into man as if it were an alien invader ... By "the Holy Spirit" we should not mean an intermediary divine agent, or even a third "Person", but God himself considered in respect of his outreach and immanence.'[52]

(*iii*) *The world within God (pan-en-theism).* However, it may well be thought that these two 'models' which attempt to hold together God's transcendence and immanence need supplementing today in the light of the kind of basis for affirming transcendence and immanence which we have found in reflecting on the world today in the perspective of our present scientific knowledge of its origins, processes and content.[53] It was in this context that we earlier[54] referred to the model of 'pan-en-theism' whereby the world is regarded as being, as it were, 'within' God, but the being of God is regarded as not exhausted by, or subsumed within, the world. It was then that feminine images of God as Creator were useful as a corrective to purely masculine images with their stress on God as creating 'externally' to himself a world from which he might then be too readily deemed as absent (the tendency of deism).

---

[49] G. W. H. Lampe, *God as Spirit* (Oxford University Press, Oxford, 1977)—see especially Ch. VIII for a discussion of the transcendence–immanence relation.

[50] Lampe, op. cit., p. 11.

[51] Lampe, op. cit., p. 133.

[52] G. W. H. Lampe, 'The Essence of Christianity—IV', in *Expository Times*, 87 (1976), 135.

[53] §§IV, A and B above, pp. 204, 205.

[54] p. 141.

*D.   The God who unveils his meaning in the various and distinctive
levels of nature's hierarchies*

Evolved man seeks meaning and intelligibility in the world,
that is, from the viewpoint of the doctrine of creation, he seeks
to discern the meanings expressed by God in his creation. These
are meanings which, alone among created organisms, man has
evolved to be capable, not only of consciously discerning, but
also of freely appropriating to give meaning to his life—or of
freely rejecting. Although, as we said earlier, God is not more
present at one time or place than at others (he is not a substance)—all is of God at all times—nevertheless man finds that
in some sequences of events in created nature and history God
unveils his meaning more than in others. God is equally and
totally present to all times and places but man's awareness
of that presence is uniform neither in intensity nor in content.
God may well communicate meaning which is neither comprehended nor apprehended. So, though in one sense, God as
Creator acts in all events, yet not all events are received as
'acts of God'. There are meanings of God to be unveiled but
not all are read: some events will be more revealing than others.

Everywhere, in all the heavens you will find his footprints,
all regions are filled with his mysterious letters,
all heights and depths with his handwriting that only he can decipher.
All powerful-one, why do you not teach us to read your book?
Why do you not move your finger along the letters
and teach us to piece them together and understand like children?
But no, that you do not do. You are no schoolmaster,
You let things be as they are, incomprehensible as they are.
Then, one day in the evening of time, will you delete them all again,
let everything become darkness, as it was before you arose from your
                                                            thoughts
and wandered off to set them down while on your way with the
                                        burning coal in your hand?[55]

In this notion of varied degrees of unveiling of the meaning
God has written in his creation, we are simply elaborating
further the analogy between God-and-the world and human
agency. Our bodies are a causal nexus of law-like events and

----

[55] *Evening Land* (Aftonland) by Pär Lagerkvist, trans. W. H. Auden and Leif Sjöberg
(Conder Book, Souvenir Press, London, 1977), p. 103.

we are agents of all their activities—yet some of our actions, gestures, responses are more characteristic and revelatory of our distinctive selves than are others. Thus it is not improper to seek for those events and entities, or patterns of them, in the world which reveal God's meaning most coherently and effectively. Some events, that is, in the language of process thought, are more 'important' than others.

In such a survey of the events and entities of the world, we have to recognize the existence of the natural hierarchy (or, rather, hierarchies) of complexity which we examined earlier.[56] The aspect of God's meaning expressed by any one level in these hierarchies is limited to what it alone can itself distinctively express, hence the 'meanings' so unveiled in *its various and distinctive levels* are complementary, though individually incomplete without the others. What is expressed in the different orders of creation and in the pattern of events involving these levels of complexity will not all have the same pertinence to men in their search for meaning and intelligibility. They would be expected to vary in what they communicate to us of God's meaning(s), in their ability to unveil God's purposes, according to the level at which they operate in the natural hierarchies of complexity, levels of which we have distinctive kinds of knowledge.[57]

E. God as 'exploring' and 'composing' through a continuous, open-ended process of emergence

We have found that the processes of the world are *continuous* and that in them there are *emergent* in space–time, through the interplay of chance and law, new organizations of the matter–energy that constitutes the universe. Any new emergent appears in continuity with the old by natural processes, yet such new emergent levels of organization frequently require epistemologically *non-reducible* concepts and language to articulate their distinctiveness. Any new meaning[58] which God is able to express in such new levels of organization is thus not discontinuous with the meanings expressed in that out of which it has emerged. If the new emergent requires new non-reducible con-

---

[56] Lecture IV.
[57] Cf. the quotation above (p. 198) from C. E. Raven.
[58] See §IV D, pp. 208, 209.

cepts and language to describe it, and so to convey any meaning from God, this would have continuity with its predecessors, both in the natural process and in the meaning it conveys, even though it also has a uniqueness of its own. So we anticipate continuity, with new meanings emerging out of the old, subsuming them, perhaps, but not denying them. *Both* continuity *and* emergence are inherent features of the observed world.

The processes of that world are also *open-ended* and so we developed the notion of God as 'exploring' in creation, of actualizing all the potentialities of his creation; of unfolding fugally all the variations and combinations inherently possible for and derivable from the tune he originally called; of bringing forth new modes of existence, requiring epistemologically irreducible and distinctive concepts and languages to describe them.

The 'openness' of the world processes has been particularly stressed recently by J. Moltmann,[59] who employs the concept of an 'open system'[60] developed in modern thermodynamic studies of living systems (which are 'open' to the exchange of *both* matter and energy):

When we pass from atomic structures to more complex systems, we discover a greater openness to time and a growing number of possibilities. With the evolution of complex systems indeterminate behaviour increases in that new possibilities also increase. The human person and human societies are the most complex systems which we know. They exhibit the highest level of indeterminate behaviour as well as the broadest degree of openness to time and the future. Because any actualization of a possibility by open systems itself creates a new openness for possibilities and does not merely actualize a given possibility and, thereby, transfer the future into the past, we cannot conceive of the kingdom of glory (consummating the process of creation with the indwelling of God) as a system that is finally brought to its conclusion and, as such, closed but, on the contrary, as the openness of all finite life systems for the infinity of God. This means, to be sure, that we cannot think of the being of God as the highest

---

[59] Above, p. 194 n. 22.

[60] Moltmann defines the openness of a system to mean: (1) that the system has various potentialities for change; (2) that its future behaviour is not wholly determined by the present; (3) that it is open to communication with other systems; (4) that the final condition of the system is different from that at the beginning. (Moltmann, op. cit., p. 124 n. 2.)

actuality for all realized possibilities but, rather, as the transcendent source for all possibilities.[61]

This last description of God as 'the source for all possibilities' is reminiscent of the postulate of process theology of God as the provider of the 'initial aims' of any 'occasion', which are the units constituting the world in Whitehead's thought:

Whitehead's fundamentally new conception of divine creativity in the world centres around the notion that God provides each worldly actuality with an 'initial aim'. This is an impulse, initially felt conformally by the occasion, to actualize the best possibility open to it, given its concrete situation.... God seeks to persuade each occasion towards that possibility for its own existence which would be best for it...'[62]

In the context of a discussion on creative self-determination ensuing in enjoyment, J. Cobb and D. R. Griffin describe this provision of an 'aim' by God in the following way:

The aim at enjoyment is not simply one among many aspects of an experience. It is the one element in terms of which the entity achieves its unity. This aim is not derived from the past world, for it is unique to the new occasion. The occasion chooses its own 'subjective aim'. Still it does not make this choice in a vacuum. The attractive possibility, the lure, in relation to which its act of self-determination is made, is derived from God. This lure is called the 'initial aim'.[63]

The stress of Moltmann and the process thinkers on 'openness' to the future is also a theme of Wolfhart Pannenberg for whom the concept of 'the ontological priority of the future' is central to his theology and Christology.[64]

F.   The possibility of God conveying meaning through the transcendence-in-immanence of the personal ('incarnation')

The concept of 'openness' suggests an incompleteness and a something-yet-to-be-achieved in the future and this is certainly how we have earlier diagnosed the state of man. Yet the mean-

[61] Moltmann, op. cit., p. 131.
[62] Cobb and Griffin, op. cit., p. 53.
[63] Cobb and Griffin, op. cit., p. 26.
[64] W. Pannenberg, *Jesus—God and Man*, English trans. L. L. Wilkins and D. A. Priebe (SCM Press, London, 1968); and *Theology and the Kingdom of God*, ed. R. J. Neuhaus (Westminster Press, Philadelphia, 1971).

ings of God unveiled to and for man will be even more partial, broken, and incomplete the more the level of creation being examined departs from the human and personal, in which the transcendence of the 'I' is experienced as immanent in our bodies. Thus although God is, in some sense, supra-personal, we may well expect in the personal—that is, in persons, in history, in personal experience, in personal encounter—to find meanings of God unveiled in a way not possibly communicated by the meanings God has written in those non-human, impersonal levels of existence with which we have hitherto been principally concerned.

The level of the personal (with all its uniqueness, new language, non-reducible concepts, new modes of experiencing, etc.) allows expression of a new aspect of God's creative Being (i.e. of the meaning and purpose he is expressing in creation), which has hitherto, at earlier levels, been only incompletely expressed, if at all. The more personal and *self*-conscious is the entity in which God is immanent, the more capable is it of expressing God's supra-*personal* characteristics, the more God can be immanent personally in that entity. Any meaning of God expressed in a higher, personal level would be complementary to the meanings expressed in the lower ones, and would not supersede them but, rather, would incorporate them into a more comprehensive framework, which would inevitably utilize personalistic language.

In man, the processes within creation become aware of themselves and seek their own meaning—that is, the processes (expressing the immanence of the Creator God) acquire a dimension of self-transcendence, that of the 'I', the subjectivity of man over against the objectivity of his own body and its environment. This raises the possibility (and so the hope) that the immanence of God in the world might display, in man at least, a hint of, a first distorted reflection of, the transcendence of God. The transcendence-in-immanence of man's experience raises the hope and conjecture that in man immanence might be able to display a transcendent dimension to a degree which would unveil, without distortion, the transcendent-Creator-who-is-immanent in a uniquely new emergent manner—that is, that *in man* (in a man, or in men), the presence of *God the Creator might be unveiled* with a clarity, in a glory, not hitherto perceived. Man, as we know him is, as we have elaborated, a broken and distorted 'image of God'. But might it not be possible for a man so to reflect God, to be so wholly open to God, that God's presence was clearly unveiled to other men in a new, emergent, and unexpected manner? Would it not then be accurate to say that, in such a person, the immanence of God had displayed a transcendent dimension to such a degree that the presence of God in his actual psychosomatic unity as a person required new non-reducible concepts and language (that of 'incarnation'?) to express a unique transcendence in and through immanence?

G.   The conjecture of God as self-offering and suffering Love active in creation

From a consideration of the character of the natural processes of suffering and death being the means to new life and from a recognition that God's continuously creative actions have evoked free, independent, self-conscious persons from his creation, which limit God's own freedom, we have tentatively recognized[65] that *God suffers with creation and in the creative process.* For this reason I suggested[66] that *love* may justifiably be attributed (with all the reservations such analogies necessitate) as a primary characteristic of the Creator in relation to his creation, for amongst human beings love is basically character-ized by self-limitation and self-denial on behalf of the ultimate good of another. But, in the absence of any other ground for such an assertion, it remains simply an intuition and only a possible insight and a hazardous one at that, in face of the personal and cosmic tragedies which always threaten to over-whelm us and precipitate us into scepticism and despair. Any unveiling of the meaning in his creation which God intends to vouchsafe to man, perhaps by means described in the previous section, would be inadequate and misleadingly tran-quillizing if it failed to do justice to the suffering of man in resonance with the suffering of God, which we have only obscurely perceived as we peer into that ultimately limiting horizon which is the inner nature of the Godhead.

[65] §III, above.
[66] pp. 198, 199.

H.   Summary

We have been recalling in the light of the scientific account of the world—of the processes and the kinds of entities that occur and have evolved in it—how we might formulate our understanding of God's relation as Creator to the world so described, that is, how we might coherently talk of God's action in the world. Although this understanding of God's action in the world has, of course, deep roots in past theológical reflection, nevertheless certain new models, metaphors, and images are called for by our present scientific insights into the world and its development.

To summarize: we have, from this stance,[67] come to see God the Creator as *immanent* in a world that he is still creating (A), and with respect to which he is the *transcendent* creative agent (B); a Creator who is more than the world, but in whom the world subsists and exists (C(iii)—pan-en-theism); and who *unveils his meaning* for man in the *various and distinctive levels* of creation (D)—which are, in their uniqueness, describable only by epistemologically *non-reducible* concepts and which evolve and are *continuously* transformed by processes that are *open-ended* and *emergent* in character (E). Because each level has, or had, only its own distinctive capacity for expressing God's meaning to man, we conceived the hope that perhaps *God might convey his meaning in and through the transcendence-in-immanence of a person(s)* adequate to do so (F); and that such a self-communication of God to man through man would, in some way, illuminate the but faintly discerned mystery of the inner life of *God as self-offering and suffering Love active* in creation (G). However if God does express his meanings in the created world, where and how can we read them? So it is we come to

V.   THE 'LONG SEARCH'

This was the title of a notable series of BBC television and radio programmes in 1977 which displayed for our reflection, as well as for the pleasures of our sight, the immensely variegated ways in which God's meaning in the world is discerned

[67] Described in the preceding sections which are referred to in the brackets of the following paragraph.

and the rich kaleidoscope of man's awareness of God. It seems that man has indulged with extraordinary fecundity the propensity of his unique self-consciousness to search for meaning and intelligibility, a search which has led him to see the world itself as non-self-explanatory and so as created. We earlier adduced grounds for understanding the Creator thus implied as One who could not misleadingly be regarded as self-communicating to man. Indeed a non-communicating Creator seems almost a self-contradiction as succinctly pointed out by Jesus in the parallel he draws between an earthly and heavenly father.

Ask, and it shall be given you; seek, and ye shall find; knock, and it shall be opened unto you: For everyone that asketh receiveth; and he that seeketh findeth; and to him that knocketh it shall be opened. Or what man is there of you, whom if his son ask bread, will he give him a stone? Or if he ask a fish, will he give him a serpent?[68]

So, indeed it is, that man's 'long search' has not been in vain—men have read God's meanings in his creation. The search has a long history and many have followed Karl Jaspers[69] in pointing to an 'axial period' around 500 BC, *c* 800–200 BC, when in the three distinct and culturally disconnected areas of China, India, and the West there was, through the insights of particular individuals, a genuine expansion of human consciousness beyond the confines of that prevailing in the ancient civilizations based on the river valleys of the Nile, of Mesopotamia, the Indus, and the Hwang-Ho (the Yellow River):

The most extraordinary events are concentrated in this period. Confucius and Lao-tse were living in China, all the schools of Chinese philosophy came into being, including those of Mo-ti, Chuang-tse, Lieh-tsu and a host of others; India produced the Upanishads and Buddha and, like China, ran the whole gamut of philosophical possibilities down to scepticism, to materialism, sophism and nihilism; in Iran Zarathustra taught a challenging view of the world as a struggle between good and evil; in Palestine the prophets made their appearance, from Elijah, by way of Isaiah and Jeremiah to Deutero-Isaiah; Greece witnessed the appearance of

---

[68] Matt. 7: 7–9 = Luke 11: 9–11 (AV).
[69] K. Jaspers, *The Origin and Goal of History* (Routledge & Kegan Paul, London, 1953).

Homer, of the philosophers—Parmenides, Heraclitus and Plato—of the tragedians, Thucydides and Archimedes. Everything implied by these names developed during these few centuries almost simultaneously in China, India, and the West, without any one of these regions knowing of the others.

What is new about this age, in all three areas of the world, is that man becomes conscious of Being as a whole, of himself and his limitations. He experiences the terror of the world and his own powerlessness. He asks radical questions. Face to face with the void he strives for liberation and redemption. By consciously recognising his limits he sets himself the highest goals. He experiences absoluteness in the depths of selfhood and in the lucidity of transcendence.

All this took place in reflection. Consciousness became once more conscious of itself, thinking became its own object. Spiritual conflicts arose, accompanied by attempts to convince others through the communication of thoughts, reasons and experiences. The most contradictory possibilities were essayed. Discussion, the formation of parties and the division of the spiritual realm into opposites which nonetheless remained related to one another, created unrest and movement to the very brink of spiritual chaos.

In this age were born the fundamental categories within which we still think today, and the beginnings of the world religions, by which human beings still live, were created. The step into universality was taken in every sense.[70]

In Western civilization we stand on the road that leads from the merger of two of the trails started in this axial period within the West (polarized in Orient and Occident)—that of ancient Israel, as transmitted and transmuted by 2,000 years of Christian interpretation and expansion; and that of ancient Greece, via medieval scholasticism, and the so-called 'Renaissance' and 'Enlightenment'. We are the recipients of this double heritage (in our language, art, literature, science, ethics, and institutions) and which has made us all the persons we are. We have no other cultural resources immediately to hand whereby to articulate and to formulate our search today for meaning and intelligibility. So it is to these resources that we must inevitably revert as we try to read the meanings the Creator has written in his world, open though we must remain to the more exotic resources of those other cultures of the Far East whose awakening occurred along with that of our progeni-

[70] Jaspers, op. cit., p. 2.

tors in the 'axial period' of man's developing self-consciousness. Unique among the formative influences in our culture, and uniquely challenging in his person and teaching when we ask 'What can we know of God's meaning for man?', stands the figure of Jesus of Nazareth. He himself was a child of the unshakable monotheistic tradition of the people of Israel which itself has strong claims to uniqueness as powerfully argued, for example, by G. E. Wright.[71] The beliefs and practices of ancient Israel have, in more recent scholarship, proved to be less monolithic and more eclectic than Wright, perhaps, allowed in 1956 but the overall distinctiveness still remains, in the judgement of many.[72]

For us, the figure of Jesus constitutes a basic 'statement' or 'proposition' concerning the nature and purpose of God the Creator and being members, as we are, of this Western civilization and not of some other, we cannot avoid asking whether the 'proposition' which *is* Jesus is plausible and per-suasive—indeed whether it makes any coherent sense to us today. It is true, as Hans Küng rightly says: 'The word "Christian" today is more of a soporific than a slogan. So much —too much—is Christian: Churches, schools, political parties, cultural associations and of course Europe, the West, the Middle Ages ...'[73] But however weary we may be of Christianity and the Christians, the person of Jesus is the reference point, the claimed resource in our culture for our search for meaning, the central question for us as we look for God's meaning written in a world now described by the sciences. As Küng again so powerfully expresses it:

Christian does not mean everything that is true, good, beautiful, human. Who could deny that truth, goodness, beauty and humanity exist also outside Christianity? But everything can be called Christian which in theory and practice has an explicit positive reference to Jesus Christ.

A Christian is not just any human being with genuine conviction, sincere faith and good will. No one can fail to see that genuine con-

---

[71] G. E. Wright, *The Old Testament against its Environment*, Studies in Biblical Theology, No. 2 (SCM Press, London, 1956).

[72] See Baker, op. cit. (above, p. 188 n. 2), for an account of just how distinctive is the Old Testament understanding of man, for example.

[73] H. Küng, *On Being a Christian* (Doubleday, Garden City, New York, 1976), p. 119.

viction, sincere faith and good will exist also outside Christianity. But all those can be called Christians for whom in life and death Jesus Christ is ultimately decisive.

Christian Church does not mean any meditation or action group, any community or committed human beings who try to lead a decent life in order to gain salvation. It could never be disputed that commitment, action, meditation, a decent life and salvation can exist also in other groups outside the Church. But any human community, great or small, for whom Jesus Christ is ultimately decisive can be called a Christian Church.

Christianity does not exist wherever inhumanity is opposed and humanity realized. It is a simple truth that inhumanity is opposed and humanity realized also outside Christianity—among Jews, Muslims, Hindus and Buddhists, among post-Christian humanists and outspoken atheists. But Christianity exists only where the memory of Jesus Christ is activated in theory and practice.[74]

No doubt more global, objective, and detached reasons could be given, in terms of the long-term influence of Christianity (and of Judaism as transmuted and transmitted by Christianity) on the beliefs and institutions of mankind, which would demonstrate the unique significance of Jesus even for Buddhists, Muslims, Shinto-ists, Marxists, Maoists, and others. But for the moment I rest my case for even considering the character of Jesus on his unique influence, at once both charismatic and didactic, in the intellectual climate we have experienced from our first breath. He has been a common point of reference and a common resource for nearly 2,000 years of our culture and so he remains a question and a challenge. So we are bound to ask

VI. WHY IS JESUS OF NAZARETH RELEVANT TO
MAN'S SEARCH FOR MEANING AND INTELLIGIBILITY?

This is the question we cannot avoid asking today, not only because of the cultural and sociological forces impelling us towards it, but also because the context in which it is raised now has been transformed during the last century as a result of the revolution in man's understanding of the world and of himself that have resulted from both scientific inquiry and from

[74] Küng, op. cit., pp. 125–6.

the modern historical perspective which, while relativizing all the past experience of mankind, simultaneously renders ambiguous our own reflections on our present viewpoint.

It is not easy for the non-expert to steer his way between the Scylla of a 'biblicism' which too readily underestimates the presumptive beliefs of the early Church in shaping what at first appears to be biographical reportage concerning Jesus; and the Charybdis of a scepticism about the possibility of discerning anything reliable about the historical Jesus which is so deep that it goes far beyond the normal canons of historical and literary criticism of ancient documents.

But non-expert though we may be in the minutiae of New Testament studies, it behoves every one of us who claims to have an intelligent awareness of his cultural heritage to have made some kind of judgement about these issues, because the question of Jesus of Nazareth will simply not run away when we ask about the meanings that God is expressing in his creation.

So may I now briefly indicate what I think are those key features concerning this Jesus which are sufficient in themselves to justify further inquiry about how the meaning that he conveys can be expressed adequately in the light of what we have given grounds for regarding as the mode of God's action in the world?

Because of limitations of time and space (and indeed of expertise), I state these key points without any supporting evidence, though I believe all can be justified in detail and would, by and large, I surmise, command the support of a good number of the authors in *both* the recent books[75] on the myth, or truth, of 'God Incarnate', namely:

(1) (a preliminary point) that the effect of the brief life and death of this obscure Jew, Jesus, of no distinguished parentage, in a backwater of the Roman Empire, produced an effect, first on his disciples and then on his culture, which resulted from focusing primarily on his person, and only secondarily on his teaching, and which was of a magnitude and quality that requires explanation;

(2) that his teachings, his personal, private, and public life and his interaction with his contemporaries, provide evidence that Jesus' relation with God was uniquely intense and intimate

---

[75] *The Myth of God Incarnate*, ed. J. Hick (SCM Press, London, 1977); *The Truth of God Incarnate*, ed. M. Green (Hodder & Stoughton, London, 1977).

(one can instance his use of the intimate 'Abba', as a form for 'father', in prayer addressed to God and its widely agreed significance[76])—we would say, in our terms, that he was 'open' to God to an extent that was qualitatively unique;

(3) that the primary stress in Jesus' teaching was the coming of the Kingdom of God, of its quality, of its demands upon man and its call to man, and that in his own coming and teaching and being present among the people of first-century Israel that Kingdom of God was being, at least, inaugurated, if not consummated (Mark 1: 14 (NEB): 'The time has come; the Kingdom of God is upon you; repent, and believe the Gospel'); that is, he identified his coming to his contemporaries with the coming of the Kingdom of God among men and with the cause of God in the world[77]('. . . if it is by the finger of God that I drive out the devils, then be sure the Kingdom of God has already come upon you'[78])—an identification, a unity with God, which was ratified and authenticated by the resurrection experiences of the disciples;[79]

(4) that Jesus spoke and acted with an authority (in his teaching, his forgiveness of sins, in his treatment of the sabbath, the law and temple, etc.) that is self-contradictory, inexplicable, and insupportable, except on the basis of Jesus' personal unity with the purposes of God;[80]

(5) that Jesus' death was uniquely tragic—both in its implications for his message, for the death of Jesus was 'also the death of his eschatological message through which he brought God to utterance and made the Kingdom of God imminent . . . His preaching then as it were goes down with him in the grave'[81] and in its manner—

Socrates died as a wise man. . . . For him, death was a breakthrough to a higher, purer life. . . . The death of Socrates was a festival of liberty . . . The Zealot martyrs who were crucified after the un-

[76] See, e.g., J. Jeremias, *New Testament Theology* (SCM Press, London, 1971), Vol. 1, pp. 63 ff.

[77] Moltmann, op. cit. (above, p. 201 n. 40), pp. 121 ff.

[78] Luke 11: 20 (NEB).

[79] W. Pannenberg, *The Apostles Creed in the Light of Today's Questions* (SCM Press, London, 1972), pp. 52 ff.; see also idem (1968), (above, p. 211 n. 64), Ch. 3.

[80] Pannenberg, op. cit. (1968) (above, p. 211 n. 64), Ch. 9; Jeremias, op. cit., Ch. VI, §22; cf. also the treatment of G. Bornkamm, *Jesus of Nazareth* (Hodder & Stoughton, London, 1960, 1963).

[81] Moltmann, op. cit., p. 122.

successful revolts against the Romans . . . died for their righteous cause, the cause of the righteousness of God, conscious that this would ultimately triumph over their enemies . . . The wise men of the Stoics demonstrated to the tyrants in the arena, where they were torn to pieces by wild animals, their inner liberty and their superiority. . . . Christian martyrs too went calmly and in faith to their death . . . Jesus clearly died in a different way. His death was not a 'fine death'. The synoptic gospels agree that he was 'greatly distressed and troubled' (Mark 14.33 par.) and that his soul was sorrowful even to death. . . . According to Mark 15 v.37 he died with a loud, incoherent cry. Because, as the Christian tradition developed, this terrible cry of the dying Jesus was gradually weakened in the passion narratives and replaced by words of comfort and triumph, we can probably rely upon it as the kernel of historical truth. Jesus clearly died with every expression of the most profound horror. How can this be explained? The comparison with Socrates, and with Stoic and Christian martyrs, shows that there is something special here about the death of Jesus. We can understand it only if we see his death not against his relationship to the Jews and Romans, to the law and to the political power, but in relation to his God and Father, whose closeness and whose grace he himself had proclaimed. Here we come upon the theological dimension of his life and death. Mark 15.34 reproduces the cry of the dying Jesus in the words of Psalm 22.2: 'My God, why hast thou forsaken me?' This is certainly an interpretation of the Church after Easter, and indeed Psalm 22 as a whole had a formative influence on the Christian passion narratives. But it seems to be as near as possible to the historical reality of the death of Jesus. . . . The history of the tradition being as it is, it can be accepted that the difficult reading of Mark is as close as may be to historical reality . . . therefore, we start from the assumption that Jesus died with the signs and expressions of a profound abandonment by God;[82]

(6) that there was a movement of faith among the early disciples of Jesus, very soon after his death, which found expression in their meeting to break bread on the first day of the Jewish week after the sabbath, and that this early practice was associated with their proclamation that Jesus was one whom God had 'raised from the dead', and that this faith and practice were triggered off by an actual nexus of events in which Jesus is described as personally encountering his disciples after his death in unexpected and, to us, still baffling ways, but sufficient

[82] Moltmann, op. cit., pp. 145, 147.

to convince them that the whole personality of Jesus had been taken through death by an act of God, so that the risen Jesus was in the presence of God and still, somehow, present to them.

It is perhaps not, after all, so surprising that the 'Jesus of history' became the 'Christ of faith', but at least these features of the 'things about Jesus'—and I have deliberately chosen what seems to me to be a minimal historically authenticated set— point to a new departure *in actual history* in what men can read of God's meaning in his creation, a new apprehension and comprehension of what God can and is doing for man. Clearly, something has occurred here in the events surrounding Jesus, of immense significance for man's search for meaning and intelligibility.

This judgement on the significance of the life, death, and resurrection of Jesus (which I have sometimes called 'the things about Jesus' and which others call the 'Christ-event' when they also want to include explicitly the response to Jesus in faith by the first disciples and the early Church) rests on all these (here six) decisive features taken together. I would not want to rest this postulate of his significance on any supposed historical evidence for his sinlessness, in the sense of moral perfection, for, as Dr D. Nineham has rightly pointed out,[83] *no* historical evidence, however complete, could ever establish

---

[83] D. Nineham, 'Epilogue', in *The Myth of God Incarnate*, pp. 186 f. If I have given the impression (e.g. in *Science and the Christian Experiment*, Ch. 6, quoted by Dr Nineham) that there is good historical evidence for Jesus' 'sinlessness' in the sense of moral perfection I would here like to correct this. However, 'sinlessness' attributed to Jesus in the sense of 'the man who lived in closest unity with the Father' (so: J. Macquarrie on 'The sinlessness of Jesus' in *Christian World*, 25 May 1978, p. 16) is another matter, as discussed in the text. When (loc. cit.) I have spoken of the humanity of Jesus as 'potentially what all men have it in their nature to be', and 'the realization of all that men might be, all that God intended men should be' I had in mind his relation to God and not his *moral* perfection as such. To speak of 'perfection' in relation to any attribute of a historical person, such as Jesus of Nazareth, is best avoided, especially in view of the ambiguity of the concept of perfectibility in man demonstrated by J. Passmore (*The Perfectibility of Man* (Duckworth, London, 1970), Ch. 1: see discussion below, §VIII). However this does not debar us from making a judgement to the effect that the historical evidence for the uniqueness of Jesus' openness to God is very strong, even if historical scepticism must still allow the caveat that, in principle, Jesus might one day be surpassable even in this. With respect to Jesus' *moral* character, there does, in fact, seem to be good evidence, in the tradition, of his moral sensitivity and perception; and his teaching concerning human relationships (even if, as we now know, many elements in it can be found in a number of other Jewish rabbis and thinkers of those times) still has in its total impact a pungency and incisive power which can

such a negative proposition. More positively, however, I do think the historical evidence for the special character of Jesus' relation to God, his 'openness' to God as I have preferred to call it,[84] is cumulatively good and I do not by this mean that Jesus' relation to God is necessarily different in kind from what is potentially available to all men—that is a matter for careful consideration and formulation in the light of the framework of thought about God's action in the world in general, to which we must return later. So I think we have good grounds, on the basis of the historical evidence, for affirming that Jesus represents a unique focus for the unveiling of God's presence in human life and for reading the meaning(s) God seeks to communicate to man.

However, and it is the crux of the present concern with the whole hermeneutical problem, this claimed historical 'evidence' comes to us already interpreted by the early Church but that *they* believed it is validated by the fact of its emergence and survival. We can judge only if their witness is basically reliable, that is, whether they got the main points right and were not fundamentally misled or deceived. There can be little doubt, from the earliest *kerugma* onwards, of the belief of the early Church in the universal significance for all men of what was revealed in Jesus concerning what God was doing in his life, death, and resurrection. Their 'gospel' consisted of just this: Jesus is 'Lord', the 'Christ', the anointed 'Son of God' (and not necessarily in a sense in which all men could not also become 'sons of God' too, but, at any rate, actually the case for him). This assignment of universal significance to the 'things about Jesus' arose very early and constitutes the problem of what theologians clumsily call Christology. As Martin Hengel has formulated it:

---

cut deeply into the conscience of even modern readers of the Gospels. In his teaching and person we do encounter a moral force for good which, when released in the world, has time and again in history changed individuals, and even societies, in an astonishing way. Strictly, though this is historically the case, it is not immediately relevant to our assessment of the significance of Jesus as a person, even though it is bound, and there is no betrayal of intellectual integrity involved therein, to enhance our willingness to consider seriously the meaning of the 'things about Jesus'. Any assertion of Jesus' moral perfection, if it is made at all, could only be regarded as a deduction from beliefs about his person and not as their 'historical' ground.

[84] Cf. E. Käsemann, *Jesus Means Freedom* (SCM Press, London, 1969).

At the feast of the Passover in the year 30, in Jerusalem, a Galilean Jew was nailed to the cross for claiming to be Messiah. About twenty-five years later, the former Pharisee Paul quotes a hymn about this crucified man in a letter which he writes to one of the communities of the messianic sect which he has founded in the Roman colony of Philippi:

He was in the form of God,
(but) did not count equality with God a thing to be grasped,
but emptied himself,
taking the form of a slave,
being born in the likeness of man and found in human form.
He humbled himself
and became obedient unto death,
even death on a cross (*Phil.* 2.6–8).

The discrepancy between the shameful death of a Jewish state criminal and the confession that depicts this executed man as a pre-existent divine figure who becomes man and humbles himself to a slave's death is, as far as I can see, without analogy in the ancient world. It also illuminates the riddle of the origin of the christology of the early church. Paul founded the community at Philippi in about the year AD 49, and in the letter which he wrote to the believers there about six or seven years later he will have presented the same Christ as in the preaching which brought the community into being. This means that the 'apotheosis of the crucified Jesus' must already have taken place in the forties, and one is tempted to say *that more happened in this period of less than two decades than in the whole of the next seven centuries, up to the time when the doctrine of the early church was completed.* Indeed, one might even ask whether the formation of doctrine in the early church was essentially more than a consistent development and completion of what had already been unfolded in the primal event of the first two decades, but in the language and thought-forms of Greek, which was its necessary setting.[85]

This understanding of the genesis of Christology in the early Church as 'development' rather than 'evolution' has also been urged by Professor C. F. D. Moule.[86] By 'development', Professor Moule means 'growth, from immaturity to maturity, of a single specimen from within itself'[87] as distinct from 'evolution', meaning the 'genesis of successive new species by

---

[85] M. Hengel, *The Son of God* (SCM Press, London, 1976), pp. 1, 2.
[86] C. F. D. Moule, *The Origin of Christology* (Cambridge University Press, Cambridge, 1977).
[87] Moule, op. cit., p. 2.

mutations and natural selection along the way'.[87] He challenges
the 'evolutionary' tendency

> to explain the change from (say) invoking Jesus as a revered Master
> to the acclamation of him as a divine Lord by the theory that, when
> the Christian movement spread beyond Palestinian soil, it began to
> come under the influence of non-Semitic Saviour-cults to assimilate
> some of their ideas; and also by appeal to the effect of the lapse of
> time, which may itself lead to the intensification of terms of
> adoration.[88]

By contrast, the tendency which he advocates as closer to
the evidence is 'developmental', that is it aims

> ... to explain all the various estimates of Jesus reflected in the New
> Testament as, in essence, only attempts to describe what was already
> there from the beginning. They are not successive additions of some-
> thing new, but only the drawing out and articulating of what is there.
> They represent various stages in the development of perception, but
> they do not represent the accretion of any alien factors that were
> not inherent from the beginning: they are analogous not so much
> to the emergence of a new species, as to the unfolding (if you like)
> of flower from bud and the growth of fruit from flower. Moreover,
> when one assumes that the changes are, in the main, changes only
> in perception, one is at the same time acknowledging that it may
> not be possible, a priori, to arrange such changes in any firm chrono-
> logical order. In evolution, the more complex species generally belong
> to a later stage than the more simple; but in development, there
> is nothing to prevent a profoundly perceptive estimate occurring at
> an early stage, and a more superficial one at a later stage: degrees
> of perception will depend upon individual persons and upon circum-
> stances which it may be impossible to identify in any intelligibly
> chronological sequence.[89]

So he argues that whatever came later was already there in
the early experience of Jesus by others[90] (and even in Jesus'
own consciousness) and was not an unwarranted accumulation of supernatural qualities from other cults. Thus, he
urges, there was for the early believers a finality, ultimacy,
uniqueness (as well as originality) about Jesus' revelation of

---

[88] Ibid.

[89] Ibid., pp. 2–3.

[90] The earliest Christology is that of Paul, cf. Phil. 2: 6–8, quoted above in the extract
from Hengel (p. 224 n. 85).

God. However any attempts by the New Testament writers to 'describe what was already there from the beginning' cannot occur without the very descriptions themselves being profoundly imbued with the presuppositions of the new and changing environments within which these attempts are successively essayed. Can a sharp contrast between 'development' and 'evolution' be maintained in the light of the intensive nineteenth- and twentieth-century discussions of the idea of 'development' of doctrine?[91] For, the bud–flower concept is far from being unquestioned as an analogy for 'development' of theological concepts. Professor Moule does, indeed, recognize this problem,[92] but thinks that the New Testament evidence is that a 'high' Christology was appropriate from the first, and was not the last term in an evolutionary series of new 'species' (of description); that the descriptions of and significance attributed to Jesus did not move successively further and further from the reality.

Generations of Christians have indeed shared in the experience of the early witnesses through their writings, through the continuous life of the communities those events generated, through the visual arts, music, and architecture and (so they believe) through their direct apprehension of God through Christ, who is revered as the universalized human Jesus[93] 'raised' to the presence of God. This continuity of experience of the presence of God in and through Jesus the Christ is received by us not only through words but also (and today perhaps more powerfully than ever) through the visual arts, through a musical tradition which is one of the unique spiritual legacies of Western man to human civilization in general, and through a numinous architecture. Thus that arrow which was shot into history in the Christ-event lands

[91] Cf. W. O. Chadwick, *From Bossuet to Newman: The Idea of Doctrinal Development* (Cambridge University Press, Cambridge, 1957).

[92] Moule, op. cit., p. 4 n. 4.

[93] Professor Moule has, as is well known, developed an understanding of the 'corporate Christ' of St. Paul's theology (in *The Phenomenon of the New Testament* (SCM Press, London, 1967), Ch. II, and in *The Origin of Christology*, Ch. 2) according to which the one who had been known as the individual, Jesus, of history turned out, after the resurrection, to be one who transcended individuality—to be the unconfined, unrestricted, more than individual, universal 'Christ' to all man—an inclusive personality. In the New Testament, he argues, Jesus is experienced as personal, but as more than individual, even though he had recently been known as such historically.

fairly and squarely here today and we cannot avoid interpreting both the early historical experience of the first witnesses and the continuous experience this has generated. Questions he roused in them are still questions for us now. Whether traditional terminology about Jesus is opaque and anathema to us, or whether it has proved a 'door to life', we cannot avoid reassessing what such a biography with such an influence can possibly mean for us today. The question of the universality of its significance cannot be easily set aside when any impartial study is made, whatever the statistics may be concerning the de-Christianization of Western contemporary society and its institutions.

However 'revelation' is relative to circumstances—the meanings which God can express in his creation are relative to the receptiveness and outlook of those to whom he is communicating. So however strong a case New Testament scholars such as Hengel and Moule may make for a 'high' Christology having its roots in the very earliest witnesses of Jesus, we cannot avoid asking whether what they saw in him, we can see too. Even if we were to accept that the New Testament represents a 'development' of seeds of judgement and reflection on Jesus, rather than an 'evolution' with mutations, we would still be bound to ask the question about Jesus classically formulated by Leonard Hodgson in relation to all such hermeneutical questions 'What must the truth have been and be if that is how it looked to men who thought and wrote like that?',[94] with J. A. Baker's added proviso that 'when as far as possible we know what the words meant to them then as far as possible we know what the truth was to them'.[95] So we come to face the question

VII. WHAT IS THE SIGNIFICANCE OF THE LIFE, DEATH, AND RESURRECTION OF JESUS FOR MAN (in his search today for God's meaning in a creation described by the natural sciences)?

The two publications[96] of 1977 on the myth/truth of God

[94] L. Hodgson, *For Faith and Freedom* (Oxford University Press, Oxford, 1956), p. x.
[95] J. A. Baker, *The Foolishness of God* (Darton, Longman, & Todd, London, 1970), pp. 364–5.
[96] See above, p. 219 n. 75.

Incarnate and their aftermath have made this a key question for the self-identity of Christianity in Britain today, and I suspect it is the central question for other post-Christian societies (it constitutes, for example, the fulcrum of Hans Küng's book[97]). Unless Christians have *some* public consensus, *some* agreed range of expressive discourse, about their understanding of the founder Figure of their community, Christianity could revert to a private opinion of no more significance to man in general than our private assessments of any great figure of the past. So the debate is timely and pertinent. The slogan word on which the debate has centred is 'Incarnation' (with a capital 'I') since it is the traditional label for the doctrine of Jesus Christ as being one person recognized in two natures, Godhead and manhood, the doctrine classically formulated by the Council of Chalcedon in 451 AD in its famous Definition which, while solving little, at least proposed the paradox succinctly and accurately. We still today have the interpretative problem proposed by the 'evidence' about Jesus (even if, indeed especially if, we accept the thesis of C. F. D. Moule for the Christology of the early Church as a development rather than an evolution)—a problem now posed in an entirely different world of thought from those of the first or fifth centuries AD. We cannot avoid an attempt to respond in the way Leonard Hodgson advised.[98] There are, of course, philosophical problems here about the use of words such as 'person', 'nature', 'substance',[99] 'being' and 'essence' in the light of modern critical (on the whole, non-metaphysical) philosophy. But there is, it seems to me, another prior problem, which has to be examined and on which the approach of these lectures can perhaps shed some light. It is the question of the way God is understood to be acting in the world, of how we conceive of his presence in creation, and so of how communication might occur between the creator and self-conscious creation, namely man. These issues seem to me to be prior to those discussed by both groups of authors in the myth/truth controversy about the Incarnation; they are issues which must be resolved before we could hope to formulate satisfactorily

[97] Above, p. 217 n. 73.
[98] Above, p. 227.
[99] See G. C. Stead, *Divine Substance* (Clarendon Press, Oxford, 1977).

today the way in which God might be 'in Christ reconciling the world to himself'.[100] This lack of analysis of how God may be conceived of as acting and being present in creation has, it seems to me, led to confusion and perhaps even unnecessary polarization in the discussion of incarnation, in general, and the Incarnation, in particular.

So we ask, can we find coherent expression of any meaning that God might have expressed in Jesus the Christ which could be seen to be congruent with our understanding of the relation of God the Creator to the created world, a world most accurately now described by the sciences?

In § IV, we recapitulated some aspects of our understanding of this relation and summarized them.[101] Let us, then, consider (in reverse of the order previously given) these perceptions of the way we must now conceive of God's action and presence in the created world in relation to those central features of our knowledge of Jesus and his impact on his contemporaries which we have just outlined.

(i) *Self-offering and suffering Love active in creation.*[102] The unity of Jesus with God his Father, his 'openness to God' as we have called it, implies that in Jesus God's presence was unveiled to us with a special clarity—yet the outcome of his life was the suffering and death of a shameful cross. So the God who was one with Jesus must have been one with him in his suffering and death. Thus to affirm Jesus' unity with God his Father is also to affirm that God suffered in and with Jesus. The God whom Jesus therefore unveiled in his life and death is indeed a 'crucified God' and the cry of dereliction can thus come to be seen as an expression of the anguish also of God in creation, an anguish which is the concomitant, paradoxically, of his over-flowing joy and generosity in that same creation. If Jesus is indeed the paradigm, and paragon, of the potential unity of the created with the Creator, then the tragedy of his actual human life can be seen as a drawing back of the curtain to unveil a God suffering in and with the sufferings of creative and created man and so implicitly, by a natural extension, with

---

[100] 2 Cor. 5: 19 (NEB).
[101] p. 214.
[102] Cf. §IV G., p. 213.

all creation. Jesus then is, as it were, a bearer of *God's* pain, the pain of the creative process.[103] The suffering and self-limitation in God, which we have inferred from the creation, and is entailed if Jesus is one with God in the way the evidence indicates, was, this implies, at this point in time concentrated into a point of unique intensity and transparency for us all to perceive. Moreover, standing as we do on *this* side of these events, we also recognize that point as a new source of life and creative outreach of God in those experiences we call the resurrection of Jesus. It was indeed a death which was a gateway to life of new significance for mankind. Here then, what Jesus did and was unveils that inner life of God as creative, self-offering, and suffering Love active in creation which we had come to apprehend, on other grounds, as a real, if hidden,[104] aspect of God's relation to the world.

(*ii*) *God conveying meaning through the personal: 'incarnation'?*[105] Because of the distinctive character of different levels in the natural hierarchy of complexity, we have recognized that what God might unveil to man of the mystery of his being and purposes is distinctive for each level. In particular, we conjectured that God's immanence might be capable of being unveiled with a transcendent dimension only in a creature such as man who already possesses a limited (and created) transcendence-in-immanence. The combination of the evidence for Jesus' intimacy with God his Father, the identity he affirmed between his message of the Kingdom of God and his own presence among men, his authority and, above all, the events of his death and resurrection all serve to impel us to a recognition that in this man Jesus, at least (with no judgement about anyone else), we encounter a transcendent vector of God's immanence in all

[103] Cf. above, p. 201, n. 40.

[104] I hope that the treatment here, by virtue of its wider setting in the context of these lectures as a whole, avoids the strictures of R. S. Barbour: 'It is all too easy, for example, to find some kind of principle of sacrifice and renewal, of "death and resurrection", running right through the universe, and to link that in a facile way with the death and resurrection of Christ.' (R. S. Barbour on 'Creation, Wisdom and Christ', in *Creation, Christ and Culture*, ed. by R. W. A. McKinney (T. & T. Clark, Edinburgh, 1976), p. 41.) There is always the danger, as he says, of imposing an artificial unity on diverse material. The point here, rather, is that the nature of the suffering God revealed in Christ is coherent with an understanding of God's relation to the world which has been shaped by our present knowledge *of* that world.

[105] Cf. §IV F (and also §IV E).

men which was so distinctive and intensive that new non-reducible concepts and language might well be required to express the uniqueness of what he was and did. I concur with using the word 'incarnation' (but with a small 'i') to denote the unique degree of God's transcendence that was personally immanent in that psychosomatic unity which was the man Jesus. On the basis of what we have seen about the relationship between levels in natural hierarchies, of emergence of the new out of old continuities, we should not be surprised, indeed we should require, that new language should be brought into play to express what men saw of God in Jesus whom they came to call the Christ: the new wine needs new bottles. And this is precisely what happened in the period ranged over by the New Testament. That new concept, sown in man's minds by what Jesus was and did and what happened to him, is what we have come to call 'incarnation'. The relation of that seed to the 'doctrine of the Incarnation' (with a capital 'I') as classically formulated at Chalcedon, via the Logos–Christology of the Fourth Gospel ('the Word became Flesh'[106]), is complex and controversial. In the present context, I simply wish to make the points (1) that the exercise of raising that seed to full flower was necessary and not misconceived, even if our present husbandry is bound, with our present philosophical resources, to produce a new variety; (2) that any unveiling of God to man through a man would necessitate such an exercise; and (3) that such an unveiling is congruent with that understanding of God's relation to the world that we have developed here in the light of our present scientific knowledge of the world. If in Jesus God's immanent presence had a transcendent dimension which was uniquely personal then new non-reducible language, concepts, and modes of experiencing this new kind of reality would have to be developed. For his uniqueness could not be expected to be reducible to the terms previously employed to explicate 'man', or even 'God'. This, it seems to me, is what justifies the use of special, 'incarnational', language concerning Jesus and, indeed, historically to have motivated the development of the doctrine of the Incarnation in the first centuries of the Church's existence.

[106] John 1: 14 (NEB).

(*iii*) '*Non-reducible*', '*open-ended*', '*emergent*', '*continuous*'.[107] The continuous processes of the created world whereby new and non-reducible emergents are brought into existence are open-ended—and it was 'openness' to God which we came to see that Jesus possessed to a unique degree. In Jesus, the open-endedness of what is going on in the world, self-consciously and overtly by a willing act of the creature himself must therefore be conceived as an open-endedness which is united with the purposes of God for the still open future. In other words, in Jesus' oneness with God his Father, the open-endedness of the creative process in Jesus himself as created man must have become identified fully and self-consciously with the 'God ahead'; with the God who is the source of the future—and so with the future that is God's intention for men and the world. But is not this just that very identification[108] between the advent of Jesus and the initiation of the Kingdom of God which is so well testified as distinctive of Jesus' own teaching?

The historical evidence is indeed that Jesus *was* so open to God, that he entrusted his whole future to him unequivocally to the point, in the cry of dereliction, of abandoning even his sense of God's presence to himself. The historical Jesus, the evidence attests, staked all on God's future for him and thereby made possible the resurrection wherein God was able to unveil further the way ahead for Jesus the Christ to draw all men after him into the fullness of life with God. Thereby the individual historical Jesus of Nazareth became the all-inclusive corporate 'Christ' of faith[109] who now represents in his totality (that is, in his life, death, and resurrection) a new departure point in the creative process, a new beginning in human life, allowing new potentialities to be anticipated and actualized in those who are willing to share in *his human* open response to God.

From this perspective, Jesus by virtue of his openness to God as his 'Father' and Creator was able to express with a unique originality the transcendence of the Creator who is immanent in the world process. Thus men encountered in Jesus a presence of God which fused God's transcendence and immanence in

107 Cf. §IV E.
108 See above, §VI (3) p. 220.
109 See C. F. D. Moule, op cit. (p. 226 n. 93 above).

a way which engendered the language of 'incarnation'. However, when such language becomes confined to assertions about Jesus' 'nature' and about what kind of 'substances' do (or did) constitute him then it loses its force to convey significant meaning to many today who, quite rightly from our viewpoint, are concerned not so much with what Jesus (or God or man) is 'in himself', but rather with the dynamic nature of the relation between God's immanent creative *activity* focused and unveiled in him and the *processes* of nature and of human history and experience, all of which are 'in God' and so from which God is never absent.

(*iv*) *The God who unveils his meaning in various and distinctive levels*.[110] What light is thrown on the various and distinctive levels of creation, other than man, by this unveiling of God's Being as transcendence-in-immanence in creation through Jesus' openness to that Being? The Nicene Creed affirms '. . . one Lord Jesus Christ . . . By whom all things were made...' and the Thanksgiving of the Series 3 rite of Holy Communion of the Church of England acclaims 'Jesus Christ . . . he is your living Word: through him you have created all things from the beginning...' The prologue to the Fourth Gospel tells of the Word (the 'Logos') through whom 'all things came to be' (v.3), that Word later attested (v.14) as becoming 'flesh', in the person of Jesus Christ. What can such language really mean for us now in the light of our understanding of God's relation to his world? The patristic Logos-Christology, in the form which postulated Jesus as the pre-existent 'Son of God', the divine Logos, who was the mediator of creation and was historically incarnate in Jesus, could be held together effectively with the more general Stoic philosophy according to which the Logos was the unifier of the whole cosmos. But this philosophy is not at hand for us today in the same form and there are cogent reasons for trying to avoid language which seems to imply that 'Christ' was somehow pre-existent before the birth of Jesus of Nazareth.[111] As Pannenberg puts it:

Today, in contrast [to the Logos-Christology], the Son's mediation

---

[110] Cf. §IV D.
[111] Lampe, op. cit. (above, p. 207 n. 49), Ch. V.

of creation must be strictly established through the concept of revelation; it is not established as something given in the philosophy of nature. We can only ask subsequently whether our understanding of the world permits us to perceive something of the relation of the Son to the Father, thus whether the world may be understood as aimed at the relation of the Son to the Father that is revealed in Jesus Christ. Certainly, to fuse in such a way the modern understanding of the world into an understanding of reality derived from the relevation in Christ demands an extraordinary effort on the part of theological thinking. But this method would probably correspond more closely to the way in which the faith in creation emerged—or better, was appropriated—from the perspective of the concrete experience of salvation in ancient Israel than did the patristic identification of the Son of God with a definite concept available in the philosophical understanding of the world at that time.[112]

Thus, we should understand 'mediation of creation by Jesus Christ' not on the basis of the postulate of 'Christ' as pre-existent before his historical birth. Rather we should think of God's intention in creation, to bring his purposes to fulfilment at all levels, as existing 'from all eternity',[113] that is within the inner life of God who transcends even time in his own being; and that Jesus unveils by his openness to God (and so 'unity' in that sense) the character of God's intentions in creation, which begins to be consummated in his life, death, and resurrection. In this sense Jesus (now seen as the Christ) could

---

[112] Pannenberg (1968), op cit. (above, p. 211 n. 64), pp. 168-9.

[113] According to G. B. Caird ('The Development of the Doctrine of Christ in the New Testament', in *Christ for us Today*, ed. N. Pittenger (SCM Press, London, 1968), pp. 4–80), both in Hellenistic and non-Hellenistic Judaism, 'pre-existence is simply another, more picturesque way of describing purpose or predestination' (op. cit., p. 77) and 'all pre-existent things could be said to exist in one mode or another, within the purpose of God' (op. cit., p. 78). He goes on to argue that all three New Testament (John, Colossians, Hebrews) writers who speak of the pre-existence of Christ do so in express contradiction of similar Jewish claims—'they ascribed pre-existence to Jesus because they wanted to claim for him all that the Jews had claimed for the Torah, because they believed that in him God's purpose for man, and therefore for the whole cosmos, had become an earthly reality ... They held that the union of the human and the divine which had been achieved in Jesus was precisely that which God had intended from all eternity as the destiny of man' (op. cit., p. 79). This interpretation of the New Testament understanding of 'pre-existence' as meaning 'in the purpose and intent of God from all eternity' certainly blunts the edge of some of the controversy concerning pre-existence. However, this still reckons without Paul for whom, as Caird points out: 'because in the earthly life of Jesus the eternal purpose of God had appeared as a person ... Paul and others after him found it impossible to imagine his pre-cosmic existence as anything other than personal' (op. cit., p. 80).

throw light on the significance of the various levels of the world order which both preceded and exist in man—for he unveils at least one aspect of their 'meaning', i.e. their place in God's unfolding purposes, as part of the exploration of these creative possibilities which have led to man. But only *one* aspect of their meaning—as I have emphasized before, we must allow a creator God to have his own inscrutable purposes and a joy in a creation not confined to man and his potentialities. So, with this important *caveat*, we can still affirm that, because we have seen that through the processes of the world there have in fact emerged self-conscious persons whose ultimate potentialities (as we shall discuss) are revealed through Jesus the Christ, then it would be true to say that the significance and potentiality of all levels of creation, as necessary intermediates on the way to the consummation of personhood, have been unveiled in Jesus the Christ, in his relation as created man to God the Creator. This seems also to be Pannenberg's position:

> The statement that all things and beings are created through Jesus Christ means that the *eschaton* that has appeared beforehand in Jesus represents the time and point from which the creation took place. According to the Biblical understanding, the essence of things will be decided only in the future. *What they are is decided by what they will become.* Thus the creation happens from the end, from the ultimate future.[112]

Thus it is not that, in any sense, the man Jesus, or even 'Jesus the Christ', is the agent of creation but that he mediates to us the meaning of creation. Through him we see for what all things were made and such an understanding of his mediatorship is coherent with the way we have come to see that God has been shaping the creation in time. As Emil Brunner has put it, in the context of a very different systematic theology from our own, 'Hence the revelation of this love of God [in Jesus Christ] is at the same time the revelation of the purpose of His Creation, and this purpose of creation is the reason why he posits a creation. The love of God is the *causa finalis* of the Creation. In Jesus Christ this ideal reason for the creation is revealed.'[114] This has been more fully argued, from the same general theological standpoint, by H. Berkhof:

[114] E. Brunner, *The Christian Doctrine of Cration and Redemption* (Lutterworth Press, London), *Dogmatics*, Vol. ii, p. 13.

To take seriously the final events in Christ, must also mean that he is confessed as the ultimate secret of *creation*.... This confession of Christ as the agent of creation is found in a particularly articulated form in three traditions, in John 1, Col. 1 and Heb. 1.... Without interruption, however, they pass from the work in creation to the work in history (cf. Col. 1: 17 f. and Heb. 1: 3).... Apparently this historical work is considered as the consequence and completion of his creative work.... They point to history as the only realm where the secret of creation is revealed and fulfilled. On the other hand, we must also say that what is revealed in history is no unrelated incident, but the realization of a condition which had been God's purpose from the very beginning. The crucified and risen Jesus is the key to the understanding of the meaning of the whole created world.... This close connection of what God meant in creation and what he accomplished in Christ was expressed by these writers, using contemporary patterns of thought, in the confession that the world was created in and through Jesus Christ.... Most classical theologians ... saw the Incarnation as the great emergency-measure by which God decided to bring the world back to its original perfection. A minority, however, maintained that Christ is more than that, that he is also the crown of creation, the new man for which creation has been waiting from the beginning (Antiochene School, Duns Scotus, several forms of liberal theology, Barth).... when a choice has to be made, the decision has to be in favour of the second doctrine, because the first cannot give a satisfactory explanation of the three passages in the New Testament which deal with Jesus Christ as mediator of creation.[115]

We have, in the previous paragraphs, been concerned with the 'purposes' of God in creation as revealed in Jesus the Christ. But to say that there are such 'purposes' is also to say that the events and processes of creation have a meaning to be discerned, for 'meaning' is that which is *meant*, i.e. intended or purposed.[116] Earlier we noted that man was distinctive, not in being evolved out of matter, but as being a form of matter who seeks and asks for meaning in the natural process whereby he has emerged. God is encountered by man in the natural events and processes

[115] H. Berkhof, pp. 12, 13 of 'God in Nature and History', in *Faith and Order Studies*, 1964–7 (World Council of Churches, Geneva, 1968), Faith and Order Paper No. 50, *New Directions in Faith and Order*; also published in a preliminary form as a study document in *Study Encounter*, Vol. i, No. 3 (World Council of Churches, Geneva, 1965), pp. 6, 7.

[116] G. D. Kaufman, *Systematic Theology: A Historicist Perspective* (Charles Scribner's Sons, New York, 1968), p. 347.

in so far as he discerns and reads the meanings in those events and processes of the God in whom they exist and who is present *in* all, if not equally present *to* all who seek him there. That is, God's meaning must be regarded as veiled: he communicates his meaning with greater clarity and richness of content through some events and processes more than through others.

We have found grounds for asserting that Jesus' oneness with God his Father was such that in him the purposes and nature of God have been unveiled in new ways, emergent from the processes of nature and history, yet distinctive, non-reducible, and *sui generis*. Moreover, the meaning of God communicated through the life, death, and resurrection of Jesus is the meaning of God which is both *about* man as well as *for* man. Thus we may say that in Jesus, the meaning he (Jesus) discerns, proclaims, expresses, and reveals is the meaning that he himself *is*. The Christian claim is that Jesus' historical appearance is properly described as 'disclosing the ultimate meaning of the whole indivisible process of creation, nature and history'.[117] This is a claim of overwhelming arrogance unless we can begin to understand, in perhaps the kind of way we have been sketching, how the meaning of God that is communicated through Jesus is related to the meaning that God has and is conveying in the creation itself. So regarded, Jesus' life, death, and resurrection could then be seen as a kind of focus of many shafts of meaningful light dispersed throughout creation. He would then be seen as a particular, even unique, focal point in which the diverse rays of meaning written in creation converge to combine and reinforce with an intensity which so illuminates the purposes of God that we are then able to interpret God's meaning communicated in his creative activity over a wider range of nature and history. It almost seems as if we can identify this meaning and this purpose of God with what the prologue to the Fourth Gospel calls the Logos, the Word, that comes out of God as the expression of his inner intent. Just as there is a tension, in our discussion above, between the meaning*s* hidden in the events and processes of nature and history and *the* meaning disclosed in Jesus the

117 H. Berkhof, op. cit. (1968), p. 13.

Christ, so there is between, on the one hand, the Word through whom 'all things came to be' (John 1; 3) which (who) is omni-present so that 'all that came to be was alive with his life' (v. 4a) in such a way that men might discern it, for 'that life was the light of men' (v. 4b); and, on the other hand, that localized, temporally constricted, Word that 'became flesh' (v. 14) and whose glory men saw 'full of grace and truth' (v. 14). The one is local, historical, and particular and is the focus, the paradigm, the definitive illuminating exemplar of, and clue to, the other which is dispersed, perennial, and general. What was manifest in Jesus gave insight into what was and is already there and this, it seems to me, is one of the permissible interpretations of:

It was there from the beginning; we have heard it; we have seen it with our own eyes; we looked upon it, and felt it with our hands; and it is of this we tell. Our theme is the word of life. This life was made visible; we have seen it and bear our testimony; we here declare to you the eternal life which dwelt with the Father and was made visible to us. What we have seen and heard we declare to you, so that you and we together may share in a common life, that life which we share with the Father and his Son Jesus Christ.[118]

What Jesus was and what happened to him can, on this view, be seen as a new source and resource for reading God's meaning for man and for all creation that leads to man—the clue that enables us to discern a meaning which is more than that embodied in the clue itself, a key that unlocks the door into a more ample room than that which constitutes the ante-chamber, a focus of rays coming from a range beyond that of its own confines, a characteristic gesture from the hand of God revealing his meaning and purpose.

(v) *The world 'within God': 'pan-en-theism'*.[119] However, unique though Jesus is, the whole world, including man and his history, in general, and the man Jesus and *his* history, in particular, subsist and exist within the 'divine milieu' of God the Creator. So that, even the human response of Jesus to God his Father is kindled and enabled by the ever-present agency of God within his creation. So that Jesus' response to God, like

[118] I John 1: 1–3 (NEB).
[119] Cf. §IV C (iii).

the lesser reactions of all human beings to God, is the result
of the personal outreach of God immanently into the depths
of a created human will—that is, it was 'in the Spirit' that Jesus
responded to his Creator (which is an aspect of the general
thesis of G. W. H. Lampe[120]). To the question 'Why was
the human will of Jesus fully open to God?' the traditional
answer would have been that God as Spirit was at work in
him. The initiative[121] was, in this sense, 'from God' and, in
this sense again, Jesus was an 'only-begotten' exemplar of the
sonship of God into which all men are called—for contingently,
we know of no other response and openness to God of a
character like his.[122]

It might, on first thought, be regarded as a somewhat
Pickwickian sense of 'initiative from God' which is being
employed here, since in this sense all activities are 'from God'
in that, but for God's creative action, there would be nothing,
and nothing happening, at all. Nevertheless, I think it is not
improper to identify particular events and processes (in this
case the 'event' of Jesus' response and openness to God and
the 'process' of his life, death, and resurrection) as being one
result of a particular 'initiative from God' when these events
and processes constitute an especially significant communication
of God's meaning to man. As agents we are all the time present
in and through our bodies, yet at times we *choose* to communicate our inner selves through our words and actions; so,
by analogy, might it be with God. It was from such a special
awareness of God experienced through Jesus that, a matter
already referred to briefly, there 'developed' the New Testament images of Jesus as the 'Christ', 'Son of God', 'Son of Man',
'Lord', 'Wisdom', 'Logos', etc., and so doctrines of incarnation,
and later of 'The Incarnation'.

(*vi*) *God transcendent and immanent*.[123] In Jesus, his Jewish
followers encountered, especially in the light of his resurrection,
a dimension of that transcendence which, as good monotheists,

---

[120] Above, p. 207 n. 49.

[121] The action of God as Spirit within the inner life of man to enable him to respond
personally to personal God (i.e. to become himself 'spirit' or 'spiritual') is scarcely
to be distinguished from that action of God sometimes denoted as 'prevenient grace'.

[122] Cf. §VI (2), pp. 219, 220.

[123] Cf. §IV A, B, pp. 219, 220.

they attributed to God alone. But they also encountered him as fully man; and in his manhood, what he was *qua* human, they also experienced, in a way different from hitherto, an intensity of God's immanence in the very stuff of existence. The fusion of these two aspects of awareness of the presence of God in the human person of Jesus gave rise to the conviction that in Jesus something new had appeared in the world—as *we* would say, a new emergent had appeared within creation—and they ransacked their cultural stock of available images, both Hebraic and Hellenistic, to give expression to this new non-reducible distinctive mode of existence that the life, death, and resurrection of Jesus unfolded.

As we have already seen, one of the abstract ideas later used to denote this new emergent mode of existence was that of 'incarnation', the three essential presuppositions of which have been distinguished by J. Macquarrie[124] as: (a) the initiative is from God, not man; (b) God is deeply involved in his creation; (c) the centre of this initiative and involvement is Jesus Christ. We have earlier adumbrated the use of 'incarnation'[125] as denoting immanence-in-a-human-person intensified to the point where God's transcendence begins to be displayed and of this as having been, at least contingently, actually the case in Jesus Christ. This is in accord with Macquarrie's second and third essential presuppositions and we have agreed that there is a divine initiative involved even in the fully human response of Jesus (criterion (a)). So I hope it is not misleading to go on using the term 'incarnation'[126] to denote the understanding of Jesus being developed here in the light of our way of regarding God's action in the world. Nevertheless when we do use this term in reference to Jesus, we are using it with a particular stress on what happened in him as being

---

[124] J. Macquarrie, *Theology*, 53 (1977), 372; reprinted in *The Truth of God Incarnate*.
[125] In §IV F.
[126] Etymologically, it must be recognized that 'incarnation' is the anglicization of the Latin equivalent (*incarnatio*) of the Greek term *ensarkosis* and means, literally, 'enfleshing', where it is the divine that is the subject—i.e. it refers to the entry of the divine into human. (See C. F. D. Moule, 'Three points of conflict in the Christological debate', in *Incarnation and Myth: The Debate Continued*, ed. M. Goulder (SCM Press, London, 1979.) So at this etymological level there is only a fine line between 'incarnation' and 'inspiration', if the subject of the latter is also God. However, in the Christian tradition the term 'incarnation' (*incarnatio*) has been more distinctly appropriated to refer, following John 1: 14, to the divine Word *becoming* a man, not

a particular form of God's immanence in, in this case, created man. Our starting-point was the recognition that God was present unveiling his meaning in the whole of his creation and could not be more or less present in some parts of it than others. So the *continuity* of Jesus with the rest of humanity, and so with the rest of nature, must be stressed more explicitly than the wording of criterion (b) of Macquarrie seems to suggest ('God is deeply involved in his creation'). We must say the creation is in God and God is the agent of its events and processes.

This means that the manifestation of God which his contemporaries encountered in Jesus must have been a manifestation emanating from within creation, deep within those events and processes which led to Jesus, and which were his life, death and resurrection. In other words, 'incarnation' in the light of our understanding of God's creation and presence in the world, does not involve any 'descent' of a God, conceived of as 'above' man. Rather, the man Jesus is, by virtue of his human response and openness to God, the locus where there is unveiled that which, or rather the One Who, is present continuously creating and bringing his purpose to fruition in the order of energy–matter–space–time. Because of the continuity of the creative activity of God throughout time acting through the inherent creativity of the universe, it seems to me that we have to come to see Jesus, not as unique in being an invasion of the personhood of a man by the external transcendent Divine Person (as in the 'doctrine of the Incarnation', capital 'I'), but rather as being a unique manifestation of a possibility always inherently there for man by his potential nature, i.e. by virtue of what man was, or rather might be, in himself (which is, of course, as God evolved him).

---

just *entering* a man. Whether or not this distinction can be properly and usefully maintained in the light of the way we have come, in these lectures, to understand how God is at work in the world is the issue which lies behind any assessment of the continued viability, or otherwise, of incarnational language. In this context, it seems to me we do not have to be impaled on the horns of the dilemma of choice between 'incarnation' *or* 'inspiration'. Indeed it could be argued that in John 1 it is precisely this dichotomy which is being repudiated by the juxtaposition, on the one hand, of 'all that came to be was alive with his [the Word's] life, and that life was the light of men' (v. 4) and 'all who did receive him ... he gave the right to become children of God ... the offspring of God himself' (v. 13) with, on the other hand, the (same) 'Word became flesh' (v. 14).

The 'incarnation' which occurred 'in' Jesus is an example of that emergence-from-continuity that we have seen characterizes the creative process. There is both continuity with all that preceded him and with him there emerges a new mode of human existence which by virtue of its openness to God was and is a new revelation of God's meaning *in* creating man and *for* man—*for* man, because man is a creature who asks 'Why?' and seeks for meaning and intelligibility in his created life. I cannot help thinking such an emphasis on continuity (immanence) as well as on emergence (incarnation) is vital to any account of Jesus which is going to make what he *was* relevant to what we *might* be. We shall return to this later, but, for the moment, let us note that nothing we have affirmed about Jesus is, in principle, impossible for all men—even if, as a matter of historical fact, we think that manifest 'incarnation' is only to be seen in him, it is not excluded as a possibility for all men.

It is at this point that the advantage of the use of 'Spirit' language in terms of which to elaborate the significance of Jesus has its strength, as urged by Professor Lampe.[127] For then, the God, who as Spirit, is manifest in the life, death, and resurrection of Jesus, is clearly designated as the same mode of being of God who *as* Spirit reaches out to all mankind and can dwell in man's inner life—i.e. can be immanent in man as a person. No attempt is then made to distinguish between the mode of the being of God revealed in Jesus, and that which might be manifest in us too.

The patristic Logos-Christology, revived by K. Barth and E. Brunner, also attempted to bridge the concepts of man, of Jesus as God Incarnate and of God in the world. However, Pannenberg has argued that the Logos concept, in the form developed by the Apologists, cannot be accommodated to our modern understanding of nature; and that in the second-century form of the concept in Irenaeus, of the Word 'in which God broke his silence', it has value only as 'a metaphor'.[128] It is then subsumed to the concept of revelation or, in the terminology used here, of unveiling of God's meaning in Jesus. Such a 'concept of the Word does not have the ontological significance of an independent hypostasis beside God the Father

[127] Above, p. 207 n. 49.
[128] Pannenberg, *Jesus—God and Man*, p. 167.

and thus does not have the significance of the patristic Logos concept'.[129] He even asserts, with Trinitarian doctrine in mind,

Today the idea of revelation must take the place of the Logos concept as the point of departure for Christology. This is largely also the case where one pursues a Christology of the Word, insofar as the concept of word here is used as a figurative expression for the revelatory event. The insight into Jesus' unity with God's essence and into the differentiation between Father and Son within the essence of God himself, which remains in spite of this unity, can be substantiated only through the perception of Jesus as God's revelation. The unity with God's essence and the differentiation of Jesus' divinity from the Father's are elements that are implicitly established already in the recognition of Jesus as God's revelation. Their explicit formulation only unfolds in the content of the perception of revelation.[130]

I am less sure of this apparently total rejection of the use of the idea of Logos: it might well be possible to formulate a consistent non-hypostatized concept of the Logos which could express the creative immanence of God in the world, and in the self-conscious rationality of man in particular, and which could also be that which is explicitly manifest in Jesus, rather than implicitly, as it is in the rest of creation. I have tried to develop such a line of thought in an earlier work:[131] it may be that we shall not, after all, be able to avoid entirely accounts of the *ontological* significance of Jesus the Christ.

It is clear that, whatever model of incarnation in Jesus is deployed, the exercise of trying to relate the encounter with God in him, experienced by both the early witnesses and the subsequent Church, cannot be conducted without constant reference to what may be plausibly believed about the way God is related to and acts in the world—and such beliefs are all the time being subtly modified as our scientific understanding of that world develops and our philosophical tools become sharpened. With this understanding of the significance of Jesus the Christ, developed in this contemporary context, we finally

---

[129] Ibid.

[130] Ibid., p. 168.

[131] Peacocke, *Science and the Christian Experiment*, Ch. 6, esp. pp. 154–64—where the treatment owes much to the interpretation of the Definition of Chalcedon developed by D. E. Jenkins, *The Glory of Man* (SCM Press, London, 1967).

turn to the much more urgent, existential and personal question of the

VIII.   IMPLICATIONS OF THE MEANING FOR EVOLVED MAN OF WHAT GOD WAS UNVEILING IN JESUS THE CHRIST

We have argued that any assessment today of the significance of the life, death, and resurrection of Jesus has to be made both in the light of the way we have to conceive of God's action in a world now best described from the perspective of the sciences; and in the light of what historical scholarship tells we can reasonably know about Jesus' teaching and the events surrounding his life, death, and resurrection. This has led us to affirm, correspondingly, both the *continuity* of Jesus, in his manhood, with the rest of creation, with a stress on the meaning of God's continuous action in that creation being focused, realized, unveiled, and illuminated in him; and a recognition of the distinctively new and *emergent* in Jesus and his relation to God. This latter aspect and the status of the historically developing language and concepts the Christian community has employed to express this new emergent have been our concern, but now we have to realize that what we have been saying about the continuity of Jesus with creation has profound implications for our understanding of man.[132] So let us now examine briefly how the unveiling of meaning we claim is available in and through Jesus relates to the non-biological needs of man we discerned in the previous lecture (V).

Man, we saw, needs to come to terms with his *awareness of death*,[133] that dissolution into disorder of the physical matrix, the stuff of materiality, which is the locus of our personal agency and presence in the world. The man Jesus existed in the world as we do; he was made of carbon, nitrogen, oxygen and so on, as we are. His body bore all the marks of its evolutionary history, as ours do. His DNA was patterned on the same genetic code as is ours, and as is that of all other living

[132] It also has, needless to say, profound implications for our understanding of the nature of God—see, e.g., Peacocke, *Science and the Christian Experiment*, Ch. 6, and the bold logic of J. Moltmann, *The Crucified God*, pp. 214–16, 230, 255) that recognizing that God was one with the Jesus who died on the cross entails also a recognition of a transition within God's inner being as creative Love—and a total rejection of the unchangeable, impassible, immovable God of philosophical 'theism'.

[133] Cf. Lecture V:§V B, p. 179.

creatures from microbes to animals. He, too, like us, represented
an apparently temporary configuration of the stuff of the world
—but a configuration which thinks, loves, and knows itself, as
we do. In himself, as man, he (like us) represented the fundamental mystery, glory, and tragedy of persons emergent in a
physical cosmos. Yet his openness to God—to the point of
offering not only his life, but also his relationship to God itself
to God to fulfil his purposes—was the occasion and opportunity
for that unveiling of God's action on behalf of man we call
the resurrection. In that action those who had known the
human person of Jesus became convinced that he had in all
his human personhood been taken through death, with all its
dissolution and apparent reversion to primeval chaos, into a
new mode of life within the very being of the God who
transcends all matter–energy–space–time. In what happened
to Jesus then, we have to say that God has, as it were, un-
mistakably shown his hand, has unveiled further his purposes
in the cosmos and the meaning he has written in man. Thereby
God in and through Jesus has afforded us a new interpretation
of personalness, a new definition (if you like) of what it is, or
rather might be, to be human, of the end God purposes for
man. More particularly, in Jesus we see what kind of life it
is (and the kind of death he suffered, for it was the direct
consequence of the character of the life) that can be taken up
into the life of the God its Creator, so that death becomes the
opportunity of a new kind of existence, emergent from its
matrix of matter–energy–space–time. It is a life of openness to
God, of oneness with God's purposes to bring his Kingdom into
the life of man, of unstinting self-offering love of man through
love of God.

So in the life, death, and resurrection of Jesus (taken
together as a unity) we face a judgement on death in relation
to God's purposes for man which, once apprehended, transforms the landscape of human self-awareness. This glow on the
horizon casts an entirely new light on and gives a new direction
to the path man treads from birth to death. For the life, death,
and resurrection of Jesus shows us that all of our existence
that is truly offered to God and his purposes, which in Jesus'
case was his whole life, is, through the gateway of death, taken
up by God into his own realm of existence. This life, death,

and resurrection of Jesus, moreover, demonstrates the possibility of transcending that *finitude*[134] which is most dramatically exhibited in death but the sense of which permeates our whole existence. For these 'things about Jesus' now assure us that whatever offering of ourselves we make to God in unity with his creative purposes—whether or not seen by our fellow men, whether or not imperfect and incomplete and whether or not frustrated by those different kinds of limitations that constitute our finitude—is taken up into the transcendent life of God.

We also saw that man needs to learn how to bear *suffering*.[135] This need finds a new context when it is understood that God as Creator has been revealed, not only as 'the Love that moves the heavens and the other stars', but also as the Love that offers itself and suffers in and with its creation. No awareness of a new context can diminish the suffering itself, only active love by human beings reflecting the Love of the Creator can do that. But the awareness of this context can allow us to see suffering as less pointless than we would otherwise—to see it, for example, as the cost of the existence of self-conscious, aware persons and as the consequence of allowing that free play of randomness which generates the new emergent entities of the cosmos and enables all its potentialities to be explored. However absurd and irrational suffering may be in its immediate incidence we are through Jesus enabled at least to begin to see how it might fit into an overarching and unfolding purpose whose fulfilment is supremely valuable, even if the way is costly. Healthy, positive, unimpeded, happy, self-conscious human life is then seen for what it is—as a rare occurrence, an occasional gift from the Creator and, perhaps, also, as a necessary recuperative intermission within that more intense creativity (in human relationships, as well as the more traditionally 'creative' pursuits of man) which its converse alone seems capable of eliciting.

Man is a self-conscious creature who is now aware that he has evolved and that his future, both individual and social, depends on which of his *potentialities* are realized, in which

---

[134] Cf. Lecture V:§V C, p. 181.
[135] Cf. Lecture V:§V D, p. 182.

direction he decides to go.[136] Men have often responded to these challenges by seeking 'perfection' but this can be a neurosis-inducing quest, not least because of the multiple ambiguities of what 'perfection' could possibly mean. As John Passmore[137] has demonstrated the question 'Are men perfectible?' does not admit of any easy straightforward answer.

To assert that man is perfectible may mean either:
(1) there is some task in which each and every man can perfect himself technically;
(2) he is capable of wholly subordinating himself to God's will;
(3) he can attain to his natural ends;
(4) he can be entirely free of any moral defects;
(5) he can make of himself a being who is metaphysically perfect;
(6) he can make of himself a being who is harmonious and orderly;
(7) he can live in the manner of an ideally perfect human being;
(8) he can become godlike.[138]

Moreover, as he points out, it is necessary also to distinguish between perfectibility for an élite and for all men. So how do we relate Jesus the Christ to man's aspirations to realize his potentialities and to determine his direction if we are to avoid, as I now think we should,[139] talk of 'perfection' in him? To talk of 'potentialities' and 'directions' is to imply criteria for judging them—and it is in relation to such criteria that 'perfection' has often been described. We will not pursue this chimera but ask, more pertinently to the present context, 'What guidance about, what insight into, human life is afforded by the life, death, and resurrection of Jesus?'

I have already concurred with Dr Nineham that the historical proof that Jesus was 'sinless', in the sense of moral perfection (even if we knew what it was), is never going to be forthcoming.[140] And, *a fortiori*, it is clear that Jesus is never going to represent 'perfection' in other highly valued areas of human activity—in art, or science, or statesmanship. Indeed, if he had been 'perfect' in any particular aspect of human activity of this kind, then what his humanity was, and became, would

---

[136] Cf. Lecture V:§V E, p. 182.
[137] J. Passmore, *The Perfectibility of Man* (Duckworth, London, 1970), Ch. 1.
[138] Passmore, op. cit., p. 27.
[139] See above, p. 222 n. 83.
[140] Ibid.

not have that universal significance for all men which has been attributed to it. What, I argued,[141] we do find is that there is good cumulative evidence for Jesus' unique openness to and oneness with God, an openness which evoked the response of both his life and his death.[142] But it was the human Jesus who so responded to God and in the uniqueness of his responses he was not only a paradigm ('a pattern, examplar, example' (OED)) but also the unique paragon ('a pattern of excellence; a person or thing of supreme excellence' (OED)), the archetype, the chief examplar of what it is for a man to be united in self-offering will and purpose with God his Creator, so that the more intimate term 'Abba', Father, becomes appropriate. Such oneness and harmony with one's Creator is a universal possibility for all men and therefore may, if one wishes, be described as the kind of 'perfection' they should seek. However, since the God, openness to whom is the realization of human potential, is God the Creator who all the time is making 'things new' in his world, the content of and the attributes appropriate to a life so united with God themselves remain entirely undefined —except in so far as a human person who is one with God will reflect the nature of that same God who was manifested in Jesus the Christ who was uniquely open to him.

In this sense all mankind can aspire to become 'Christlike': because of what Christ was and did all men can hope, as St. Paul did for the Galatians, that they may 'take the shape of Christ'.[143] Such is also the significance of Jesus' 'Sonship' of God which seems to be a sonship in which all can share, to which all are called, as Professor Lampe has expressed it in relation to the 'post-existent Christ':

Resurrection is something much wider and more far-reaching than the return of Jesus to friends who had let him down. It is, rather, a taking up of those friends, and of all subsequent believers, into his life of sonship. It is the broadening out of the union of God's Spirit with man from its embodiment in the individual life of Jesus to include

---

[141] §VI (2), above pp. 219, 220.

[142] In the circumstances of his time (which would be the circumstances of *any* time, men being what they are) his death on a criminal's cross was the consequence of the quality and character of his life and teaching, so that his life and death have to be judged together.

[143] Galatians 4: 19 (NEB).

all those who are indwelt and taught and guided into all the truth by the Spirit that was his.[144]

The title 'Jesus Christ' represents the fusion of what the man Jesus was in history and the significance (Christ) that came to be attributed to him. But this significance is always being viewed within the moving perspective conditioned by man's cultural resources in directions opened up by his expanding consciousness resulting from his newly won knowledge, not least in the sciences. I am suggesting, furthermore, that for us with our combination of historical scepticism and relativism—both with respect to much of the purported 'history' of Jesus and with respect to the stability of our own viewpoint—the significance of Jesus is to be found in his being a model of the mode of all mankind's relationship to God whose character as Love was itself expressed in Jesus' life, death, and resurrection. Therein Jesus is the supreme examplar and original archetype of the way God can bring all human beings to actualize that potentiality which all share—the ability to respond to, to be open to, the God who is our Creator and calls us into *his* future.

Jesus' life, death, and resurrection show that God is that creative Love who suffers in and with the created self-consciousness of man and that that same God wills to take us into his life. Jesus by constituting this archetype of man's relation to God exercises a critical function over all other such purported relationships by revealing in himself both man's capacity to respond to God and what such a response might entail. Thereby Jesus shows us what God is intending for man through his creation and the route of self-offering love along which God beckons us. Each generation of those who follow Jesus along that route fill out their description of the scenery through which it passes and the character of the terrain. Nevertheless it is still Jesus the Christ who defines the direction of the exploration and gives us, through his own life with God, the expectation that we can arrive at God's destination for us.[145]

It is worth digressing, briefly, to note that in the foregoing

[144] Lampe, op. cit., p. 157.

[145] This account has affinities with traditional understandings of Jesus Christ as, in the first instance (or, as first proposition), an indicative revelation, or archetype, of the will of God (*Urbild*); and in the second instance (or, as second proposition), as imperative (*Vorbild*).

I have been trying to assess the meaning for evolved man of what God was unveiling and doing in the man Jesus the Christ in relation to what man needs to 'live by', which we discerned earlier[146] in broadly psychological and anthropological terms. But I also outlined[147] some of the profound theological diagnoses of man's state and predicament: of his sin (and so 'Fall) as a falling short from what God intends for him and therein a failure to realize his potential and a defacing of the 'image of God' in him; of the tension between his self-centredness and the 'openness' to the world which distinguishes him from other organisms; and, so, as an unfulfilled paradox in the perspective of evolution. To all of these more theological diagnoses of man our assessment of the significance of Jesus, of the particular meaning of God he unveils at that time and place in the history of man, is relevant, as merely restating them at this point makes abundantly apparent. We cannot follow this trail now but it is worth reaffirming that the starting-point for that assessment of Jesus must be in the context of our world, of which the sciences have actually demonstrated us to be part. It is, I would urge, only from such a base that a more systematic theology, including a Christology (and indeed Jesuology) might then be legitimately developed which might have any hope of being understood, let alone believed, by twentieth-century human beings. But we leave such a task for the moment and return to our main theme.

We have seen that the life, death, and resurrection of Jesus the Christ tells us more about man himself than we could have otherwise discovered. In manifesting to us God as Creator Spirit immanently at work to evoke in that part of his creation which is self-aware a conscious response to himself and a call to unity with his purposes, the 'things about Jesus' afford a definition of what it is to be human, or rather to become human. Jesus the Christ is the expressed, intelligible answer (i.e. 'Word') by God to the question 'What should man become?' What man encounters in Jesus the Christ is, in Philip Hefner's phrase[148] the 'self-definition' of human life,

---

[146] Ibid. Lecture V.

[147] §II, above, pp. 188 ff.

[148] P. Hefner. 'The Self-Definition of Life and Human Purpose: Reflections upon the Divine Spirit and the Human Spirit', *Zygon*, 8 (1973), 345–411.

which he describes as a process of understanding who man is and for what end he exists, and of acting upon this understanding so as to actualize it concretely—a process he sees as particularly manifested through God as Holy Spirit in the self-transcendence of all life in relation to its environment.[149] In this respect, Hefner writes in consonance with Professor Lampe's own understanding of God as Spirit:

If, then, we ask again, 'What has God in Jesus done for man that man himself could not do?', our answer can be: 'Created him'; or, rather, 'Brought the process of creation to the point where perfect man appears for the first time'. 'Perfect', in this context, means 'perfect in respect of his relationship to God'.

Creation is a continuing process, and for God's continuous creation of man in ever deeper and richer communion with himself the model of God as Spirit is very apt; for the term 'Spirit' properly refers, not to God's essence but to his activity, that is to say, his creativity.[150]

The definition of man afforded by Jesus the Christ is not entirely *self*-definition, however, for man is defined not by what he begins as, nor by what he believes himself to be, but by that to which God intends to bring him. However we may define man from the viewpoint of the physical, biological, or social sciences this is no match for a definition coming, as it were, from the other direction: more precisely, from the direction of that Other who is God the Creator. In this sense Jesus is the definition of the divine end of man—he defines man not by his origins in the physical, biological, and social world but in terms of what God intends him to become. Thus we might well say that through Jesus we have come to see what personalness might amount to. In his life, death, and resurrection we have seen a concentration of the activity of the immanent Creator to bring created personalness out of materiality into the divine life.

In thus speaking, we come very close to patristic teaching on the 'deification', or 'divinization', of man, through Jesus

---

[149] For further discussion of this, in relation to an incarnational interpretation of creation see also, in the same volume, by the present author, 'The Nature and Purpose of Man in Science and Christian Theology', *Zygon*, 8 (1973), 373–94, esp. 390–1.

[150] Lampe, op. cit., p. 17.

Christ.[151] Moreover this growth in union with and knowledge of God is the work of God as Spirit; for where the 'Spirit of the Lord' is 'there is no veil over the face, we all reflect as in a mirror the splendour of the Lord; thus we are transfigured into his likeness, from splendour to splendour [or, "glory to glory", RV]; such is the influence of the Lord who is Spirit.'[152] This theme of the 'deification' of man also underlies the concept of the participation of man in the 'sonship' of man to God which was realized in Jesus: 'In Jesus, however, we do see one who for a short while was made lower than the angels, crowned now with glory and honour because he suffered death, so that by God's gracious will, in tasting death he should stand for us all. It was clearly fitting that God for whom and through whom all things exist should, in bringing many sons to glory, make the leader who delivers them perfect through sufferings.'[153]

What happened to Jesus, it is claimed, is universalizable and communicable to all human persons. But why should this be so? The only basis for this, it seems to me, must be in the continuities which Jesus has with us: that is, because what is unveiled in Jesus is the continuous immanent creative activity of God in man (as 'Spirit', or as 'Logos') that is there all the time. God's acts in Jesus, which are not to be distinguished from what Jesus did *qua* man, unveil the meaning God intends for man both within his creation and beyond. In Jesus the Christ, man comes to know of his capacity for sharing in the life of God as self-offering creative Love and the meaning and intelligibility of the existence that God intends for him. In Jesus, then, there is revealed what God has *all the time* been doing

---

[151] 'Our Lord Jesus Christ, the word of God, of his boundless love, became what we are that he might make us what he himself is' Irenaeus, *Adversus Haereses*, 5, praef. (trans. H. Bettenson, *The Early Christian Fathers* (Oxford University Press, London, 1956), p. 77); 'The Word ... of God, who became man just that you may learn from a man how it may be that man should become God", Clement of Alexandria, *Protrepticus* 1 (8, 4) (Bettenson, op. cit., p. 177); 'For the Word was not degraded by receiving a body, so that he should seek to "receive" God's gift. Rather he deified what he put on; and, more than that, he bestowed this gift upon the race of men', Athanasius, *Contra Arianos*, i. 42 (Bettenson, op. cit., p. 279); 'The Word was made man in order that we might be made divine. He displayed himself through a body, that we might receive knowledge of the invisible Father', Athanasius, *De Incarnatione*, 54 (Bettenson, op. cit., p. 293).

[152] 2 Cor. 3: 17, 18 (NEB).

[153] Hebrews 2: 9, 10 (NEB).

and intending for man and so man is, because of this, now able freely and consciously to respond to God and to participate with God in his continuously creative work.[154] In taking the self-offered life and death of Jesus into his own life, God has shown that this is what he intends for all—it is what human life is meant to be and become—and he has unveiled this meaning within the very warp and woof of the earthy, physical, frustrated, tragic existence which constitutes human life, the very matrix of matter–energy–space–time within which as Creator he has chosen to express himself. But all talk of 'deification' of man, of a hope for man which incorporates him into the life of God runs out into the mysterious and ineffable and inexpressible[155]—for it is then the inner being of the God who is Other and Creator of which we have to speak. Even so, this is the unthinkable possibility which God incarnate in evolved man has unveiled for us—that God can dwell in man in such a way that man can come to dwell in God—the vision ultimately vouchsafed to Dante of the life of God Himself:

> Eternal light, that in Thyself alone
> Dwelling, alone dost know Thyself, and smile
> On Thy self-love, so knowing and so known!

---

[154] The theme of the next Lecture (VII).

[155] This emphasis has been a constant theme, expressed in their own way, of the Eastern Fathers, expounded thus by A. M. Allchin: 'There is that in man which desires to make things perfect and complete, in a limited, finite sense. He wants to make things safe, and to hold them as his own, not as a gift with unconfined implications and possibilities. He wants to define himself and even, we may say, to define God. In seeking to do this he shows that he has understood neither God nor himself. The quality of openness is a quality of all true humanity; openness to a God who however intimately present in his world he may be, always goes beyond all that we can desire or think of him ... But the deepest root of this necessity of openness is not to be found in the created and creative possibilities of man, but in the unknowability of the riches of God. This theme of the unknowability of the God who makes himself known in Jesus is again one of the absolute presuppositions of all patristic theology. And again it is one which needs particular emphasis in our own time. The ... preference [of Eastern theology] for the way of negation in the approach to God, is a witness to the superabundant generosity of the divine being which always goes beyond what we can see or know of him, and thus, in a paradoxical way it is also a witness to the capacity for the infinite which is planted at the heart of man, created in the divine image' ('The Doctrine of Man—an Eastern Perspective', in *Man: Fallen and Free*, ed. E. W. Kemp (Hodder & Stoughton, London, 1969), p. 154).

The sphering thus begot, perceptible
In Thee like mirrored light, now to my view—
When I had looked on it a little while—

Seemed in itself, and in its own self-hue,
Limned with our image; for which cause mine eyes
Were altogether drawn and held thereto.[156]

---

[156] Dante, *Il Paradiso*, Canto XXXIII, ll. 124–33, trans. Barbara Reynolds (her completion of Dorothy Sayers's translation) (Penguin Books, Harmondsworth, 1962).

VII

Man in Creation

I. INTRODUCTION

ON Christmas Day 1968, three American astronauts (Frank Borman, James Lovell, and William Anders) were the first human beings ever to go round the 'dark' side of the moon away from the Earth. Firing their rockets at the crucial point, they headed Apollo 8 for home and it was then that these three men beheld the planet Earth in a way vouchsafed to only a small number of human beings. They saw Earthrise over the horizon of the moon—and they saw it in its bright blue and white beauty, wreathed in cloud and glistening by the light of the sun against the black void of space. The photographs that others since have taken on such voyages behind the moon are part of the imperishable memories of our times and the image they have implanted has played its part in the radical change in our consciousness of our earthly home. For they, and we through them, began to see the Earth as a spaceship. But spaceships are vulnerable for they are dependent on a highly interlocking system of working units each of which is essential to the functioning of the whole, which includes the life of the astronauts—as became dramatically apparent to all when, on 14 April 1970, at 0404 BST, from Apollo 13, already then fifty-six hours and over 200,000 miles from the Earth on its way to the moon, the cryptic message was received 'Hey, we've got a problem here!' An oxygen tank had been damaged by an (unexplained) explosion. Only by a *tour de force* of technical and medical intelligence were the astronauts restored safely to Earth. The percipient had been aware of the vulnerability of spaceship Earth for many decades; for example, four years before Apollo 13, Barbara Ward had written (borrowing a comparison of Buckminster Fuller):

The most rational way of considering the whole human race today is to see it as the ship's crew of a single space ship on which all of us, with a remarkable combination of security and vulnerability, are making our pilgrimage through infinity. Our planet is not much more than the capsule within which we have to live as human beings if we are to survive the vast space voyage upon which we have been engaged for hundreds of millenia—but without noticing yet our condition. This space voyage is totally precarious. We depend upon a little envelope of soil and a rather larger envelope of atmosphere for life itself. And both can be contaminated and destroyed.... We are a ship's company on a small ship. Rational behaviour is the condition of survival.[1]

—but it had not become part of the common consciousness of mankind. Today, *Torrey Canyon* and *Amoco Cadiz* disasters, and almost daily newspaper reports of other new kinds of pollution and scarcities in non-renewable resources of material and energy serve to reinforce that dramatic, and beautiful initiation into our newly won global awareness.

Such are the rapidity and facility of communications today that, all over the industrialized world, at least, a new literature on the environment has burgeoned. The range and presuppositions of this literature are astonishingly wide-ranging, from the romantic and hippy to the cautious and governmental. Somewhere between these two extremes lie the publications of the World Council of Churches who, for a decade or more, have made wide-ranging studies[2] of the impact of science and technology in the context of the need to bring into existence a just, participatory, and sustainable society; and also the publications of individual churches.[3]

The sheer bulk of the literature on the environment (one wonders how much of our timber resources have been devoted

---

[1] Barbara Ward, *Space Ship Earth* (Hamish Hamilton, London, 1966), p. 18.

[2] e.g. T. S. Derr, *Ecology and Human Need* (Westminster Press, Philadelphia, 1975, first published as *Ecology and Human Liberation* (WSCF Books, World Council of Churches, Geneva, 1973, Vol. iii, No. 1, Serial No. 7)); H. Berkhof, 'God in Nature and History', *Faith and Order Studies*, 1964–7, No. 50, pp. 7–31; and most issues of *Anticipation* (published by the World Council of Churches, Geneva).

[3] By the *Church of England: Man in his living environment* (Board for Social Responsibility of the Church Assembly, Church Information Office, Church House, Westminster, 1970); *Man and Nature*—a report of a sub-group (of the former Doctrine Commission of the Church of England) set up in 1972 to 'investigate the relevance of Christian doctrine to the problems of man in his environment' (published Collins,

to it!) testifies both to the immense interest, at least in the *reading* public—this itself hints at the restricted social range of environmentally concerned groups—and to the diversity of human reactions to nature.

This diversity was never better exemplified (as T. S. Derr has reported)[4] than in the year following that of the Apollo 13 events, in 1971, when nature staged one of her own autonomous 'happenings' devoid of any human influence. For at that time Mount Etna erupted with terrifying rapidity and force, spewing a destructive and incandescent stream of lava on to the populated hillsides below. Human witnesses to this event reacted as follows: a group of tourists in Sicily, imbued with misplaced sporting instincts, *cheered* when the lava flowed across its first road as it came down the hillside; local farmers, enraged by such behaviour, attacked the tourists; a whole village took part in a special mass in front of the lava and implored the Virgin and local saints, whose relics they possessed for just such purposes, to stem its inexorable flow; and the Italian government could think of nothing better to do than to drop bombs on the flowing rock to divert it! In these reactions, we have in miniature a reflection of the ambiguities in some of the traditional attitudes of man to nature. Now superimposed upon these or, rather, embedding them in a new context, comes our new global awareness of our planetary home.

Our concern, in these lectures, has been with the doctrine of creation. What contribution to our global environmental problems, if any, is afforded by this perspective of man as created in a created world? To this question we shall revert later, but first we must clear what it is that environmental science, the science (ecology)[5] of our planetary home (*oikos*),

---

London, 1975), ed. H. W. Montefiore—who had earlier written *Can Man Survive?* (Fontana, Collins, London, 1969). By the *Church of Scotland*: the extensive publications of their Science, Religion and Technology Project (obtainable from the Church of Scotland Home Board, 121 George St., Edinburgh EH2 4YN). By the *American churches: Human Values on Spaceship Earth* (National Council of Churches, New York, 1966).

[4] Derr, op. cit., 1973, 1975, Ch. 1.

[5] *Ecology* may be defined as the scientific study of the relation between living organisms and their environment. *Human ecology*, as a subdivision, is then the relation between man and his environment (rather than man with man).

is telling us about the complexity of its interlocking dynamic processes.

II. THE WORLD ECOSYSTEM

A. Ecosystems

The energy source for all living organisms, including man, is the Sun whose energy is absorbed through green plants, on which all animals depend ultimately for food and which themselves depend on the activities of bacteria decomposing dead organisms and making nitrogen available. So all life is interdependent—indeed many creatures can only live in concert with, and often literally on, particular other organisms (symbiosis). Modern man is misguided if he thinks he can live and operate independently of the rest of the living world. Although he is an omnivore, capable of living in many habitats, he is still just as dependent on plants and bacteria, and on other animals, as was primitive man. All plants and animals live in complex systems consisting of many crossflows and exchanges of energy and matter in various chemical forms of such baffling complexity that only the advent of computers, and the development of systems theory, have given any hope of analysing them. 'It is hard to be a reductionist ecologist' according to an eminent ecologist.[6] These 'ecosystems' and their ramifications and mutual interlocking relations are, by and large, little understood. Pollution studies nearly always demonstrate them to be more complex and with longer tentacles than previously realized. The boundaries of such ecosystems are very blurred, for an ecosystem can be perceived at different levels: that of the whole world or (more usefully), that of the rain-forest or oakwood ecosystems, or, even, the ecosystem centred on a single plant—it includes everything contributing to the maintenance of life within a specified place and time.

In such systems all species are dependent for their survival on the system operating but not all are essential to its operations. Ecologists distinguish various 'trophic levels', a term which includes different kinds of exchanges of both food materials and

---

[6] Dr Norman Moore, to whom I am indebted for a lecture he gave on ecology at St. George's, Windsor, in September 1973.

of energy. These levels are: *producers*, photosynthetic plants converting the sun's radiant energy into stored chemical energy (as carbohydrates); *primary consumers*, herbivorous animals feeding on plants; *secondary consumers*, carnivorous animals feeding on primary consumers—that is, predators, parasites, and scavengers (of dead animals); *tertiary*, animal and other higher-order, *consumers* feeding on levels lower down in the food chain (though not 'lower' in any evolutionary sense—some bacteria are the highest-order consumers of all). Some consumers are opportunist and can switch between trophic levels (a bear feeding on fish and berries is both a tertiary and a primary consumer). Where an organism comes in the food web will depend on many factors, such as age and size. D. J. Owen[7] compares the food web of a large (4 kg) pike, living in the Thames, with a small one (a few centimetres long). The latter occupies the place of water beetles in the food web of the former since it feeds on smaller items (crustaceans, tadpoles, and insects) and is itself a source of food for perch on which the pike feeds; however, if it reaches full size, it will itself feed on perch (and roach) and become a top predator in the ecosystem. Consideration of such interrelationships in respect of the capture and transfer of energy at different trophic levels leads to the elaboration of an 'ecological pyramid' in which the width of the horizontal band representing energy transferred at each trophic level diminishes, in steps, as one goes from producers (plants) at the bottom, up to primary consumers (crustaceans, in this example) and secondary consumers (roach) to the large pike as tertiary consumer. Construction of such ecological pyramids is highly instructive and can be extended to much more complex systems—for example, all the organisms in a pond or lake, or all the insects in a field. The next stage in representation is a 'trophic model' which attempts to represent all processes of energy transfer in the ecosystem on one diagram and these can become extremely complex when the system includes organisms operating simultaneously at more than one trophic level.

Most living organisms procreate at rates which, if all survived to reproduce themselves, would produce a high surplus but

[7] D. J. Owen, *What is Ecology?* (Oxford University Press, London, 1974), from which much of this brief account here is derived.

because of the finiteness of the Earth, and so of resources and habitats, such exponential increase is impossible. It is prevented by inter-species competition and predation which is mitigated, at least among the higher animals, by birth control (reabsorption of embryos), the relation of brood size to available food, by territorial behaviour (often through ritualized fighting), etc.

Such ecosystems—communities of very different species mutually interacting and interdependent—tend to a steady state, or dynamic equilibrium, which is characteristic of their habitat and climate—tropical rain forest, desert, island, etc. Even so, ecosystems display both sequential and cyclical changes, which may involve any particular part of a forest, say, looking different at various times, while the forest as a whole is statistically stable; and the relative proportion of different species in an ecosystem may change cyclically. Natural ecosystems are, in fact, relatively stable—indeed evolution has ensured, by natural selection, that they are very durable, homeostatic, and resilient to wide variations in agents and influences present during their evolution (which in most cases does not include the effects of human action). In particular, it seems to be the rule that the greater the diversity, that is, the greater the number of component species present, the greater is its stability likely to be. Moreover, diversity itself depends on a number of factors—it increases from the poles to the equator, and it is lower on islands than on continental land masses.

B. Man and the ecosystems

Man, as we have stressed, has evolved out of the inorganic and biological world and is inherently a part of nature from this historical viewpoint. But, more pertinently, and urgently, it is necessary also to be alert to the fact that man is a part of nature today and cannot be considered outside the ecological network. Those features of man which render him distinctive, indeed unique, and which we have already had cause to emphasize, do not in any way place him outside the system. He has always been a factor in ecology—shedding waste, corpses, and food residues into the environment—and he has always depended on other species for food and energy and for replenishing the oxygen we consume from the air and for recycling nutrients. In fact, man (even more than the large pike we considered earlier) stands at the apex of a many-layered 'ecological pyramid'. But man is a special case in so far as the food we eat has been killed or prepared for us by other people. We eat bread as 'primary' consumers, to use the 'trophic' terms, although we do not individually grow our own wheat; we eat beef as 'secondary' consumers (the cattle having been killed by others); and, apart from fish, few of our eating habits place us in the 'tertiary' or higher levels (we do not eat predators very much nor feed on naturally dead organisms—though we consume huge quantities of such 'dead' organic material in the form of oil, coal, and natural gas). Moreover, man is not peculiar in needing to control his population and it has in fact been controlled ecologically and automatically in the past by disease, limited food resources, and climate. However, although man's destructive character does not place us outside the natural ecosystems of the world nevertheless his unique combination of intelligence and social organization, with its modern fruit of technology, adds a new and overwhelming factor to his effect on his own and other ecosystems.

Ever since man has emerged as *homo sapiens* (and even as Neanderthal man) he has been having a distinctive impact on natural ecosystems, from the time he first employed fire-drive methods to hunt game, thereby destroying forest and expanding grazing land—to the development of agriculture, which liberated at least some of the human population from food-gathering to make things, build cities, and to create the arts of civilization—to the destruction of the forests of the Lebanon and North Africa and the enclosure of common land in eighteenth-century England—right up to the present century.

But with man's increased ability to grow food for himself and now, in the twentieth century to prolong his life by medical technology and by chemical and other agents which destroy anti-human predators, his population has grown so steeply that he swarms over the finite surface of this global planet and is now a major factor in the ecosystems of all living creatures— and indeed of the natural inorganic systems of the Earth too. It probably took hundreds of thousands of years for the human population to reach its first billion, i.e. 1,000 million, in 1830.

It took only a hundred years to reach its second billion (in 1930), another thirty years its third (in 1960), and fifteen years its fourth (1975), and even if the birth and death rates equalize in the near future (which they show no sign of doing) the world population will still go on rising until well into the next century (possibly reach its seventh billion by the year 2000). Some of the poorer countries, in which of the order of half the population are under eighteen, will face disastrous situations by the end of the century.

The compounding of population and of technology has suddenly within recent decades accelerated to awake us to an inescapable new fact—that man has the capability of rendering unstable the ecosystems of the Earth through the massive doses of technology which have been injected into it since World War II. No longer can we delude ourselves that pollution is essentially local in scale—if only because the evidence about DDT which, while giving new possibilities of life (indeed life itself) to millions of people in previously malaria-infested regions, has spread through the food-chains of the globe being found, for example, in Arctic penguins and in fishes all over the world.[8] The time-scale of such effects is long compared with biological generation times—even if we stop using DDT now it will go on increasing in the oceans for the next twenty years, so we need to take thought much further ahead for the benefit of organisms alive in the future than we have ever had to do in the past.

But the effects of man on ecosystems are more subtle and profound than is suggested by straightforward examples of pollution (such as DDT, or mercury in the sea, or alteration of the carbon dioxide content of the atmosphere with consequent effects on temperature and climate). For man's impact on ecological systems is nearly always, often mistakenly on his own behalf, to simplify, to change complex ecological systems of many species to systems of fewer species, single ones even

[8] See 'Pollution and Worldwide Catastrophe', J. Maddox, *Nature*, 236 (1972), 433–6. The levels of DDT found in human beings have now been shown not to have caused damage to health, except in a few accidents (*Health Hazards of the Human Environment*, World Health Organisation, Geneva, 1972), though it is highly inimical to other living species, e.g. to many predatory birds and marine organisms (see Maddox, loc. cit., with references).

—as when forests are changed to grass lands, or even to mono-cultures of one cereal crop of high productivity. Cereal monocultures are highly vulnerable to changes in climate or to insects and man then has to take over the attempt to manage the ecological balance.

To convert an area of rain forest to a rice field is to replace an organized stable ecosystem that has taken thousands of years to put together with a simple monoculture dominated by one species and the organisms that happen to be able to exploit that species. The result is man is constantly faced with the depredations of weeds and pests able to adjust themselves to the monoculture he has created. This in turn leads to campaigns designed to destroy the weeds and the pests.[9]

Frequently he finds it hard to foresee the long-term effects of his pesticides and fertilizers on other organisms and thus to himself. Thus the 'Green Revolution' in rice has rendered the increased crops more vulnerable to accident and has neces-sitated greater use of pesticides to maintain these new strains —is this a case of short-term gain at the expense of long-term loss? It is hard to know, for man is all the time introducing *extra* imbalances into natural ecosystems (it must be remem-bered that not all natural systems can be regarded as 'balanced' and steady).

So almost everything man does to natural ecosystems for his own benefit is of such a kind and has such global effects that he is forced into becoming the manager of the Earth. The space-ship Earth, which is man's home, shows symptoms of becoming crippled in a way no less real than that of Apollo 13.

We have to visualize the earth as a small, rather crowded spaceship, destination unknown, in which man has to find a slender thread of a way of life in the midst of a continually repeatable cycle of material transformations. In a spaceship, there can be no inputs or outputs. The water must circulate through the kidneys and the algae, food likewise, the air likewise.... Up to now the human population has been small enough so that we have not had to regard the earth as a spaceship. We have been able to regard the atmosphere and the oceans and even the soil as an inexhaustible reservoir, from which we can draw at will and which we can pollute at will. There is hand-

[9] Owen, op. cit., p. 160.

writing on the wall, however ... Even now we may be doing universal damage to this precious little spaceship.[10]

Man, whether by intent or not, now finds himself at the helm of his spaceship and his own fate is linked with that of all its systems. For man needs, as much as other living organisms, the natural dynamic steady states of the oceans, of the atmosphere, and of the global cycles of carbon, oxygen, carbon dioxide, nitrogen, and water. So he now finds he has little option but to monitor and control, as it were from the apex of his 'ecological pyramid', his impacts on the balance of the great systems further down the pyramid which are themselves already interlocked with the urban life of the majority of mankind. For man lives in a 'made' world and to a world so organized in mind and practice we need, as Joseph Sittler has put it, a fresh approach, that is:

... a vast expansion of the notion of nature itself. For the reference of the term must now go beyond the given nonhuman world of land and sea and forest and wind and rain and petroleum and the entire range of plant and animal life. *Homo operator* is as ultimately dependent upon this primal nature as man has always been; but the *sense* for this dependence is distanced and muted in virtue of the astounding transformations science-based technology has wrought. The 'made' world that has come into being following the work of the chemist, the physicist, the biologist, the engineer, is closer to the common life of the millions than the 'natural' world of his fathers. Forests meet him as paper and plywood; oil and coal as energy, saran wrap, tires, and pharmaceuticals.... For so adaptable is man to the world that science has made possible and technology has realized, that in this new, 'made', extrapolated world most men feel at home. Here he 'belongs', in the company of fellow operators in the world he finds his 'natural' community; here he feels secure, for he knows the rules of the game; here he sees and works with astounding fabrications out of primal nature and deals with them with familiar, even playful recognition.[11]

This is a necessary qualification of the term 'nature',[12] for in most long-populated regions of the earth it is an earlier system

---

[10] K. E. Boulding, *Human Values on the Spaceship Earth* (National Council of Churches, New York, 1966), p. 6, quoted by Braaten, op. cit. below, p. 269 n. 27.

[11] J. Sittler, *Essays on Nature and Grace* (Fortress Press, Philadelphia, 1972), pp. 103–4.

[12] See Appendix B for a discussion of this term.

of man-in-nature which is now being given an extra impulse towards imbalance by the pressure of human population increase compounded by human technology. However this qualification should not diminish the sense of urgency which is generated by our newly acquired awareness of our planetary home as a great ecosystem—an awareness never better expressed than by Barbara Ward and Rene Dubos in the material they prepared for the United Nations Stockholm Conference on the Human Environment in 1972:

... we have lacked a wider rationale of unity. Our prophets have sought it. Our poets have dreamed it. But it is only in our own day that astronomers, physicists, geologists, chemists, biologists, anthropologists, ethnologists and archeologists have all combined in a single witness of advanced science to tell us that in every alphabet of our being, we do indeed belong to a single system, powered by a single energy, manifesting a fundamental unity under all its variations, depending for its survival on the balance and health of the total system.[13]

III. PROGNOSES

For more than a decade, there have been raised strident voices from prophets of the doom which is imminent for mankind as the consequence of what is already happening to his environment and population. One of the most famous deliverances of this kind was the 1972 report[14] sponsored by the Club of Rome which, on the basis of a computerized 'world model', predicted collapse of the economic and industrial systems of 'developed' countries by about the year 2100, unless the birth rate should come to equal the death rate and capital investment should come to equal capital depreciation. Almost as great in its impact, in the United Kingdom at least, was *A Blue-Print for Survival*[15] which made our flesh creep in the following terms.

The principle defect of the industrial way of life with its ethos of

[13] B. Ward and R. Dubos, *Only One Earth* (Penguin Books, Harmondsworth, 1972), p. 297.
[14] D. H. Meadows *et al.*, *The Limits of Growth* (MIT Press and Potomac Association, New York and Earth Island, London, 1972); a short account is given in 'The Carrying Capacity of our Global Environment' by J. Randers and D. H. Meadows, in *Western Man and Environmental Ethics*, ed. I. G. Barbour (Addison–Wesley, Reading, Mass., and London, 1972), pp. 253–76.
[15] *Ecologist*, Vol. 2, No. 1 (1972).

expansion is that it is not sustainable. Its termination within the lifetime of someone born today is inevitable—unless it continues to be sustained for a while longer by an entrenched minority at the cost of imposing great suffering on the rest of mankind. We can be certain, however, that sooner or later it will end (only the precise time and circumstances are in doubt) ... Radical change is both necessary and inevitable because the present increase in human numbers and *per capita* consumption, by disrupting ecosystems and depleting resources, are undermining the very foundations of survival.

And again we had 2,400 environmental scientists in a published message:

Widely separated though we are geographically, with very different cultures, languages, attitudes, political and religious loyalties, we are united in our time by an unprecedented common danger. This danger, of a nature and magnitude never before faced by man, is born of a confluence of several phenomena. Each of them would present us with almost unmanageable problems: together they present not only the probability of vast increases in human suffering in the immediate future, but the possibility of the extinction, or virtual extinction, of human life on Earth.[16]

Does not one hear echoes here of a more ancient voice?

I beheld the earth, and, lo, it was waste and void; and the heavens, and they had no light. I beheld the mountains, and, lo, they trembled and all the hills moved to and fro. I beheld, and, lo, there was no man, and all the birds of the heavens were fled. I beheld, and, lo, the fruitful field was a wilderness, and all the cities thereof were broken down at the presence of the Lord, and before his fierce anger.[17]

Indeed Jeremiah now seems a veritable novice by comparison with the authors of some of our modern scientific jeremiads!

Some six years after the *Blue-Print*'s call to action we still have disasters such as that of the oil spill from the *Amoco Cadiz* (the giant oil tanker wrecked on the Brittany coast in March 1978), the Mediterranean increasingly becomes a cess-pit and more and more of our beaches become unusable for recreation and are left to be occupied by plastic refuse and

---

[16] Issued by Dai Dong (Community of Man), a project of the Fellowship of Reconciliation (9 Coombe Rd., New Malden, Surrey).

[17] Jeremiah 4: 23–6 (RV).

lumps of congealed oil—so one could go on. Occasionally a shock event catalyses public opinion and government action (as when publicity about the secret dumping of cyanide on waste tips finally forced the British government into action long advised by the informed); and, slowly, environmental issues are being taken seriously by politicians even though, when weighed against loss of jobs or economic growth, there are not many votes in them. More cautious and less pessimistic assessments are not illfounded especially when the actual social and political responses to environmental change are taken into account.[18] Progress has been real—for example, the United Nations Stockholm declaration and its environment programme, the EEC environment legislation, the Royal Commission on Environmental Pollution in the UK and translation of its proposals into legislation, the planning of a Law of the Sea Conference (up till now still abortive)—but painfully slow. Even if some governments have begun to accept responsibility, the awakening of the general public opinion has only begun. H. Skolimowski, Professor in Engineering Humanities at the University of Michigan, even avers that

The ecology movement is in trouble because it has promised so much and delivered so little.... When one looks at the field, one sees an extraordinary proliferation of ideas, efforts, activities and publications. Now, there are lots of tributaries, but they do not connect to make up a river; lots of mini-influences, but they do not add up to make a significant difference to the existing socio-economic paradigm.... The ecology movement has succeeded in making us see the negative aspects of the present socio-economic paradigm; indeed, the negative aspects of the whole western materialistic civilisation. But it has not succeeded in its positive role, in instilling into us new, positive attitudes.... The technological society has deliberately cultivated a careless, consumptive, egoistic and slovenly human being. The frugal society which the ecology movement implicitly postulates must start with re-directing our attitudes and re-educating our values.[19]

[18] See, e.g., Lord Ashby, *A Second Look at Doom*, the 21st Fawley Foundation Lecture, University of Southampton, 1975, later published in *Encounter*, 46, 3 (1976), 16–24; and the evidence he gives in his Leon Sloss Junior Memorial Lectures, Stanford University, *Reconciling Man with the Environment* (Stanford University Press, Stanford, Calif. and Oxford University Press, Oxford, 1978) for a definite trend towards a higher valuation by the public of the environment.

[19] H. Skolimowski, *Listener*, 2 Dec. 1976, pp. 702–3.

He argues that, although the ecology movement has begun to devise alternative technologies on the basis of a developing ecological knowledge, it 'has made few inroads into rethinking the value basis ... which would be compatible with the new technology and the new world picture'[20]—and even less with developing what he calls a 'theology' which might integrate and include technology, knowledge, and values. He has tried to formulate a 'new moral imperative'[21] because of his belief in the need, engendered by our new-found ecological awareness, to generate a value system appropriate to the new situation in which man now finds himself in relation to the world—and so to other men and other living creatures.[22]

A similar emphasis occurs in the writings of Lord Ashby, based on his experience as Chairman of the Royal Commission on Environmental Pollution and on involvement in making its recommendations legislatively effective. He summarizes part of his 1976 Jephcott Lecture thus:

(1) Decisions on the protection of the environment are not just deductions from scientific and technical and economic data; there is an important, and sometimes a decisive, contribution based on 'fragile' social values which ... cannot be quantified without draining them of their content. That is one aspect of the human dimension.
(2) It is very difficult to assess these social values because public perception of an environmental hazard does not coincide with the expert's prediction of the probability of its occurrence and the damage it may do ...[23]

He agrees with the realism of Edmund Burke's dictum[24] that 'the public interest requires doing today those things that men of intelligence and goodwill would wish, five or ten years hence, had been done' and says this applies also to ecological questions both because of the fluidity of social values today, with the consequent unpredictability of future public opinion, and because of the complexity and frequent unavailability of

[20] Ibid.
[21] H. Skolimowski, *Ecological Humanism* Tract 19 and 20 (The Gryphon Press, Lewes, Sussex).
[22] See below, § V C.
[23] Lord Ashby, 'Protection of the Environment: The Human Dimension', Jephcott Lecture, *Proc. Roy. Soc. of Medicine*, 69 (1976), 721-30.
[24] Ashby, op. cit., 1976, pp. 727, 728.

hard data on the problems. To work with such a short time-scale (a 'horizon' of *c*. ten years) has the further advantage, he argues, of recognizing that the choices we make influence the values we come to hold: 'The environmental ethic is not a fixed goal, an immutable concept: it is an evolving idea.'[25] He sees the principle emerging, to which I have already referred, of recognition of man's interdependence on and involvement with other living organisms and of the risk of our disturbing nature's equilibria in a way dangerous even to our-selves: he echoes the view of Mr Justice Douglas of the US Supreme Court that environmental objects should have legal 'standing' conferred on them to allow those concerned to sue for their preservation.[26]

It has thus become increasingly clear that one of the vital components in the ecological situation we now face is the set of values we regard as operative in the process of making public and private decisions on the ecological data. These 'ecological values' are in process of change in a situation where personal ethical values are themselves in disarray and confusion. In the ecological situation, as Carl Braaten has said:

... our traditional ethic tends to lean backward to the past and therefore becomes speechless and helpless in coping with the actions which bear heavily on the destiny of the coming generations.

The attempt of some contemporary ethicists to free ethics from this bondage to past norms and principles in favor of a 'situation ethics' is a total failure with respect to the ecological problem. We cannot wait until we get into the situation of crisis and decision and then intuit the right thing to do, for then it will be too late; our society will have reached the point of no return.[27]

The ethical questions raised by our environmental dilemmas continually project us into the future in the sense that we have to include in our decisions a weighing of the consequences of our actions on mankind in the future (even if only ten years ahead), as well as on man and other living organisms now. To include 'living organisms' in that last phrase begs the

[25] Ibid.

[26] Quoted by C. D. Stone, *Should Trees Have Standing?* (Kaufman, Los Altos, Calif., 1974).

[27] C. Braaten, 'Caring for the future: where ethics and ecology meet', *Zygon*, 9 (1974), 316.

question of whether the interests of other living organisms should be weighed in our decisions, should even have 'rights', legal 'standing', conferred upon them. Such questions, the answers to which may necessitate new values and objectives for mankind in his relation to nature, cannot be considered without presuppositions concerning man's relation to nature —and it is to these presuppositions in this context that, I would claim, the understanding of nature as *creation* is acutely relevant. *How* these values make themselves effective in the complex chain which terminates in public decision-making is a different and complex problem which is commanding increasing attention:[28] *that* such value judgements are involved or presupposed is clear.

IV. THEOLOGY AND ECOLOGICAL VALUES

A. Are they connected?

The claim that the understanding of nature as *creation* is relevant to the generation of ecological values needs a more general justification before any closer study of the relation of the doctrine of creation to our ecological situation is merited. Do religious beliefs, as articulated intellectually in theological models, matter? Does any distinctive attitude to nature logically follow from theological statements?

Before following up such questions, it is worth while to take note that there have in recent years been significant statements, from a distinctively scientific viewpoint, of the role of religion in the cultural history of mankind. For example, in his 1975 Presidential Address to the American Psychological Association, Donald Campbell,[29] who describes himself as speaking from a physicalistic (materialistic) world view and as a 'hard-

---

[28] Lord Ashby (op. cit., 1978, pp. 14 f.) distinguishes three stages: (i) the 'ignition stage' in which public opinion is raised to a temperature which stimulates political action; (ii) the hazard is examined objectively, to find out how genuine and how dangerous it is and just what is the risk; and (iii) this objective information has to be combined with the pressures of advocacy and with subjective judgement to produce a formula for political decision. (i) involves explicit journalism; (ii) requires inputs from the scientist and economist (as 'objective' as possible) and (iii) involves inputs from spokesmen for public and private interests and the politician's 'hunch'. Values are involved primarily in (iii) but often, latently, in (ii) also.

[29] D. T. Campbell, 'On the conflicts between biological and social evolution and between psychology and moral tradition', *American Psychologist*, 30 (1975), 1103–26; reprinted in *Zygon*, 11 (1976), 167–208, along with other articles discussing his address.

line neo-Darwinian', analysed social evolution in terms, such as 'natural selection', analogous to those of biological evolution (not unlike R. Dawkins,[30] though without his nomenclature). He urged his fellow-psychologists to give up their traditionally anti-religious stance and to recognize that religions, with their associated ethical norms, have possibly been largely responsible for changing man from a primate defending only genetic kin into civilized man capable of co-operating with the whole of his species in societal living. In his own words: '... I have taken social evolution seriously and thus have included in the total range of facts to be explained the religious systems that emerged with ancient urban civilizations, treating these as having, or having had, an evolutionary adaptive value, an underlying functional truth, which modern social and behavioral scientists need to understand.'[31] Human urban social complexity, he argued, has been made possible by *social* evolution which, in optimizing social system functioning, has had to counter individual selfish tendencies which *biological* evolution continued to select as a result of genetic competition among the co-operators—and religion has been the principal countering agency.

Committing oneself to living for a transcendent Good's purposes, not one's own, is a commitment to optimize the social system rather than the individual system. Social groups effectively indoctrinating such individual commitments might well have had a social-evolutionary advantage and thus have discovered a functional, adaptive truth. It seems from cross-cultural surveys that belief in transcendent deities that are concerned with morality of human behavior toward other human beings occurs more frequently in more complex societies [G. Lenski, *Human Societies: A Macrolevel Introduction to Sociology*, McGraw-Hill Book Co., New York, 1970]. This fits in with the view that such an influence furthering altruistic behavior was more needed in urban civilizations than in more primitive ones either because of the greater complex social coordination required or because urban humankind lacked the genetic support for altruistic behavior that their predecessors had.[32]

This view also constitutes part of the foundation on which

[30] See above, Lecture V.
[31] Campbell, op. cit., p. 188.
[32] Campbell, op. cit., p. 192.

Ralph Burhoe[33] develops a 'scientific theology', a theology of the human prospect and of the 'Lord of History' which incorporates more completely than any other current 'theology' the scientific account of man's biological and cultural history. He argues, in concord with D. T. Campbell and S. H. Katz,[34] that

The emergence of the conscious feelings of self as more than the body, as a larger being with sociocultural loyalties and cosmic connections, has been provided by the evolving systems of socially transmitted rituals and beliefs, usually called religions.... evidence is becoming overwhelming that religion is a part of man's basic and perennial nature and is simultaneously biological and cultural. The perennial necessity for *Homo* to produce adaptive behavior to meet the requirements of a sociocultural life in the real world and the impossibility of this being done genetically assure us that religious rituals and beliefs (or their equivalents) will continue to flourish and evolve with man as long as he survives as a sociocultural animal. From this history of the total ecosystem controlling human destiny in the long and short ranges of its biological and cultural evolution, one could properly conclude that the system has ordained the evolving of religious systems and their rituals, myths, and theologies to enculturate a deepest reverence of this total system, which contains our ultimate resources and specifies what is required that we may have life. It is this system which thus far has produced such an awe-inspiring transformation of the dust of the earth into living form so fascinating to us as ours.[35]

So there is a prima-facie case, on the basis of man's cultural history at least, for taking religious beliefs, and the theological statements articulating them, very seriously indeed in relation to man's values, and so attitudes and actions towards the environment. But does any particular attitude logically follow from theological beliefs? There have been those, of course, who have argued that theological utterances have no 'cash value' in terms of actual statements about reality, since they are not empirically falsifiable, even if they do express attitudes. This is not the view being take in these lectures in which theological

[33] R. W. Burhoe, 'The Human Prospect and the "Lord of History"', *Zygon*, 10 (1975), 299–375.
[34] S. H. Katz, 'Evolutionary Perspectives on Purpose and Man', *Zygon*, 8 (1973), 325–40; see this whole issue of *Zygon* (Sept.–Dec. 1973).
[35] Burhoe, op. cit., pp. 316–18.

discourse is regarded as meaningful and, in respect of the doctrine of creation in particular, as functioning to produce conceptual models which give both intelligibility to all-that-is (as here viewed largely through the spectacles of the sciences) and also meaning to individuals in steering their path through life. Some religious statements, even if they (like some scientific ones) do not generate falsifiable hypotheses and experiments, do at least

> seem to be expressing belief that the world is one way rather than another possible way. They [religious statements] seem to indicate less than precise but identifiable expectations *and firm commitments to values which imply ethical duties*. It is the nature of theological utterances that they cannot be reduced to factual statements, that is, statements which are central to scientific language games; but theistic affirmations, for example, seem to be cashable in terms of the world being created and therefore dependent upon a power transcending it. Events in the world can be explained in terms of a transcendent source of power and the purposes of a transcendent reason. Theism says, at least, that man is not fully comprehended when seen as a creature only of the world.[36]

In this important article, Marietta goes on to argue, I think correctly, that although the grounds of conduct seem usually to be beneath the level of conscious reasoning (the so-called 'reasons' people give for their behaviour often being quite irrelevant) yet the cultural, social and economic institutions which are affecting their conduct have, in fact, been shaped by intellectual beliefs. Even more importantly, he argues, on the basis of Wittgensteinian linguistic theories, Gestalt psychology, and studies of perception, that 'Beliefs influence the meaning and value which consciousness will place on a thing. This bestowal of meaning and value precedes any deliberate reasoning.'[37] So all belief models and, in particular in the present context, theological models, such as those pertaining to God as Creator, are effective at the most basic level of perception, that is at the level of what the world of nature, of the environment, is seen *as*. Often a problem, such as an environmental one, is only seen *as a problem* through the per-

---

[36] D. F. Marietta, Jr., 'Religious models and ecological decision making', *Zygon*, 12 (1977), 154. Italics mine.
[37] Marietta, op. cit., p. 156.

ception shaped by a particular set of beliefs. For such reasons, we may expect religious beliefs to be influential in determining attitudes to the non-human world. In particular, theological models of God as Creator, of all-that-is as created, and theological understandings of man in relation to God and nature cannot fail to shape what we see the non-human world *as* and thus to influence our environmental attitudes and actions. Whether or not there is a positive contribution from the Judeo-Christian tradition in respect of these models of creation and of man is what we must investigate.

Any model in order to facilitate the making of correct decisions about personal and social ecological action will need, Marietta argues,[38] to be: (1) *believable*, that is, 'connectable' with the world of our experience (which now means consistent also with current scientific knowledge); (2) *an adequate 'picture'* (or *model*, in our terminology) *of reality* so as to elicit the desired perceptions of the world (so that problems are seen as problems, changes as changes, etc.) and must therefore incorporate the understanding of man within the global ecosystem that we have described above in terms of current ecological science (i.e. interdependence, finiteness, role of diversity, etc.); (3) *able to provide motivation for people to act for the future good of humanity* and the whole ecosystem; and (4) *a help to people to adjust deliberately and creatively* to changes necessary for survival and preservation of a dynamically equilibrated ecosystem.

The earlier lectures have given grounds for thinking criterion (1) (is it believable?) and criterion (2) (adequacy of a 'picture', or model, of reality) can be satisfied by the Judeo-Christian doctrine of creation, amplified and enriched by new models pertinent to what science discovers the world to be like— although we have not yet inquired into the kinds of perception on the world this doctrine might evoke. Criteria (3) and (4) (on motivation for a futuristic ethic and on helping to adjust to change, respectively) are directly relevant to ecological issues and have yet to be applied.

B.   The Judeo-Christian doctrine of creation and attitudes to nature[39]

   (i) *The biblical doctrine of creation.*   In a much quoted and

---

[38] Marietta, op. cit., pp. 157 ff.
[39] See Appendix A.

reprinted essay, Lynn White[40] urges that the exploitative outlook which has engendered the ecological crisis in Western industrialized nations is itself the direct result of the Judeo-Christian tradition which, he says, basing itself on Genesis 1: 26 ff., has conceived of man as superior to, and dominant over, nature which, in this tradition, he claims, 'has no reason for existence save to serve man'. Indeed, he calls this last a 'Christian axiom'; he asserts that 'Christianity bears a huge burden of guilt' (for the possession by man of technological powers now out of control) and speaks of the 'orthodox Christian arrogance toward nature'. Max Nicholson, a former Director-General of the Nature Conservancy, has written as follows:

Historically the core of the cultural complex disseminating and maintaining errors of attitude and practice on these matters, and obstructing the way to harmony between man and nature has been organised religion ... Inevitable though it may have been as a step towards progressive civilization, it was a tragedy that of all the religions in the world it should have been one of the very few which preached man's unqualified right of dominance over nature which became the most powerful and influential, through the agencies of ancient Judaism and modern Christianity. Although it is arguable that the Old Testament implies some limits to man's right ruthlessly to trample upon nature and recklessly to multiply his own numbers at its expense, any qualifications and restraints are feeble compared with its chronic and uninhibited incitement towards aggressive, exploitative and reproductively irresponsible behaviour in the human species.... The inherent dangers and distortions enshrined in their [Judaism and Christianity] dominant myths of man's role on earth have been aggravated by increasing blindness and neglect to keep alive even those by no means negligible sympathetic contacts with nature which were part of the heritage of such earlier Christians as St Jerome, St Cuthbert and St Francis.[41]

Lynn White's position has been readily adopted by those who are only too eager to find yet another stick with which to beat Christianity (even if, ironically, only yesterday they were deploring Christianity's supposed dogmatic antagonism to

[40] Lynn White, 'The Historical Roots of our Ecologic Crisis', *Science*, 155 (1967), 1203-7.
[41] Max Nicholson, *The Environmental Revolution* (Hodder & Stoughton, London, 1970), pp. 264-5.

science and technology!) and by those Christians, such as Lynn White himself, who accept it more in sorrow than in anger in hope that the Church might then emerge purified from its sackcloth and ashes to provide the moral lead for ecological renewal.

This view has joined forces with a more romantic view of nature held by exponents of the 'counter culture', which sets itself against Western technical society and experiments with Eastern religions, often in the setting of new modes of communal life. All of these threads are entangled in the following statement of the 'Berkeley Ecological Revolutionary Organization':

It seems evident that there are throughout the world certain social and religious forces which have worked through history toward an ecologically and culturally enlightened state of affairs. Let these be encouraged: Gnostics, hip Marxists, Teilhard de Chardin Catholics, Druids, Taoists, Biologists, Witches, Yogins, Bhikkus, Quakers, Sufis, Tibetans, Zens, Shamans, Bushmen, American Indians, Polynesians, Anarchists, Alchemists ... the list is long. All primitive cultures, all communal and ashram movements.[42]

There are no Jews, no Protestants, Anglicans, or Orthodox Christians, and only a subgroup of Roman Catholics, in that list! So the stigma of Lynn White has certainly been found useful for beating what is thought to be a Judeo-Christian dogma.

That there have been and are Western Christians who hold this particular constellation of beliefs and that at some times and places they may even have been held by a majority of Christians seems quite likely. But to substantiate White's hypothesis, which has been made even more dogmatic and has been more widely generalized by others, it would be necessary to show that men in the 'Judeo-Christian tradition' have uniquely generated the eco-disasters of our planet; that an exploitative view of nature was actually and generally held in that tradition; and that this tradition actually does involve such an exploitative view. In fact, none of these three statements can be adequately substantiated and his hypothesis also emerges as

---

[42] Quoted by G. Fackre, 'Ecology and Theology', in *Western Man and Environmental Ethics*, ed. I. G. Barbour (Addison–Wesley, Reading, Mass., London, etc., 1973), p. 117, from *The Lancaster Independent Press*, 14 Feb. 1970.

much too simplistic. We shall indicate very briefly why this is so.

Firstly, it is quite clear that man's exploitation of his natural environment, leading to irreversible ecological changes of a kind inimical to the welfare of subsequent generations of men, has occurred from the time of primitive man onwards and is not specifically associated with Judeo-Christian societies. Long before the Jewish prophets and the advent of Jesus primitive man had hunted by 'fire-drive' methods and Mediterranean man had stripped the trees and turned into barren terrain both the hills and plains of much of the lands bordering that sea. Disastrous interference with nature is not confined to the Christian West as a visit to modern industrial Japan quickly establishes.

Secondly, even among the followers of the Judeo-Christian[43] tradition, there have been marked divergences between their attitudes to science and technology—which, broadly speaking, developed most in the Latin form of Christianity of Western Europe and, more particularly, found their most congenial climate in the Protestant variant of that form. Technology did not flourish in the Orthodox Byzantine Empire of the East, although—just to controvert all attempts at historical generalizations—it did develop strongly in the non-Christian cultures of China, and both science and technology have distinct roots in ancient Greece and medieval Islam.

Even with reference to Western Latin Christianity, it cannot be maintained that the exploitative, rapacious attitude to nature was uniformly encouraged in a society which could produce both a St. Francis, with his sense of oneness with all the creatures and creations of God, and a St. Benedict who, through the working symbiotic communities that he initiated, fostered the habit of an ordered balanced interplay with natural cycles which increased the fertility and fecundity of the areas where Benedictines and Cistercians settled.

---

[43] J. Passmore has recently argued, in *Man's Responsibility for Nature* (Duckworth, London, and Scribner's, New York, 1974), that it was *Graeco*-Christian 'arrogance which generated a rapacious attitude to nature'. But this generalization also needs qualification since, although Stoicism (as Passmore argues) may have contributed to such an attitude, the Platonic tradition encouraged a gentler and more harmonious relationship of man with nature.

The Western medieval bestiaries testify not only to the interest of a more rural society in all kinds of living creatures but also to the meaning which was attributed to everything in a universe that was governed by a controlling mind and was capable of rational explanation. For example, the activities of some animals are seen as types of Christ and of others as moral lessons for man. Moreover:

The Bestiary is a compassionate book. It has its bugaboos, of course, but these are only there to thrill us. It loves dogs, which never was usual in the East from which it originated; it is polite to bees, and even praises them for being communists like the modern Scythians [the Russians of their day]; it is tender to poor, blind Echinus [the sea-urchin]; the horse moves it, as Sidney's heart was moved, 'more than with a trumpet'; above all, it has a reverence for the wonders of life, and praises the Creator of them: in whom, in those days, it was still possible absolutely to believe.[44]

Thirdly, the Judeo-Christian tradition, at least as represented in its main written documents, the Bible, does not, in fact, depict man's dominion over nature as simply brutally exploitative, as if nature is there only for man's benefit. As with all the neat headings within which theological discourse would like to confine the richly variegated books of the Bible, it is almost impossible to produce a 'biblical doctrine' of nature and man's relation to it. The evidence has been widely surveyed[45] in relation to ecological concerns, not to mention the more standard works on the theology of the Bible.[46]

The fruits of these scholarly labours concerning the main

---

[44] Appendix, p. 247, by T. H. White, following his translation and edition of a Latin bestiary of the twelfth century, published as *The Book of Beasts* (Jonathan Cape, London, 1954).

[45] 'Biblical Attitudes to Nature', by J. Baker in *Man and Nature*, ed. H. W. Montefiore (Collins, London, 1975), pp. 87 ff.; C. F. D. Moule, *Man and Nature in the New Testament* (Facet Books, Fortress Press, Philadelphia, 1967); I. G. Barbour, in *Earth Might Be Fair*, ed. I. G. Barbour (Prentice-Hall, Englewood Cliffs and Hemel Hempstead, 1972), Chs. 1, 9; T. S. Derr, op. cit. (above, p. 256 n. 2); J. Barr, 'Man and Nature—The Ecological Controversy and the Old Testament', *Bull J. Rylands Lib.* 55 (1972), 9–32, see also Barr's article in *Ecology and Religion in History*, ed. D. and E. Spring (Harper Torchbook No. 1829, New York, 1974)—and other articles by J. Macquarrie and Lynn White in this collection.

[46] e.g. W. Eichrodt, *Theology of the Old Testament*, trans. J. A. Baker (SCM Press, London, 1967).

thrust of the biblical (primarily Old Testament) understanding of nature and man's relation to it may be summarized as follows:

(a) Creation as good, ordered, and of value to God

The determining and controlling factor in thinking about nature, and man in nature, is the sovereignty of God as Creator. 'The earth is the Lord's and the fullness thereof.'[47] Moreover, *God*, according to the Priestly author(s), has said of each aspect of the creation that 'it was good',[48] indeed he has declared that it was all 'very good'[49]—which 'can only mean good for that for which God intends it'.[50] This is the underlying basis for Jesus' declaration[51] that there is no food which is 'unclean' and also for the belief that ultimately, because of the character of God, all things can be a revelation of the divine wisdom and goodness. Moreover 'the world of the Genesis creation story is an ordered world. The story is built upon a process of separation and ordering; it is interested in different levels of created being, in different functions and different species.'[52] God created the world, for the most part, for its own sake and he delights in his creation in virtue of the qualities he has accorded it, regardless of man for whom God's purposes in much of nature may for ever be inscrutable.[53] For Jesus, God's providential care extends even to the most insignificant creatures and the beauty of the 'lilies of the field' (the spring flowers of Galilee) are in accord with his intention.[54]

(b) Nature as desacralized, revalued, and historicized

Because God is One and Creator, there is no other transcendent power other than his and so nature is not divine and not to be worshipped for itself but valued *as* God's creation.[55] It is to be received by man as God's gift. Nature is not the realm of operation of powers, divine or demonic, which exist over

---

[47] Psalm 24:1.
[48] Genesis 1: 4, 10, 12, 19, 21, 25.
[49] Genesis 1: 31.
[50] C. Westermann, *Creation* (SPCK, London, 1974), p. 61.
[51] Mark 7: 19.
[52] J. Barr, op. cit. (1972), p. 31.
[53] See above, Lecture II, pp. 84, 85.
[54] Matthew 6: 26, 28; 10: 29.
[55] Psalm 19: 1; 104: 24–31; Job 38, 39.

against God the Creator himself and are not subject to him. 'Man did not face a world full of ambiguous and capricious gods who were alive in the objects of the natural world. He had to do with one supreme creator God whose will was steadfast'[56]—and so the created order should in principal be a regular manifestation of the supreme 'mind' of the Creator (though it was to be many centuries before this was seen as the justification it is, *inter alia*, for nature being amenable to human empirical inquiry, that questions may be 'put' to nature). It is not clear to what extent the religion of the people of Israel was distinctive in this respect,[57] but there is no doubt of this being a characteristic attitude of their religion, in view of the recorded and continuous pressure of both prophet and priest against any backsliding into nature religions always ready at hand to seduce the people away from their loyalty to Yahweh. So the valuation that is placed upon nature is that it is God's creation, that is, it is God's not man's and this goes so far as to be expressed in legislation, as in the Law of Jubilee[58] whereby man does not own land but is regarded as a tenant installed by God.

[56] Derr, op. cit. (1973), p. 11.

[57] e.g. J. Barr quotes (op. cit. (1972), p. 29, n. 1) W. G. Lambert (in his *Babylonian Wisdom Literature*) as suggesting that in Akkadian myths the gods have ceased to be aspects of nature.

[58] Leviticus 25: 1–34. 'No land shall be sold outright, because the land is mine' (v. 23, NEB), the Lord said to Moses. A phenomenological perspective of what land meant to the people of ancient Israel has been offered by W. Bruegemann (*The Land: Place as Gift, Promise, and Challenge in Biblical Faith* (Fortress Press, Philadelphia, 1977)). To them land was a physical source of fertility and life; it was 'a place for the gathering of the hopes of the covenant people and a vibrant theological symbol' (op. cit., p. xii). Among his 'Concluding Hermeneutical Reflections', Bruegemann includes the following: 'Of the God of the Bible then, it is likely that we can no longer settle for the antithesis of the God of history versus the gods of the land. As Yahweh is lord of events so he is also fructifier of the land. As he comes "in that day", so also he watched over the land. He not only intrudes to do saving deeds but he also governs in ways to assure abiding blessings.... He is Lord of places as well as times' (op. cit., p. 185). His theme 'reasserts faith in Yahweh as land-governor and -maintainer, and creation not simply as innovative act but as resilient sustenance' (op. cit., p. 188)— a theme in accord with the understanding of creation pursued in these lectures, with a not dissimilar conclusion: '... the land is not only gift from God, transcendent Promiser. It is also land in history, land not usurped or simply mastered, but a land with its own history. Therefore his people [of Israel] does not own the land but also belongs to the land. In that way, we are warned about presuming upon it, upon controlling it in scientific and rational ways, so that its own claim, indeed its own voice, is not heard or is disregarded' (op. cit., p. 192).

In the biblical literature, nature is historicized; it has a history with God at the beginning and the end. There are cycles within nature but, because it is the creation of a God who is working his purpose out, it is not a repetition of endlessly repeated fixed patterns. This understanding of created nature developed in the people of Israel as a consequence of their belief in God's creative actions within the time of their own history as a people, for the Old Testament is essentially anthropocentric.

In her [Israel's] scriptures, particularly in the Psalms, nature plays a great role, but almost without exception in connection with God's acts in history and his covenant with Israel, to which nature also bears witness and responds (cf. *Psalms* 19, 29, 65, 67, 74, 75, 89, 96, 104, 136, 147 and 148). After God's character in his historical deeds is discovered, this character can also be discerned and these deeds seen prefigured in the processes of nature, and nature can be invested with the same grace as history discloses.[59]

It is because of this historicization of nature and its processes that New Testament visions of the consummation of God's purposes can also include the whole of nature as in Romans 8: 21 ('the creation itself also shall be delivered from the bondage of corruption into the liberty of the glory of the children of God' (RV)) and the vision of Revelation 21: 1 of a 'new heaven and a new earth'.

(c)   Man's place in nature: 'dominion'

Only within the ambience of the understanding of creation, including man, in relation to God as outlined in (a) and (b) can the relation that God assigns to man in nature, in the biblical literature, be understood. As J. Barr puts it: 'The whole framework of Genesis i is intended to suggest that man is man when he is in his place within nature. His dominion over nature is given little definition; but, in general, its content is less exploitation and more leadership, a sort of primary liturgical place.'[60] Man exercises the 'dominion' that is accorded him under a delegated authority from God who is the Creator of both man and that over which man is given this derived

[59] H. Berkhof, 'God in Nature and History', *Faith and Order Studies*, Paper No. 50 (World Council of Churches, Geneva, 1968), p. 10.
[60] Barr, op. cit. (1972), p. 31.

'dominion', and which independently of man has value to God as his creation. The *locus classicus* of this concept is, of course, Genesis 1:

v. 26.   Then God said,
   'Let us make man in our image, after our likeness;
   and let them have dominion over the fish of
    the sea and over the birds of the air, and over the
    cattle, and over all the earth,
   and over every creeping thing that creeps upon the
    earth.'
 27.   So God created man in his own image, in the image of
   God he created them;
    male and female he created them.
 28.   And God blessed them, and God said to them,
   'Be fruitful and multiply, and fill the earth and
    subdue it;
   and have dominion over the fish of the sea and over
    the birds of the air,
   and over every living thing that moves upon the earth.'
 29.   And God said,
   'Behold I have given you every plant yielding seed
   which is upon the face of all the earth, and every
   tree with seed in its fruit; you shall have them
   for food ...'[61]

So man is created, not to minister to the gods as in some Sumerian-Babylonian narratives, but to civilize the earth and this is seen in the context of the history of mankind. The 'dominion' which he is described as being assigned is that of a king (as can be shown by a detailed comparison with the court-styles of Babylon and Egypt, according to C. Westermann[62]). The kingly quality of man is seen in his rule over the animals and in accordance with the concept of kingship in antiquity:

As lord of his realm, the king is responsible not only for the realm; he is the one who bears and mediates blessings for the realm entrusted to him. Man would fail in his royal office of dominion over the earth were he to exploit the earth's resources to the detriment of the land, plant life, animals, rivers and seas ... What is decisive is the

---

[61] Genesis 1: 26 f. (RSV).
[62] Westermann, op. cit., pp. 52–3.

responsibility of man for the preservation of what has been entrusted to him; and he can show this responsibility by exercising his royal office of mediator of prosperity and well-being, like the kings of the ancient world.[63]

Although 'dominion' has this kingly reference, it is a caring 'dominion' exercised under the authority of the Creator, and so it is a more accurate reflection of the meaning of the Genesis myth to say that it describes man as vicegerent, or steward, or manager, or trustee (as of a property, or a charity) as well as exercising the leadership of a king of creation. He is, in the myth, called to tend the earth and its creatures in responsibility to its Creator. He is accountable. He is responsible.

His 'dominion' is thus far from being one of simple exploitative power. J. Barr[64] has pointed out that, in the P source, in the beginning, man (like the animals) was vegetarian until the Deluge. Moreover the Hebrew words translated 'have dominion' and 'subdue', he says, do not necessarily have the sense of strong, forceful submission that some authors have claimed.[65] Barr suggests that in Genesis 1 we have a paradise picture, a period at the beginning of the world when there is peace in the animal world and between man and animal and so man's 'dominion' there depicted 'contains no markedly exploitative aspect; it approximates to the well-known Oriental idea of the Shepherd King'.[66]

(d) Man: the image and likeness of God

What has been said of man's dominion must now be considered in the wider context of the destiny claimed in Genesis 1: 26 for man in God's creative act: 'Let us make man in our image, after our likeness'. It is important to note that this notion of

---

[63] Ibid.

[64] Barr, op. cit. (1972), pp. 21 f.

[65] J. Black, *The Dominion of Man: the Search for Ecological Responsibility* (Edinburgh University Press, Edinburgh, 1970), p. 37. Although this particular textual interpretation of Black has now proved to be untenable, nevertheless his book provides a valuable account of how the 'dominating' attitudes of Western man towards nature have developed and have continued, until recently, to constitute an uncriticized presupposition of the *Weltanschauung* of the West. What was, conveniently, *believed* to be the biblical understanding of man's relation to nature was more important in this respect than what the biblical view actually was.

[66] Barr, op. cit. (1972), p. 72.

man as created in the 'image' of God was held in conjunction with the Hebrew understanding of man as a psychosomatic unity—'You are dust and to dust you shall return.'[67] It is the total psychosomatic person who is made in the 'image' of God. Interpretation of this phrase 'image of God' has a history as long and as complex as the cultural situations in which the Bible has been expounded. It is noteworthy, as Barr points out,[68] that at the time during which critics, such as Lynn White, say the technological exploitation of nature arose from the Judeo-Christian doctrine of creation, the image of God in man was regarded, in Christian theological exegesis, as man's immortal soul and reason. So that man's 'dominion' tended at that time to be thought of, not as control and exploitation, but as man's *superiority* as a rational being over the soulless and mortal. This gives rise to doubt whether Genesis 1: 28 really has had the effect these critics propose.

What, then, is the meaning of the 'image' in modern exegesis? C. Westermann concludes,[69] after surveying all the culturally dependent earlier interpretations, that there is now impressive evidence that what is said of the king as the image of God in Egypt and Mesopotamia is the basis of the Genesis text and concludes (in accordance with W. H. Schmidt and H. Wildberger) that the image of God is to be understood in the sense of viceroy or representative: 'man is ... God's representative ... there is but one legitimate image through which God shows himself in the world and that is man'.[70] Barr,[71] too, rejects the identification of the 'image of God' with man's position of dominion over nature: 'The point was not that man had a likeness to God through acting as God's representative towards the rest of created nature, but that he himself was like God. In what way he was like God is not stated.'[72] 'Dominion' is then likely to be consequential upon being such an image of God but is only one aspect of what being 'in the image of God'

[67] Genesis 3: 19; and cf. Lecture IV.
[68] Barr, op. cit. (1972), pp. 23–4.
[69] Westermann, op. cit., pp. 58 ff.
[70] W. Wildberger, quoted by Westermann, op. cit., p. 59.
[71] J. Barr, op. cit. (1972), pp. 19 ff., and also 'The Image of God in the Book of Genesis—A Study of Terminology', *Bull. J. Rylands Lib.* 51 (1968–9), 11–26.
[72] Barr, op. cit. (1972), p. 20.

entails.[73] So dominion over nature tends to be over-emphasized in exegesis which identifies it with the image of God in man. Westermann concurs with Barr in this and stresses that it is man's simply being man, and not by virtue of any one particular quality ('dominion' or anything else), that man is in the 'image of God': 'Man's dignity is founded on his being a creature; God, by creating man in his own image, has given man his human dignity ... man—everyman—is created for this purpose: namely, that something may happen between him and God and that thereby his life may receive a meaning.'[74]

(e)   Man: in rebellion

We have already discussed, in relation to contemporary understandings of man, the 'Fall' of man that is so vividly recounted in the older myths of the J school preserved in Genesis 2, 3. It is not my purpose to describe in detail the profound meaning of these stories that modern exegesis has made accessible to our generation.[75] It is though, en passant, worth noticing that one exegete[76] points out that the command from God to man (not to eat of 'the tree of the knowledge of good and evil'[77]) introduces man to freedom and puts him into relationship with the one who commands (God)—it is an act of confidence in man in his relationship to God. Man uses this freedom to succumb to the temptation to 'be like God, knowing good and evil'[78] and from this arises the 'disturbance and a destruction of the proper relation between God and man, when man in his drive after knowledge oversteps or tries to overstep his limits'.[79] The significance of this for our present concern, is that, in the myth, man's disobedience defaces the image of God in him. His relation to nature is now no longer one of pastoral 'dominion', kingly and caring, but one of contention and

---

[73] Cf. Genesis 5: 3 and 9: 6 for implications of other meanings.

[74] Westermann, op. cit., p. 60.

[75] For detailed accounts, see C. Westermann, op. cit., and his Biblischer Kommentar, Altes Testament, i. 1 (Neukirchener Verlag, Neukirchen—Vluyn, 1974); G. von Rad, Genesis (SCM Press, London, 1961); W. Eichrodt, Theology of the Old Testament, trans. J. A. Baker (SCM Press, London, 1967); the biblical themes are well expounded in Creator, Creation and Faith by Norman Young (Collins, London, 1976).

[76] Westermann, op. cit., pp. 90 ff.

[77] Genesis 2: 16, 17.

[78] Genesis 3: 5.

[79] Westermann, op. cit., p. 93.

opposition. These ancient myths shrewdly make a close link between man's corrupt exercise of his latent powers over nature and his broken relation with his Creator. He still stands over nature but the exercise of his power is now subject to the possibility of causing disharmony in the created order.

Although this idea of the 'Fall' of man has been of far-reaching significance in Christian interpretation and elsewhere, it is 'nowhere cited or presumed in the Old Testament; its significance is limited to the primeval events'[80] but it has influenced New Testament writers, such as Paul, who took a pessimistic and anxious view of the world of man, and by association that of nature, too, both of which to him and to much of the Mediterranean world of his time seemed, in Romans 8: 21, to be in 'the bondage of corruption', 'the shackles of mortality', 'its servitude to decay'.[81] The assumption is that, in man's 'Fall', man has pulled down nature with him. C. F. D. Moule[82] argues that in Hebrew thought a connection had been made between non-human nature and human morals, degradation in the latter being closely related, causally by implication, to the former.

The modern scientific world-view, while, in general, rendering such a connection unintelligible has, curiously enough, now made it possible to see through modern ecological science how in practice *today* man with his powers can introduce a gross disorder and disharmony into nature, whereas previously his activities have been too small in number and intensity to alter the world's ecosystem anything other than locally and marginally. So there is prophetic if not ontological force in making this link between man's character and the state of the natural world.[83] The situation has been put well by H. Berkhof:

There is yet a second and even more serious reason to see a cleavage between the biblical and the modern world-view on this point. That is the way in which sin, according to the Bible, affects human and non-human nature, by introducing evil and suffering, thorns and thistles, and human death. Passages like Genesis 3 and Romans 5 give the

[80] Westermann, op. cit., p. 89.
[81] Translations, respectively, of RV, NEB, and of Moule, op. cit. (1967), p. 10.
[82] Moule, op. cit. (1967), pp. 5 ff.
[83] See Moule, op. cit. (1967), for an interesting discussion of these issues in relation to man's responsibility towards nature.

impression of a 'fallen creation'. In modern scientific thinking, however, there is no place for the conception that an alteration and
deterioration took place in man's physical nature, and in the biological world around him, as a consequence of his culpability. According to our experience, death is inherent in all life. Strife and suffering
belong to nature. Floods and earthquakes are part of the same reality
to which majestic mountains and fertile valleys belong. In Scripture,
an identifiable connection between sin and suffering is sometimes
definitely denied (Job, Luke 13: 1–5; John 9: 3), but more often it
is strongly posited. In the latter case, the biblical writers—basing
themselves on the world-view, and using the common mythological
language, of their time—tried to express something which is as near
to modern man as it was to them: the unity of man and nature and
of soul and body, and the decisive role which man plays in the process
of nature. Man, who is in fact sinful man, on the one hand is rooted
in nature and, on the other hand, transforms nature. He lives in three
relations: as child of God, as his neighbour's partner, and as master
of nature. If one relation is distorted, it also affects the others. When
man, as the master of nature, fails to put his mastery to the service
of God and of his neighbour, he denies the true purpose of his
dominion, and thereby harms nature.[84]

(*ii*) *Traditional post-biblical Christian theology and attitudes to
nature.*   So far we have been considering the 'biblical' doctrine
of creation and its understanding of the triangle of relationships
of God–man–nature. For the most part it has been the Old
Testament which has been under contribution and the much
smaller and temporally more restricted New Testament has
relatively little to say directly about man's proper attitude to
nature. The reasons for this are partly sociological and partly
because of the nature of the primitive Christian community and
its world-view.[85] The Christians of the first century used the
Old Testament (it was their 'Bible') primarily as a sourcebook
of supposed predictions of Christ, his work and his effects. Their
message was initially a gospel of personal salvation and, probably most significantly of all, the earliest Christians felt they
were living at 'the end of the ages', and the created order had
only a short time before the 'Second Coming' of Christ and
all was to be swept away. The process of abandonment of this
view is already apparent in the New Testament itself but the

[84] H. Berkhof, op. cit., pp. 19, 20.
[85] See J. A. Baker, op. cit. (above, p. 278 n. 45), whom I largely follow here.

process has not gone far enough in what became the canon of the New Testament, to redirect interest explicitly to the created order and man's continuing life in it under God, although the author of 1 Timothy inveighs against those who 'forbid marriage and inculcate abstinence from certain foods, though God created them to be enjoyed with thanksgiving by believers who have inward knowledge of the truth'.[86]

More significant is the idea of the 'cosmic Christ' in John 1, Colossians 1, and Hebrews 1—the idea that Christ as divine existed before his historical Incarnation and was the agent, the mediator of creation.[87] As J. Baker says:

The implications of this idea for a theology of nature are not, of course, worked out in the New Testament itself; but, obscure as the thought-forms undoubtedly are to us, there does shine through them a conviction that the whole universe, could we but see it, is in its essential nature in harmony not merely with some unknown divine power but with God as revealed in Jesus, and that therefore there must be some *modus vivendi* between man and nature which is in keeping with all that is best in both.[88]

As we saw earlier, the doctrine of *creatio ex nihilo*, even if not explicitly stated in the Old Testament, was certainly accepted by the inter-testamental period[89] and we find it twice in the New Testament.[90] It soon became the presupposition of Christian faith, notably in its intense effort of self-identification in confrontation with the various Gnostic modes of thought—the world of nature, the stuff of the world, had been created by God, it had a dependent existence, but it was good because made by God and because (cf. Genesis 1) he was regarded as having declared it to be so.

So, by and large, it would be true to say that Christians came to value creation and to resist Gnosticism and Manichaeism (which regard matter, and so the world, as inherently evil) on the same grounds as the Jews. However they had an even stronger reason for a positive affirmation of both the reality

---

[86] 1 Timothy 4: 3 (NEB).
[87] See, however, the discussion of this idea in Lecture VI: § VII (iv), pp. 233 ff.
[88] Baker, op. cit., p. 108.
[89] 2 Macc. 7: 28.
[90] Hebrews 11: 3 and Romans 4: 17.

and the worth of the created order—namely, the doctrine of the incarnation.

Whether Christians understand this doctrine in its classical more 'mythical' form (which I have denoted by 'Incarnation', with a capital 'I') or in the more continuous, immanentist form ('incarnation', with a small 'i') for which I argued in the previous lecture, it had profound implications for man's understanding of nature. For if God was able to express the nature of his own being, not only implicitly by sustaining the world in being, but explicitly in and through the life, death, and resurrection of the man Jesus, then the world of matter organized in the form we call a man must be of such a kind as to make this possible. As I have written elsewhere,

This [incarnation] constituted a repudiation of all attitudes to the stuff of the world which saw it as evil, alien to its Creator, a prison from which a non-material reason, or 'soul', must seek release. God was to be seen as achieving his ends by involvement with, immanence in, expression through the very stuff of the world and its events in space and time. Moreover, the assertion that Jesus was the ultimate revelation of God's being to men in a mode they could understand and appropriate, amounted, we can now see, to an affirmation that 'nature' in its actuality, materiality and evolution, of which Jesus was indubitably a part, is both potentially at least an expression of God's being and the instrument of his action. Paradoxically, the Christian claim asserts that God fulfils man's personalness, and satisfies his most 'spiritual' aspirations, by entering the temporal process of materiality as a man, made like all men of the component units of the stuff of the world.[91]

The Incarnation of the Word of God is, in the writings of many of the fathers of the Church, seen, not as an isolated wonder, but as the focusing and bringing to a consummation of a universal pattern of activity, in the way I have preferred to denote as *incarnation* (see Lecture VI): 'The Word of God, who is God, wills at all times and in all things to work the mystery of his incarnation', declares Maximus the Confessor, one of the profoundest of the Byzantines. But if, in the Christian understanding, the world of matter has both the *symbolic* function of expressing his mind and the *instrumental* function

[91] A. R. Peacocke, *Science and the Christian Experiment* (Oxford University Press, London, 1971), p. 157.

of being the means whereby he effects his purposes, then we can say, broadly, that the world is a sacrament or, at least, sacramental.

This recognition of the presence of God 'in, with, and under' the life of a real man had other consequences for the whole cycle of Christian teaching. For by their character some of the central practices of the Christian faith (I refer to the sacramental use of bread, wine, and water) predispose and point to the highest possible valuation of the natural, of the stuff of the world in its very materiality. In the developed Christian understanding of God's relation to physical reality, the world of matter is seen as both expressing and revealing the mind of God, its Creator, and as effecting his purposes. For the physical, material world which he has brought into existence is the matrix within which and the means whereby autonomous, personal agents can be brought into existence and into harmony and union with himself. Thus, in the Christian understanding, the world of matter, in its relation to God, has both the symbolic function of expressing his mind and the instrumental function of being the means whereby he effects his purpose. We could perhaps put it thus: the created world is seen by Christians as a symbol because it is a mode of God's revelation, an expression of his truth and beauty which are the 'spiritual' aspects of its reality;[92] it is also valued by them for what God is effecting instrumentally through it, what he does for men in and through it. But these two functions of matter, the symbolic and the instrumental, also constitute the special character of the use of matter in the particular Christian sacraments. Hence there is, in each particular sacrament, a universal reference[93] to this double character of created physical reality and, correspondingly, meaning can be attached to speaking of the created world as a sacrament or as sacramental.

This intuition is central to the Christian attitude to the world and it stems from the doctrine of the incarnation and the meaning invested in the sacraments in the tradition, a meaning for which there are good grounds for believing originated, at least as regards the Eucharist, in the words and intentions of

[92] Cf. W. Temple, *Nature, Man and God* (Macmillan, London, 1934, repr. 1964), Ch. IV.
[93] Cf. O. C. Quick, *The Christian Sacraments* (Nisbet, London, 1927).

Jesus himself.[94] This unity of man and nature as the vehicle of the divine is a feature of Eastern Orthodox Christianity (which often seemed so 'physical' to Western theologians) and of Lutheran and Anglican theology which maintained, as F. J. A. Hort, Cambridge New Testament scholar and natural scientist, put it:

All Christian life is sacramental. Not alone in our highest act of Communion are we partaking of heavenly powers through earthly signs and vehicles. This neglected faith may be revived through increased sympathy with the earth derived from fuller knowledge, through the fearless love of all things ... The Eucharist is on the one side of the 'perfection' of the sustenance of life in personal communion, on the other a use of the products of the earth as instruments of communion, implying the necessity of taking the whole [of] nature into communion if it is to be real, the symbols of creation and of the Lord's body in one.[95]

C. Assessment of the traditional Judeo-Christian 'models' of creation in relation to ecological values

Even if the foregoing brief excursus into traditional Judeo-Christian theology has correctly delineated its genuine features, it certainly does no justice to the vast complexity of the varieties of *actual* Christian attitudes to nature.[96] In all traditions from Calvinist to Roman Catholic, there can be found those who approach nature with a caring and sensitive attitude and those who exploit it. The attitudes are difficult to designate as specifically 'Christian' for they come intertwined with other themes in the development of Western thought which, since the rise of natural science and the 'Enlightenment', has not been particularly sympathetic to Christian belief. Often, because of the prevalence of 'official' Christendom in all Western societies until relatively recently, those who wish to exploit nature have often latched on to the 'dominion' theme as a licence for all their depredations, however little a proper understanding of

[94] See J. Jeremias, *The Eucharistic Words of Jesus* (SCM Press, London, 1966).
[95] F. J. A. Hort, *The Way, the Truth and the Life* (Macmillan, Cambridge and London, 1893), pp. 213–14.
[96] The articles of I. G. Barbour and the collection of essays he has edited are useful starting-points: *Earth Might be Fair*, ed. I. G. Barbour (Prentice-Hall, Englewood Cliffs, 1972); *Western Man and Environmental Ethics* (Addison–Wesley, London, 1973); and J. Passmore, op. cit., for a magisterial historical survey.

its meaning and its context in the doctrine of creation actually justifies them. But men have never been inhibited from genuflecting towards spiritual values while at the same time furthering in their name their own cupidity and social power.

As a question of social, cultural, and ideological history, it may be of interest to disentangle the complex factors that have led to destructive ecological attitudes. But I hope it has become clear that, *in themselves*, that complex of ideas about nature, man and God we have called the Judeo-Christian doctrine of creation far from instilling attitudes inimical to harmony with nature provides a strong motivation, to those who hold them, towards action based on desirable ecological values. That they have not always done so must be admitted and perhaps there is some stress or emphasis which has rendered them more readily distorted to underpin Western man's aggressive attitudes than we have yet discerned—or perhaps the total Judeo-Christian outlook on created nature lacks a particular emphasis which is especially important when science shapes man's ideas and technology, the child of science, gives him new powers over non-human nature. So the Judeo–Christian doctrine of creation will need reassessing in relation to its ecological consequences not so much in its traditional form as in the form we have been developing in these lectures in the light of the scientific perspective on the world.

For the moment we examine briefly the Judeo-Christian constellation of ideas on nature, man, and God, in the more traditional form just outlined, in the light of the four criteria of Marietta[97] for any model, theological or otherwise, which may be regarded as satisfactory for facilitating correct decisions about personal and social action, i.e. satisfactory for creating suitable contemporary ecological values.

Criterion (*1*) (Is it believable?) concerns the wider question of the justification of and the coherence of the Judeo-Christian belief in God as Creator. I hope I have given grounds at least for entertaining this as a working hypothesis.

Criterion (*2*) was: Is the model (or 'picture') of reality adequate to elicit perceptions in the world that are such that the world may be perceived more clearly—ecological problems seen *as*

---

[97] See above, pp. 273, 274, and Marietta, op. cit.

problems, dangers as dangers, etc.? It is hard to know how to apply this criterion, but it seems to me that consciously and reflectively holding to the Judeo-Christian doctrine of creation (meaning the whole constellation of ideas outlined hitherto), since it makes one see all that is as created by God, as of value in itself to God, as vehicles of his purpose and symbols of his meaning, cannot fail to heighten the sensibilities and increase the awareness of the ecological situation for any who pursues its implications.

Criterion (3) was: does the model (or 'picture') of reality provide motivation for people to act for the future good of humanity and for the whole ecosystem? It seems to me that an awareness that man stands before God as his Creator with power over, and immense responsibility for, the rest of the created world, present and future, provides such a motivation and so meets this criterion. Moreover, for those who accept belief in God as Creator (not just as a proposition but as a commitment and with recognition of his sovereignty in all they undertake), a transcendent reference of the utmost significance is brought to bear on their understanding of their relation to the rest of the world thereby seen *as* created. Even responsibility to *future* generations takes on an added gravity when we realize that we hold the balance of the Earth's ecosystems in trust, and that we are answerable to that God who, as the Creator 'in whom we live and move and have our being', is the pivotal reference of intellectual intelligibility and personal meaning in our whole existence.

Criterion (4) was: does the model (or 'picture') of reality help people to adjust deliberately and creatively to changes necessary for survival and preservation of a dynamically equilibrated ecosystem? This is a pragmatic criterion only applicable after sociological inquiry. The supporter of the Judeo-Christian doctrine of creation could point to the actual efforts being made by believers in that doctrine, as a consequence of that belief (they would urge), to assess the problems, think out courses of action and to influence governments and politicians. The efforts of the World Council of Churches[98] in this regard

[98] Outlined in an article by Paul Abrecht, Director of the subunit on Church and Society of the World Council of Churches in 'Impact of Science and Technology on Society: New Directions in Ecumenical Social Ethics', *Zygon*, 12 (1977), 185–98.

have been notably intense and have brought them even into
the environmental debates initiated by the United Nations, for
example their representation at the United Nations Conference
on the Human Environment in Stockholm, 1972; their direct
role in the international discussion of the future uses of nuclear
energy, to which their earlier, fairly technical, preparatory work
made an important contribution; their acute awareness of the
particular problems of the under-developed Third World (who
are largely sceptical of the ecological sensitivity of the affluent
West), because the membership of the Christian churches from
these regions is strongly and very vocally represented on the
WCC; and their, still quite recent, attempts to increase
ecological awareness among ordinary Western church members
through its 'Energy for My Neighbour' programme. Others
must judge, indeed only time will do so, whether these efforts
of a Christian body have resulted in more effective ecological
action. But at least they are being made by an organization
which is genuinely international and which enables its members
to 'speak the truth in love' to each other.

So far we have been speaking of the Judeo-Christian doctrine
of creation as it has, by and large, been conceived as a result
of reflection on its primary sources in the biblical literature and
in the Christian experience before the rise of science. But we
have found, in the course of these lectures, that there are good
grounds for amplifying and enriching that doctrine, so received,
in the light of the perspective on the world afforded by the
natural sciences, a context to which theological questions
cannot avoid being directed if they are to have meaning for
contemporary man. So we must now consider again those ways
of seeing the world and God's action in it, which have resulted
from our earlier inquiries, in relation to our assessment of man's
role in relation to nature.

V. MAN'S ROLE IN CREATION RECONSIDERED

We must now assess both the kind of response from man to
nature which is called for and his role in creation, in the light
of the understanding of God's relation to the world which we
have developed in relation to the scientific perspective on that

world.[99] We shall then go on[100] to relate this response and this role, conceived within a theological approach itself shaped by the context of science, to the criteria for 'ecological values' already propounded.[101]

A.   Man as priest of creation

Our earlier exposition stressed particularly, and intentionally more than has traditionally been the case, that God the Creator is immanent[102] in a world that he is still creating. We conceived of God acting through the world as creative agent, so that God is acting in and through its natural processes (as described by the sciences) in a way analogous to the immanence involved in our acting in and expressing ourselves as personal agents through our bodies, also describable in the terms of the natural sciences. God is everywhere and at all times in the processes and events of the natural world which are to be seen as the vehicle and instrument of God's action and as capable of expressing his intentions and purposes—as our bodies are agents of ourselves.

This immediately suggests that man should respond to nature with a respect of the same kind as a man accords to his own body and those of other people—as agents of those other 'selves'—a respect which does not treat them simply as mere aggregates of flesh, hair, bone, protein, haemoglobin, etc. For a human person respects the body of another person as being the expression of that other 'self'—the body is seen as the mode and arena of the agency of that other 'self'. In the case of the natural world, if it is God who is the agent who is expressed therein, man's attitude to nature should show a respect which is transmuted into reverence at the presence of God in and through the whole of the created order, which thereby has, as it were, a derived sacredness or holiness as the vehicle and instrument of God's own creative action. (It is not, as the Old Testament has clarified once and for all, holy in itself.)

[99] We shall follow broadly the headings (and labels A ... etc.) of Lecture VI: § IV, pp. 204 ff.
[100] § VI, below, pp. 312 ff.
[101] Above, p. 273 n. 36.
[102] Cf. Lecture VI: § IV A, p. 204.

But this is only to say that the world is sacramental,[103] to use the traditional term in Christian theology which by its etymology and its long-hallowed associations also conveys the sense of 'holy' in the sense of 'set aside for God's purposes'.

This complex of proper responses of man to nature at once suggests that man's role may be conceived as that of *priest of creation*, as a result of whose activity, the sacrament of creation is reverenced; and who, because he alone is conscious of God, himself, and nature, can mediate between insentient nature and God—for a priest is characterized by activity directed towards God on behalf of others. Man alone can contemplate and offer the action of the created world to God. But a priest is also active towards others on God's behalf and in this sense, too, man is the priest of creation. He alone, having reflected on God's purposes, can be active towards the created world; he alone can consciously seek to further and fulfil God's purposes within it.

> Of all the creatures both in sea and land
> Onely to Man thou hast made known thy wayes,
> And put the penne alone into his hand,
> And made him Secretarie of thy praise.

> Beasts fain would sing; birds dittie to their notes;
> Trees would be tuning on their native lute
> To thy renown: but all their hands and throats
> Are brought to Man, while they are lame and mute.

---

[103] 'There are some signs that the old unitary view of creation and salvation maintained itself much later in the West [than some authors have implied]. Renaissance and Counter-Reformation Catholicism contain splendid affirmations of the goodness of the material creation, and of its capacity for reflecting the divine glory. In England also, the view of a man as a microcosm and the vision of the whole world as potentially sacramental, full of God's presence, still survived. It received a striking statement in the preaching, poetry and theology of the writers of the first part of the seventeenth century. Only in the latter part of that century, under the impact of a new science and a new philosophy, did the old way of seeing the interrelationship of man's inner world with the world around him, and of both with God, finally break down. Indeed, the English romantics, notably Coleridge and Wordsworth, made a remarkable if not wholly successful attempt to reaffirm it at the very time when, in the thought of Kant and Schleiermacher, religion was finally becoming restricted to man's subjectivity. From this has come a wealth of poetic writing which has helped greatly to maintain the vision of the world as potentially sacramental', *Man and Nature* (ed. Montefiore), pp. 47–8; see also A. R. Peacocke, op. cit., Ch. 7, on 'Matter in the theological and scientific perspectives'.

Man is the worlds High Priest: he doth present
The sacrifice for all: while they below
Unto the service mutter an assent,
Such as springs use that fall, and windes that blow.[104]

To be a priest is also, as the foregoing suggests, to be a
mediator, one who, in the thought of the Greek fathers of the
Church, can gather together the offering of creation in order
to present it to the Creator: 'The [Byzantine] Liturgy itself
is an offering of the world to God by man, it is a passing over;
in no sense a static thing, but rather a movement from this
world to the world to come, from earth to heaven ... the whole
of mankind and indeed the whole universe is conceived to be
in some way associated with this movement of offering, this
coming to God.'[105]

B.   Man as vicegerent, steward, manager of creation

Like the traditional Judeo-Christian doctrine of creation, stemming as it does from the biblical tradition, my earlier exposition
of that doctrine has been based on the proposition of God as
transcendent creative agent.[106] We had already seen that this
evokes 'monarchical' models of God as Creator and emphasizes
the otherness of the selfhood of God in relation to the dependent world that he creates *ex nihilo*. The consequences of the
recognition by man of himself and the whole of nature *as*
created, of the concepts of man's 'dominion' and of man as
made in the 'image of God' for man's response to nature have
already been elaborated.[107] In this theological development,
man may be regarded as the 'Lord of creation', though this
is a misleading term, for he has only a delegated power from
the divine authority. So we used (or could have used) such terms
as *vicegerent, steward, manager* to represent man's role in relation
to nature in this theological perspective. However, these terms
still introduce a nuance of 'domination' into the biblical concept
of 'dominion' and, in modern English, do not adequately

---

[104] G. Herbert, *Providence*, ll. 5–16 (Works of George Herbert, Clarendon Press,
Oxford, 1941 edn., pp. 116 ff.).
[105] Allchin, in *Man and Nature*, ed. Montefiore, pp. 148–9.
[106] Cf. Lecture VI: § IV B, p. 204, and also Lecture I.
[107] § IV B, C, above, pp. 274 ff.

convey the 'caring' component in ancient ideas of kingship. So they all leave much to be desired in this respect.

C. Man as symbiont, with reverence for creation

That the world, with all its ecosystems, exists 'in God' and that the creation is going on in this world 'in God'[108] reinforces the attitudes already set out as the proper response to God's immanence in the world. God is present 'in, with, and under' (a set of prepositions usually used with a sacramental reference) all the world processes which, as an aspect of God's being and action, therefore command respect and reverence and have value. So apprehension of God's immanence in the world[109] and of the continuing creation being 'in God' give grounds for a reverence for all creation that incorporates that 'reverence for life' which Albert Schweitzer advocated:

> The great fault of all ethics hitherto has been that they believed themselves to have to deal only with the relation of man to man. In reality, however, the question is what is his attitude to the world and all life that comes within his reach. A man is ethical only when life, as such, is sacred to him, that of plants and animals as [well as] that of his fellow-men, and when he devotes himself helpfully to all life that is in need of help.[110]

H. Skolimowski also accepts this principle of reverence for all creation (which he takes as basic, the Christian ethic of love of man being, in his view, derivative, rather than vice versa) and he expresses his second 'consequence' of 'Ecological Humanism'—the first is the impending 'age of stewardship'— in notably religious language, urging that 'the world is to be conceived as a sanctuary: we belong to certain habitats, which are the roots of our culture and our spiritual sustenance. These habitats are the places in which we, like birds, temporarily reside: they are the sanctuaries in which people, like rare birds, must be taken care of.'[111]

For the natural world to be respected and reverenced by man is for man to value it in such a way that he refuses to disturb

---

[108] Cf. Lecture VI: § IV C, p. 207.

[109] §V A, above, pp. 295 ff.

[110] A. Schweitzer, *My Life and Thought*, ed. C. T. Campion (Allen & Unwin, London, 1933), p. 188.

[111] Skolimowski, op. cit. (above, p. 268 n. 21), p. 39.

it without careful consideration of his aims in doing so and of the consequences of his interference. To have such a disposition, to instill and to practise such reverence, is for man indeed to be the priest of creation and Lord Ashby attributes such attitudes to pragmatic biologists:

> Man-made ecosystems lack the stability and durability that natural systems acquire from their slow and relentless evolution. We have to live with this mystery and its sobering moral influence. It is no wonder that biologists who have reflected on complexity regard it as an act of vandalism to upset an ecosystem without good cause for doing so. We had better respect and preserve the stability of natural ecosystems and try to learn the secret of their stability, so that if we succeed we can apply the secret to our man-made imitations.[112]

On these kind of grounds—an emphasis on the interdependent, symbiotic character of all life, and indeed, of the whole natural world—could, he goes on to suggest, be based a purely secular case for gentle and discriminatory attitudes to nature. Man as *symbiont* does not injure his partners in living.

> Considerations such as these are enough to provide the rudiments of an environmental ethic. Its premise is that respect for nature is more moral than lack of respect for nature. Its logic is to put the Teesdale Sandwort [a 'modest little plant' whose existence in its last site in England was threatened by a proposal to build a reservoir there] ... into the same category of value as a piece of Ming porcelain; the Yosemite Valley in the same category as Chartres Cathedral; a Suffolk landscape in the same category as a painting of the landscape by Constable. Its justification for preserving these and similar things is that they are unique, or irreplaceable, or simply part of the fabric of nature, just as Chartres and the painting by Constable are part of the fabric of civilization; also that we do not understand how they have acquired their durability and what all the consequences would be if we destroyed them.[113]

But the extension of the argument in this second part of the quotation, seems, with its aesthetic undertones, to go beyond what biology *per se* can underpin. For even with its emphasis on symbiosis, it is still the motivation of human self-survival which appears to be determining policy towards nature, even

[112] Ashby, op. cit. (1978), pp. 84–5.
[113] Ashby, loc. cit.

if that policy is the prudent one of maintaining organisms to which man is symbiotically related. The question is, is this enough? Whatever the sympathies of individual biologists, biology as such seems able only to generate a human survival policy towards nature, even when symbiotically informed. For could not one always argue against any particular natural ecosystem that was not closely connected to man that its removal could be justified if that contributed to man's biological need to survive? So although biology may provide a starting-point for the 'rudiments of an environmental ethic' one wonders whether, in itself, it can go any further. That is why we are exploring the possibility of developing 'ecological values' by seeing nature *as* created. For, as Moltmann points out, symbiosis is the essential fact of life for all living organisms and has important consequences for man's relation both to nature and to God:

Investigations into the ecology of survival have demonstrated, on the sub-human plane, that where competing organisms adapt to one another (*symbiosis*) they have a much better chance of survival than those which continue to conflict with one another in the 'struggle for existence'. The subject–object relation between man and nature and the model of domination and exploitation do not provide a viable basis for the survival of both human and non-human systems: rather they lead to the mutilation of nature and to the ecological death of both man and nature.

Now all the factors which alter our natural environment have their roots in economic and social processes within human society and these are themselves rooted in man's self-expression; this being so, the task of Christian theology would appear to be that of cultivating a re-evaluation of contemporary values. Man will not rediscover the image of God upon earth through the domination of nature or by the exploitation, in demonic fashion, of natural systems for his own ends.[114]

D. Man as interpreter, prophet, lover, trustee, and preserver of creation
God as Creator, we have argued,[115] is expressing his intentions and purposes, is unveiling his meaning, in the various and distinctive levels of the created natural world and in its pro-

[114] J. Moltmann, 'Creation and Redemption', in *Creation, Christ and Culture*, ed. R. W. A. McKinney (T. & T. Clark, Edinburgh, 1976), p. 133.
[115] Cf. Lecture VI: § IV D, p. 208.

cesses, which thereby have the meaning with which he endows them. But, if the analogy is to hold, God has also to be recognized as a self-communicating agent, for 'meaning' is futile and sterile if never communicated. So it is we came to speak of God as actively unveiling his meaning, of speaking his word, to that part of his creation, man, capable of seeing and hearing him. This allows man to see the natural world as a symbol of God's meaning, as the means whereby his intentions and purposes are made known. This understanding is, indeed, included in the concept of the world as a sacrament, for the matter of a sacrament always has two functions: the symbolic function, whereby the outward expresses what is inward, so that the inward is known thereby; and the instrumental function whereby the outward takes it character from what the inward reality is effecting by it.[116] So the aspect of the created world as the instrument of God's action, whereby his purposes are effected, conjoined with its aspect as a symbol of God's meaning, supports and amplifies the concept of the natural world as a sacrament, with its implications of the need for reverence in man's attitude to nature and of man's role as the priest of creation, previously urged.

Furthermore it serves to emphasize another aspect of man's functions, namely, man as *interpreter* of creation's meaning, value, beauty, and destiny. Man alone in the natural world reads, articulates, and communicates to others the meanings he reads. If those meanings are correctly and surely discerned, then we may say that in man God has created through evolution a creature who is able to be aware of his (God's) purposes and to discern them and articulate them consciously. In man, creation becomes conscious of itself *as* created and the emergence of man's consciousness and intelligence, whereby he is capable of reading God's meaning, must be seen as an intention of God's creative work. That is, God meant the creation to be able eventually to respond to the meaning of his Self that he had communicated through his creation. So man is interpreter of God, and, as such, he acts as *prophet*, a role which historically has always complemented the priestly in man's corporate relation to God. Like Hamlet's players, man is 'to hold, as

[116] Cf. W. Temple, *Nature, Man and God*, Ch. IV.

t'were, the mirror up to nature': like the poet, he too sees that 'nature is never spent', that 'There lives the dearest freshness deep down things'.[117]

As we have seen,[118] the created world consists of natural hierarchies of complexity, of immense variety and distinctiveness. Their uniqueness often consists in them being describable only by epistemologically non-reducible concepts, which are *sui generis* for the level in question. The natural world is an integrated whole of parts themselves intricately complex and all interlocked in a ramifying web of multiple connections and the Earth's ecosystems represent that level in the hierarchy which is the highest and most complex that has come under scientific scrutiny. The ecologist sees each level in the hierarchy of complexity of ecosystems as essential to other levels, as part of a whole, and yet as of significance in itself. 'It is hard to be a reductionist ecologist', to repeat that remark of Dr Moore. Each organism and level depends on the whole and the whole depends on it. Thus man, in his relation to nature, must make a sensitive response to its integrated complexity and not succumb to the temptation, which inertia and laziness of mind and convenience lure him towards, to see it and react to it merely as an assembly of more easily manageable units which science has already analysed and which current technology can shape as man desires. To do so, would be analogous to the error of treating a person as a mere aggregate of flesh, hair, bone, protein, etc., and so never really to encounter the real person, the real 'Thou' to our 'I'. Some authors, seeing that man should not be reductionist towards the Earth's complex ecosystems, have urged him to regard the natural world as a 'Thou' to his 'I'; they press for an 'I–Thou relation' to our environment, in which a sophisticated technology interacts sensitively with it and is always under the control of an information 'feedback' from that same environment.[119] This pressure, significantly enough, arises from the scientists' own understanding of ecological complexity, of the interdependence of things in nature, so that the idea of man as 'lord of nature' is, in the

[117] Gerard Manley Hopkins, 'God's Grandeur'.
[118] Lecture IV.
[119] W. H. Klink, 'Environmental concerns and the need for a new image of man', *Zygon*, 9 (1974), 307.

minds of biological scientists, replaced by the idea of man in symbiosis with nature.[120]

These authors are not wanting to personify nature, to write it as 'Nature', in any romanticizing manner. They want to emphasize the unique non-reducible wholeness and integration of the ecosystems of the Earth and see parallels in personal relations. In a way, they are asking mankind to adopt the role of *lover of nature*,[121] for the lover supremely in I–Thou relationships is sensitive to the full personhood of the beloved. It is this kind of motivation which seems to have led Barbara Ward and Rene Dubos to conclude their book with the following plea:

Alone in space, alone in its life-supporting systems, powered by inconceivable energies, mediating them to us through the most delicate adjustments, wayward, unlikely, unpredictable, but nourishing, enlivening and enriching in the largest degree—is this [Earth] not a precious home for all of us earthlings? Is it not worth our love? Does it not deserve all the inventiveness and courage and generosity of which we are capable to preserve it from degradation and destruction and, by doing so, to secure our own survival?[122]

Perhaps such language may be too emotive for some, but if we are 'to put the Teesdale Sandwort ... into the same category of value as a piece of Ming porcelain' then man must come to regard himself as a *trustee* and *preserver* of nature, for much of it is unique and irreplaceable—just as the trustees of an art gallery preserve works of human creative art for future generations—who may, indeed, appreciate and understand their significance better than any of those responsible for the preserving at any given time. In this role of trustee and preserver of nature, there is, it seems to me, an added incentive and dimension when we see nature as created so that man's trusteeship is, as it were, 'before God'—we are, or should be, caring for what is of value to God, for he made it thus for its own sake and not just for its utility to man.[123] He values it for itself and for its part in expressing his purposes: 'from atom

[120] Ashby, op. cit. (1978), pp. 82–3.
[121] One of the most striking expressions of this attitude appears in an early novel of Hermann Hesse, *Peter Camenzind* (See end-note, p. 317).
[122] Ward and Dubos, op. cit., p. 298.
[123] Recall God's answer to Job out of the whirlwind in Job 38, quoted on p. 85.

and molecule to mammal and man, each by its appropriate order and function expresses the design inherent in it, and contributes, so far as it can by failure or success, to the fulfilment of the common purpose.'[124]

To see nature *as* creation is to see it from a quite different perspective—a perspective the adoption of which may well prove to be crucial, in the full etymological meaning of that word, in the coming decades. It is to view man and nature *sub specie aeternitatis*—a perspective at once sobering and invigorating. Such a perspective is as necessary to ecology as it is to theology, as Joseph Sittler has well said:

It is a fallacy to suppose that because we know about and think about atoms, genes, astro-physical space and organisation we are thereby thinking about the creation ... *Creation* is a religious and philosophical term; it is not a term whose proper reference is simply the fact of, or the possible structure and process of, the world. The term 'creation' contains and requires a God-postulation. Until we ... admit nature as the *creation* into our reflective nexus, and permit nature there to retain its intransigent reality, we shall neither theologize soberly nor be theologically guided to act constructively.[125]

E.   Man as co-creator, co-worker, and co-explorer with God the Creator

The scientific perspective on the world and life as evolving has resuscitated the theme of *creatio continua* and consideration of the interplay of chance and law (necessity) led us to stress the open-ended character of this process of emergence of new forms.[126] In trying to articulate our resulting understanding of God's action in the world we deployed the model of God as the composer of the fugue of creation, as the leader in a dance of creation (Shiva Nataraja) and as exploring possibilities and actualizing potentialities in a spirit of delight and play. We recognized that creation is still going on—the fugue is still being developed—the choreography is still being elaborated. But man, too, finds himself with creative energies both within and for himself and in relation to nature through his newly acquired technology. So he is faced with a choice—does he join in with

---

[124] C. E. Raven, Gifford Lectures 1952, *Natural Religion and Christian Theology*, Vol. ii, *Experience and Interpretation* (Cambridge University Press, Cambridge, 1953), p. 157.
[125] Sittler, op. cit., p. 99.
[126] Cf. Lecture VI: § IV E, p. 209.

the creative work of God harmoniously integrating his own material creations (which are never *ex nihilo*) into what God is already doing? Or does he introduce a discordant note, an entanglement of and confusion within the dance?

It is as if man has the possibility of acting as a participant in creation, as it were the leader of the orchestra of creation in the performance which is God's continuing composition. In other words man now has, at his present stage of intellectual, cultural, and social evolution, the opportunity of consciously becoming *co-creator*[127] and *co-worker* with God in his work on Earth, and perhaps even a little beyond Earth. To ask how to fulfil this role without the *hubris* that entails the downfall classically brought upon those who 'would be as gods' is but to pose in dramatic fashion the whole ecological problem. But at least one who sees his role as that of *co*-creator and *co*-worker with God might have a reasonable hope of avoiding this nemesis, by virtue of his recognition of his role *ipso facto* as auxiliary and co-operative rather than as dominating and exploitative.

Moreover if man recognizes that God is always active, 'making things new', then his response to created nature must be flexible, open-minded, expecting change and sensitively observing and adjusting to modifications in the world's eco-systems, seeing these as part of God's subtle mechanisms whereby stability is the pre-condition of innovation and

---

[127] The image of man as co-creator with God was a major theme of the Christian humanists of the Italian Renaissance and was based on their Christian appraisal of man, whose endowments and creativities they were concerned to extol, as C. E. Trinkhaus (*In Our Image and Likeness: Humanity and Divinity in Italian Humanist Thought* (Constable, London, 1970), 2 vols.) has amply demonstrated. Thus, eg., Trinkhaus argues that the conception of the Florentine Giannozzi Manetti (1396–1459) of man's creation in the image of God and his vision of man's heavenly destiny represented 'an important new conception of man as actor, creator, shaper of nature and history, all of which qualities he possesses for the very reason that he is made "in the image and likeness" of the Trinity' (op. cit., p. 248). For Manetti, 'man's ingenuity or inventiveness was so great that man himself should be regarded as a second creator of the human historical world that was superimposed on the original divine creation of the natural world' (op. cit., p. 247). The Florentine Marsilio Ficino (1433–99) too had 'an irrepressible admiration for the works of human industry with which he was surrounded in Renaissance Florence.... he cannot help seeing in man's mastery of the world ... further evidence of man's similarity to God if not of his divinity itself' (op. cit., p. 482). It was Ficino who said that man 'acts as the vicar of God, since he inhabits all the elements and cultivates all, and present on earth, he is not absent from the ether' (quoted, Trinkhaus, op. cit., p. 483).

fluctuation in dynamic equilibrium the means of change. Man, with his new powers of technology and with new scientific knowledge of the ecosystems, if he chooses to acquire and apply it, could become that part of God's creation consciously and intelligently co-operating in the processes of creative change taking due account both of man's and nature's proper needs, with duly assigned priorities for each. The exploration which *is* science and its progeny, technology, might then, and only then, come to be seen as an aspect of the fulfilment of man's personal and social development in co-operation with the God who all the time is creating the new. Man would then, through his science and technology, be exploring with God the creative possibilities within the universe God has brought into being. This is to see man as *co-explorer* with God. But these themes, of co-creation and co-exploration, imply intelligent participation by man in God's work of creation. And for that God's meaning has to be discerned.

F. 'Incarnation' and man as co-creator with God

Although God the Creator can express his meaning and intentions at all levels in the hierarchies of created nature, nevertheless we had intimations[128] that the immanence of his transcendence in the natural order might reach a unique intensity in that least reducible of all the levels of created entities—the human person. We also gave reasons for thinking that this possibility of the immanence-of-transcendence-in-a-person, which we called 'incarnation', occurred pre-eminently in history in one who was uniquely open to God, Jesus of Nazareth. In him 'incarnation' occurred—an unveiling of God's meaning within creation to man. But, I also argued, unique though this incarnation was historically and contingently (so that the Church has called it *the* Incarnation), it was expressive of an open possibility for and potentiality of all mankind. Jesus in his life, death, and resurrection, showed that complete openness of man to God was possible and that it led to a new fullness of the life of man with God—and indeed beyond biological life. 'The Incarnation', in Jesus, shows that incarnation—becoming the conscious vehicle of the divine

---

[128] Cf. Lecture VI: § IV F, p. 211.

creative process—is a real possibility for all men. But the locus of this unique intensity of the immanence of the transcendent was the human personality of Jesus.

It has always been the Christian claim that Jesus was fully and completely human and from this it follows that one of the meanings of Jesus' life, death, resurrection—and teaching— for us is that the transcendent Creator can be immanent in man at the fully personal level. But since God is Creator, and still creating, then we must conclude that the continuing incarnation of God 'in us' is identical with God's creative work in and through us. In other words, when we as persons are most creative—whether in the arts, science, and literature, or in intellectual reflection, or in our work, or in personal and social relations, in general, our distinctively human activities— then we are fulfilling those human potentialities that were unveiled in Jesus uniquely and seminally as the continuous creative work of God in man. Man has a derived creativity from God and all genuine activities of man which attain excellence, and are in accord with God's intentions to build his reign of love (his 'kingdom'), may be regarded as man exerting his role as *co-creator* with God. Since 'incarnation' is the 'bodying forth', giving a human personal form to, the transcendent Creator in the immanent, then in all aspects of human creativity man is co-creating with God. As Teilhard de Chardin would put it—he is 'building the earth'. This seems to be what William Blake had in mind when he spoke of 'building up Jerusalem' (even though we dissent from his Platonic-Manichaean distaste for matter). His great series of *Illustrations of the Book of Job* begins with Job and his family depicted as 'worshipping God'—so-called 'worship' and so-called 'God', Blake would have us understand. They *sit* under the Tree of Life from which hang musical instruments, as 'untouched as on a Calvinist Sabbath', Kathleen Raine des-cribes them. But at the end of this monumental series, Job's restored family all *stand* around him playing the instruments, now taken down from the tree, and enthusiastically join in making the music of both heaven and earth. As Kathleen Raine writes in her percipient study,

The series begins and ends with a symbolic expression of Blake's belief that Christianity is 'the liberty both of body and of mind to exercise the Divine Arts of Imagination, Imagination the real and eternal World of which this Vegetable Universe is but a faint shadow ... Let every Christian, as much as in him lies, engage himself openly and publicly before all the World in some Mental pursuit for the Building up of Jerusalem'.... In the last plate each has taken his intrument, and all are playing and singing with that joyful and tireless industry of spirit which for Blake was the essence of Christianity.[129]

Kathleen Raine refers to 'spirit' and this is probably a more appropriate word to denote that continuous creative activity of God immanent in man's inner life wherein God responds to man's endeavours and enables him to transcend his finite limitation in creative works and deeds.[130]

In the doctrine of creation, associated with an awareness of incarnation, we have the basis of a genuinely Christian humanism,[131] in which all human excellence is seen as man making his distinctive human contribution as co-creator to that ceaseless activity of creation which is God's action in and for the world. When its implications are fully followed, we would then have a sure corrective to that arrogant Philistinism which is, sadly and mistakenly I think, one of the least endearing of the cultural features of some of the most active parts of the Christian Church in our society today. Failure to see all creative human excellence—in whatever sphere of life—as part of a never-ceasing *opus Dei* is a blight on human joy and well-being and sadly it is often inflicted for mistakenly and supposedly Christian 'otherworldly' reasons. Joseph Sittler sees human life as the recipient of the grace of God expressed in creation:

When men experience as a positive good the activities of their lives, the range of the work of their brains and imagination and hands ... they do not feel either sinful, pretentious or subhuman. They know, rather, that it is precisely in such work and works that some healthful reality of their nature is being fulfilled in joy and creativity, some significant element in their constitution as men is being realized.

---

[129] Kathleen Raine, *William Blake* (Thames & Hudson, London, 1970), pp. 186, 187.
[130] See Lecture VI, p. 242 for a discussion of the relation of 'spirit' to 'incarnation' language.
[131] For which I have argued elsewhere (Peacocke, op. cit., pp. 174–6).

The theological requirement of this anthropological fact is clear and commanding. The grace of joy and creativity, the possibility of life-understanding and life-enhancement thus experienced, the sense of a self-transcending engagement with the allure and power and mystery of the world refuses to be identified as absolutely separate from the grace and joy and new possibility given to human life in that Christically focused grace, greater than all, which is forgiveness of sin.... For while nature and history may be mute about both the reality of God and meaning in life, man's experiences engender pre-hensions which become occasions within which the announced presence of a gracious God and the divine redemption is, by a necessary momentum, postulated as the meaning of the creation.[132]

Such an apprehension of the life of man engraced by God does, in the light of what we have been saying about God's creative action in the world, perhaps now allow us to make a more positive assessment of human civilization, in general, and technology, in particular. For it is not without significance that the biblical account of man begins in a garden in Genesis but is consummated in the new Jerusalem—a city, symbol of culture.

For one who believes in, is committed to, God as Creator[133] can affirm that it must have been God's intention that human society should have attained its present economic and techno-logical complexity, since he created man, through evolution, with just those abilities which made such complexities inevitable and he at least must have known that it would be so. Such a believer could thus see his work, not as a kind of sacrificial offering to God, but actually as a genuine *opus Dei* of its own; in building up human society one is joining in the creative activity of God who made it all possible. Even the humblest job in the complex society created by scientific technology in satisfaction of real and legitimate needs could take on a new point, if seen as part of that creative process which brought man and society into existence. Provision of such a wider context could, in principle at least, give a new significance to

[132] Sittler, op. cit., p. 115.

[133] This, of course, includes many others besides Christians, even though I believe there is a distinctive enrichment and expansion of the doctrine of creation afforded through what the life, death, and resurrection of Jesus entail.

man's daily work, and so counteract the pointlessness and vacuousness which many feel about it.[134]

However, to speak of 'work' in this way as a problem of individual response is to ignore the social context of work, which actually constitutes that activity *as* work. Because of the vastly increased complexity of society today any implications for man's life of belief in God as Creator, and of more specifically Christian belief, has a social context and reference which is ignored at the peril of irrelevance. No doubt these are 'the greater' works than his own which in the Fourth Gospel Jesus is said to predict his followers would do.[135] As William Temple comments on this passage:

In scale, if not in quality, the *works* of Christ wrought through His disciples are greater than those wrought by Him in His earthly ministry. It is a greater thing to have founded hospitals all over Europe and in many parts of Asia and Africa than to have healed some scores or some hundreds of sick folk in Palestine; and it is to the Spirit of Christ at work in the hearts of men that we owe the establishment of hospitals.[136]

Human action to be effective has to be social and it is as social action that it is judged. We cannot avoid what Gabriel Fackre[137] has called 'the social bundle'—we all affect each other and are affected by each other, beyond the boundaries of our local space and time.

The Christian faith is not insensitive to this—indeed, the New Testament emphasis on 'koinonia', fellowship, in the Holy Spirit and the doctrine of the church as a community held together by Spirit-endowed love and constituted by sacramental worship[138] can, with some justification, be said to have initiated a new understanding of what community might actually mean and become. There is always a communal reference even in what has often been taken to be the most personal aspects of the Christian religion—for example, man's response to Jesus' crucifixion with reference to which J. Moltmann affirms '... the

[134] Cf. Peacocke, op. cit., pp. 194–6; and Teilhard de Chardin, *Le Milieu Divin* (Fontana Books, Collins, London, 1964), pp. 64–7.

[135] John 4: 12.

[136] W. Temple, *Readings in St. John's Gospel* (Macmillan, London, 1955), p. 235.

[137] Fackre, in Barbour (ed.), op. cit. (above, p. 276 n. 42), p. 127.

[138] The Eucharist, from the earliest times, included a thanksgiving for creation in the offering of the bread and wine made by man from corn and grapes.

"crucified God" accepts men in their *shared* lack of full humanness.'[139]

Time and space exclude a proper exploration of this social dimension of man's relation to nature—for example, the politics of the environment;[140] of the problem of technology as an ideology in relation to political ideologies;[141] of the need to politicize appropriately the whole environmental movement;[142] of the urge to develop a new life style;[143] of the politics of conservation;[144] and of the relation of technology to political responsibility.[145]

G. Man as fellow-sufferer in creation

The theme of God the Creator as self-offering and suffering love in action was one of which we could catch only a fitful and baffling hint as we looked at the actual processes of evolution, the mode of creation of living organisms.[146] The life and death —in conjunction with the teaching—of Jesus afforded a profounder revelation of the truth that God as Creator suffers in and with his creations—it is *Love* that 'moves the heaven and the other stars'. But if this is so, that God is self-offering and suffering Love in the processes of creation, then man cannot expect to participate in the creative process, to be, as we said a co-creator and co-worker with God, without cost and without love—he must be a *fellow-sufferer* in creation with God the Creator. There can then, from this perspective, in the long run be no readjustment to their interrelation that is adequate to the needs of both man and nature without cost to man, without sacrifice of the selfish ends of both the individual and

---

[139] J. Moltmann, *Man* (SPCK, London, 1974), p. 20 (italics mine).

[140] See Ashby, op. cit. (1978), and references therein.

[141] See Abrecht, op. cit. (above, p. 293 n. 98), and *Anticipation*, No. 25 (1978), 4 (World Council of Churches, Geneva), Cambridge Consultation on The Ideological and Theological Debate about Science, June, 1977.

[142] See Derr, op. cit., Ch. 6; D. D. Williams, 'Changing concepts of nature', in *Western Man and Environmental Ethics*, ed. Barbour, pp. 48–61.

[143] Cf. the 'Life-Style' prescriptions of the fellowship instituted by H. Dammers, Dean of Bristol, in 1971 and the accounts of other communities by J. V. Taylor, *Enough is Enough* (SCM Press, London, 1975).

[144] See D. W. Morley (ed.), *The Sensitive Scientist* (SCM Press, London, 1978), Ch. 8 (a report of a British Association Study Group).

[145] Barbour, op. cit. (above, p. 276 n. 42), pp. 146–65, § IV on 'Attitudes towards Nature and Technology'.

[146] Cf. Lecture VI § IV G, p. 213.

of the community. What this 'cost' might be and what kind of new communal awareness and altruism will be called for has scarcely begun to be discerned. Too much contemporary ecological discussion has been in terms of a sophisticated projection of *man's* desire for survival—not wrong in itself, but inadequate for providing the larger perspective the mounting climacteric demands.[147] But, until enough people in even the affluent communities of the world come to see the natural world in at least some of the ways here adumbrated further development of this theme, except perhaps in a context purely within the Christian community, is premature.

VI. 'ECOLOGICAL VALUES' AND THE DOCTRINE OF CREATION

What is the relation of the foregoing to the generation of the best 'ecological values', meaning by this term the principles on which to base the making of wise personal and social decisions, with respect to those of our actions that impinge on the environment? This apparently simple question is more complex than first appears. No simple answer can be given, but nevertheless I wish to argue for the vital relevance to the development of appropriate ecological values in the coming decades of man's understanding of his and nature's relation to God as Creator.

There are, however, certain prior unresolved issues. I have spoken loosely, in company with other writers on these matters, of 'ecological values'. But the word 'values' can be very slippery.[148] In the relation to discussion of the environment at least four different meanings have been usefully distinguished by Lord Ashby:[149] (1) 'value' as cost in the market place, quantified as cash—a value in relation to that of other things;

---

[147] Cf. A similar point made by J. Cobb, *Is it too late?* (Bruce, Beverley Hills, Calif., 1972), p. 90, concerning those who argue for the protection of the wilderness because of its importance for *man*.

[148] See the article by W. K. Frankera on 'Values and Valuation', *The Encyclopaedia of Philosophy*, ed. P. Edwards (Collier–Macmillan, London, 1967), Vol. 8, pp. 229–32, and for references. A biological account of values has been given by G. Pugh, *The Biological Origin of Human Values* (Basic Books, New York, 1977), see above, Lecture V, p. 154 n. 13.

[149] Ashby, op. cit. (1978), pp. 6 ff.

(2) 'value' as usefulness, utility for persons or welfare for society; (3) 'intrinsic value', an objective quality of the thing itself; and (4) 'value' as symbols or in relation to a concept. Economists, with varying degrees of success, attempt to quantify senses (1) and (2).[150] Values in the sense of (3) and (4) play a much bigger part in the pattern and direction of man's relation to the natural world and cannot be quantified without reducing them to meaninglessness (one of the principal themes of Lord Ashby's 1977 Leon Sloss Junior Memorial Lectures).[151]

Of these it is 'value' as intrinsic worth (3) and as symbol or concept (4) that is most likely to be related to belief systems in general and the theistic doctrine of creation, in particular. But our more immediate concern, the relation between Christian belief and value judgements in decision making, is more complex than is usually realized. It has been clear for some time that Christian belief, including faithfulness to the New Testament, does *not* lead necessarily or directly to a simple ordering of ethical prescriptions which thereby constitute a system of 'values'.[152] Many writers on Christian ethics and values have concluded, rather, that Christian theology should aim to provide a context of reference concerning what man and nature are and what they may both become, in the light of the overall purposes of God, and it is this that theology *can* attempt to articulate in an intellectually coherent way. Such articulation provides a distinctive framework of reference which can then be judged for its usefulness as a framework and not as a system which, of itself, will generate 'ecological values' or ethical prescriptions concerning practical environmental decisions.[153]

---

[150] e.g. Talbot Page, *Conservation and Economic Efficiency* (Johns Hopkins University Press, Baltimore, 1978).

[151] Above, p. 267 n. 18.

[152] See J. L. Houlden, *Ethics and the New Testament* (Pelican Original, Penguin Books, Harmondsworth, 1973); J. T. Sanders, *Ethics in the New Testament* (SCM Press, London, 1976); T. W. Manson, *Ethics and the Gospel* (SCM Press, London, 1978 ed.); articles on 'New Testament Ethics' by E. Clinton Gardner, and 'Jesus: Ethical Teachings of' by H. K. McArthur in *A Dictionary of Christian Ethics*, ed. J. Macquarrie (SCM Press, London, 1967), pp. 175 ff. and 229 ff., resp., and references therein.

[153] In addition to references already cited, the following may also be consulted for assessment of the present relation of theology and ecology: 'Problems of Biology and the Quality of Life', D. Jenkins, *Anticipation*, 10 (1972), 21–9 (World Council of Churches, Geneva); 'Rights for Both, Man and Nature?' (an ecumenical debate about

In the foregoing section, I took as a starting-point that understanding of God's relation as Creator to the natural world which we have been working out in the light of our scientific knowledge of the world.[154] The aspects of the scientific account of the world on which we have drawn hitherto in these lectures have not, as a matter of fact, until the present lecture, included much of the contemporary understanding of ecology as such,[155] though it has rested heavily on the account of man's continuity, as an evolved biological organism, with the rest of the natural world. We found that taking the scientific perspective on the world seriously has afforded an amplification and enrichment of our understanding of God's creative relation to the natural world, including man. I then tried to infer what attitudes to nature and roles for man in relation to nature such an amplified understanding of the doctrine of creation might entail—attitudes that would go beyond the biblical concept of 'dominion' with man cast as *vicegerent*, *steward*, or *manager* on behalf of a transcendent Creator. This process of inference was, it seemed to me, quite legitimately pursued with, as its presupposition, the scientific account of the natural world as a complex of interlocking ecosystems.

Recognition of the immanence of God as Creator led to the development of the notion of man's role as that of *priest* of creation, to which reverence is due as the medium of God's creative work. This creation, being a symbol of God's meaning

---

process theology's perspective on the ecological crisis), T. S. Derr, J. B. Cobb, D. R. Griffin, C. Birch, P. Verghese, *Anticipation*, 16 (1974), 20–36; 'New Approaches to Creation', A. Dumas, *Anticipation*, 18 (1974), 7–9; 'The Theological Understanding of Humanity and Nature in a Technological Era', Part 6, of the findings of a conference concluding the five-year World Council of Churches' Study Programme on the Future of Man and Society in a World of Science-based Technology, *Anticipation*, 19 (1974), 33–6; 'Toward a New Theology of Nature', O. Jensen, *Bangalore Theological Forum*, VII. 1 (Jan.–June, 1975), 37–51; 'The Whole Earth is the Lord's: toward a holistic ethic', H. K. Schilling, in *Earth Might Be Fair*, ed. I. G. Barbour (Prentice-Hall, Englewood Cliffs, N.J., 1972), pp. 100–22; *Small is Beautiful*, E. F. Schumacher (Abacus, London, 1974); *A Guide for the Perplexed*, E. F. Schumacher (Jonathan Cape, London, 1977); 'Man and Nature: A Theological Assessment', H. Montefiore, *Zygon*, 12 (1977), 199–211.

[154] As summarized in Lecture VI: § IV, pp. 203 ff.

[155] Had we done so, the present *interconnectedness* of the natural world, within and between the various levels of the hierarchies of complexity, would certainly have had to be stressed more than we have done, in addition to its continuity in time (cf. Appendix A (i)).

and a vehicle and instrument of his purposes, can properly be seen as sacramental—as a 'sanctuary' even—and is worthy of man's reverence. Such a reverential attitude to all creation was, indeed, also a consequence of biological appraisals of man as *symbiont* in relation to other living organisms. With respect to the purposes and meaning of God expressed in the world, man appeared as *interpreter* and *prophet* of creation. Consideration of the way in which God is continuously creating at various and distinctive levels of interlocking and subtle complexity indicated that man's attitude to such a symbiotic world should be one of sensitivity and responsiveness, more akin to what is involved in I–Thou relationships. Man might then conceive of himself as the *lover*, or at least the *trustee* and *preserver*, of the natural world. But the role for man in relation to nature which most distinctively arose from the understanding of God's action in the world that we have been developing was that of man as *co-creator* (or *co-worker* and *co-explorer*) with God. For God's continuously creative presence in the world is characterized by being open-ended and emergent, so that man can now exercise his own created free creativity consciously in co-operation with the Creator. The advance of science, which has influenced such a concept, itself provides the means whereby man can consciously co-operate in God's creative processes, for through science man comes to know what these processes actually are— both individually and in all their web of ecological and hierarchical interactions. But to be committed to work with and alongside God in his creative work, is to be prepared to make the sacrifice of love involved in creation, to be a *fellow-sufferer* with God in creation, and it is this which was uniquely illumined, indeed, made possible, by the historical incarnation of transcendence-in-immanence, wherein Jesus of Nazareth became the Christ of faith. For that, above all, showed what was possible for man in the light of God's purposes.

VII. CONCLUSION

It seems to me that to accept a doctrine of creation of the kind I have been developing is in fact to deploy a model which allows one to recognize ecological changes, problems, value-judgements, evils, etc. for what they are. This satisfies the second criterion, that a model of reality must facilitate wise ecological decisions, in that such a picture (or model) of nature as creation can incorporate current scientific understandings of man in his global ecosystems and can elicit ecologically desirable and realistic perceptions on the world. For the doctrine of creation as here elaborated directs the eyes and attention of one who accepts it away from himself towards the natural world, including other people, as the *locus* where God is to be encountered.

Furthermore, since the sphere of God's creative work is always from the present into the future (He is the God Ahead), to aspire to be co-creator with God involves *ipso facto* acting for the future good of both humanity and the Earth's ecosystems—for these will in the future, as now, continue to be the assumed sphere of God's creative work and for man to be participant in creation (co-creator, co-worker, and co-explorer with God) is nothing else than to seek to act in accord with that action of God which always goes on from the present into the future. For man to see himself as co-creator with God therefore provides a powerful motivation to act for the future good. The model therefore satisfies another (the third) criterion[156] of ecological suitability.

Finally, to be co-creator with the 'living God' who always actualizes in his creation new possibilities, previously unimagined humanly speaking, is to be prepared always to adjust creatively and deliberately to the changes necessary for God's purposes to be fulfilled—which includes maintaining the environment in such a way that it can go on being the medium through which life can continue and explore new modes of existence under the guidance of God. In this way is satisfied the fourth criterion[157] of a model of reality that facilitates wise ecological decisions, namely, one that helps man to adjust to changes necessary for survival and for the preservation of a dynamically equilibrated system. The dynamic interaction of nature, man and God that is implicated here has been finely expressed by D. D. Williams, in relation to the thought of H. N. Wieman:[158]

[156] See above, p. 274, and n. 38.

[157] See above, p. 274.

[158] In H. N. Wieman, *Man's Ultimate Commitment* (Southern Illinois University Press, Carbondale, 1958).

For Wieman, faith achieves its maturity in a commitment to the creative activity of God. In this activity the diverse experiences of life are welded into new integrations, new forms emerge, and new values and sensitivities are born. A response in the biblical spirit to man's situation in nature need not be blind worship of what is, nor sentimental affirmation of automatic progress. It need not retreat from the scientific attitude in exploring the possibilities of existence. It can be the hopeful, sacrificial determination to discover those conditions of man's relationship to his environment that release the great possibilities of his creative freedom. Our concepts of nature are being ploughed up, and we have to reconsider our human task in the light of the new concepts. In the Christian outlook, God himself is in the ploughing up and in the remaking.[159]

I cannot pretend, at this stage, that *how* man is to become such a co-creator with God, that *how* this could be possible at all, seeing men as they are, does not raise profound questions to which, it seems to me, the resources of the whole Christian faith are the response. Nevertheless I hope that the understanding of God as Creator that has been developed up to this point, is of such a kind that it might unite all those who are engaged in the 'Long Search' for God and that such an understanding might enable men of widely diverse theistic traditions, to join in that perpetual *Benedicite* which, no doubt, the morning stars first sang together when the sons of God shouted for joy:

O, All ye Works of the Lord, bless ye the Lord:
     praise him, and magnify him for ever.
O, ye holy and humble men of heart, bless ye the Lord:
     praise him, and magnify him for ever.

END-NOTE

Excerpt from Hermann Hesse, *Peter Camenzind* (1904), trans. W. J. Strachan (Penguin Modern Classics, Harmondsworth, 1973), pp. 82–4:

Plenty of people say they 'love nature'. They mean that sometimes they are not averse to allowing its proffered charms to delight them. They go out and enjoy the beauty of the earth, trample down the

---

[159] D. D. Williams, 'Changing Concepts of Nature', in *Western Man and Environmental Ethics*, ed. I. G. Barbour, pp. 60–1.

meadows and gather bunches of flowers, sprays of foliage, only to throw them down or see them wilt at home. That is how they love nature. They remember this love on Sundays when the weather is fine and are then carried away by their own sentiment. And this is generous of them for is not 'Man the crowning glory of Nature'? Alas, yes, 'the crown!'

And so more enthusiastically than ever I explored the basic things of life. I heard the wind sighing in the tree-tops, mountain-torrents roaring down the gorges and quiet streams purling across the plains, and I knew that God was speaking in these sounds and that to gain an understanding of that mysterious tongue with its primitive beauty would be to regain Paradise. There was little of it in books; the Bible alone contains the wonderful expression of the 'groaning and travailing of creation'. Yet I knew deep down inside me that at all times men, similarly overcome by things beyond their comprehension, had abandoned their daily work and gone forth in search of tranquility so to listen to the hum of creation, contemplate the movements of the clouds, and anchorites, penitents and saints alike, filled with restless longing, stretch out their arms towards the Eternal....

St. Francis expressed it in a more mature, yet more childlike way. Now, for the first time in my life I understood him. By his inclusion of the whole earth, plants, animals, the heavenly bodies, winds and water in his love for God, he anticipated the Middle Ages, even Dante himself, and discovered a language to express the eternally human. He deemed all powers and natural phenomena his 'dear brothers and sisters'. When in his later years the doctors condemned him to let them sear his forehead with a red-hot iron, even in the middle of his dread of the agonizing torture he was able to greet his 'dear brother, fire' in this fearful iron.

As this personal love of nature began to grow in me and I listened to her voice as to a friend and travelling companion who speaks in a foreign language, my melancholy, though not cured, was ennobled and cleansed. My ear and eye became more acute, I learned to grasp subtleties and fine distinctions, and longed to hear the pulsation of life in all its manifestations more clearly and at close quarters— perhaps even to understand and enjoy the gift of expressing it in poetic form so that others also could get closer to it and seek out the springs of all refreshment, purification and childish innocence with deeper understanding. For the time being it remained a wish, a dream. I did not know whether it could ever be fulfilled, and I did what was nearest by loving everything visible and by no longer treating anything surrounding me with scorn or indifference.

VIII

Creation and Hope

I. INTRODUCTION

THERE is a natural human curiosity and enchantment about the future—for it is undoubtedly true that that is where we all plan to spend the rest of our lives! Yet do not most of us feel, now, that even the future isn't what it used to be? The hopeful 1960s—the decade of Kennedy, of Vatican II, of 'socialism with a human face' in Czechoslovakia, of the first space-flights to the moon, of expanding educational systems, of a new-found and hopeful environmental awareness, of economic expansion (we could all give our own list)—have given way to the tired cynicism of the 1970s as the hopes placed in these features of our life then have become increasingly manifest as misplaced. As Jurgen Moltmann has said 'Everywhere people feel deceived, abused, dispirited, exploited, and estranged so that they no longer trust the inbuilt goals and hopes of our progressive societies, universities, churches and sciences. They refuse to live goal-oriented and future-conscious, since they refuse to freeze that future in its present image.'[1] Hope has become one of the lost virtues of our age and its loss infects every aspect of our cultural and social life. 'Where there is no vision, the people perish' (Proverbs 29: 18) applies as ever. In the Western industrialized world, the sensitive experience *Angst* and despair, and the insensitive indulge in a frenetic search for substitute ends—in domestic mechanization and other manifestations of private affluence, in elaborate holidays, in lethal speeds, in world-escaping religions of personal salvation, in cults of UFO's and space fiction and even in the occult. Ironically, if we, the

[1] J. Moltmann, 'Hope and the Biomedical Future of Man', p. 90 in *Hope and the Future of Man*, ed. E. H. Cousins (Fortress Press, Philadelphia, 1972, and Garnstone Press, London).

Western and industrialized, are the oppressors, it is clear that the struggle for freedom from our oppression at least gives the oppressed of the Third World meaning to life and hope for the future. Those in control of the world's resources of power become more and more apprehensive of the future. We suspect that 'we've never had it so good' and we'll never have it again. There seems to be a widespread loss of faith in the ability of the future to bring something which is actually *more* fulfilling into men's lives. Many thinking people fear that what they have experienced as the 'Death of God' is being followed by the 'Death of Man', as man's spontaneity becomes paralysed and as he becomes interred in a tomb of technical-economic structures of his own making. Increasingly many feel that the Orwellian '1984' has already, proleptically, arrived in 1978.

Yet man lives by hope and he needs a zest in life that relishes creative tasks taken within the ambience of a sense of duty, to drive out the vertiginous fear induced both by his new lofty experience of ascendancy over the world and by the concomitant challenge to control the evolutionary processes of the world's ecosystems. Without such a taste, such a zest, for life, how can man seize the tiller that his intelligence and science have put within his grasp? As Lewis Ford, the process theologian, has said, 'Hope releases the energies of man, and the lure of a better future is the only reason for any striving. Proximate hopes, however, must be situated within an horizon of ultimate hope.'[2] So that hope is not based on fantasy, however pious, we would be wise to make as realistic assessment as we can of what the future holds.

II. THE FUTURE—ACCORDING TO SCIENCE

Not surprisingly, the resources of science, with its confidence in its powers of predicting natural events, have been evoked to peer into the future, generating an exercise graced with the title 'futurology'.[3] This exercise produces results of varying

[2] L. S. Ford, pp. 135–6 in Cousins, op. cit.
[3] For pungent comments on the relation of 'futurology' to Christian eschatology see the Introduction to *On the Way to the Future* (*A Christian view of eschatology in the light of current trends in religion, philosophy and science*) by H. Schwarz (Augsburg Publ. House, Minneapolis, 1972).

reliability, as we shall see—and it is not always the case that the long-term, large-scale predictions are less reliable than the short-term and small-scale.

Even to use the term 'future' implies that we are contemplating time from the transient viewpoint of the now-instant of our consciousness from which events are described as past, present, or future and with different degrees of pastness and futurity. It is *our* future, or the future of *our* planet, galaxy, etc. in which we are interested. So we naturally employ what McTaggart[4] denoted as the 'A' linear temporal series. In this 'A' series, our now-instant is the continually moving point from which events are viewed as past, present or future. It is as if our consciousness constituted a sliding pointer, a continually moving reference point, gliding over a linear scale of time. This he distinguished from the 'B' series, whereby a set of events X, Y, and Z are permanently ranked by their before–after relationship (on whether X occurs *before* Y and Y *before* Z). The A-series is clearly dependent on certain peculiarities of human consciousness whereas the B-series, at least, purports to objectivity, though it too depends on the asymmetric and transitive character of our temporal awareness.[5]

The relation of these two views of time to that employed in physics, as measured by clocks or atomic frequencies, is highly complex (and still controversial), involving both philosophical and scientific problems[6]—*inter alia*, the question of whether or not directionality in time can be securely based on thermodynamics. In discussions of the 'future' we shall frequently find ourselves setting a before–after (series B) relation on to the sliding scale of our own past–present–future (series A) perspective. For our immediate purposes in reviewing scientific projections into the future, these considerations need not impede us, but they raise very fundamental and difficult questions with respect to God's relation to time. The scientific projections of

[4] J. McTaggart, *The Nature of Existence* (Cambridge University Press, Cambridge, 1927).

[5] See discussion by K. Denbigh, *The Inventive Universe* (Hutchinson, London, 1975), Ch. 1.

[6] See e.g. J. C. C. Smart, *Problems of Space and Time* (Macmillan, New York, and Collier, Macmillan, London, 1976); G. T. Whitrow, *The Natural Philosophy of Time* (Nelson, London, 1961); J. R. Lucas, *A Treatise on Time and Space* (Methuen, London, 1973); all of which contain extensive references to the relevant literature.

the future have various physical time-scales which we will consider in increasing order of magnitude.

A. The future on the Earth

In our discussion (VII) of man in creation, I referred to various prognoses of the future of Spaceship Earth—some horrendous, others cautiously and provisionally optimistic. Lord Ashby, whose prognosis is included among the latter, advised,[7] as we saw, following Edmund Burke in 'doing today those things that men of intelligence and good will would wish, five or ten years hence, had been done', because the choices we make influence the values we come to hold. Because man has, willy-nilly, come to be manager of the earth and its resources, his attitudes and decisions resulting therefrom determine the future, so the content of 'futurology' is itself a factor in influencing the future on the earth. With such 'feedback', where new information is all the time influencing decisions the outcomes of which themselves constitute new information, one has to utilize new intellectual techniques, new *Tools for Thought*, as C. H. Waddington called his (sadly, posthumous) book outlining them for the general public.[8] Not surprisingly the theory of games plays a large part in these new approaches to our terrestrial future— also brilliantly expounded in *Das Spiel* by Eigen and Winkler[9] to which I already referred in connection with the role of chance and law in the origin of life. Study of these fascinating works serves to reinforce the wisdom of Lord Ashby's short-term horizon for ecological decision-making—in the spirit of Newman's 'I do not ask to see / The distant scene; one step enough for me'.

According to the German nuclear scientist W. Häfele, there is no way of overcoming the uncertainties inherent in the use of high technologies such as nuclear engineering—a situation he denotes as 'hypotheticality':

The process of iteration between theory and experiment which leads to truth in its traditional sense is no longer possible. Such truth can no longer be fully experienced. This means that arguments in the

[7] Lord Ashby, Jephcott Lecture, 'Protection of the Environment: The Human Dimension', *Proc. Roy. Soc. Med.* 69 (1976), 727–8.

[8] C. H. Waddington, *Tools for Thought* (Jonathan Cape, London, 1977).

[9] M. Eigen and R. Winkler, *Das Spiel* (Piper, Munich/Zürich, 1976).

hypothetical domain necessarily and ultimately remain inconclusive
... this ultimate inconclusiveness which is inherent in our task
explains, to some extent, the peculiarities of the public debate on
nuclear reactor safety. The strange and often unreal features of that
debate ... are connected with the 'hypotheticality' of the domain
below the level of the residual risks.... It is impossible [to apply the
method of trial error to ultimate reactor safety] because the consequences of so doing would be too far-reaching.[10]

... It is probable that ' "hypotheticality" will characterize the
next stages of human enterprise. The magnitude of technological
enterprises will be so great that it will not be possible to proceed
with the absolute certainty that there will be no negative consequences.'[11]

The irony, challenge, and tragedy of this new feature of
'hypotheticality', of permanent uncertainty, in human decision-
making is now conjoined with the new human capacity, by
means of nuclear weapons, of doing what the Hebrew apocalyptic literature affirmed only God could do—namely, foreclose
the history of human (indeed all) life on earth. The advent
of Overkill undoubtedly ushers in an apocalyptic era but one
brought within the realm of *human* decision-making. Even at
a level less dramatic than that of the effects of nuclear
weapons, the ambiguities and ignorance involved in human
decision-making could, because of its feedback character,
induce oscillations of increasing amplitude in the ecological
effects of such decisions beyond the limits of toleration of
terrestrial ecosystems.

This consequence of high technology has its roots in a paradox
concerning man which is implicit also in the application of
technology to himself. It is the paradox of the 'myth', as
Langdon Gilkey calls it,[12] which 'promises to man freedom *over*
necessitating destiny on the basis of man's complete subservi-
ence *to* necessitating determination.'[13] Gilkey depicts this

[10] W. Häfele, 'Hypotheticality and the New Challenges: The Pathfinder Role of
Nuclear Energy', *Minerva*, 12 (1974), 314–15, and reprinted in *Anticipation* (World
Council of Churches, Geneva), May 1975, No. 20, pp. 19, 20. See also Lord
Rothschild's 1978 Richard Dimbleby Lecture on 'Risk', *The Listener*, 30 Nov. 1978,
pp. 715–18.
[11] Häfele, op. cit. (1974), p. 319, and (1975), p. 22.
[12] L. Gilkey, *Religion and the Scientific Future* (SCM Press, London, 1970).
[13] Gilkey, op. cit., p. 82.

anthropocentric myth of the new scientific or technological man as 'the man in the white coat' who *knows* the secrets of things, what their structures are and how they work; so he is the man who can control these forces he understands and bring them into the service of human purposes. The paradox lurks in the assumption that for scientific inquiry man can be exhaustively understood as the determined *object* of inquiry, to be comprehended precisely as a non-intentional creature operating under determining laws of necessity—man as a being to whom the category of freedom is inapplicable to those who know. But as Gilkey says,

... if the man in the white coat is as free to control, and as intentionally motivated by creative and moral purposes, as the mythical image proclaims ... then the man on the table, the object of the inquiry of the same scientist, must *also* be in part free.... Since in this case both controller and controlled represent instances of the same sort of being, this myth about man tends to contradict itself.[14]

This contradictory modern myth, of man as helpless patient in the backless white hospital garment and yet as mighty doctor in the sacral white coat who knows the secrets of things,[15] is nevertheless endemic in our culture. The future *on* the earth is therefore intimately interlocked with the paradoxes of the human situation[16] that are not resolvable from within the scientific perspective alone.[17]

B. The future of the Earth

Curiously, however opaque the immediate future *on* the earth may be on a time-scale of decades and centuries because of man's waywardness, the longer-term fate of the Earth as a planet can be predicted with more confidence. Because the fundamental source of energy of the Earth—and so of all its living forms—is the Sun,[18] the fate of the Earth is entirely dependent on its future, and that can be predicted with

[14] Gilkey, op. cit., p. 82.
[15] Gilkey, op. cit., p. 85.
[16] Never better characterized than by Reinhold Niebuhr, *The Nature and Destiny of Man* (Charles Scribner's Sons, New York, 1941–3).
[17] As previously argued in Lectures V–VII.
[18] Cf. pp. 258 ff.

certainty in the long run. For the basic energy-producing process in the Sun is the reaction in which four hydrogen nuclei unite to give a helium nucleus and its content of hydrogen is sufficient to go on producing energy for perhaps another 5,000 million years by this process. There will certainly come a stage when the hydrogen in the central regions becomes depleted so that the supply of energy drops and the freshly produced helium forms itself into a core and starts to contract under its own weight. What follows this initial stage in the life of a star is complicated and depends on its mass and composition though the general patterns of change are predictable. In the case of our Sun, the first stage will be a *rise* in temperature as the core shrinks and, oddly, this will be concomitant with an increase in brightness and an expansion and cooling of the outer layers of the star where nuclear 'burning' still continues. This cooling will change its colour to red and the Sun will by then have become a 'red giant', like Aldabaran. With this increase in the Sun's luminosity the heat striking the surface of the Earth will melt the polar icecaps, causing widespread floods and, although natural selection for many millions of years may evolve organisms capable of withstanding the higher temperatures, there will undoubtedly come a time when all land will be baked desert, the oceans will boil and all life will be literally incinerated. Then the Earth will be slowly but inexorably vaporized and will then probably be engulfed by an expanding Sun. The planet on which life as we know it evolved will have disappeared for ever from the universe.

Perhaps we now lose interest in the fate of the expanded Sun which has taken the Earth back into its maw, but the astrophysicists have a reasonably confident understanding of its future development from observations of other stars in their various stages and by means of calculations based on knowledge of nuclear reactions and the relevant forces. As the temperature in its core increases, new nuclear reactions will occur (e.g. $3\,He \rightarrow C$), producing a sharper rise in temperature and a kind of internal flash which can be contained. The Sun will then settle down to be a much hotter and bluer 'giant', possibly pulsating. Eventually, when all nuclear fuel is exhausted, it will cool down to become a white and then a black 'dwarf'. Thus, after unimaginably long periods of time, of orders of magnitude far greater than its present age, energy production in the Sun (and in other stars less than three times its original mass) will cease and it will become a ball of crushed 'burnt out' matter.

Our Sun and its satellite Earth is, on this time-scale, just an intermediary stage of evolution of a dispersed cloud of gas on its way to becoming a ball of crushed matter. The emergence of ordered molecular living systems, including man, on a fragment of matter spun off during this evolution constitutes, it seems, only a temporary hiatus in the relentless and irreversible movement of the galaxy towards an end that we can actually observe as the fate of other planetary systems and which Shakespeare presaged in his last play and farewell to the theatre, when Prospero lifts his spell:

> Our revels now are ended. These our actors,
> As I foretold you, were all spirits and
> Are melted into air, into thin air:
> And, like the baseless fabric of this vision,
> The cloud-capp'd towers, the gorgeous palaces,
> The solemn temples, the great globe itself,
> Yes, all which it inherit, shall dissolve
> And, like this insubstantial pageant faded,
> Leave not a rack behind.[19]

C.   The future of the galaxy and of the universe

Although the second law predicts a running down of the universe towards equilibrium[20] it cannot say how fast this will

[19] *The Tempest*, IV. i. 148.

[20] The application of the Second Law of Thermodynamics to the universe *as a whole* is problematic in so far as that law asserts that entropy (disorder) always increases with time in an *isolated* system and one has to assume that the 'universe' is isolated (no matter or energy entering or leaving) for the law to be applicable. This means that the Second Law cannot be applied to limited regions such as the solar system or the galaxy or even the observable universe, which has a 'horizon' fixed by the impossibility of observing galaxies so distant and moving so fast that their spectrally shifted emitted light is not detectable by us, and not likely to be. However, even though these regions, large as they are, cannot be regarded as isolated, *sensu stricto*, if we define the universe as 'all matter and energy', this is *ipso facto* 'isolated' in the sense required, and eventually the Second Law says equilibrium (maximum entropy) will prevail throughout—which will include the sub-regions of the observable universe, our galaxy and the solar system. So the predictions outlined later in this section remain valid possibilities on the basis of the Second Law. (See A. R. Peacocke, *Science and the Christian Experiment* (Oxford University Press, London, 1971), p. 198.)

occur. Stars in other parts of the universe will at different times follow a sequence similar to the Sun, if of approximately the same mass, but otherwise somewhat different histories. Heavier stars burn up their nuclear fuel more quickly, explode as supernovae, or collapse into 'black holes';[21] smaller stars last longer. New stars can still form in the universe from scattered clouds of matter but eventually this supply will become too depleted for any new stars to form. From then on, stars will gradually disappear from a universe already spatially dilated beyond the present scale, leaving black dwarfs and black holes, and these latter will slowly accumulate in an increasingly dark and colder space. Eventually the temperature in space of its 'black body radiation' will be lower than that (10^{-7} °K) of these stellar black holes, which will then begin to lose energy by the process of quantum evaporation discovered by Hawking.[22] They will then over a period of the order of 10^{67} years rise in temperature, as they contract, to a size of only 10^{-6} cm. when they will shine like stars for about another 10^{33} years and will finally disappear as radiation. Or, it may be that most of the stellar black holes from a galaxy will be absorbed first into a gigantic black hole which will take 10^{100} years to evaporate into radiation. As Paul Davies (to whose writings I am indebted for much of this account) says: 'The final feeble resources of free energy will be exhausted, the whole cosmic machine will have run down to a standstill and the second law of thermodynamics will have claimed its last victims. After this, equilibrium will prevail and the entropy of the universe will have risen to its maximum.'[23]

There is, as astronomers have realized for some time, an alternative to this slow heat death of a for-ever expanding universe. If the total quantity of matter in the universe in relation to its scale is sufficiently great, the force of gravity will continuously slow down the present cosmological expansion until the galaxies cease to recede and start to contract, with

---

[21] A black hole is a star that has contracted under gravitation to less than a certain critical radius after which no electromagnetic radiation can escape from it (it is 'black').

[22] S. W. Hawking, 'Particle creation by black holes', *Comm. Math. Phys.* 43 (1975), 199–220.

[23] Paul Davies, *The Runaway Universe* (Dent, London, 1978), p. 162. (See also his *Space and Time in the Modern Universe* (Cambridge University Press, Cambridge, 1977).)

increasing velocity—that is, the universe will *im*plode. Galaxies cease to be distinguishable and the interstellar spaces would contract with an increasing interstellar 'temperature' of the background radiation. With increasing rapidity the universe would pass in reverse through the various earlier stages of the expansion from the hot big bang—until quantum processes take over, space–time breaks down and present physics can predict no more. The universe will end in a singularity in which 'all matter will be squeezed out of existence at an infinite density.'[24]

Both of these alternatives are catastrophic and both constitute a scientific 'end' in which the organization of the universe, as we know it, will have gone. At the moment, the first (a slow heat death through continuous expansion) seems more probable from the evidence, but there are many uncertainties still to be resolved.[25] One set of uncertainties concerns the singularities that have been postulated in both of these proposals. If these can be avoided, so that at a limiting fantastically high density the contraction of the second model reverses into an expansion again then (for a number of possible theoretical reasons) 'a recontracting universe may survive its encounter with the future singularity and emerge, phoenix-like, from another primeval fireball to re-expand in a new cycle of activity. Furthermore this process of expansion and recontraction could then he repeated *ad infinitum*, thereby endowing the universe with immortality'[26]—more precisely, endowing the *cycles* of universes with 'immortality', for this has to be qualified to allow for the inevitable operation of the Second Law. It was in such a context that, in Lecture II, I drew attention to the realization that there is a close connection between the values of the fundamental physical parameters and the existence of life and so of intelligent creatures capable of observing the universe—the so-called 'anthropic principle'.

In any case, the demise of living organisms, including man, is inevitable long before the final slow heat death of the first prospect or the obliteration of matter in the other two. All that intelligent man, or machine intelligence created initially by man, could hope to do would be to delay his (or its) demise

[24] Davies, op. cit., p. 165.
[25] See above, p. 326 n. 20.
[26] Davies, op. cit., p. 183.

—with greater difficulty in a contracting universe than in a still-expanding one which might allow our descendants to transmigrate to other planets, possibly in another stellar system. Nevertheless, however much intelligent beings could extend their communal existence, eventually the remorseless increase in entropy will bring about a collapse of technological and material organization. In brief: 'The unpalatable truth appears to be that the inexorable disintegration of the universe as we know it seems assured, the organization which sustains all ordered activity, from men to galaxies, is slowly but inevitably running down, and may even be overtaken by total gravitational collapse into oblivion.'[27]

Thus science fails to answer 'the ultimate question of hope',[28] not only because of the ambiguity of man's exercise of the powers with which science endows his freedom, but also because science raises questions about the ultimate significance of human life in a universe that will eventually surely obliterate it. However far ahead may be the demise of life in the cosmos, the fact of its inevitability undermines any intelligible grounds for hope being generated from within the purely scientific prospect itself.

The apocalyptic character of the scientific end, both of the Earth and of the universe, is far more bizarre and dramatic than anything that the Hebrew imagination conceived in the centuries immediately around the beginning of the Christian era. The Revelation of John is but a pale document compared with these modern scientific apocalypses! Yet while the biblical apocalypses (e.g. Mark, chapter 13, as well as the Revelation) fundamentally address themselves to the same questions as we now raise in the light of scientific prediction of the End, and while they too portend sequences of events of an awesome character, they nevertheless are illumined from beginning to end with a radiant hope. We must now therefore, briefly, examine the biblical perspective and inquire as to the source of its hope.

[27] Davies, op. cit., p. 197.
[28] Gilkey, op. cit., p. 99.

III. BEGINNING AND END IN THE BIBLE[29]

There is indeed a stark contrast between the scientific picture of the end of the Earth and of the universe and those which conclude the Bible. The Revelation of John speaks[30] of a 'new heaven and a new earth' and a 'new Jerusalem' whose light will be the glory of God and from which suffering and death and pain will have been expunged. The images are drawn from a rich literary tradition and the use of them is highly mythological. Indeed it is clear that the greater part of the Revelation does not place its events (perhaps they could more properly be called 'happenings' in the contemporary argot) on the time scale of history. It begins with the particular, in history, with the state and possible plight of the seven churches to whom it is addressed. However, as it develops its highly formalized structure[31] it moves towards the goal of universal history, when the limitations on human existence are removed (e.g. the barriers between man and God, exclusion from paradise, death, sorrow, suffering). In so doing, it is the mirror image of the Beginning as depicted in Genesis 1–11, where the movement is from the universal and trans-temporal, 'events' which none can witness and are therefore beyond history, to a partial history, that of the people of Israel. The language of mythology is there in Genesis, though it lies submerged beneath the surface. These early chapters move in a world beyond our understanding, standards, and concepts of reality —for example, only in these early chapters of Genesis does man (Adam) confront God face to face, something not allowed historical man elsewhere in the Old Testament without some kind of intermediary.

The primal 'time' and end 'time', to which these biblical accounts of the Beginning and the End refer, both lie beyond historical time—'beyond' not in the sense of being an extra extension of historical time, but essentially different from it. With respect to it they act rather as a framework from another

---

[29] See C. Westermann, *Beginning and End in the Bible*, trans. K. Crim (Facet Books, Fortress Press, Philadelphia, 1972), whose account is largely followed here.

[30] Revelation 21: 1, 23.

[31] See G. B. Caird, *A Commentary on the Revelation of St. John the Divine* (A. & C. Black, London, 1966).

dimension. The Beginning and End in the Bible delimit historical time as boundaries which are 'not-time', for they represent
the origin and goal, respectively, *of* time. Both the Beginning
and the End have a universal scope in a trans-temporal
setting. Within these boundaries, this framework, the history
of salvation, the history of man's well-being, is worked out.

The two accounts also interrelate for in Genesis, the Creator
holds the key to the fate of the world and the possibility of
its destruction is never absent—the existence of creation is not
to be taken for granted, as the story of the Flood makes clear.
Indeed, according to Westermann,[32] the constant ritualistic
repetition of creation by the narrating of the creation stories
contributes to and celebrates the preserving of creation from
a relapse into chaos, never far away. However, God's purposes
are not frustrated for, in Revelation, the End is the consummation of his purposes, not in a return to chaos, but in a 'new
heaven and new earth' with its 'new Jerusalem'. C. Westermann
sums up the biblical themes thus:

> The message of the beginning and the end means that God's activity
> is not confined to salvation history but extends to universal history
> as well. It means that God is the creator of all mankind, including
> all the stages of human development and all the possibilities of human
> existence, human activity, and human thought. The sciences also,
> with all their possibilities and consequences, have their basis in the
> plan of the creator of mankind. This means that God, the creator
> of mankind, intends to bring this creation of his to a goal that only
> he knows. Mankind was created for a significant purpose, a purpose
> that man himself can neither accomplish nor frustrate.... The
> message about the beginning and the end means that God created
> the entire universe for a purpose. It also means that the universe
> has a history, a history with a beginning and an end. When we speak
> of God and to God, we are acknowledging that everything has a
> meaning and a purpose.[33]

This account of the biblical understanding of the Beginning
and the End as representing a non-temporal boundary for
temporal history has introduced a distinction that serves to
warn us against too readily identifying scientific (and
pseudo-scientific) futurology, which makes predictions con-

[32] Cf. p. 32.
[33] Westermann, op. cit., p. 38.

cerning historical time, with eschatology, which is about the ultimate destiny and goal of man and also, in many apocalypses, of the universe too. It is this destiny which is hidden within the purposes of God and hope, in the Old Testament, is based on the character of God as trustworthy for the good of man and of his creation.

For Paul, too, hope is founded unequivocally on the nature of the transcendent God and not on our immanent potentialities, except in so far as they have been shown to be consummated in the taking of our lives into God, a destiny revealed and made possible to us through Jesus Christ. '. . . we labour and struggle, because we have set our hope on the Living God, who is the Saviour of all men', he writes.[34] It is the stress it places on the reliability, conjoined with the novelty, of the 'future' as something to be hoped for which is a notable feature of biblical religion, according to Pannenberg.[35] However, what Pannenberg means by the 'future' is far from straightforward, as we shall see. For 'futurology', the 'future' lies on the familiar time scale of clocks, and on the less familiar scale based on atomic frequencies as chronometers that the physicist measures.

The distinction between what 'futurology' and 'eschatology', respectively, seek to explicate is nicely demonstrated by the ambiguity of the English word 'end', meaning (*inter alia*) both a *terminus ad quem* in time and a goal or aim. One may well have hope based on one's discernment of the 'end' of all things in the second sense (of goal, or aim) while being pessimistic (or should one say, realistic?) about the 'end' of all things in the first sense (of a temporal terminus). It is with such problems that theology has wrestled since Schweitzer rediscovered the eschatological thrust of the New Testament[36] in the first decades of this century so we must now consider some contemporary theological understandings of hope in relation to the 'future'.

[34] 1 Tim. 4: 10 (NEB).

[35] See the account of his ideas by A. D. Galloway, in *Wolfhart Pannenberg* (Allen & Unwin, London, 1973), pp. 21–3.

[36] For the complexities of the biblical words for time, see James Barr, *Biblical Words for Time* (SCM Press, London, 1962, and 2nd revised edn., 1969), in particular for his discussion (pp. 50 ff.) of O. Cullman's *Christ and Time* (Eng. trans. Floyd V. Filson, SCM Press, London, 1951). Philosophical distinctions (such as those of McTaggart or even those concerning eternity and time) must not, it seems, be read into the different biblical words for time.

IV. FUTURE AND HOPE IN CONTEMPORARY THEOLOGY

A. The meaning of the future

Christian reflection on the relation between the 'last things' and present reality, with its hopes and fears, inevitably involves conclusions about the interrelations of past, present, and future. This cannot but be interlocked with the developments in the concept of time which have resulted from relativity and quantum theory and which philosophy is still in the process of digesting. For our present purposes it is perhaps enough to recognize that time as measured and used by the physicist is intimately related to space and energy, and so to matter, and must be considered as an aspect of the total created order. Thus any doctrine of creation must take physicists' time to be created along with matter, space, and energy with which it is integrated in our current conceptualization of the universe.[37] Time, so regarded, is then an aspect of creation and creation is not an event on such a time scale. Furthermore, we recall that this does not necessarily mean that God must be conceived of as purely 'timeless'. For, as Karl Barth has expressed it,

Even the eternal God does not live without time. He is supremely temporal. For His eternity is authentic temporality, and therefore the source of all time. But in His eternity, in the uncreated self-subsistent time which is one of the perfections of His divine nature, present, past and future, yesterday, today and tomorrow, are not successive, but simultaneous. It is in this way, in this eternity of His, that God lives to the extent that He lives His own life.... We speak of 'created time', but it would be more accurate to say 'co-created'. For time is not a something, a creature with other creatures, but a form of all the reality distinct from God, posited with it, and therefore a real form of its being and nature.... Time is the form of the created world by which the world is ordained to be the field for the acts of God and for the corresponding reactions of His creatures, or, in more general terms, for creaturely life.[38]

---

[37] See above, Lecture II, pp. 55, 79; and A. R. Peacocke, 'Cosmos and Creation' in *Cosmology, History and Theology*, ed. W. Yourgrau and A. D. Breck (Plenum Press, New York and London, 1977), pp. 376–9.

[38] K. Barth, *Church Dogmatics*, Eng. trans. (T. & T. Clark, Edinburgh, 1960), iii. 2, pp. 437–8; also see above, Lecture II, p. 80 and n. 53; and Peacocke, op. cit., p. 379.

The philosophical discussion of time is beyond our present scope, but we have already had to note MacTaggart's distinctions between time as a ranking of before–after (the B-series) and time viewed as past–present–future from an ever-moving transient 'now' moment (the A-series)—a view which implicates the human consciousness, with its sense of succession, in the concept of time. As Denbigh remarks in his summing up of his study on the 'construction of time':

... time in human experience has a 'one-way-only' character and is felt as a creative ongoing; scientific theory itself neither favours nor excludes such a view, but good reasons may be advanced why the sense of time's directions which is available from conscious awareness should not be disregarded. In an important sense 'time' seems to provide a kind of link between the mental and the physical.[39]

In the present context of relating the doctrine of creation to man's need for hope it is however the understanding of contemporary theologians of the *meaning* of the future with which we must be concerned, rather than with philosophical inquiries into time itself, a still active field.

The theological understanding has been formulated in the light of the biblical exegesis I have outlined; against the background of a spirit of the age, and of theology itself, which stresses the existential; and, for some of them, with an awareness of the continuous, open-ended nature of the creative evolutionary process. Many contemporary theologians see the meaning of the Christian faith as eschatologically determined, that is, they understand life through what they believe the Christian faith gives us hope we shall become. There seem, at present, to be three movements in contemporary theological thinking that is seriously concerned with the future: (i) the 'theologians of hope', principally from Germany or of American Lutheran provenance; (ii) the 'Teilhardian' theologians, those developing the ideas of Teilhard de Chardin; and (iii) the 'process theologians', mainly in the USA but also in Britain, to whom we have already had cause to refer.

(i) *The theologians of hope* work from within the biblical message, as they see it, of God's promise of future fulfilment and

---

[39] Denbigh, op. cit., p. 53.

the hope this generates.[40] For these theologians the significance of the future lies in its relation to the present and these two are bridged by symbolic language ('eternal life', 'the beyond and the transcendent', 'heaven and the Kingdom of God'), which conveys a message that they believe can generate the hope, energy and encouragement to work for change. Biblical religion, they argue, was driven into world history by the force of its belief in the future—it was the power and promise of the future that kept Israel moving forward to ever more universal roles. This future, with its promise, is not seen as a simple extrapolation from, and prolongation of, the present, but as a reality in its own right—for ultimately it is what is meant by God. 'God is our Future, the fulfilling power of the future of all things', writes Carl Braaten.[41]

Because eschatology was the centre of Jesus' message, the Jesus of history is linked, for Christians, to the future of God, so the reality of God as our future has, for them, an implicit Christological reference:

It may seem paradoxical that the Christian faith is simultaneously rooted in the past history of Jesus Christ, grounded in the present experience of the believing church, and still oriented to the future as no other religion. The paradox may be only apparent, for it is the real history of Jesus Christ that mediates the power to attract faith in him today, thus constituting the church, and also to generate anticipations of the future. The history of Jesus has such inexhaustible power because the eschatological future of God's kingdom became really present in him, giving us a vision of the shape of things to come.[42]

Taking seriously the idea of *creatio continua*, Pannenberg stresses that God confronts each present with a future different

[40] C. Braaten, *The Future of God* (Harper & Row, New York, 1969) and *Eschatology and Ethics* (Augsburg Publ. House, Minneapolis, 1974), Chs. 1, 2; H. Schwarz, *On the Way to the Future* (Augsburg Publ. House, Minneapolis, 1972) and *Our Cosmic Journey* (Augsburg Publ. House, Minneapolis, 1977); W. Pannenberg, *Jesus—God and Man* (SCM Press, London, 1968) and *Theology and the Kingdom of God*, ed. R. J. Neuhaus (Westminster Press, Philadelphia, 1971); J. Moltmann, *Theology of Hope* (SCM Press, London, 1967) and *The Experiment Hope* (Fortress Press, Philadelphia, 1975); J. B. Metz, *Theology of the World* (Herder & Herder, New York, 1969). See also: P. Hefner, 'Questions for Moltmann and Pannenberg', *Una Sancta* 25 (1968), 32–51.
[41] C. E. Braaten, 'The Significance of the Future: An Eschatological Perspective', in Cousins, op. cit. (above, p. 319 n. 1), p. 53.
[42] Braaten, op. cit. (1974), p. 42.

from itself. Even on a more transcendentalist view of God's relation to the world, it has been traditionally held that all creation is destined to participate in God's glory and thereby to be itself glorified.[43] Because of this creative character of *God's* action on the present, there is the possibility or, rather, the opportunity for man to be open to this transcendent element in his immediate present and so to commit himself to the open future. This commitment can occur either with fretful anxiety or with the hope of unlimited fulfilment, or with both—as finely depicted by Reinhold Niebuhr's description of man's condition as that 'of the sailor, climbing the mast ... with the abyss of the waves beneath him and the "crow's nest" above him. He is anxious about both the end toward which he strives and the abyss of nothingness into which he may fall.'[44] It was the hope of fulfilment that, as we have seen, characterized the faith of Israel in *both* the novelty *and* the reliability of the future-to-be-hoped-for.

It is intriguing to note that this theme of fulfilment finds an echo in the inaugurating address that the biologist Julian Huxley gave to a CIBA Foundation symposium on *Man and His Future* in which he characterized his main theme thus:

> ... biologists have to think of the future of man in the unfamiliar terms of psycho-social or cultural evolution. Looking back, we see that evolving man has lurched from one crisis to another ... The present phase of the process is rapidly becoming self-limiting and self-defeating.... The new and central factor in the present situation is that the evolutionary process, in the person of mankind, has for the first time become conscious of itself. We are realizing that we need a global evolutionary policy ... To succeed in this we need to reorganize our science ... In particular, we must switch more and more of our scientific efforts from the exploration of outer space to that of inner space—the realm of our own minds, and the psycho-metabolic processes at work in it.... We should set about planning a Fulfilment Society, rather than a Wealthy Society, or an Efficiency Society or a Power Society. Greater fulfilment can only come about by the realization of more of our potentialities.... Our knowledge

---

[43] Pannenberg, 'Future and Unity' in Cousins, op. cit., pp. 62–3.
[44] R. Niebuhr, *The Nature and Destiny of Man*, Vol. 1 (Charles Scribner's Sons, New York, 1941), p. 185 (1964 printing).

of the evolutionary past makes it clear that any new psychosocial system should be open-ended, not liable to become self-limiting.[45]

This passage is redolent of that optimism of the 1960s, to which I have already referred, yet, nevertheless, represents a sensitive *biological* diagnosis of man's needs—even as this scientific ideology (Evolution with a capital 'E') proves incapable of advising[46] *which* possibilities for man should be fulfilled, and which not, in the striving for fulfilment which is to follow, so Huxley predicted, the struggle for existence.

The theme of 'openness to the future' has characterized the theological approach of J. Moltmann[47] who has stressed that creation is an 'open system', open in relation to time and to its own alteration within time. But he goes on to raise an important question for the 'future' which leads to an apparent impasse:

Is the completion of the process of creation to be understood as the final conclusion of the open and opened system? Is the kingdom of glory the final conclusion to the universe? Then the new creation would be the end of time and in itself timeless. Man, understood as an open system, would then be only an unfinished system and the open systems of nature would be no more than systems that were not-yet-closed.... The consummation would then be the end of human freedom and the end of new possibilities for God. Time would be destroyed by eternity and possibility by reality.[48]

Such a conclusion would frustrate the purposes of the God who as Creator all the time 'makes things new', so the ultimate end of man and nature must be of a kind that is consistent with the character of the God that is unveiled in his creation so far. The consummated life in God must be, for Moltmann, one of unlimited possibilities for glorified man in which he is free to participate in the freedom of God—

... time and history, future and possibility may be admitted into the kingdom of glory and, moreover, both to an unimpeded extent and

[45] J. Huxley, 'The Future of Man—Evolutionary Aspects', in *Man and His Future*, ed. G. Wolstenholme (Churchill, London, 1963), pp. 20, 21.

[46] Moltmann, op. cit. (above, p. 319 n. 1), p. 94.

[47] See above, Lecture VI, pp. 210, 211.

[48] J. Moltmann, 'Creation and Redemption', in *Creation, Christ and Culture*, ed. R. W. A. McKinney (T. & T. Clark, Edinburgh, 1976), p. 130.

in a way that is no longer ambivalent. Instead of a timeless eternity we should talk about 'eternal time'; instead of the 'end of history' we should talk rather about the end of pre-history and the beginning of the 'eternal history' of God, man and nature. We must, above all else, think of change without passing away, time without the past and life without death.[49]

This stress on the open possibilities of the present as being a manifestation of our confidence in the openness of the future has led Moltmann to stress that a future which does not begin in the transformation of the present is no genuine future—and leads him to a *liberation* theology in which a future that is related to the ultimate good, that is, to the Godhead of God, must begin with overcoming the oppression of the present.[50]

(ii) *The Teilhardian theologians*, whose theme is probably more generally known in Britain, draw upon the scientific perspective of the world in evolution from atom to the consciousness of man to underpin an eschatological vision of a final unity. In this ultimate unity, complexity will reach its zenith of consciousness within what they call an 'Omega Point', which is itself the energizing focal point of the process and seems to be identified by Teilhard, at least, with the glorified Christ, who stands at the end of time—the Pantocrator.[51]

In the Teilhardian perspective the future is only intelligible as the future or destiny of what is now and has been. It is impossible to understand the future except relative to a deep probing of the past–present of which it *is* the future. This probing reveals, and indeed selects, man with his peculiar gifts of consciousness and self-consciousness as the leading edge of evolution, which cannot be understood correctly unless it is interpreted in the light of man. Matter–energy has a tendency to become more complex—meaning thereby a tendency to intensification of multiplicity (or aggregation) and centredness (or organization of identity)—that reaches its present point of highest development in man's self-consciousness as individual-in-society. The future is then, from this perspective, the fulfilment of this trend of evolving forms of matter–energy, i.e. the

[49] Ibid.

[50] Moltmann, op. cit. (above, p. 319 n. 1), pp. 57, 59.

[51] See the account of P. Hefner, *The Promise of Teilhard* (Lippincott, Philadelphia and New York, 1970), Ch. IV.

destiny of man and the world is to fulfil this trend. This vision allows human self-consciousness to give itself to action that is responsible for the destiny of the world by being convinced that the world does indeed have a destiny that is consonant with the personhood of man and his species. 'To be at home in the world is to find it in basic consonance with the human enterprise; to find that world comprehensible is to find that the environment is consonant with man's mind as well as with his body and will.'[52] On this basis, P. Hefner has developed the Teilhardian perspective and has characterized the future: as one of convergence and unification; as one of progressive personalization; as open, not closed; as implying the worth and reliability of creation;[53] as activating human energy; and as exemplifying love as the term which covers the action in which activated human energy contributes towards the fulfilment of the evolutionary process, at the present time focused in man.[54]

The emphasis in the Teilhardian perspective is more upon the vision which makes it possible for persons here and now to live by participation in the slow rise of mankind towards unity with itself and with God, than with any detailed cosmological scheme, or particular metaphysic. It is the mystical and moral passion for sharing the creative action that is God's work in the world[55] that, at the end of the day, is one of the most impressive features (according to D. D. Williams,[56] and I concur) of the optimism and hopefulness about a significant ethical and religious life in the present age that the Teilhardian view induces.

(*iii*) *The process theologians.* We have had occasion elsewhere in these lectures to refer to various aspects of process theology;

---

[52] P. Hefner, 'The Future as Our Future: A Teilhardian Perspective', in Cousins, op. cit. (above, p. 319 n. 1), p. 24.

[53] See below, p. 348.

[54] The concept of love in Hefner's account of the Teilhardian perspective includes: (1) love defined as the action of union between centred persons that is freely entered into; (2) a great emphasis on the centring effects of true love; (3) love as engaged in all its forms in world-building; and (4) love as by definition earthy and material, because world-building is contributing to the physical development of persons, the world, mercy, politics, psychotherapy, as well as the organization of human energies.

[55] As 'co-creator', in the terminology of Lecture VII.

[56] D. D. Williams, 'Hope and the Future of Man: A Reflection', in Cousins, op. cit., p. 143.

here it is its perspective on the future with which we are concerned.[57] Process theology is derived from the metaphysics of A. N. Whitehead which he developed in response to the transformation of the scientific perspective brought about by relativity (and to a lesser extent) quantum theory. Whitehead saw the fundamental units of the world as events, rather than substances, and for him process was fundamental both to the world and to God. Process theologians have found his metaphysics a more effective tool than any other available metaphysical scheme for interpreting the biblical tradition of the living God active in history and nature. John Cobb describes[58] the Whiteheadian view as one which, while being dissatisfied with the existentialist understanding of each moment as being the point of decisive judgement and an end in itself (so displacing the 'future' from this role), nevertheless finds itself in a mediating position between two active and well-known alternatives to existentialism. These are, on the one hand, Bultmann's account of Christian eschatology as openness to the immediate future and, on the other hand, the conclusion of the Teilhardians and the theologians of hope. According to Cobb, Whitehead, like the existentialists, focuses on the present moment as the locus of decision but, unlike them, sees the decision as necessarily 'polar'[59] in the sense that it is *both* repetition of the past *and* response to the new God-given possibility, fulfilment of which is then the actualization of potentiality brought to the present from the past. This doctrine of decision as novel realization of God-given possibilities is, in fact, very similar, Cobb argues, to Bultmann's call to openness to God's future. However, unlike Bultmann, Whitehead adopts a 'polar' view of the importance to every moment of *both* the immediate future *and* the ordinary temporal future, the 'future beyond itself':

[57] See the following, in addition to other references cited below: J. B. Cobb, *God and the World* (Westminster Press, Philadelphia, 1969), Ch. 2; J. B. Cobb and D. R. Griffin, *Process Theology: An Introductory Exposition* (Christian Journals, Belfast, 1977), Ch. 7.

[58] J. B. Cobb, 'What is the Future? A Process Perspective', in Cousins, op. cit., pp. 1 f.

[59] This use of 'polar' recalls the description by Professor Basil Mitchell of Oxford (in an unpublished paper) of theological paradoxes, and contrary positions 'held in tension', as 'theological ping-pong'!

The awareness that its [immediate] realization [of possibility] can be a positive contribution to the temporal future is itself a part of the value realized in the moment.... there is little value or interest in life when it is devoid of the sense that what is going on has value beyond itself.... Whitehead's view is that the only locus of value is the present moment, but that the richness of that value depends on anticipation of its value to others.[60]

But, Cobb continues, if meaning in the present depends on anticipation of the temporal future, what kind of future is that? For even the limited satisfaction we can derive from anticipation of the proximate future runs out into wider issues of personal and social destiny, because the proximate future is but one thread of an expanding web of interconnections. So, to ensure the meaning of the present moment, that wider destiny must be conceived of as hopeful. Whitehead saw the need for this hope but did not base it on eschatologies of the kinds we have already considered. He took seriously the scientific evidence, now stronger in our day than in his, that human history will have an end in time as we know it, as well as a beginning, and that end will be simply extinction in that time. For him it ultimately matters little, in principle, whether that extinction is within the near future or billions of years hence:

... on the scale of history, to which our imaginations are more attuned, process does not guarantee progress. Cultural epochs succeed each other, thereby realizing new and different values. Novelty is necessary if zest is to be regained after one culture has exhausted its fundamental possibilities. But whether the artistic achievements, for example, of the later epoch are greater or less of those of the earlier is an open question. This is not a cyclic view. Whitehead stresses real novelty and radical change. Also, progress is possible. Over hundreds of millions of years and culminating in man, despite temporary reversals, there was fundamental progress on this planet in the realization of greater values. Within human history, too, threads of progress can be discerned. God's activity in the world makes for progress, as well as mere change. But there is no guarantee of progress in the short run, and in the long run it is inevitable that life on this planet will become extinct.[61]

For Whitehead, each moment of experience receives much

[60] Cobb, op. cit. (above, p. 340 n. 58), p. 5.
[61] Ibid., p. 7.

of its internal value from its anticipation of its contribution to the future beyond itself—and this has the requisite feature of ultimacy, the process theologians would claim, since this future, in his understanding, is simply *God's* future. Following this lead, process theologians take the issue of hope to refer both to expectation in the present and to possibilities in the future of divine redemptive action. This divine action of creative love is persuasive, not coercive, promoting enjoyment, and it is adventurous; it is the 'lure' of God whereby he draws his creation on to fulfil his purposes.

It is because God exercises power upon us, persuasive power, that a space is opened up for us within which we are free. If there were no God, there would be no freedom, and the freedom would not be open to be shaped by human decision. The future is open and we are free because of God. The power to open the future and give us freedom is a greater power than the supposed power of absolute control [as in the notion of God as Controlling Power (ch. 3 and p. 119)], for a power effective over free beings is a far greater power than what would be involved in the manipulation of robots.[62]

It thus becomes clear again that in this theology, as in the others, the meaning of the future is ultimately located in God. We must now consider how the different theologies conceive of this relation.

B. *The future and God*

(i) The *theologians of hope* see hope for the future as closely linked with belief in God. For Carl Braaten the process of removing any reference to the future from eschatology, that has been the response to the grotesque eschatological mythology of some Christian sects, and the further process of removing eschatology from theology paved the way for the 'death of God' both culturally and theologically.

Ultimately what we mean by the future is what we mean by God. For God is our Future, the fulfilling power of the future of all things. If the symbolism of the future which holds the hope for a radical transformation of this world and its people into a new world and a new humanity is eliminated from the consciousness of mankind, then the medium of God-language is also destroyed. For God is always

---

[62] Cobb and Griffin, op. cit., p. 120.

introduced in human language as one who will make the difference, bringing another dimension and doing a new thing.[63]

For Pannenberg, too, the futurity of God is of primary importance. God is not timeless yet, as its Creator, he is Lord over time. This is not a restriction upon God and time is, for Pannenberg, the locus and occasion of the divine free creativity. All times are present to God. The 'time' referred to here by Pannenberg seems to be close to the 'physicists' time' which is so intertwined conceptually with space, matter and energy as to be part of the created order. However, that is not to say God is 'timeless' in some other sense of time, and Pannenberg accepts that there must be succession (or, better, the ranking of temporal events) within God, if God is to have any significant self-disclosing relation to our historical time.[64] Yet how is God going to be involved in consummation and fulfilment in the history of man (and of nature?) without there being development in God himself, without there being an element of 'not yet' in God? As a response to this problem, Pannenberg introduces the idea of 'the ontological priority of the future', which develops the creation's relation to God in terms of its future rather than its present. Whatever Pannenberg means by this—and it is not entirely clear in the absence of an agreed philosophy of time—it is clear that he rejects any idea of development in God, in the way that Whitehead and the process theologians allow in their concept of the 'consequent', temporally developing 'pole' in God, as distinct from the 'primordial', eternally unchanging 'pole'. For, for Pannenberg, although the future is not yet decided, 'what turns out to be true in the future will be evident as having been true all along'.[65] So the movement of time contributes to deciding what the definite truth is going to be also with regard to the essence of God.

Pannenberg perhaps comes nearer to the Teilhardian theologians when he stresses that the idea of the creative unification of man is necessarily implicated in the idea of one God as soon as that one God is considered, not only as the origin of creation, but also as its ultimate destiny and consummation, provided

[63] Braaten in Cousins, op. cit., pp. 53, 54.
[64] See above, p. 333 n. 38.
[65] W. Pannenberg, *Theology and the Kingdom of God*, ed. R. J. Neuhaus (Westminster Press, Philadelphia, 1971), pp. 62 ff.

that God's creative activity is not separated from, but related to, his future. So he believes, with Teilhard, that the future evolution of man will tend towards a unity of mankind:

... if love is considered to represent the ultimate motivation of God's creative activity, and if it belongs to love that the one who loves communicates himself to the beloved one to the degree that is beneficial for the beloved one, then the consummation of the process of evolution in a convergent unity by participation in the unity of the creator seems intimately connected with the act of creation as such. This does not constitute a claim of the creatures on God, but it lies in the intrinsic logic of the creative love of God himself.[66]

Moltmann also stresses, as we have seen, the theme of 'openness to the future'. Earlier (p. 337) I quoted the passage where he recognizes the apparent impasse in such thinking which arises if the disappearance of this openness is taken to be an aspect of God's consummation of his creative work. This he resolves by postulating that the life of man in God must be one of unlimited possibilities:

If the process of creation is to be completed through the indwelling of God, then the unlimited possibilities open to God indwell the new creation and glorified man is free to participate in the unlimited freedom of God. The indwelling of unlimited possibilities open to God signifies, moreover, the openness (par excellence) of all life-systems and, for that reason, their eternal qualities for life not their rigidity[67]

—and this has implications for our understanding of God:

Because any actualisation of a possibility by open systems itself creates a new openness for possibilities and does not merely actualize a given possibility and, thereby, transfer the future into the past, we cannot conceive of the kingdom of glory (consummating the process of creation with the indwelling of God) as a system that is finally brought to its conclusion and, as such, closed but, on the contrary, as the openness of all finite life systems for the infinity of God. This means, to be sure, that we must think of the being of God not as the higher actuality for all realized possibilities but, rather, as the transcendent source of all possibilities.[68]

[66] W. Pannenberg, in Cousins, op. cit., pp. 64–5.
[67] Above, p. 337 n. 48.
[68] Moltmann, op. cit. (above, p. 337 n. 48), p. 131.

So in Moltmann's thought, too, the character of man's ultimate 'future' eschaton is closely linked with the concept of God and his relation to the world.

(*ii*) The *Teilhardian theologians*[69] see meaning given to human existence and the wider evolutionary process by that image of the future which is the destiny of the world and which is discerned in the nature of the past–present reality that we are. This image of the future also gives focus to our actions which, together with the meaning it affords, points us towards a unification of all reality of a kind that preserves our identity. The images here referred to are manifested in concrete sets of symbols and in specific historical communities—those (largely political) for whom destiny is a call forward towards the 'Ahead' in the temporal process, and those (largely religious) for whom the call is upward towards an ultimate 'Above'. Neither kind of community is, from the Teilhardian perspective, adequate for man today: thus, the religious communities, in particular, must recognize that the reality they worship as the God Above is *also* the God Ahead (and thereby provide the transcendent dimension needed by the other, political, kind of community). God is, then, for the Teilhardian theologians the 'Prime Mover Ahead', the 'Mover, Collector, Consolidator, the God-Forward of evolution'.[70] In this perspective:

the Christian symbols are the concrete vehicles for understanding the meaning of the process of which we are a part, the direction in which it is going, the shape of our actions. Christ is the Omega toward which the process is tending—ultimate unification of all things, with the most intense personalization of the individual value and identity— and Omega, which is both presence and eschaton, both source and goal, both context and direction. Christ reveals to us that the process is in God, and that his transcendence lies in his being the future of our past–present rather than in his being distant from our material realm.[71]

However this leads to no inevitable 'progress' into God for, on

---

[69] P. Hefner, op. cit. (above, p. 339 n. 52), whose account I largely follow here.

[70] Quoted by Hefner, op. cit., p. 34, from *La Place de l'homme dans la nature*, by Teilhard de Chardin (Seuil, Paris, 1963), p. 173, Eng. trans. by G. Shriver, in G. Crespy, *From Science to Theology: An Essay on Teilhard de Chardin* (Abingdon, Nashville, 1969), p. 74.

[71] Hefner, op. cit., pp. 34–5.

this view, God has so incarnated himself and the future into the self-conscious frontier of his creation, namely man, that the future in fact rests upon man.

(*iii*) The *process theologians* also stress the importance of belief in God. For them, the supreme importance of religion is that it gives a vision of something beyond the passing flux of transient experience. The impossibility of locating fulfilment or consummation at the temporal end of the endless procession of new events focuses religious concern on the dimension of reality that has permanence, namely, God. Nevertheless, for the process theologians, following Whitehead, concern for God apart from a concern for the world would be being faithless to God. God in his 'consequent' nature, in process theology, acts upon the world which also acts upon him and thereby grows by being the sympathetic recipient of all the values realized in the world.

The value of the present is woven upon the values of the past, and together they are transformed into a new unity in God.... Each moment of experience receives ... much of its internal value from its anticipation of its contribution to the future beyond itself. Insofar as it recognizes that this future contains, quite literally, God's future, its meaning has the requisite ultimacy.[72]

So in process theology God has a 'future' which will be an enrichment and enhancement of the present by an incorporation into himself of the emerging value in the 'passing flux' of events: this incorporation is itself based on the 'eternal' nature of God as the source of value in all events. To this kind of 'future' of God man contributes and thereby finds the significance of his own human present in this relationship to 'God's future', that is, to God's life and being. As Lewis Ford puts it:

Process theism ... radically shifts the locus for our hope; the ultimate meaning of the world is not to be found in its future, but in its ongoing contribution to the life of God. The ultimate horizon of hope is situated not at the end of history but in the present experience of God. All of our deeds and actions finally come to nought in this temporal scene, but not before they have become a permanent enrichment of the divine life.[73]

[72] Cobb, op. cit. (above, p. 340 n. 58), p. 9.
[73] L. S. Ford, in Cousins, op. cit., p. 136.

V. CREATION AND HOPE IN CONTEMPORARY THEOLOGY

'All of our deeds and actions finally come to nought in this temporal scene', says Ford—from what science can tell us, not only *our* deeds and actions, as well as those of our predecessors, but also of those who, down the corridors of time, will succeed us—until the Earth is burnt up into the Sun, and the Sun and its galaxy go to *their* 'long home', of 'slow refrigeration through everlasting expansion or dramatic cremation and complete obliteration of the physical world.'[74] Thus, just as we are sure human life had a beginning, not earlier than 3 billion[75] years ago when all life began, it is most likely to perish with its earthly home 5 billion years hence—or else be so transformed that to call it 'human' would be inappropriate. The wisdom of the Bible in setting its 'salvation history' within a trans-temporal framework is thus made manifest to our scientific perspective in a way impossible to many of our immediate fore-bears who conceived of infinite space enduring for an infinite time as a kind of unlimited stage for the dance of matter, energy, and life. This backdrop we now know has its limits, not only conceptually (because of the curvature of space–time), but also because along any scale of time we may devise, the planet Earth, together with its galactic purlieus is destined to undergo profound changes that will sweep away the molecular structures which constitute living matter. Hence the wisdom of the biblical setting of the Beginning and End as a trans-temporal framework for salvation history, yet included in God's work, for it is essential to God being God that he is the first and the last (the Alpha and the Omega), that his activity includes everything.[76]

How do the various theologies of God's purposes in and for time fare in the light of this scientific perspective? For its solemnity and reality is not one whit diminished by the almost unimaginable time scale on which it is based. Even that comes within reach of our minds, when we note that radio signals are now being received on radio telescopes in this country which started their journey across the universe before the Sun and

[74] P. Davies, op. cit. (above, p. 327 n. 23), p. 165.
[75] US billion = 10^9 = 1,000 million.
[76] Cf. Westermann, op. cit. (above, p. 330 n. 29), p. 39.

the planets, including Earth, existed (*c.* 5 billion years ago); and furthermore that the signals are already on their way which, on arrival at this corner of the universe, will encounter a Sun 'burning' its last hydrogen into helium and an Earth already incinerated, if still locatable at all.[77] What do our theologies of the future amount to against *that* backdrop?

(*i*) The *theologians of hope*, true to their grounding in biblical exegesis, stress (as we have seen) that the 'future' with which they are concerned is not an extrapolation of the past and present; it is a reality in its own right, of an ultimacy which gives it 'ontological priority' of a kind which locates it in God himself. So if we were to ask them in which direction to look in order to perceive the 'future' to which they refer, it is clearly not along any 'ordinary' time axis known to physics, to our clocks or to our ordinary experience of terrestrial, 'daily' (i.e. Sun-regulated) life. To look for the 'future' they describe, we must look towards God and he it is indeed on whom their hope is grounded. Hope, then, becomes for them in fact the attitude appropriate to the experience engendered when we look towards God in the present.

(*ii*) A similar conclusion, it seems to me, emerges from placing the perspective of the *Teilhardian theologians* against this same scientific backdrop. They extrapolate into the future from the past, stressing especially the past emergence of consciousness from complexity, but their confidence in making such an extrapolation at all depends on that character of the Creator and of his dynamic work that they deduce from their inter-pretation of the evolutionary past leading to our present. Teilhard identifies his 'Omega Point', that 'far-off divine event to which all creation moves', with Christ and so implicitly, since he was a Christian theologian, he locates it within the being of God himself. Thus again hope is, for this group of theologians too, based on the character of God, and on the reliability of his creation, and so is located on an axis which runs between man and God, rather than along the 'ordinary' time-scale already mentioned.

[77] The time implicit in these statements is one based on the Earth (and, effectively also, the Sun) as the inertial reference system, with the qualifications this involves concerning its actual scale, if not its sequence of events.

(*iii*) The *process theologians* are quite explicit about this, as illustrated in the earlier quotation from Lewis Ford (p. 346), whence he continues, even more pointedly,

> There are strong metaphysical reasons why Whiteheadians resist any notion to an ultimate end of history or a final consummation of the evolutionary process. If all being lies in becoming, the end of becoming would signify the annihilation of all things, including God, for the continuation of the divine concrescence requires a constant enrichment of novelty from the world ... God's appetition for the actualization of all pure possibilities requires an infinity of cosmic epochs for the world. I envision an endless series of expansions and contractions of the universe, in which all the outcomes and achievements of each cosmic epoch are crushed to bits in a final cataclysmic contraction, to provide a mass/energy capable of assuming a novel physical organisation in the next expansion.... Only in some such fashion will it be possible for God to pursue his aim at the actualization of all pure possibilities, each in its due season.... it is more important to recognize that there are no religious reasons for insisting on an end to the process *if* the meaning of the world and the ground of our hope is to be found in the enrichment of divine experience. There can be all sorts of penultimate consummations in the future, but none need be the bearers of such ultimate significance which demands that it must necessarily be unambiguously good. We have hope in God, but it is equally true that God has hope in all of his creatures, trusting us to accomplish his purposes by actualizing the lures he provides.[78]

Of course, for Ford, as for other process theologians, there is an incompleteness in God who, though 'infinitely rich in possibility', is 'deficient in actuality'—a concept of God which we have already found itself to be deficient in other respects. Even so, the process theologian clearly locates 'the ultimate horizon of hope ... in the present experience of God',[79] and it is within such an horizon that proximate hopes must be situated. The 'ultimate meaning of the world is not to be found in its future, but in its on-going contribution to the life of God'.[79] Here 'future' really does mean 'on the ordinary time scale' but again hope is located on the axis between man and God in the *present* experience.

---

[78] Ford, op. cit. (above, p. 346 n. 73), pp. 136 f.
[79] Ibid.

VI. HOPE IN CREATION

Of these three theological perspectives on the future and of God's relation to it the Teilhardian and process theologians explicitly take into account a scientific world-view, the 'theologians of hope' being primarily biblically orientated. If one allows for their different ways of expounding that 'future' which is God's concern (or even God himself, it almost seems in some of these expositions), then these three theologies of the future prove to be more convergent than at first appears to be the case. There is also a congruity between this common understanding of the basis of hope that, so it seems to me, underlies their apparently divergent expositions and that which can be developed, more positively in my view, from the relation of God and the world that I have been expounding as resulting from taking the scientific perspective and the questions it raises as our starting-point.

Before developing this, there is a submerged paradox, contradiction possibly, which must be brought to the surface, in the finitude of the time-scale of the existence of *homo sapiens* and the challenge and exhortation I developed in my last lecture for him to become a co-creator with God in his continuous work of creation. What is the point of being a co-creator if all is eventually to be obliterated? This dilemma must be kept in mind when we expound the relevance of God's relation to the world, as we have been developing it, to the question of hope. Such an exposition will be based on the presumption that, if the question 'What is God's purpose in creation?' can be answered in a way which gives significance to human life in the purposes of God, then there is a basis for hope.

Our special emphasis has been on God's *immanence*[80] in the created world and we developed the model of God as agent of the world through which he expresses his meaning and purpose. Our basis for this stress is the trustworthiness and viability of the created order, as manifest in its regularity and ability to be subsumed under scientific laws and interpretative concepts. The experience of this trustworthiness and viability of the created order is an *unveiling* of God's *meaning*[81] and purpose

[80] Lecture VI: § IV A, p. 204.
[81] Lecture VI: § IV D, p. 208.

and is a primary ground for hope—for that created order has been the matrix of our own emergence and evolution. As Hefner put it at the 1971 New York conference on the 'Hope and Future of Man': 'The God question *is* the question of the reliability of the creation order, and it is difficult to speak of the future or of God apart from that reliability.'[82] And, earlier:

We must recognise that the question concerning the trustworthiness of the evolutionary process *is* the question concerning God. We must resist the temptation to say that it *leads to* or implies the God-question ... the reality and the nature of God will be unfolded in the course of our probing the nature of the world processes in which we live and move, and as we seek to understand man's relationship to those processes, their trustworthiness for or hostility to human life, and the question of man's survival within the milieu which these processes have engendered.[83]

That is, if our model of God as agent is at all applicable, then in experiencing the world *as* trustworthy and *as* viable, that is, as amenable to scientific analysis, we are encountering God *as* generator of and basis for hope.

This experience of God immanent in the world must not, however, be confined only to those who see it through scientific spectacles—far from it, as countless lines of Wordsworth and other poets of nature could illustrate. The author who exhibits, at least for me, most clearly the link between God's immanence in the world and the dimension of hope is Thomas Traherne, for whom their union is the source of all 'felicity',[84] as he calls it:

The WORLD is not this little Cottage of Heaven and Earth. Though this be fair, it is too small a Gift. When God made the World He made the Heavens, and the Heavens of Heavens, and the Angels, and the Celestial Powers. These also are parts of the World: So are all those infinite and eternal Treasures that are to abide for ever, after the Day of Judgment. Neither are these, some here, and some there, but all everywhere, and at once to be enjoyed. The WORLD is unknown, till the Value and Glory of it is seen: till the Beauty and the Serviceableness of its parts is considered. When you enter into it, it is an illimited field of Variety and Beauty: where you may lose

[82] Hefner, op. cit., p. 37.
[83] P. Hefner, 'The Relocation of the God-Question', *Zygon*, 5 (1970), 13, 15.
[84] 'Intense happiness, bliss' (OED).

yourself in the multitude of Wonder and Delights. But it is an happy loss to lose yourself in admiration at one's own Felicity: and to find GOD in exchange for oneself. Which we then do when we see Him in His Gifts, and adore His Glory.[85]

This special emphasis on God's immanence we have held, however uncomfortably, with a recognition of his transcendence.[86] It is this vision, common to all monotheistic religions, of something beyond the passing flux of transient experience[87] that has been the mainstay of the hope the religions have, since their inception, engendered in beleaguered mankind. Even today—

... the ultimate horizon of our future is as shrouded in mystery as that of any other age, for the ambiguity of our freedom and our fate, and the strange way they can interact in history, remain as impenetrable as ever, giving to our feelings for the future the deep tone of anxiety. In our age as in any other, therefore, confidence and hope depend on a sense of the transcendent Lord of all things—for unless the Lord builds the house, the builders do labor in vain.[88]

We also had reason for affirming that we must regard the world as being *within God* (pan-en-theism).[89] This implies that God is closer to us than we realize, that 'indeed he is not far from each one of us, for in him we live and move, in him we exist.'[90] Paul here, in this Athens speech attributed to him by Luke, is referring to a general sense of the intimacy of the presence of God, one also recognized in the tradition he had received:

For this commandment which I command thee this day, it is not hidden from thee, neither is it far off. It is not in heaven, that thou shouldest say, Who shall go up for us to heaven, and bring it unto us, that we may hear it, and do it? Neither is it beyond the sea, that thou shouldest say, Who shall go over the sea for us, and bring it unto us, that we may hear it, and do it? But the word in very nigh unto thee, in thy mouth, and in thy heart that thou mayest do it.[91]

---

[85] Thomas Traherne, *Centuries*, I. 18.
[86] Lecture VI: § IV B, p. 204.
[87] Cf. p. 346.
[88] Gilkey, op. cit., p. 100.
[89] Lecture VI: § IV C (iii), p. 207.
[90] Acts 18: 27, 28 (NEB).
[91] Deuteronomy 30: 11–14 (AV).

In other words, our hope is grounded on an apprehension of God within the very stuff of human and natural existence. Hope is to be found as we look towards God within present actualities, as the transcendent that is immanent in all we experience.

We saw, too, that we had to conceive of the Creator God as *continuously* active in the *open-ended, emergent*[92] processes of the world. All events participate in one continuous process that is the expression of the divine purpose which includes ourselves. Because the process has produced man, with all the vulnerable autonomy and creativity of his self-consciousness, in spite of all setbacks, detours, disasters, and tragedies, and through the operation of its own in-built systems (its own natural 'wisdom', as R. W. Burhoe[93] likes to call it) we can rely on its long-term capabilities, provided we work with these processes and not against them. It is here that the paradox of the need for us to be co-creators with God on an Earth with a *terminus ad quem* can begin to be resolved. For our hope is in *God*, in his ability to work out his purposes, partially, at least, manifest in his eliciting consciousness from insentient matter. However, that hope depends for its consummation and fulfilment on our response to God, on our apprehension of his purposes and mode of working in his universe—for God as Love (we saw) put himself and his purposes at risk in endowing man with the freedom to participate in implementing his purposes or to go his own way. These purposes of God, however dimly we apprehend them, must *ex hypothesi*, because they are *God*'s, finally achieve their fulfilment beyond space and time within the very being of God himself. All we can perceive at the moment is how God works out his purposes in space and time, conveying his meaning to man in the diverse ways we have discerned—and it is up to man to listen and respond to that meaning.

Man cannot believe himself to be the sole arbiter of his own destiny without intellectual contradiction and historical self-destruction. If he is to have confidence in his destiny, therefore, *he must recapture that sense of the creativity, wonder, and sacrality of the given*, as the source and ground of his own powers, of his potentialities, and of his hopes. And

[92] Lecture VI: § IV E, p. 209.
[93] R. W. Burhoe, 'The Human Prospect and the "Lord of History"', *Zygon*, 10 (1975), 209–375.

he must understand that the present and the future course of his history is not just the *servant* of his autonomy and creativity as in a 'secular' understanding, but that in a mysterious way that destiny manifests as well He who is his Lord. For judgment on his misuse of his autonomous powers, and grace to re-create them, must be mediated to him through the events of his historical destiny if man is to have any confidence at all.[94]

Yet, however carefully we try to perceive God's meaning, to hear the leitmotifs he is developing in creation, it comes through to us muffled and distorted by our own ignorance and waywardness, obscured by our intellectual inertia and blurred by our sufferings. We need a more ample and clearer communication[95] of his meaning in and through created transcendence-in-immanence, that is, through a person. So it was that man learnt, as we have seen, that

God who at sundry times and in divers manners spake in time past unto the fathers by the prophets,
Hath in these last days spoken unto us by his Son.[96]

Or, to put it in the nutshell of the Oxford Bidding Prayer: '... above all, ye shall praise God for his inestimable love in the redemption of the world by our Lord Jesus Christ; for the means of grace, and for the hope of glory'.

We have seen reason to believe that the traces we have detected in creation of the ways of a loving Lord of creation have opened up into the Way of the truth unveiled in the life, death, and resurrection of Jesus the Christ. In him, transcendence-in-immanance became incarnate; the possibilities in man were actualized. In him, the faint, sometimes hardly caught resonances, have swelled out into the rich harmony of God's revealed possibilities for creative man in creation. For in Jesus we are able to hear that Word (the Logos) imprinted in creation in an unmistakable fashion. In him we see how a rich life of openness to God, and self-offering love to man as a reflection of the love of God[97] can, through the deepest imaginable suffering, be taken up into the life of God himself. The

---

[94] Gilkey, op. cit., p. 18 (first italics mine).
[95] Lecture VI: § IV F, p. 211.
[96] Hebrews 1: 1, 2 (AV).
[97] Lecture VI: § IV G, p. 213.

intimations and hints that we so laboriously picked up in the
created order in him became illuminating revelation of that
which was there all the time—which seems to be at least one
of the possible interpretations of the opening of the First Epistle
of John:

It was there from the beginning; we have heard it; we have seen
it with our own eyes; we looked upon it, and felt it with our own
hands; and it is of this we tell. Our theme is the word of life. This
life was made visible; we have seen it and bear our testimony; we
here declare to you the eternal life which dwelt with the Father
and was made visible to us. What we have seen and heard we declare
to you, so that you and we together may share in a common life,
that life which we share with the Father and his Son Jesus Christ.
And we write this in order that the joy of us all may be complete.[98]

—and what is hope but the anticipation of the completion
of joy?

So we find that what, earlier in this exposition appeared as
the dilemma of the challenge to become a co-creator with God
in a world with a *terminus ad quem*, is transmuted into a call
to participate in the costly, open-ended, risk-taking creative
work of love that God himself is implementing in the world.
The role of co-creator involves the way of the cross, for within
the centre of the being of Creator, did not the Seer truly
perceive that 'Lamb slain *from the foundation of the* world'?[99]

VII. CONCLUSION

Thus the understanding of God's relation to the world, of the
doctrine of creation, that we have been developing in the light
of the sciences, is congruent with an understanding of hope that
is grounded on the character as Love of the transcendent God
who is immanently active in all events, most notably in the
personal, and uniquely transparently in Jesus the Christ. The
immediacy of God's creativity in and through the actual events
of the hierarchical complexities of the stuff of the world is what
constitutes the dimension along which hope is generated in
man as he apprehends that loving, urgent, and fulfilling

[98] 1 John 1: 1–4 (NEB).
[99] Revelation 13: 8 (AV).

Presence. The 'future' which is the concern of theologians of hope and of the Teilhardians does indeed seem to be most relevant only when it is a symbol for that line from man to God which can be drawn in the present actualities. It is along this line that, in accordance with the process theologians, I see that hope may actually be engendered.

It seems that the doctrine of creation, here elaborated, when the threads of its implications and consequences are drawn out, can provide man with a vision and hope in actual existence that no secular ideology can match in its depth and sensitivity to the various levels of man's needs and aspiration. As a group of us expressed it a few years ago, relating the doctrine of creation to other major Christian beliefs and to the basis of man's hope in the world:

To accept God as the Creator of all things implies that man's own creative activity should be in co-operation with the purposes of the Creator who has made all things good. To accept man's sinfulness is to recognize the limitation of human goals and the uncertainty of human achievement. To accept God as Saviour is to work out our own salvation in union with him, and so to do our part in restoring and recreating what by our folly and frailty we have defaced or destroyed, and in helping to come to birth those good possibilities of the creation that have not yet been realized. To 'renounce the world, the flesh and the devil' is to turn from grasping and greed and to enjoy people and things for their own sake and not because we possess them. To accept the Christian doctrine of the Resurrection is to persevere in spite of setback and disaster, to resist the temptation to slip into a mood of fatalistic resignation, to believe that success can be attained through failures and so to live in hope. To accept God as the Sanctifier of all things implies a respect for all existence, which is upheld by his Spirit and instinct with his energy. To accept our nature as created in God's image and likeness and as destined to grow toward him involves responsible use of those godlike powers over the natural environment which God has put into our hands. To hold that God has created the world for a purpose gives man a worthy goal in life, and a hope to lift up his heart and to strengthen his efforts. To believe that man's true citizenship is in heaven and that his true destiny lies beyond space and time enables him both to be involved in this world and yet to have a measure of detachment from it that permits radical changes such as would scarcely be possible if all his hopes were centred on this world. To believe that all things will be restored and nothing wasted gives added meaning to all man's efforts and strivings. Only by the inspiration of such a vision is society likely to be able to re-order this world and to find the symbols to interpret man's place within it.[100]

So it is we come to the end of this, quite sufficiently long, trail that began by recalling the not infrequent *naïvetés* of the exchanges between science and religion. No doctrine of creation can for long stand alone in isolation from other central themes in the Christian faith, if only because, at the end of the day, the whole loving activity of God in creation—redemption—sanctification has to be conceived of as one continuous action in which he implements his one purpose. No act of creation, of redemption, or of sanctification is 'once for all' in the sense that it does not have to be perpetually operative. Points in time may be 'once for all' in the sense that they clarify and bring to the surface what is going on all the time, but God as Creator, Redeemer, and Sanctifier is a living energy who never ceases to create, redeem, and sanctify us and none of these activities can, for long, be considered in isolation from the others.

I hope the exercise that we have been undertaking illustrates how beginning with one activity, natural science, through which man's mind has expanded into new areas of awareness and apprehension of his world, questions may be raised and trails started that at least point to the central concerns of the theological enterprise. There is, indeed, a case for regarding theology as the intellectual formulation of non-reducible concepts (certainly with respect to creation) for articulating the unique triangular relation of nature, man, and God.[101] For making the world as described by the natural sciences our starting-point for raising questions which turn out to be theological ones does not, of itself, preclude the possibility that those questions so raised may refer to a distinctive level of discourse. But if that is so, the way such questions are answered could possibly involve resources and experiences quite other than those used and undergone in intellectual and scientific activities, as such. In other words, nothing in the position developed here, and the way in which problems have been raised and their

---

[100] *Man and Nature*, ed. H. W. Montefiore (Collins, London, 1975), pp. 77–8.
[101] See Appendix C.

resolution explored, precludes the possibility that God himself may be a resource of knowledge and illumination. That is, we have left open the possibility of specific revelatory acts of God towards man both in nature and history. Our aim has not been directed to examining *that* possibility but rather (with the possible exception of Lecture VI on incarnation, where we examined historical evidence about Jesus which pointed to a uniqueness that was irreducible) seeing how far we can get without resorting to it. But to pursue that would be quite another exercise.

CODA

I would not like to leave the impression that the doctrine of creation is merely an arid formulation of the abstracting intellect for making coherent a number of otherwise unintelligible features of the world and of our lives in it. It is, or rather should be, I believe, one of the throbbing arteries of the Christian life. For to believe in God as Creator, is simply to acknowledge that we live and move and have our being in One who is not far from any of us. Furthermore, this belief entails that in our being and acting creatively and responsively to other people and our environment, both man-made and natural, we *are* manifesting *ipso facto* the very creativity of God himself—for God as Creator is operating in and through us to be and do those very things. And God could not be closer than *that*—and therein lies our hope. We start from where we are in our created lives in the world and we find that

> We shall not cease from exploration
> And the end of all our exploring
> Will be to arrive where we started
> And know the place for the first time[102]

In that end, which is also the beginning here-and-now, the apprehension of God as Creator is not a cold, intellectual 'doctrine' suitable only for the study, or the lecture room (even when it is a church!)—the affirmation of creation is about the very presence of God in *his* world that is also *our* world. We

---

[102] T. S. Eliot, *Little Gidding*.

have been much concerned in this last lecture, with the mystery of God's relation to time, our time, our future. For he has made us in time and has given us time enough in which to be made as he proposes. Indeed 'all times are his seasons' and I know of no passage in which the immediacy of the presence of the eternal God the Creator to us creatures of time, on the way to being fully created, is more amply expressed than the 'Sermon preached at Paul's upon Christmas Day in the Evening, 1624' by John Donne:

GOD made Sun and Moon to distinguish seasons, and day, and night, and we cannot have the fruits of the earth but in their seasons: But God hath made no decree to distinguish the seasons of his mercies; In paradise, the fruits were ripe, the first minute, and in heaven it is alwaies Autumne, his mercies are ever in their maturity. We ask *panem quotidianum*, our daily bread, and God never sayes you should have come yesterday, he never sayes you must againe to morrow, but *today if you will heare his voice*, today he will heare you. If some King of the earth have so large an extent of Dominion, in North, and South, as that he hath Winter and Summer together in his Dominions, so large an extent East and West, as that he hath day and night together in his Dominions, much more hath God mercy and judgement together: He brought light out of darknesse, not out of a lesser light; he can bring thy Summer out of Winter, though thou have no Spring; though in the wayes of fortune, or understanding, or conscience, thou have been benighted till now, wintred and frozen, clouded and eclypsed, damped and benummed, smothered and stupified till now, and God comes to thee, not as in the dawning of the day, not as in the bud of the spring, but as the Sun at noon to illustrate all shadowes, as the sheaves in harvest, to fill all penuries, all occasions invite his mercies, and all times are his seasons.[103]

---

[103] John Donne, in *LXXX Sermons*, 1640.

Modern Atomic Physics and Eastern Mystical Thought

SINCE Lecture III was delivered and its last two sections (III C and III D) written, F. Capra's *The Tao of Physics*[1] has come into my hands and has made me aware of many other parallels between Eastern mystical thought and some of the radically new concepts that prevail in modern physics, especially in its application of quantum and relativity theory to the sub-atomic domain. Capra points out many fascinating correspondences between the new concepts the physicists have had to adopt under pressure of observation of sub-atomic phenomena and certain general features of ancient Hindu, Buddhist, and Taoist mysticism. These correspondences between modern physics and Eastern mysticism consist in:

(i) the awareness in both of the unity and mutual interconnectedness and interdependence of all things and events, that is the experience of all phenomena in the world as different manifestations of the one ultimate reality, so that the universe is a complicated web of relations between the parts of a unified whole;

(ii) the acceptance in both of opposites as polarities within a unity;

(iii) the recognition in both of the limitations of all creations of the human mind, such as space and time, and so the need to transcend them in other dimensions;

(iv) the stressing in both of the dynamic character of the universe, that it consists of myriad forms which come into being and disintegrate, transforming themselves into one another without end;

(v) the rejection by both of the picture of nature as consisting of solid indestructible objects moving in a void that is strictly 'nothing' and its replacement, in physics (in quantum field theory), by a 'field' which is present everywhere in space yet, in its particle aspect, capable of a discontinuous 'granular structure', and, in Eastern thought, by the 'Void' with an infinite creative potentiality;

(vi) the stress on the dynamic and rhythmic character of the interplay and transformations which occur in the universe, in the physical

[1] F. Capra, *The Tao of Physics* (Collins, Fontana, London, 1976).

picture of sub-atomic particles as engaged in a ceaseless flow of energy and matter, in which particles are created and destroyed without end, and (as in my treatment in III C of Lecture III) the cosmic dance of Eastern thought;

(vii) the occurrence in both sub-atomic physics (*w.r.t.* particle groups and the concept of 'quarks') and in Eastern thought (e.g. the 'koans' of the Zen masters) of paradoxes which nevertheless serve to draw attention to an otherwise inexpressible feature of reality;

(viii) the realization in both that patterns of change that are discernible within the dynamic flux of the universe ((iv) above) may themselves well be critically dependent on the character of the human consciousness that perceives—and may even be regarded [though this is highly disputable] as 'nothing but creations of our measuring and categorizing mind' (Capra, op. cit., p. 292);

(ix) the parallel between, on the one hand, the putative [and still disputed] 'bootstrap hypothesis'[2] of sub-atomic physics which, rejecting the older methodology of attempting to analyse complex structures of the world into 'fundamental' components, sees the structure of the dynamic web of interrelated events that constitutes the sub-atomic world as determined by the very self-consistency of these mutual inter-relations that the inquiring consciousness itself requires—and, on the other hand, the stress in Eastern thought (especially Taoism) that in the universe everything is connected to everything else and no part of it is fundamental ('Carried to its logical extreme, the bootstrap conjecture implies that the existence of consciousness, along with all other aspects of nature, is necessary for self consistency of the whole'.)[3]

Capra concludes that modern sub-atomic physics and Eastern mysticism converge because: 'Both emerge when man enquires into the essential nature of things—into the deeper realms of matter in physics; into the deeper realms of consciousness in mysticism—when he discovers a different reality behind the superficial mechanistic appearance of everyday life.'[4]

Although this conclusion does not face up squarely to the philo-

---

[2] G. Chew, '"Bootstrap": A Scientific Idea?', *Science*, 161 (1968), 762–5; 'Hadron Bootstrap: Triumph or Frustration?', *Physics Today*, 23 (1970), 23–8. Each hadron (the sub-particular 'family' of baryons and mesons, both particles and anti-particles: it includes protons, neutrons and π-mesons) is held together by forces associated with the exchange of other hadrons in the 'cross-channel' (see Capra, pp. 285 ff.), each of which is, in turn, held together by forces to which the first hadrons makes its contribution. Each particle helps to generate other particles which in turn generate it. The whole set of hadrons generates itself in this way and thus pulls itself up, as it were, 'by its own bootstraps'.

[3] G. Chew, op. cit. (1968), p. 763.

[4] Capra, op. cit., p. 322.

sophical (specifically, the epistemological) problems posed by postulating that physics and mysticism discover 'a different reality' than
that given by appearances, we are nevertheless greatly indebted to
Dr Capra for pointing out these extensive correspondences, and so
complementarity, between modern physics and Eastern mysticism.
However this account is deficient in so far as it ignores certain
characteristics of the Judeo-Christian tradition that are equally
germane to the new concepts of modern physics he expounds so
skilfully.

Thus he accords no overt recognition that there has been a
genuinely Christian mystical tradition which in many of its broad
characteristics (and it is only at such a broad level of generalization
that Capra, in fact, is able to unify such diverse and multiparous
traditions as the Hindu, Buddhist, and Taoist) exhibits many of those
features he attributes only to the East.[5]

Secondly, he speaks in only one passage[6] of the Judeo-Christian
concept of God but confines himself entirely to its 'monarchical
model' of God[7]—and then only to God as divine lawgiver—and he
entirely ignores the parallel emphasis in the Judeo-Christian tradition
on the immanence of God in all that is, especially as represented by
the Christian use of the concepts of 'Logos' and of 'Spirit'.[8]

Thirdly, partly no doubt because he does not take biology into
account, he fails to recognize the growth of organic concepts of nature,
as an alternative to mechanistic ones, long before the twentieth-
century developments that he describes.[9]

These omissions need to be rectified in making any judicious assessment of the significance of the parallels he demonstrates between
modern physics and Eastern mysticism, in the context of any consideration of the relevance of the scientific world-view to models of
God as Creator. If Capra's parallels were to be so supplemented,
both modern sub-atomic physics and Eastern mysticism (as well as
its more Western counterparts) might then be seen as enlarging our
apprehension of the unity of the cosmos and of its dynamically

[5] See, as two examples of an extensive literature: *The Perennial Philosophy* by Aldous
Huxley (Collins, Fontana, London, 1958) and *Mysticism* by F. C. Happold (Penguin
Books, Harmondsworth, 1963).

[6] Capra, op. cit., p. 303.

[7] Cf. Lecture I, p. 45.

[8] See pp. 205, 206.

[9] In fact, they go back to the seventeenth-century biologists, such as John Ray,
see C. E. Raven, *Natural Religion and Christian Theology*, Gifford Lectures, 1951, First
Series, *Science and Religion*, especially Chs. VI and X (Cambridge University Press,
Cambridge, 1953).

interrelated unity—and thereby enriching our intellectual comprehension and personal awareness of the way the transcendent Creator is immanent in his creation, of the manner in which the creation manifests the agency of its immanent Creator.

APPENDIX B
(to Lecture VII)

'Nature'

So far, the term 'nature' has been used without any attempt to define it: the reluctance to do so is not without some justification for it is notorious for the ambiguity of its referent(s) and extension. So much so that R. W. Hepburn,[1] advises writers who are aware of the web of ambiguities in which 'nature' and 'natural' are involved to choose words of greater precision and stability of meaning. We shall not, here, have much cause to use the adjective 'natural', with its frequent ethical overtones and presumption of nature as a norm. But, even if we avoid the adjective, with this associated further dimension of meaning, and confine our use to the noun 'nature', we find it to be functionally diffuse in contemporary usage. For it points to a funda-mental human experience and awareness, which is, indeed, the cause of its in-built ambiguity, since its range is as wide as the cultural and linguistic horizon of its users.[2] A. O. Lovejoy and G. Boas[3] have listed at least 66 distinct meanings of the term and even the *Shorter Oxford English Dictionary*[4] devotes a whole column to the noun alone. Its range is well illustrated by noting that with which it is contrasted in various contexts, e.g., variously: 'Art', culture, human civilization; man, personal existence, 'spirit'; God, supernature, grace, Spirit; the 'un-natural', abnormal, improper; mind; and appearance.

In this present lecture, 'nature' is being used in the sense of 'the natural world', or, just 'the world' meaning 'the more or less ordered

---

[1] R. W. Hepburn, 'Nature, Philosophical Ideas of', *The Encyclopaedia of Philosophy*, ed. P. Edwards (Collier-Macmillan, London, 1972 repr.), Vol. 5, pp. 454–7.

[2] I am much indebted, in writing this Appendix, to an article entitled 'The Problem with Nature' which Mr G. P. Alcser, then of Linacre College, Oxford, made available to me in draft form in 1973.

[3] A. O. Lovejoy and G. Boas, *Primitivism and Related Ideas in Antiquity* (Johns Hopkins Press, Baltimore, 1935), pp. 447–56, who cite thirty-nine senses of *phusis* and 'nature' in literary and philosophical usage from which ethical and other normative uses are derived and twenty-seven normative uses of these terms in ethics, politics, and religion.

[4] *Shorter Oxford English Dictionary*, 1973 edn.

universe and its processes, taken as inclusive of all instances of it'[5] or 'the material world ... its collective objects and phenomena, the features and products of the earth itself *as contrasted with those of human civilization*'.[6] We shall not be using Nature (with a capital N) to denote a 'creative and regulative physical power operating in the physical world'[7] as the cause of its phenomena.

With the rise of natural science, as we now know it, 'nature' came to be identified with the realm of things which is subject to empirical inquiry[8] and for more than two centuries, after Newton, *that* meant a mechanistic, law-governed, static entity which stood over against man for his objective investigation and, eventually, exploitation. We have already seen, in Lecture II, how that scientific perspective on 'nature' ('the natural world', or just 'the world'—I have used the three almost interchangeably) has been profoundly transformed in the twentieth century into a more organismic, relational, and dynamic account which incorporates the epistemological humility generated by quantum theory and relativity. Even as we speak of 'nature' ('the natural world', or 'the world') as an entity on which man may have a perspective, we have found that man is historically, through evolution, and actually, in the world ecosystems, a part of the very entity he is in the course of describing. Thus the strict distinction between man and nature is continually breaking down. But, in so far as these terms ('nature', 'the natural world', 'the world') involve a reference to that which is viewed and described by man by means of his 'natural' science and to the sphere of man's action on non-human entities (both inorganic and living), their use seems to me to be unobjectionable, providing their limitations are borne in mind (in particular the oversharp distinction they imply between man and 'nature').

This semantic context must be appreciated in any account of the Judeo-Christian theology of nature and its doctrine of creation, for 'nature' has no equivalent in the biblical literature, primarily because this word 'in its Latin and also in its Greek meanings (*natura, phusis*)

[5] Alcser, op. cit., referring to J. Macquarrie, *The Scope of Demythologising* (SCM Press, London, 1960), pp. 143, 144, who refers to one meaning of 'nature' as 'the ordered universe and its processes'.

[6] *Shorter O.E.D.*, 1973 edn., meaning IV. 2. The italicized restriction is qualified by the discussion of man as co-creator in Lecture VII: § V E, pp. 203 ff. (N.B. the quotation from J. Sittler, p. 264.)

[7] *Shorter O.E.D.*, 1973 edn. We shall not normally be using 'nature' to refer to a very different cluster of meanings, viz. as 'the essential qualities of a thing ... the inherent and innate disposition or character of a person (or animal)' except when the context makes it clear that this is the meaning intended.

[8] Alcser, op. cit.

suggests something centred in itself, with an immanent origin and growth; dependence on the Creator God cannot be expressed by it'.[9] Instead of 'nature', the New Testament uses the word 'creation' (*ktisis*), and the verb 'create'.[10] This is a vital distinction for 'nature' connotes subsistence and autonomy whereas 'creation' connotes sourcehood and dependence[11] and, moreover, includes both man and all that is non-human within the category of the *created*. Although man may have a special role *within* creation, their relation is that of one created entity to another, for both man and non-human nature are dependent for their being on God the Creator. This is the presupposition which pervades the Old Testament, even though the word 'creation' is absent—it uses other expressions such as 'heaven and earth', 'all that lives', 'all things' (cf. *ta panta* in the Epistle to the Ephesians), and 'the earth' (which often, in the Old Testament, means 'the nations' other than Israel—and so very much the *human* world, which is usually the meaning of 'the world' (*kosmos*) in Paul and John).

So the use of the term 'creation' instead of 'nature' has theological presuppositions already built in, it is a way of 'seeing *as*' and it is these presuppositions, and their implications for ecological values, which we are concerned to bring to light in Lecture VII.

[9] H. Berkhof, 'God in Nature and History', *Faith and Order Studies* 1964–7, Paper No. 50 (World Council of Churches, Geneva, 1968), p. 14.

[10] See G. W. H. Lampe, 'The New Testament Doctrine of *KTISIS*', *Scottish J. Theol.*, 17 (1964) 449–462.

[11] Alcser, op. cit.

Reductionism and religion-and-science: 'the Queen of the sciences'?

IN Lecture IV we expanded our original discussion of interfaces between the sciences beyond the confines of the natural sciences in general, and of the biology/physics-and-chemistry interface in particular, into the sciences of the human individual and of human society. We noted the relation between a science whose focus of study is a higher level in the complex hierarchy of natural systems and one whose focus is a lower level. We noted also that there is no automatic and inevitable possibility of reducing the theories and concepts of the science of the higher level to theories and concepts of the science of the lower level. We had to make a distinction between reduction of theories, which is about the deduction of one set of empirically confirmable statements from another such set, and the reduction of processes. We found that we should not expect to derive one set of properties, or a phenomenon at a higher level, from another set of properties at a lower level. As Nagel puts it:

The conception [that reduction is a process of deriving one set of properties of one subject matter from the properties of another] is misleading because it suggests that the question of whether one science is reducible to another is to be settled by inspecting the 'properties' or alleged 'natures' of things rather than by investigating the logical consequences of certain explicitly formulated theories (that is, systems of statements). For the conception ignores the crucial point that the 'natures' of things and in particular of the 'elementary constituents' of things, are not accessible to direct inspection and that we cannot read off by simple inspection what it is they do or do not imply. Such 'natures' must be stated as a theory and not the object of observation.[1]

We have also seen that although a theory applicable to a higher

[1] E. Nagel, *The Structure of Science* (Harcourt Bruce, New York, 1961), p. 364.

level of complexity in the hierarchy of natural systems may not be reducible to a theory derived for a lower level, yet, nevertheless, there is a real justification for a methodological reductionism, in so far as the decomposing of the higher-level system into simpler sub-systems, or component units, can simplify and enhance one's understanding of the higher-level system. Indeed, it is essential for this understanding but, at the same time, does not evacuate the higher-level study (that is the study of the higher-level system in its totality with the appropriate language and methods relevant to it at that level) of any meaning or validity. I hope that this was adequately illustrated in Lecture IV by the relation of biology to physics-and-chemistry so that we can now with some confidence look at the 'science' of an even more complex and all-embracing level.

I refer to the intellectual analysis, usually called theology, of the activity of *homo religiosus*. It is certainly no longer true that Christian theology is generally regarded as 'the Queen of the sciences', as the medieval university assumed. Nevertheless it is the case that when man is exercising himself in his religious and worshipping activities he is in fact operating at a level in the hierarchy of complexity which is more intricate and cross-related than any of those we have considered when discussing the natural and social sciences. For in his religious activities man utilizes every facet of his total being: his solitariness, his interaction with other people, his interaction with nature and the universe. Man's religious activities include 'the flight of the alone to the Alone' for it is at least true in part that religion is what 'man does with his solitariness'; and yet it is equally true that there is no genuinely religious life and activity unless it is an activity in community, and for the Christian it is participation in a community which extends across both space and time. Equally religion is about the ultimate meaning that a person finds in his or her relationship to the whole of the universe, and 'Religion is a relation to the ultimate' has been proposed by Penner and Yonan as a suitable compression of some seven widely accepted definitions of religion.[2] We will not enter here the game of defining religion,[3] which the two last-mentioned authors advise us to avoid as a result of their analyses of this and other definitions, but it is at least clear that religion is

---

[2] H. H. Penner and E. A. Yonan, *J. Religion*, 52 (1972), 128.

[3] Other more defensible definitions (Penner and Yonan suggest) of religion are: 'one's way of valuing most intensively and comprehensively' (F. Ferré, *J. Amer. Acad. Rel.* 38 (1970), 11); 'a cultural system consisting of culturally patterned interaction with culturally postulated super-human beings' (M. E. Spiro, 'Religion and the Irrational', in *Symposium on New Approaches to the Study of Religion*, (ed.) June Helin (University of Washington Press, Seattle, 1964), p. 103).

deeply involved with the ultimate meanings that man finds in his relationships to the natural world, with his origins and his destiny in that natural world—and of course there are those who stress, sometimes exclusively, that the Judeo-Christian doctrines of Creation and of the End are specifically about meanings, rather than about explanations, as such. All that needs to be emphasized for the purpose of the present argument is that man in his religious activity is the whole man interacting fully as a person ('body, mind, and soul') with other people, who are equally totally interacting with him. Together they interact with the natural world and discover its meaning for them—and express the ultimacy of the significance of this complex integrated activity in their worshipful recognition of a transcendent, yet immanent, Creator as the source of all that is. It seems to me that no higher level of integration in the hierarchy of natural systems could be envisaged than this and theology is about the conceptual schemes and theories that articulate the content of this activity. Theology therefore refers to the most integrating level we know in the hierarchy of natural relationships of systems and so it should not be surprising if the theories and concepts which are developed to explicate the nature of this activity, both the felt nature and the intellectually articulated nature, are uniquely specific to and characteristic of this level. It should not be surprising, too, if special methods, techniques, and languages had to be developed to describe this supremely integrating and highly complex activity. For this reason theories and concepts which the theologian may apply objectively to religion, and its own formulations of its own self-awareness, have the right not to be prematurely reduced, without very careful proof, to the theories and concepts of other disciplines appropriate to the component units (society, man, nature, etc.), the unique integration of which in a total whole comprise the religious activity *par excellence*. It may, in fact, be proved that some of these concepts can be so reduced, but meanwhile there is a prima-facie case (as there is for biological concepts in relation to physics–chemistry) for continuing to pursue both the study and the exercise of religion. Only detailed inquiry and cross-comparison of theological concepts and theories with those of (say) sociology and psychology can establish which are irreducible. Experience of other interfaces suggests that many will be such.[4]

[4] It should be noted that the view I express here is somewhat different from that of Penner and Yonan (op. cit.). In parallel with what happens at the interfaces between the natural sciences, I would not be surprised if the processes and events which constitute the raw data of the study of religion proved not to be autonomous: but, by the same token, many of the theories and concepts, the symbolic and metaphorical

Nevertheless, one must stress that this putative autonomy which we assign to theology, which is the intellectual articulation of the life of religion, does not preclude, and indeed *should* not preclude, the careful study of the component, contributory 'sub-systems' in religious activity—just as the study of the 'sub-systems' of atoms and molecules and macromolecules can contribute to an understanding of their integration in the living organism. Studies of the 'sub-systems' of society, man, and nature are what we call 'science'—the individual sciences of sociology, psychology, biology, and all the way down the scale. The theories, concepts, laws, and experimental discoveries, which constitute these respective sciences, provide a developing and changing context within which reflection on religion has to be set. These theological reflections may well prove to have their own conceptual autonomy and appropriate language, but they cannot be studied in isolation from the developing knowledge of the 'sub-systems', that is of the knowledge of nature, man, and society which the sciences are all the time elaborating. Knowledge and understanding of the lower levels feeds upwards and alters the context in which our understanding of the higher levels is placed. This is as true of religion in relation to our knowledge of the natural world and of man's world as it is of biology in relation to physics and chemistry and of sociology in relation to psychology and indeed at all the other interfaces.

Thus I conceive the relation of religion and science to be on the following lines. There are in religious experience, and in the experience of the Christian community with which I am most concerned, concepts, ideas, affirmations, beliefs, metaphors, images which have a life of their own, a history of their own, and an impact of their own within their own thought world. The terms of religious discourse, and of Christian theological discourse in particular, are often very subtle in the intricacy of their relations with many levels in the life of mankind, intellectual, aesthetic, social, professional, sexual, historical, and so on, but because they refer to a total activity of man in community in his total relationship with the natural world they must not be prematurely reduced away to some lower-level scientific description. What we must do is set these 'religious' affirmations, their ways of depicting the world, their understandings of the world and

---

language which theology employs in articulating and explicating the life of religion are likely to prove not to be reducible (i.e. to be autonomous). Penner and Yonan (op. cit., pp. 130–1) seem to anticipate that theory-reduction is what goes on in the sciences and what should go on in the study of religion. My argument here is that theory-reduction, in fact, is much less frequent at the interface between the natural sciences than they assume.

of man in the world *alongside* the changing perspective of man in the world which the sciences engender through studying the various levels which the natural hierarchy of systems displays. Theology should be neither immune from the changing outlook of the sciences of man and nature nor should it be captive to them.[5]

[5] A similar understanding of the relation of the scientific to the theological enterprises seems to be being developed by Professor T. F. Torrance in his address given on 21 Mar. 1978, on the occasion of his receipt of the 6th Templeton Foundation Prize (published by Lismore Press, 4 Meadow Vale, Deans Grange, Co. Dublin, Ireland, and only to hand since these Lectures and this appendix were written). In that lecture he refers to there being 'different modes of rationality' developed in natural science and what he prefers to call 'theological science', because 'the nature of what we seek to know in each is different', yet these two modes of rationality represent 'one basic way of knowing'. Professor Torrance places a strong emphasis on 'knowing things in accordance with their natures, or what they are in themselves'—terminology from which these lectures have shied away (cf. Appendix B); but he is also strongly indebted to Michael Polanyi's analyses of the hierarchical character of natural systems, which is the basis of the argument of this appendix and of much else in the rest of this volume.

Supplementary Notes for the
Paperback Edition

It is impossible to do justice to the immense literature on the relation of science and religion, in general, and to Christian theology, in particular, that has burgeoned over the last few decades—especially in comparison with the 1970s in which this volume was prepared and first delivered as lectures. Hence these supplementary notes, making no pretensions to completeness, can refer to only a few publications which appear to me to be particularly useful resources. Noteworthy in this latter regard is the most recent major work of Ian Barbour, namely, *Religion and Science: Historical and Contemporary Issues* (SCM Press, London, and Harper, San Francisco, Harper Collins, New York, 1998); a widely-used textbook, with critical analyses and extensive references, is *God, Humanity and the Cosmos: A Textbook in Science and Religion*, by C. Southgate *et al.* (T. & T. Clark, Edinburgh, 1999); and, from a specifically Christian perspective, *Science and Christian Belief* by John Polkinghorne (SPCK, London, 1994). A useful resource is the website *www.scienceandreligionbooks.org.*

Since my first publishing of these Bampton Lectures in 1979 my widest-ranging book on these themes, including a more direct consideration of aspects of Christian theology as such, has been my *Theology for a Scientific Age: Being and Becoming—Natural, Divine and Human* (2nd enlarged edition: SCM Press, London, and Fortress Press, Minneapolis, 1993) [henceforth TSA]. My own most recent survey of many of the issues, for the general reader, is to be found in *Paths from Science towards God: The End of All Our Exploring* (Oneworld, Oxford, 2001) [henceforth PSG].

By far the most extensive and thorough investigation of the interaction between the sciences and a wide range of, at least, Christian theology is that represented by the research consultations organized roughly biennially since 1987 by the Vatican Observatory and the Center for Theology and the Natural

Sciences, Berkeley, California. The volumes, with the subtitle (for all except the first) 'Scientific Perspectives on Divine Action', which resulted from those conferences were: *Physics, Philosophy and Theology* (1988); *Quantum Cosmology and the Laws of Nature* (1993); *Chaos and Complexity* (1995); *Evolutionary and Molecular Biology* (1998); *Neuroscience and the Person* (1999); *Quantum Mechanics* (2001).[1]

These supplementary notes are subdivided according to the Roman numbers of the principal sections (lectures/chapters) of the original printing and their subsections also follow its notations, with page numbers given where reference is made to particular issues.

I   THE TWO BOOKS

I, IIA. For magisterial and insightful accounts of the historical relations between 'religion' and 'science' (the inverted commas indicating the fluid boundaries between these two enterprises) see: J. H. Brooke, *Science and Religion: Some Historical Perspectives* (Cambridge University Press, Cambridge, 1991) and J. Brooke and G. Cantor, *Reconstructing Nature: The Engagement of Science and Religion* (T. & T. Clark, Edinburgh, 1998). The nineteenth-century Oxford debate involving T. H. Huxley and Bishop Samuel Wilberforce has been the object of renewed intensive historical research which has been disentangling the myth from the history: q.v. J. H. Brooke, 'The Wilberforce–Huxley Debate: Why Did It Happen?', *Science and Christian Belief*, 13 (2001), 127–41 for references.

VB. For scholarly accounts of the context and content of the understanding of divine creation in the Judeo-Christian tradition and its relation to wider, and often more ancient traditions,

---

[1] They are, respectively, denoted here as: PPT; QCLN; CC; EMB; NP; and QM. All were published jointly by the two institutions mentioned and are distributed through the University of Notre Dame Press. The editors of these volumes were: for PPP, R. J. Russell, W. R. Stoeger, and G. Coyne; for QCLN, R. J. Russell, N. Murphy, and C. J. Isham; for CC, R. J. Russell, N. Murphy, and A. R. Peacocke; for EMB, R. J. Russell, W. R. Stoeger, and F. J. Ayala; for NP, R. J. Russell, N. Murphy, T. C. Meyering, and M. A. Arbib; for QM, R. J. Russell, P. Clayton, K. Wegter-McNelly, and J. Polkinghorne.

For a penetrating survey see also: N. Saunders, *Divine Action and Modern Science* (Cambridge University Press, Cambridge, 2002).

see: H. G. Reventlow and Y. Hoffman (eds.), *Creation in the Jewish and Christian Traditions* (Sheffield Academic Press, Sheffield, 2002); and the article on 'Cosmogony, Cosmology' by R. A. Oden in *The Anchor Bible Dictionary*, vol. 1, ed. D. N. Freedman (Doubleday, New York, 1992), pp. 1162–71.

II   COSMOS, MAN, AND CREATION

IIA, B(i), (ii). The indicative remarks in the text have been extensively amplified in intensive studies of the implications for theology of relativity and quantum theory, well represented in the volumes PPT, QCLN, and QM. New issues that have arisen include: the debate over the 'block universe' model of relativity theory and God's relation to the time of the world (q.v. QCLN, especially pp. 135–44); and, in quantum theory, quantum entanglement, decoherence, nonlocality, and the measurement problem (q.v. QCLN, QM *passim*). These issues involve philosophically profound problems whose theological import continues to be far from clear.

IIIC, IV. On the anthropic principle, *The Anthropic Cosmological Principle* by John Barrow and Frank Tipler (Clarendon Press, Oxford, 1986) has become a major source, as has *Universes* (Routledge, London and New York, 1989, rev. 1996) by John Leslie, who discusses thoroughly the philosophical issues.

The possibility of the existence of other universes (a 'multiverse') has been widely discussed. It has been raised *inter alia* by the astrophysicist Martin Rees in his *Before the Beginning: Our Universe and Others* (Simon and Schuster, New York, 1997; Free Press, 2002) and by the physicist Freeman Dyson in *Imagined Worlds* (Harvard University Press, Cambridge, Mass., 1997). Its theological implications have been the subject of interdisciplinary study in *Many Worlds: The New Universe, Extraterrestrial Life and the Theological Implications*, ed. Stephen Dick (Templeton Foundation Press, Philadelphia and London, 2000). Many (e.g. Leslie, op. cit.) have regarded the postulate of a multiverse as undermining the inference of the existence of a Creator God from the anthropic principle. In the original text (pp. 69–72), I argued that the existence of other universes would still be *consonant with, though not a proof of,* the existence of a Creator God who intends to bring a form of sentient, self-conscious life into existence through the, apparently random, exploration of all possibilities in a framework of God-given (meta-) laws controlling the sequence/existence of the various permutations of universes (rather similarly to the postulate concerning chance and law made with respect to biological evolution in Chapter III). I continue to hold this position, as expounded in PSG, pp. 70–2.

III CHANCE AND THE LIFE-GAME

II B, C. *An Introduction to the Physical Chemistry of Biological Organization* by A. R. Peacocke (Clarendon Press, Oxford, 1983, repr. 1989, with supplementary references), chapters 2, 4, and 5 give an account, with full bibliography, of the thermodynamics of living organisms and of the stochastic kinetics proposed as underlying the origin of self-replicating living molecular systems. The role of chance in divine creation was later more fully expounded by D. Bartholomew in his *God of Chance* (SCM Press, London, 1984).

IV NATURE'S HIERACHIES—'THINGS VISIBLE AND INVISIBLE'

1A. The 'hierarchy' of natural systems and of the sciences pertaining to them was later expressed by the author in a diagram in TSA, Fig. 3, p. 217, and Fig. 19 in 'Relating Genetics to Theology on the Map of Scientific Knowledge' in *Controlling Our Destinies*, ed. P. R. Sloan (University of Notre Dame Press, Notre Dame, Ind., 2000), p. 349. This diagram extended from the physics of elementary particles at the base 'up' (in the sense of increase in complexity) to the sciences of behaviour of living organisms, in general, and human beings, in particular, and, at the 'top', to aspects of human culture, including religion with its corresponding 'science', theology. This elaboration is also relevant to Appendix C ('Reductionism and religion-and-science: "the Queen of the sciences"?').

The diagram was later revised and modified by N. M. Murphy and G. F. R. Ellis in *On the Moral Nature of the Universe* (Fortress Press, Minneapolis, 1996), Fig. 4.10, p. 86, to include two branching lines from biology towards, on the one hand, ecology, geology, astrophysics, and cosmology and, on the other, psychology, social and applied sciences, motivational studies, and ethics.

11B, C, D, E. That human beings are psychosomatic unities (p. 125) was urged by me as both biblical and in accord with scientific studies in my earlier *Science and the Christian Experiment* (Oxford University Press, London, 1971), pp. 141–4, 148–54; and later both in a paper provocatively entitled 'A Christian Materialism?' (given at the XXth Nobel Conference, 1985), in *How We Know*, ed. Michael Shafto (Harper & Row, San Francisco, 1985), pp. 146–68, and in TSA, pp. 218–48. It has been a dominant theme in the science and Christian theology dialogue at the turn of the millennium in, for example, *Human Nature at the Millenium: Reflections on the Integration of Psychology and Christianity* (Apollos, Baker Books, Grand Rapids, Michigan, 1997) by M. A. Jeeves; in *Whatever Happened to the Soul?*, ed. W. S. Brown, N. Murphy, and H. Newton Malony (Fortress Press, Minneapolis, 1998); and in NP (1999).

11C. The 'pan-psychism' of process philosophers has come to be re-designated by them as 'pan-experientialism' according to which 'all individuals [that is, all entities, including the material units of the universe] have at least some slight degree of experience and spontaneity [or "feeling"]', D. R. Griffin, in a paper on 'Panentheism: A Postmodern Revelation' in *In Whom We Live and Have Our Being: Panentheistic Reflections on God's Presence in a Scientific World*, ed. Philip Clayton and Arthur Peacocke (Eerdmans, Grand Rapids, Michigan, 2004). A useful exposition of process philosophy and theology is his *Reenchantment with Supernaturalism: A Process Philosophy of Religion* (Cornell University Press, Ithaca, 2001).

p. 129. The term 'supervenience' has continued to be much employed, since D. Davidson's espousal of it, as a designation of the relation between mental and brain properties. It has been formally distinguished as having weak, strong, and global forms by J. Kim in 'Concepts of Supervenience' (*Philosophy and Phenomenological Research*, XIV, no. 2 (Dec. 1984), 153–76) and has been re-defined by Nancey Murphy in the usual terms of property covariance but with an added proviso of the need to specify the, expectedly variable, circumstances under which the covariance of mental and brain properties occurs (see her 'Supervenience and the Downward Efficacy of the Mental: A Nonreductive-Physicalist Account of Human Action' in NP, pp. 147–64; her position has been criticized by L. Cullen in 'Nancey Murphy, Supervenience and Causality', *Science and Christian Belief*, 13 (2001), 39–50—her response is on pp. 161–3).

IVC(iii). For diverse, and on the whole sympathetic, assessments of 'panentheism', see *In Whom We Live and Move and Have Our Being: Panentheistic Reflections on God's Presence in a Scientific World*, ed. Philip Clayton and Arthur Peacocke (Eerdmans, Grand Rapids, Michigan, 2004).

V THE 'SELFISH GENE' AND 'WHAT MEN LIVE BY'

pp. 158 ff. The content and philosophical and theological implications of the 'science of complexity' are made accessible to the general reader in *From Complexity to Life: On the Emergence of Life and Meaning*, ed. Niels Henrik Gregersen (Oxford University Press, Oxford, 2003), which has extensive bibliographies. Expositions of the science of complexity in living organisms are to be found in: A. R. Peacocke, *An Introduction to the Physical Chemistry of Biological Organization* (Clarendon Press, Oxford, 1983, repr. 1989 with supplementary references) and in *The Emergence of Everything* (Oxford University Press, New York, 2003) by Harold Morowitz, who covers a wider range of systems.

pp. 160 ff. Proposed mechanisms and factors considered to be involved in biological evolution, other than natural selection, include:

• the 'evolution of evolvability' (D. C. Dennett, *Darwin's Dangerous Idea* (Allen Lane, Penguin, London and New York, 1995; p. 222 and n. 20, for references), in particular the constraints and selectivity effected by self-organizational principles which shape the possibilities of elaboration of structures and even direct its course (S. A. Kaufman, *The Origins of Order: Self-Organization and Selection in Evolution* (Oxford University Press, New York and London, 1993); id., *At Home in the Universe* (Penguin Books, London, 1995); B. C. Goodwin, *How the Leopard Changed its Spots: The Evolution of Complexity* (Scribner's Sons, New York, 1994));

• the 'genetic assimilation' of C. H. Waddington (*The Strategy of the Genes: A Discussion of Some Aspects of Theoretical Biology* (Allen & Unwin, London, 1957));

• that how an organism might evolve is a consequence of itself, of its state at any given moment, and so on historical accidents, as well as on its genotype and environment (R. C. Lewontin, 'Gene, Organism and Environment', in *Evolution from Molecules to Man*, ed. D. S. Bendall (Cambridge University Press, Cambridge, 1983), pp. 273–85);

• that the innovative behaviour of an individual living creature in a particular environment can be a major factor on its survival and selection and so on evolution (A. Hardy, *The Living Stream* (Collins, London, 1985), pp. 161 ff., 189 ff.);

• that 'top–down causation' operates in evolution (D. T. Campbell, 'Downward Causation in Hierarchically Organised Systems', in *Studies in the Philosophy of Biology: Reduction and Related Problems*, ed. F. J. Ayala and T. Dobzhansky (Macmillan, London, 1974), pp. 179–86) and does so more by a flow of information between organism and environment and between different levels (q.v. TSA, p. 59) than by any obvious material or energetic causality;

• that the 'silent' substitutions in DNA are more frequent than non-silent ones (with an effect on the phenotype); in other words, the majority of molecular evolutionary change is immune to natural selection (M. Kimura, 'The Neutral Theory of Molecular Evolution', *Scientific American*, 241 (1979), 98–126);

• that group (alongside that of individual) selection, in a unified theory of natural selection, operates at different levels in a nested hierarchy of units, groups of organisms being regarded as 'vehicles of selection' (D. S. Wilson and E. Sober,

'Reintroducing Group Selection to the Human Behavioral Sciences', *Behavioral and Brain Sciences*, 17 (1994), 585–654);

• that long-term changes in the genetic composition of a population result from 'molecular drive', the process in which mutations are able to spread through a family and through a population as a consequence of a variety of mechanisms of non-reciprocal DNA transfer, thereby inducing the gain or loss of a variant gene in an individual's lifetime, leading to non-Mendelian segregation ratios (G. A. Dover, 'Molecular Drive in Multigene Families: How Biological Novelties Arise, Spread and are Assimilated', *Trends in Genetics*, 2 (1986), 159–65).

• an emphasis on the context of adaptive change (or, in many cases, non-change, stasis) in species regarded as existing in interlocking hierarchies of discrete biological entities (genes, populations, species, eco-systems, etc.) in a physical environment (N. Eldredge, *Reinventing Darwin: The Great Evolutionary Debate* (Weidenfeld & Nicolson, London, 1996)).

IVB. For a later assessment of the significance of sociobiology for theology see: Arthur Peacocke, 'Sociobiology and its Theological Implications', *Zygon*, 19 (1984), 171–84; and id., *God and the New Biology* (Dent, London, 1986; repr. Peter Smith, Gloucester, Mass., 1994), chapter 8, where there is also discussed the proposal of M. Ruse and E. O. Wilson, that ethics is an evolved illusion fobbed off on us by our genes to get us to co-operate, albeit a useful one for human survival (q.v. M. Ruse and E. O. Wilson, 'The Evolution of Ethics', *New Scientist*, 17 (1985), 50–2; and M. Ruse, 'The Morality of the Gene', *Monist*, 67 (1984), 167–99).

Sociobiology, as the study of the social behaviour and social, interacting cognition of living organisms and the role in establishing these of the evolutionary history of the organisms (and of their ecologically near-neighbours, whether as predators or as symbionts), now also contributes to the enterprise of 'evolutionary psychology'. This latter is the study of nervous systems from an evolutionary perspective and includes aspects of cognition not concerned with sociality as such (memory, vision, navigation, etc.). It often focuses explicitly on the functional organization of the brain and so on psychological adaptations and less on adaptive behaviour. To some extent the new study has absorbed the earlier one and, in spite of the differentiation noted above, 'sociobiology' as a designation has tended to be superseded by the newer term considered as of wider scope, since social cognition and behaviour can become a subfield of evolutionary psychology. Its origins can be traced back to G. C. Williams, *Adaptation and Natural Selection* (Princeton University Press, Princeton, 1966) and its development can be assessed in *The Adapted Mind: Evolutionary Psychology and the Generation of Culture*, ed. J. H. Barkow, L. Cosmides, and J. Tooby (Oxford University Press, Oxford, 1992) and from the reading lists provided by the Center for Evolutionary Psychology, University of California, Santa Barbara, on *www.psych.ucsb.edu/research/cep*.

p. 165, n. 40. See also A. R. Peacocke, *An Introduction to the Physical Chemistry of Biological Organization* (Clarendon Press, Oxford, 1983, repr. 1989 with supplementary references), pp. 1–14, 245–79.

IVC. *Memes*. This concept has been critically analysed by M. Midgley in 'Gene-juggling', *Philosophy*, 54, no. 210 (1979), 108–34; by G. S. Stent in *Morality as a Biological Phenomenon* (University of California Press, Los Angeles, 1980); and by J. Bowker in the Gresham Lectures, 1992–3, *Is God a Virus? Genes, Culture and Religion* (SPCK, London, 1995)—but adopted enthusiastically by S. Blackmore in *The Gene Machine* (Oxford University Press, Oxford, 1999). See also: W. Durham, *Coevolution: Genes, Culture and Human Diversity* (Stanford University Press, Stanford, Calif., 1991) and H. Plotkin, *Darwin Machines and the Nature of Knowledge* (Harvard University Press, Cambridge, Mass., 1993).

VII EVOLVED MAN AND GOD INCARNATE

For later reflections of the author on evolved humanity, incarnation, and the historical Jesus, see: TSA, chapters 13, 14; 'The Incarnation of the Self-Expressive Word of God' in *Religion and Science: History, Method, Dialogue*, ed. W. Mark Richardson and Wesley J. Wildman (Routledge, New York and London, 1996), pp. 321–39; and *Paths from Science towards God: The End of All Our Exploring* (Oneworld, Oxford, 2001), pp. 158–9, 164–71.

vii(i), p. 229. The theme of God as self-offering, suffering Love expressed 'in, with and under' the world of creation and supremely and explicitly in the life and death of Jesus the Christ was expanded in TSA (pp. 126–7, 308–11, 329, 331), especially in the light of P. S. Fiddes's *The Creative Suffering of God* (Clarendon Press, Oxford, 1988). This theme has since become a recurrent one in late twentieth-century Christian theology, especially by those engaged in the science and theology dialogue (q.v. the authors and references in *The Work of Love: Creation as Kenosis*, ed. J. Polkinghorne (SPCK, London, 2001)).

VII   MAN IN CREATION

p. 256, nn. 2, 3; p. 313, n. 153. Religion and Ecology. A survey of the steadily growing responses, since 1976, of the world religions to the global environmental crisis has been given in 'Introduction: The Emerging Alliance of World Religions and Ecology' by M. E. Tucker and J. A. Grim in *Daedalus* 130, no. 4 (2001), 10-13 (the whole issue is on 'Religion and Ecology: Can the Climate Change?'). Of particular value are the series of volumes published by the Center for the Study of World Religions at Harvard Divinity School and distributed by Harvard University Press, Cambridge, Mass.: *Buddhism and Ecology* (1997), *Confucianism and Ecology* (1998), *Hinduism and Ecology* (2000), *Christianity and Ecology* (2000), *Indigenous Traditions and Ecology* (2001), and *Daoism and Ecology* (2001), with forthcoming volumes on Judaism, Islam, Jainism, and Shinto and a summary volume in 2004.

vE, pp. 304–6. The concept of humanity as a 'created co-creator' with God has been impressively propounded and developed by P. Hefner in his *The Human Factor: Evolution, Culture and Religion* (Fortress Press, Minneapolis, 1993).

p. 311, nn. 140–5. An attempt to formulate principles and procedures in resolving conflicts over environmental issues, especially those between different interests, was made by a working party of wide-ranging membership over a period of three years at the Ian Ramsey Centre, Oxford, England. Its report, together with discussions of value systems and alternative approaches, has been published as *Values, Conflict and the Environment*, ed. Robin Attfield and Katharine Dell (Avebury, Ashgate Publishing, Aldershot, UK, and Brookfield, USA, 2nd edition).

VIII   CREATION AND HOPE

The relation of scientific scenarios concerning the future of planet Earth, and of life upon it, and of the cosmos to the eschatological hopes expressed in the New Testament and traditions within the Christian churches have been widely discussed since this chapter was written. Most of these discussions have been with reference to that traditional framework but F. J. Tipler , in his *The Physics of Immortality: Modern Cosmology, God and the Resurrection of the Dead* (Macmillan, London, 1995; Doubleday, New York, 1997) and F. J. Dyson, in his *Infinite in All Directions* (Harper & Row, New York, 1988) have advocated very speculative 'physical eschatologies' involving the continuation of information-processing in an infinitely collapsing or an expanding universe. Such scenarios have been criticized as bearing little relation to the hopes of fulfilment of a fully human life which characterize Christian eschatology or indeed to any other hopes which humanity might nurture. However, serious consideration by theologians and scientists of the relation of Christian eschatology to cosmological scientific predictions has continued and is well represented both in *The End of the World and the Ends of God: Science and Theology on Eschatology*, ed. J. Polkinghorne and M. Welker (Trinity Press International, Pa., 2000) and, in a style more accessible to the general reader, in J. Polkinghorne's *The God of Hope and the End of the World* (SPCK, London, 2002).

In this chapter (subsections IV ff.) I reported in regard to the form and basis of Christian hope on the writings of what were then becoming known as the 'theologians of hope', of Teilhard de Chardin and of some process theologians. I concluded there that a common theme, with which I concurred, was that human hope is to be located on the axis between humanity and God in the *present* experience as we look towards the God who is essentially Love and ever-faithful—on our intimations of transcendence in the immanent. I did not speculate on the possibility of the *transformation* of this actual world, as do those who believe that, in the resurrection of Jesus, his actual physical body was transformed to a new regime or mode of existence, based on the assumption that the accounts of the empty tomb are historical and have this implication (q.v. several authors in *Resurrection: Theological and Scientific Assessments*, ed. T. Peters, R. J. Russell, and M. Welker (Eerdmans, Grand Rapids, Michigan, 2002). I am sceptical of this latter position, not seeing it as essential to the primitive, historical, apostolic affirmation and experience that 'He is risen', as I have fully discussed in TSA, pp. 279–88. So I still draw back, *pace* the authors in the two volumes referred to at the end of the last paragraph, from speculating about the scenario, and indeed ontology, of the 'Last Things', willing as I am to allow poetry, music, and visual imagery to 'flesh out' (*mot juste!*) their content.

Index of names

Abrecht, P., 293, 311
Albright, F., 42
Alcser, G. P., 364, 365, 366
Alexander, H. G., 53
Alexander, R., 174
Allchin, A. M., 189, 253, 297
Anders, W., 255
Anderson, B. W., 81
Appleman, P., 50
Ardrey, R., 161, 174
Ashby, Lord, ix, 267, 268, 270, 299, 302, 311, 312, 313, 322
Athanasius, St., 43, 252
Auden, W. H., 208
Augustine, 79, 181
Aurobindo, Sri, 110, 111
Austin, W. H., 2, 23, 24, 25, 26
Ayala, F. J., 114, 116

Bach, J. S., 106
Bacon, F., 3, 5, 7
Baker, J. A., 84, 85, 125, 188, 189, 217, 227, 278, 285, 287, 288
Bampton, Canon John, ix
Barbour, I. G., 21, 22, 40, 136, 265, 276, 278, 291, 310, 311, 314, 317
Barbour, R. S., 230
Barker, E., 171
Barnes, B., 18
Barr, J., 189, 278, 279, 280, 281, 283, 284, 285, 332
Barth, K., 13, 14, 194, 242, 333
Beckner, M., 114, 117
Bell, R. H., 25
Benedict, St., 277
Berkhof, H., 235, 236, 237, 256, 281, 286, 287, 366
Bettenson, H., 252
Birch, C., 314
Black, J., 283
Blacker, C., 31

Blake, W., 307, 308
Blakemore, C., 121, 152
Boas, G., 364
Boer, P. A. H. de, 142, 143
Bohr, N., 56
Boltzmann, L. E., 99, 158
Borman, F., 255
Born, M., 57
Bornkamm, G., 220
Boulding, K. E., 264
Bowden, J., 201
Bowker, J., 41, 183, 184
Boyle, Robert, 4, 5, 6, 49, 58
Braaten, C., 264, 269, 335, 342, 343
Braithwaite, R. B., 24
Breck, A. D., 31, 62, 73, 79, 333
Brooke, G., 82
Brooke, J., 108
Browne, T., 5
Brownlee, W. H., 42
Bruegemann, W., 280
Brunner, E., 4, 79, 235, 242
Bruns, J. E., 144
Budd, S., 20
Bullett, G., 108
Bultmann, R., 31, 340
Burhoe, R. W., 27, 32, 34, 272, 353
Burke, E., 268, 322
Bussey, D., 14
Butler, R. J., 128

Caird, G. B., 234, 330
Cairns, D., 189
Callender, C., 43, 78
Campbell, D. T., 33, 34, 270, 271, 272
Campbell, J., 110
Campbell, J. Y., 189
Campion, C. T., 298
Capek, M., 57
Capra, F., 106, 360, 361, 362
Carlyle, T., 51, 89

Carter, B., 67, 68, 69
Caspar, M., 106, 109
Chadwick, W. O., 226
Chalmers, T., 181, 182
Chaudhuri, H., 111
Chew, G., 361
Childs, B. S., 83
Clement of Alexandria, 252
Cobb, J., 23, 105, 127, 141, 200, 211, 312, 314, 340, 341, 342, 346
Coleridge, S. T., 296
Compton, J. J., 135
Coomaraswamy, A. K., 107, 108, 109
Coulson, C. A., 14
Cousins, E. H., 319, 320, 335, 336, 339, 343, 344, 346
Cox, H., 109
Crespy, G., 345
Crick, F. H. C., 118
Crim, K., 330
Csikszentmihalyi, M., 175
Cughman, R. F., 202
Cullman, O., 332
Cuthbert, St., 275

Dante, 59, 109, 199, 253, 254, 318
Dammers, H., 311
Darlington, C. D., 173
Darwin, C., 1, 6, 7, 12, 50, 65, 78, 87, 89, 160, 161, 164
Darwin, F., 6, 65
Davidson, D., 129, 130, 131, 133, 136, 139
Davies, J., 108
Davies, P., 73, 327, 328, 329, 347
Dawkins, R., 162, 163, 164, 177, 178, 190, 271
Democritus, 113
Denbigh, K., 57, 58, 61, 155, 158, 321, 334
Derham, W., 6
Derr, T. S., 11, 256, 257, 278, 280, 311, 314
Dillistone, F. W., 14
Dobzhansky, T., 1, 72, 114, 116, 168, 169, 180
Dodd, C. H., 206
Donne, J., 359
Douglas, Justice, 269
Douglas, M., 29
Draper, J. W., 10
Dubos, R., 265, 303
Dumas, A., 314
Dummett, M., 21

Eccles, J. C., 72, 121, 170
Eddington, A., 67
Edwards, J. W., 14
Edwards, P., 312, 364
Eichrodt, W., 81, 124, 125, 189, 190, 278, 285
Eigen, M., viii, 92, 100, 101, 102, 103, 104, 163, 322
Einstein, A., 55
Eliot, T. S., 199, 358
Emerson, R. W., 89
Evans, G., 21
Evdokimov, P., 45, 81, 192

Fabre, J. H., 165
Fackre, G., 276, 310
Faraday, M., 123
Ferré, F., 368
Farrer, A., 48
Feyerabend, P. K., 115
Ficino, M., 305
Filson, F. V., 332
Fisher, L. R., 82
Flew, A. G. N., 35, 176
Fodor, J. A., 128, 131
Ford, E. B., 169
Ford, L. S., 320, 346, 347, 349
Foster, L., 129
Foster, M. B., 8, 9, 10
Francis, St., 275, 277, 318
Frankera, W. K., 312
Frazer, J., 31
Fuller, B., 255

Galileo, 52
Galloway, A. D., 332
Gardner, E. Clinton, 313
Geach, P. T., 81
Gilkey, L., 37, 323, 324, 329, 352, 354
Glansdorff, A., 106
Gore, C., 200
Goulder, M., 240
Green, M., 219
Grensted, L. W., vii
Griffin, D. R., 126, 127, 141, 200, 211, 314, 340, 342
Grislis, E., 202

Habermas, J., 19, 23, 33
Habgood, J., 2
Häfele, W., 322, 323
Haldane, J. B. S., 161
Hallam, A., 87

Hamilton, P. N., 200
Hamilton, W. D., 174
Happold, F. C., 362
Hardy, A., 72, 168, 169
Harman, G., 129
Harrelson, W., 81
Hartley, H., 3
Hartshorne, C., 140, 200
Hawking, S. W., 327
Hebblethwaite, B., 45
Hefner, P., x, 30, 31, 32, 37, 250, 251, 335, 338, 339, 345, 351
Heidemann, J., 73
Heim, K., 25, 55
Heisenberg, W., 55
Helin, J., 20, 368
Helitzer, F., 66
Hellman, D., 106
Hengel, M., 223, 224, 225, 227
Hepburn, R. W., 364
Herbert, G., 297
Heschel, A., 201
Hesse, H., 303, 317
Hesse, M., 19, 20, 23, 28, 33, 73
Hick, J., 28, 219
Hinshelwood, C. N., 72, 150
Hoagland, H., 27
Hodgson, L., 227, 228
Holst, G., 108
Hooykass, R., 8
Hopkins, G. M., 302
Hort, F. J. A., 291
Horton, R., 29, 30
Houlden, J. L., 188, 313
Hoyle, F., 64, 150
Hubble, E., 67
Hudson, W. D., 25
Huxley, A., 362
Huxley, J., 156, 169, 176, 336, 337
Huxley, T. H., 12, 50

Illingworth, J. R., 200
Irenaeus, 252

Jacobson, C., 29
Jaspers, K., 215, 216
Jenkins, D. E., viii, 243, 313
Jensen, O., 314
Jeremias, J., 220, 291
Jerome, St., 275
Justin Martyr, 79

Kant, I., 64, 65, 296

Käsemann, E., 223
Katz, S. H., 272
Kaufman, G. D., 181, 202, 236
Kemp, E. W., 188, 253
Kemp-Smith, N., 65
Kent, P. W., 97, 159
Kepler, 106, 109
Keynes, G., 6
Klink, W. H., 302
Knight, H., 14
Koestler, A., 26
Kripke, S., 129
Kung, H., 217, 218, 228
Kuhn. T. S., 34, 123

Lack, D., 12, 13
Lagerkvist, P., 208
Lambert, W. G., 280
Lampe, G. W. H., 207, 233, 239, 242, 248, 249, 251
Lane, W. R., 83
Laplace, P. S. de, 53, 54, 62
Leach, E., 29
Lenski, G., 271
Lévi-Strauss, C., 29
Libet, B., 121
Lipner, J., 109
Locke, J., 21
Loewe, M., 31
Long, C. H., 31
Longair, M. S., 67
Lorenz, K., 174
Lossky, V., 189, 195
Lovejoy, A. O., 364
Lovell, B., 51, 64, 66, 68
Lovell, J., 255
Lucas, J. R., 81, 321
Lucretius, 113
Lyell, C., 12

MacIntyre, A., 35
MacLagan, D., 28
MacKay, D. M., 25
Macquarrie, J., 39, 45, 222, 240, 241, 278, 313, 365
McArthur, H. K., 313
McDowell, J., 21
McKie, D., 3
McKinney, R. W. A., 43, 80, 194, 230, 300, 337
McTaggart, J., 321, 332, 334
Maddox, J., 262
Malinowski, B., 28

Malthus, T. R., 12
Manetti, G., 305
Manson, T. W., 313
Manuel, F. E., 3
Maranda, P., 29
Marietta, D. F., 273, 274, 292
Marks, J. H., 83
Marty, M. E., 181
Mascall, E. L., vii
Max, N., 63
Maximus the Confessor, 289
Meadows, D. H., 265
Medawar, P. B., 26, 116, 119
Metz, J. B., 335
Milton, John, 87
Misner, C. W., 62, 63, 69
Mitchell, B., 39, 340
Moltmann, J., 42, 43, 44, 80, 109, 193, 194, 195, 201, 210, 211, 220, 221, 244, 300, 310, 311, 319, 335, 337, 338, 344, 345
Monod, J., viii, 50, 51, 53, 70, 72, 86, 87, 90, 92, 93, 94, 96, 97, 104, 160
Montefiore, H. W., 85, 257, 278, 296, 297, 314, 357
Moore, N., 258, 302
Morley, D. W., 16, 311
Morowitz, H. J., 151
Morris, D., 174
Moule, C. F. D., ix, 189, 224, 226, 227, 228, 232, 240, 278, 286
Mulliken, R. S., 54
Munitz, M. K., 35, 129

Nagel, E., 92, 115, 367
Nagel, T., 130
Neuhaus, R. J., 335, 343
Newton, Isaac, 4, 5, 6, 8, 53, 365
Nicolis, G., 100
Nicholson, M., 275
Niebuhr, R., 324, 336
Nikam, N. A., 110, 111
Nineham, D., 222, 247

Otto, R., 64
Owen, D. J., 259, 263

Pailin, D., 39
Page, T., 313
Paley, W., 6, 7, 12
Pannenberg, W., 194, 195, 211, 220, 233, 234, 235, 242, 332, 335, 336, 343, 344
Pascal, B., 51, 155

Passmore, J., 222, 247, 277, 291
Paul, St., 184, 186, 224, 332
Peacocke, A. R., 40, 55, 72, 79, 97, 114, 159, 165, 189, 193, 195, 200, 243, 244, 251, 289, 296, 308, 310, 326, 333
Peake, A. S., 124
Pearman, D. G., 181
Pelikan, J., 43, 78, 79
Penner, H. H., 368, 369, 370
Phillips, D. Z., 25
Pike, N., 81
Piper, R., 101
Pittenger, N., 141, 200, 234
Planck, Max, 55, 66
Platzman, R. L., 158
Polanyi, M., 26, 72, 371
Pollard, W. G., 95, 96, 97
Pope, A., 197
Popper, K., 131, 170, 177
Prigogine, I., viii, 92, 97, 98, 100, 103, 104, 106
Pugh, G. E., 154, 179, 312
Putnam, H. W., 21

Quastler, H., 158
Quick, O. C., 290
Quinton, A. M., 176

Rad, G. von, 83, 285
Raine, K., 307, 308
Ramsey, I. T., 24, 39, 40, 176
Randers, J., 265
Raven, C. E., 14, 165, 198, 200, 209, 304, 362
Ravin, A. W., 184
Ray, J., 6, 7, 362
Redfield, R., 28
Reynolds, B., 254
Richardson, A., 189, 191
Robinson, H. Wheeler, 124
Rootselaar, B. van, 170
Rothschild, Lord, 323
Ruel, M., ix
Russell, C. A., 8
Russel, B., 89, 90

Sahlins, M., 173, 174, 175, 176
Sanders, J. T., 313
Sayers, D., 254
Schilling, H. K., 61, 155, 203, 314
Schlegel, R., 56
Schleiermacher, F., 78, 192, 296
Schmidt, W. H., 284

Schoepf, B., 29
Schumacher, E. F., 314
Schuster, P., 101
Schwarz, H., 320, 335
Schweitzer, A., 298, 332
Scullion, J. J., 189
Shakespeare, 326
Shaw, P., 4
Shepherd, J. J., 34, 36
Sherrington, C., 152
Shriver, G., 345
Simon, H. A., 165
Simpson, G. G., 72, 156, 157, 164, 165, 169
Simpson. J. Y., 10
Sittler, J., 264, 304, 308, 309, 365
Sjöberg, L., 208
Skolimowski, H., 267, 268, 298
Slater, J., 89
Smart, J. C. C., 35, 321
Sperry, R. W., 121
Spiegelberg, F., 111
Spiro, M. E., 20, 368
Sprat, T., 5
Spring, D., 278
Spring, E., 278
Staal, J. F., 170
Stace, W. T., 25
Stead, G. C., 228
Stone, C. D., 269
Strachan, W. J., 317
Swanson, J. W., 129

Tax, S., 43, 78
Taylor, J. V., 311
Teilhard de Chardin, 123, 126, 127, 131, 159, 160, 168, 201, 307, 310, 334, 338, 344, 345, 348
Temple, W., 290, 301, 310
Tennyson, A., 87–9, 164
Thekkumkal, J. S., 109
Theophilus, 79
Thorne, K. S., 69
Thorpe, W. H., 72, 153, 154
Tillich, P., 25, 192, 193
Tolstoy, L., 178, 180
Tomita, K., 73
Torrance, T. F., 371
Towers, B., 159
Traherne, T., 351, 352
Trinkhaus, C. E., 305
Trinklein, F. E., 48
Trivers, R. L., 174, 175

Tylor, E. B., 31
Tyndall, J., 53

Verghese, P., 314
Vidler, A. J., 2

Waddington, C. H., 160, 176, 322
Wald, G., 151
Wallace, A. R., 12
Wallis, J., 3
Ward, B., 255, 256, 265, 303
Ward, K., 35, 36
Weisskopf, V., 64
Weiszäcker, C. F. von, 41
Wesley, John, 7
West-Eberhard, M., 174
Westermann, C., 32, 189, 279, 282, 284, 285, 286, 330, 331, 347
Wheeler, J. A., 66, 69
White, A. D., 10
White, L., 275, 276, 278, 284
White, T. H., 278
Whitehead, A. N., 23, 126, 127, 140, 200, 211, 340, 341, 343, 346
Whitrow, G. T., 321
Wieman, H. N., 316
Wiggins, D., 128
Wilberforce, S., 12
Wildberger, W., 284
Wiles, M., 28
Williams, D. D., 311, 316, 317, 339
Wilson, B. R., 29
Wilson, E. O., 117, 162, 171, 172, 173, 174, 175, 176, 177
Wilson, R. A., 201
Winch, P., 25
Winkler, R., 101, 322
Wittgenstein, L., 7
Wolstenholme, G., 337
Wordsworth, William, 296, 351
Wright, G. E., 217
Wynne-Edwards, V. C., 161
Wyon, O., 79

Yockey, H. P., 158
Yonan, E. A., 368, 369, 370
Young, J. Z., 149
Young, N., 150, 285
Yourgrau, W., 31, 62, 73, 79, 333

Zimmer, H., 110
Zhabotinsky, A. M., 99

Subject
Index

'Abba', 248
Action, 132–3, 133, 135
Acts of the Apostles, 352
Adam, 190–1
African religious thought, 29–30
Agent, conscious, 137–8; God as, 133–5; man as, 131–3, 144
Aggression, Aggressiveness, 173, 175
Altruism, 161–4, 173, 176
Analogy, in theology, 39
Anthropic principle, 67–8, 328
Anthropocentrism, 72, 84, 158, 324
Anthropology, 33, 60, 171–6; of the Bible, 124, 188–92; Eastern, 191
Anti-discipline, 117, 171
Anti-reductionism, 118–19
Apocalyptic, 323, 329, 332
Apocrypha, 84
Apollo 8, 255
Apollo 13, 257
Apologists, 242
Arianism, 43
Astro-physicists, 59, 150
Atheism, 43
Atomic processes, 56
Axial period, 215, 217

Baal, 82
Babylon, cosmogonic myths of, 41
Beauty, 35; of nature, 48
Beginning, in the Bible, 330–2, 347
Behaviour, sciences of human, 171
Behaviourism, 131
Benedicite, 317
Bestiaries, Western medieval, 278
Biblicism, 219
Biochemists, 60, 151

Biological criteria, for man's position in evolution, 72
Biological organization, 118
Biological systems, complexity of, 58
Biology, theoretical, 97
Black body radiation, 327
Black holes, 62, 327
Blue-print for Survival, 265–6
Boltzmann principle, 99
Book of Common Prayer, ix
Book of Nature, 3–7
Book of Scripture, 3–7
'Bootstrap hypothesis', 361
Boyle's law, 58
Brahma, 107
Brain, 120–3, 134, 137, 159, 166
Bridgewater Treatises, 12, 181
British Association, 12, 15
British Council of Churches, 15–16
Buddhism, 205

California State Curriculum Commission, 1
Causality, 57
Causal chains, 90, 93, 96
Causes, multiple, 90, 96
Chance, 51, 62, 66, 70, 86–92, 103–4; in biological evolution, 97; 'due to', 51, 91, 103; in a law-regulated system, 97; in literature, 87–90; as a metaphysical principle, 70; 'pure', 91, 93; search radar of God, 95; two meanings of, 90–2
Chance and law, 100, 102, 103–5, 155, 182–3, 304; as creative, 103–4, 111; in the life-game, 103–5
Chance and Necessity, 50–1

Chaos, 71, 81, 82, 83, 84, 87, 89, 166

Chemical kinetics, physico-chemical laws of, 100, 101

China, 215

Christ, the corporate, 226, 232; cosmic, 288; of faith, 222, 232; as Pantocrator, 338; as pre-existent Son of God, 233–4; as post-existent, 248; as *Urbild*, 249; as *Vorbild*, 249

Christ-event, 222, 226

Christian, 217–18; formulations, implausibility to modern men of, 48; humanism, 308; mystical tradition, 362

Christology, 211, 223–8, 242–3; as development, 224–7; early, of Paul, 224–5; as evolution, 224–7; and revelation, 243

Church of England, 5, 256

Club of Rome, report of, 265

Colossians, Epistle to the, 234, 236, 288

Commitment, personal, in religious belief, 26

Complementarity, 55

Complexity, 59, 158–160; and consciousness, 159–60

Consciousness, 63–5, 120, 124, 126, 134, 338; and complexity, 159–60; emergence of in animals, 168, 183; as emergent, 71, 76, 120; epistemologically irreducible, 120; 'rudimentary', 126; threshold of, 121

Contingency, 37, 77, 78, 204

Continuity, of natural processes, 60, 73, 155, 204, 210, 232, 353

Copernican Revolution, 7

Corinthians, 2nd Epistle to the, 229, 252

Corpus callosum, 121

Cosmological theories, under-determined, 73

Cosmology, 51–2, 59, 84, 85; religious mythic, 20, 33; religious and scientific compared, 31

Cosmos, 50–85, 71, 77, 80, 81, 82, 87, 89, 166

Cosmos-explaining-being, 36, 38

Council of Chalcedon, Definition of, 228, 231

Counter-culture, 276

Covalent bond, theories of, 139

Creatio continua (creation as continuous), 79–80, 204, 232, 304, 335–6, 353

Creatio ex nihilo, 43, 44, 79, 81–3, 141, 297

Creatio mutabilis, 80

Creation, an article of faith, for Barthians, 14; of the 'Baal type', 82; the dance of, 106–8; death in, 200; and the 'dominion' of man, 189, 281–5, 291, 297; of the El type, 82; as expression of purpose and intention of God, 145, 236; God's relation to the world, 46; gratuitousness and joy of God in, 111; and hope, 319–55; idea of, 7; (Judeo-) Christian doctrine of, 8, 24, 37, 44, 76, 78, 292, 365, 369, (and attitudes to nature, 275–91); man in, 255–317; models of, 38–45, 196, 273–4; music of, 105–6, 107; 'original', 78; pain in, 200; the 'play' of God in, 108–11; Priestly account of in Genesis 1, 81; and redemption, 82; a relation of dependence of the cosmos on God, 43–4; reliability of, 339, 348, 351; a self-emptying by God, 199; suffering in, 199–202

Creation, biblical understanding of, 10, 32, 42–3, 81–4, 274–87; as desacralized, revalued and historicized, 279–81; as good, ordered and of value to God, 279

Creation, doctrine of, 14, 38–45, 46, 77–85, 104–11, 196–203, 356–7; and ecological values, 291–4, 312–15; and hope, 319–55; in the light of the emergence of man, 196–203

Creative self-determination, 211

Creativity, of man, 168–9, 307–8, 353; of the given, 353

'Creator', analogy to 'maker', 43

Creator, theological doctrine of God as, 37; and see under 'God'

Culture, 176, 192; autonomy of, 174

Dai Dong, 266

Dance, of creation, 106–8, 361

Darwinism, 62

DDT, 262

Death-awareness, 179–80

Deism, 44

Demons, and Christian belief, 124–5

Demon possession, 122

De-mythologizing, 31

Dependence, of world on God, 78, 138, 204

Determinism, 52–7; atomistic, 113; biological, 174; Laplacian, 53–4, 57, 59

Deterministic laws, of physics and chemistry, 128

Deuteronomy, 352

Disorder, and entropy, 158

Dissipative systems and structures, 97–100

DNA, 65, 92, 93, 121, 127, 158, 160, 167

Drugs, 15, 121

Dualism, 24, 43, 122–5, 134

Dualism, God-world, 138–9

Dynamic equilibrium, of ecosystems, 260

Earth, as a spaceship, 255, 263–4, 322

Earthrise, 255

Eastern Fathers, 253, 297

Eastern religious and mystical thought, 106–11, 360–3

Ecclesiastes, 84, 87

Ecclesiasticus, 84

Ecology, 165, 172, 257–65, 314

Ecological action, model facilitating decisions on, 274, 316

Ecological balance, 263, 274

Ecological future, prognoses of the, 265–70

Ecology movement, 267–8

Ecological pyramids, 259 (man at apex of) 261, 264

Ecological values, 269–70, (and theology) 270–94, (and the doctrine and models of creation) 291–4, 312–15

Ecosystems, 258–60, 293, 302; diversity in, 260; and man, 260–5, 293, 299, 365; of the world, 258–64, 286, 365

Eddington's relation, 67

Élan vital, 121

Electrons, 21–2

Emergence, 61, 119, 127, 155, 209–11, 232, 246, 315, 353; of conscious life, 72, 272; mental activities as, 127; of life, 95, 100, 103, 167

Emergents, non-reducible character of, 112–19, 209–10, 232

Empirical natural science (and philosophy), 10, 11

End, in the Bible, 330–2, 347, 369

Energy, 55, 66, 70, 338

Enlightenment, The, 216

Entropy, 98, 158, 327–9

Equilibrium, 98–9

Eschatology, 332, 335, 340, 342

Essences, 39

Eternal objects, in process theology, 141

Ethics, 15, 173, 269; Christian, 313; evolutionary, 176

Eucharist, 290–1

Events, as ontological categories, 130; as fundamental units, in process thought, 340; interconnectedness of, 314, 360

Evil, natural, 166

Evolution, 1, 59–60, 73, 337; becomes 'history', 169–70; biological, 96, 103, 165, 197, (mechanism of) 160–4, (synthetic theory of) 160, 172; of life, 'an inevitable process', 103; open-ended character of, 167–9; progress in, 156; psychosocial, 169; social, 271;

Evolution—*cont.*
  trends in, 155–60; trial and error in, 168
Existentialism, 96
Exorcism, 124
Explanation, 35, 36, 39, 73–4, 75

Feedback, 322
Felicity, 351–2
Fellowship, in the Holy Spirit, 310
Fertilizers, 263
'Forms of life', 25
Freedom, 71, 166, 195, 197
Frontal leucotomy, 121
Fundamental constants (or parameters), 66, 68, 166
Fundamental particles, 59
Future, of the Earth, 324–6; on the Earth, 322–4; ecological, prognoses of the, 265–70; of the galaxy and of the universe, 326–9; and God, 335, 342–6, 353; and hope, in contemporary theology, 333–46; man's, 319–21, 335, 337–8, 345, (according to science), 320–9; meaning of, 333–42; ontological priority of, 211, 343; openness to, 211, 232
Futurology, 320–1, 331–2

Galatians, Epistle to the, 248
Galaxies, 59, 326–9
Games, theory of, 102, 163, 322
Genesis, 11, 37, 41, 42, 43, 81–3, 142, 143, 189–93, 206, 279, 281–5, 330
God, abstract essence of, 140; 'acts of', 208; as agent, 133–5, 199, 203, 351; 'Ahead', 345; as communicator of meaning, 144–6, 203, 205, 208–9, 214, 216, 350, (through a person) 230, (through Jesus) 233–238; as 'composing', 209–11; concrete actuality of, 140; consequent nature of, 140, 343, 346; as creative love, 45, 140, 199, 213, 229–30, 246, 252; the Creator (archetypal image of) 39, 196, (feminine image of) 142–4, 207, (as Spirit) 250–2, (Judeo-Christian understanding of—see under 'Creation'); 'Death' of, 320; dependence of world on, 78, 138, 204; energies of, 45; the envisager and fund of universals, 140; as exploring, 209–11; the Father, 140, 207; of the gaps, 24, 78, 132, 136; immanence of, 81, 146, 204, 207, 214, 239–44, 350, 351, 363; as impassible, 200; Incarnate, myth or truth, 219, 227–8; intentions and purposes of in creation, 136, 138, 300–1, 350, 353; as Love, in creation, 45, 213, 229–30, 353; 'lure' of, 342; manifest in man, 195; motherly aspects of in Hebrew tradition, 142; *pathos* in, 198, 201; primordial nature of, 140, 343; relation to the world (analogous to human agency) 134, (asymmetry of) 139, (biological model) 142, dualism of) 138–9, (interventionist view of) 134, (in the light of the sciences) 203–14; as Responsive Love, 140; as self-offering, in creation, 213, 214, 229–30, 252, 311; *semper Creator*, 105; as Sustainer and Preserver of creation, 79; talk about, criteria for, 39; the Son, 207; as source of the future, 232; as (Holy) Spirit, 81, 140, 206–7, 242, 250–2, 308, 362; as suffering Creator, 198–202, 213, 214, 229–230, 311; as supra-personal, 202, 205, 212; taking a risk in creation, 198; transcendent source and meaning, 75; as transcendent, 200, 202, 204–5, 207, 239–44, 297, 352; as unveiling his meaning in various levels, 208–9, 233–8, 350; in the world, 205–7, 238–9, 298
God-meme, 178
Gene, 93, 160, 163; selection, 160; selfish, 161–4, 173, 175, 176
Genetic assimilation, 160
Genetic code, 65
Genetic mutations, 60

Geneticists, 60
Geology, 59
Geophysics, 60
Gnosticism, 288
Green Revolution, 263
Group selection, 160–4, 173

Hadron, 361
Hebrews, Epistle to the, 234, 236, 252, 288, 354
Hermeneutical problem, 223, 227
Hierarchy, of levels in a living organism, 115; of levels of organization, 62, 112–19, 209, 302, 355; model, 114; of natural systems, 113–15, 133, 230, 302, 369, 371; of the sciences, 116–17; of the *theories* (of the *sciences*) 114–16
Hierarchical systems, causal connections, 118
Heisenberg Uncertainty Principle, 55
Homo religiosus, 368
Hope, 319–20, 329, 349, 350, (biblical) 331, (in creation) 350–5; theologies of, 334–8, 342–5, 348, 356
Hormones, 121
'Hot big bang', 69, 73, 74, 79, 328
Hubble constant, 67
Human consciousness, expansion of, 63–5; emergence of, 71, 76, 120
Human knowledge, ambiguity of, 63
Human life, parameters of the milieu of, 71
Hypercycle, autocatalytic, 102
Hypotheses, scientific, 33
Hypotheticality, 322–3

Idea-meme, 177–8
Identity, mind-body, 125, 128–31, 137
Images, 76
Immanence of God, 45, 139, 204; see, 'God, immanence of'
'Impossible' spectator, 16
Incarnation, 211–13, 228, 230–1, 233, 239, 240–4, 289, 306–7, 346,

354, 358, (and man as co-creator with God) 306–11, (three presuppositions of) 240, (as emergence-from-continuity) 242
Incarnational theology, Anglican, 14
India, 215
Individual selection, 160–4
Initial aims, of an occasion, in process thought, 211
Information-carrying systems, 97
Integrality, defined, 158
Intelligibility, 33, 46, 74, 75, 196–7, 208
Intentions, in action, 131, 135
Interconnectedness, of events, 314, 360
Interdependence, of events, 360
Interfaces, 119–22, 369
Inter-testamental period, 288
'Interests', 19, 33
Irreconcilers, of Darwinism and Christian belief, 13
Isaiah, 82
Islam, 205
'I-Thou' relation, between man and nature, 302–3

Jesus, as archetype, 249; authority of, 220; bearer of God's pain, 230; continuity with creation, 244; cry of dereliction, 201, 217; as divine end of man, 251; effect of life and death, 219; an 'emergent' in creation, 240; as exemplar, 249; focus for unveiling God's meaning and presence, 223, 233, 237; intensity and oneness of relation with God, 219–20, 223, 229; and man's search for meaning and intelligibility, 218–27; and moral perfection, 'sinlessness' of, 222–3, 247–8; openness to God, 219–20, 223, 229, 248; as paradigm, 229, 248; as paragon, 229, 248; and personalness, 251; resurrection of, 221–2, 248–9; as self-definition of human life, 250; as Son of God, 233–4, 239; teaching about the Kingdom

Jesus—*cont.*
  of God, 220; 'the things about',
  222, 250; tragic death of, 220–1
Jesus Christ, ontological significance
  of, 243; as mediator of the meaning
  of creation, 234–8, 288
Job, Book of, 37, 84, 85, 106, 149,
  155, 287, 303, 307–8
John, first Epistle of, 146, 199, 238,
  355
John (Fourth Gospel), 42, 146, 205,
  206, 231, 234, 236, 237, 238, 241,
  287, 288, 310
Judeo-Christian tradition, 8, 27, 37,
  38, 74, 76, 205, 274, 277–8, 362,
  (attitudes to science and technology) 277, (post-biblical attitudes to nature) 287–291

Kerugma, 223
Kinship relations, 175
Koans, 361

Lamarckian inheritance, 170
Land, meaning for ancient Israel,
  280
'Language games', 7, 25, 26
Law, 86, 92, 197; 'of complexity-
  consciousness', 159; of Jubilee, 280
Laws, psycho-physical, 129; statisti-
  cal character of scientific, 95, 96
Leviticus, 280
Liberation theology, 338
Life, gift of the Creator, 83; industrial
  way of, 265–6; interdependence of,
  258–60; new, through death of old,
  164–6, 199; origin of, 59; 'struc-
  tural logic' of, 165
Life-game, 86, 92; relevance of, 104–
  105
Līla, 109–10
Logos 205–6, 233, 242–3, 252, 362;
  Jesus as, 239, 252, 354
Logos-Christology, 231, 233–4, 242–
  243
'Long Search', 214–18, 317
Love, concept of, 339
Luke, Gospel of, 142, 215, 220, 287

Lux Mundi, 200–1

Macromolecules, informational, 103;
  replicating biological, 101; self-
  organizing cycles of, 102
Man, 50, 73; as agent, 130, 131–3,
  144; anthropocentric myth of, 324;
  biblical view of, 188–91, 217;
  biological constraints on, 176; biological needs of, 154, 179; as
  co-creator with God, 304–6, 306–
  311, 315–17, 350, 355, (theme of
  Renaissance Christian humanism)
  305; as co-explorer with God, 306,
  315; continuity with biological
  world, 153; control of his own evolution, 184; as co-worker with
  God, 304–6, 315; creativity of, 195,
  307–9; and death, 179–80, 244–6;
  deification, divinization of, 251–3;
  destiny (*Bestimmung*) of, 194; dichotomous view of, 189–90; direction of, 182–4, 246–54; distinctive
  attributes of, 153–4; divine end of,
  251; 'dominion' of, 189, 281–5, 291,
  297, 314; dualistic view of, 124;
  dynamic concept of, 195; and the
  ecosystem, 260–5; emergence of,
  169; emergence of in the universe,
  72; existence of as non-necessary,
  71; 'Fall' of, 190–1, 193, 250,
  284–5; as fellow-sufferer with God
  in creation, 311–12, 315; finitude
  of, 181, 204, 245–6; freedom of,
  195, 197; Greek concepts of, 189;
  the 'highest animal', 157; as image
  of God, 189–90, 195, 213, 283–5,
  297; as interpreter of creation,
  300–1, 315; investigator, user, and
  denizen of nature, 48; in the light
  of the sciences, 149–54; as lover of
  creation, 303, 315, 317–18; as
  manager of creation, 263, 297–8,
  314, 322; as mediator of creation,
  296–7; social dimension of relation
  to nature, 311; as omnivore, 258;
  path through life, 182–4; personal,
  psychosomatic unity of, 125, 189–

Man—*cont.*

190; personhood of, 189; perfectibility of, 222–3, 246ff; population
of, 261–2; potentialities of, 182–4,
193, 246–54; presence in the
universe, significance of, 84; as
priest of creation, 295–7, 314–15;
as prophet of creation, 301–2, 315;
in rebellion, in biblical view, 285–
287; relation to nature, biblical
understanding of, 274–87; reverence of for creation, 298–300; self-
awareness of, 193; self-definition
of, 250; sin of, 192–4; state and
predicament of, 188–96, 250; as
steward of creation, 297–8, 314; as
symbiont with creation, 298–300,
315; and suffering, 182, 246;
tension between self-centredness
and openness, 194; theological
appraisals of, 188–196; trichotomous view of, 189–90; as trustee
and preserver of nature, 303–4,
315; an unfulfilled paradox, 183,
195–6; as vicegerent of creation,
297–8, 314; view of the anatomist,
151; view of the biochemist, 151;
view of the cell biologist, 151; view
of the biologist and ethologist,
153–4; view of the chemist, 150–1;
view of the cosmologist and astrophysicist, 150; view of the molecular biologist, 151; view of the
neurophysiologist, 152; view of the
physicist and physical chemist, 150;
view of the physiologist, 152; view
of theologians, 187–8

Manichaeism, 43, 288

Maccabees, Second Book of, 43, 288

Mark, Gospel of, 220, 221, 279, 329

Materialism, 128

Matter, 55; instrumental function of,
289–90; mental capabilities of,
128; symbolic function of, 289–90

Matter-energy, 66, 70, 338

Matthew, Gospel of, 142, 215, 279

Meaning, 73, 74, 75; of an action,
135; in the cosmic process, 145;

desire for, 38; discerning of personal by other personal agents,
144; of a message, 135; personal,
37, 46, 47, 74; social, 47; within the
physical nexus of the world, 135,
136, 208; in the world, 75, 216

Memes, 177–8

Memory, 100

Mental activity, functionalist view of,
133; intimate relation with
physico-chemical state of the
brain, 121

Mental events, 120, 129, 130

Mental and the material, 118–31

Mental pole, of occasions, 127

Metabolic mechanisms, 65

Metaphor, 39, 76

Mind, 121, 124

Models, 33, 38, 39, 73, 76; 'candidates for reality', 39; differences
between religious and scientific,
40; facilitating decisions on ecological action, criteria for, 274,
292–4; of an immanent God, 44;
religious, 40, 273–4; theoretical in
science, 40; of a transcendent God,
44

Molecules, 60, 66

Molecular biology, 59, 60, 93

Monism, 122, 125–7; anomalous,
129, 130

Monocultures, ecological, 263

Mutations (genetic), 92, 94, 96, 168

Motion, 57

Mystery of existence question, 34, 35

Myths, 27, 29, 30–2; of creation, 28;
functionalist account of, 28; narrative, 31; scientific, 28; 'structuralist'
account of, 29

Name of God, 42

National Academy of Sciences, 1, 8,
13, 25

Natural laws, 60

Natural theology, 6, 11, 12, 14, 23,
26, 46, 47, 145, 201

Natural religion, 23

Naturalistic fallacy, 176

Nature, 11, 264, 364–6; as corpuscular-kinetic, 57; as desacralized, revalued and historicized in biblical view, 10, 279–81; fundamental constants of, 66; history of, 11; not divine, 11; organic concepts of, 362
Necessity, 50, 69, 71, 197
neo-Darwinism, 160
Neurophysiology, 120, 137
New Jerusalem, 307, 309, 330, 331
Newtonian world-view, 76
Nicene Creed, 44, 233
'Noosphere', 131, 160
Nuclear energy, 15, 322–3
Nuclear warfare, 15, 323

Object, absolute, 52, 53, 55
Objective observer, 56
Occasion of experience, in process thought, 126, 211, (physical pole of) 126, 127, (mental pole of) 127
Occult, 122–4
Odium academicum, 112
Odium theologicum, 112
Omega Point, 338, 345, 348
On the Origin of Species, 50
Openness, 59; to the future, 210–11, 232, 337, 340, 344; to the world, 194
Open system, 80, 210, 337, 344
Order and entropy, 158
Orderliness, 158
Order-through fluctuations, 100; in chemical systems, 99
Organization, measure of, 158
Origin of life, 73, 100–3
Original righteousness, 191, 193
Original sin, 191
Orthogenesis, 167
Oscillating reactions, 99

Pain, 165–6, 200, (in creation) 201–202, 230
Panentheism, 45, 141, 201, 207, 214, 238–9, 352
Panpsychism, 125–7
Pantheism, 43, 141

Paradigm shifts, 123
Particles, fundamental, 87, 95
People of Israel, 37
Persons (and the personal), 73, 131, 144, 212, 246; as free agents, 138; non-dualist view of, 133
Pesticides, 263
Philippians, Epistle to the, 224
Philosophy of science, 22
Physical pole, of occasions, 126, 127
Physicalism, 130
Physico-theology, 6, 11, 64
Physics, twentieth-century, 52–9
Play, 109, 111
Pollution, 15, 256, 258; Environmental, Royal Commission on, 267, 268
Population genetics, 160
Population, of man, 261–2
Predestination, 54
Predictability, 56, 58, 59
Prediction and control, in science, 19
Preservation, God's continuing creative work in, 78
Priestly writer, 83
'Primeval soup', 100
Process autonomy, 117, 367
Process theology, 23, 126, 140, 200, 209, 339–42, 346, 349, 356
Processes, natural, continuity of, 60, 73, 155, 204, 210, 232, 353; inventiveness and creativity of, 61, 204; open-ended character of, 210, 214, 232, 304, 315, 353
Proton-proton interaction, 66
Proverbs, 43, 84, 111, 143, 319
Providence, 95–7
Psalms, Book of, 37, 52, 84, 221, 279, 281
Psychic explanations, 124
Psychology, 112, 369–70

Quantum theory, 55–7, 340, 360, 365
Quarks, 361

Randomness, in microscopic events constituting the macroscopic, 97, 197; of molecular event, 94, 167;

Randomness—*cont.*
at the molecular level of the DNA,
94; in natural processes, 103, 246
Realism, 21, 22
Reality, biblical understanding of,
83; models as candidates for, 21,
134; two realms of, 24
Reasons, of an agent as causes, 130; in
action, 131, 135
Reconcilers, of Darwinism and
Christian belief, 13
Reduction, methodological, 115–16;
of theories, 115, 117, 367
Reductionism, 112–19, 131, 367–71
Religion, definition of, 20, 368; functionalist-anthropological account
of, 20; intellectual aspects of, 34;
irrelevance of natural science to,
26; mystical-instrumentalist account of, 24; role for, in the survival
and development of human society,
33, 270–4; and science, relation of,
22, 367–71; study of, 369
Religious doctrines, instrumentalist
accounts of, 23–4
Religious myth, functionalist account of, 28
Religious statements, as indicating
commitment to values, 273
Renaissance, The, 216
Replicators, 163, 164
Resources, non-renewable, 256
Revelation, to John, 42, 43, 200, 281,
329, 330, 331, 335
Revelation, in relation to Christ-
ology, 243
Reverence for life, 298
Rigid designation, 129
Rituals, 27
Romans, Epistle to the, 184, 186,
202, 281, 286,
Royal Society, 3, 8, 12, 49

Sacrament, world as a, 289–91; -s,
Christian, 290
Sacrifice, law of, 165
Salvation, 48
Salvation history, 42, 331, 347

Science, changes in, 15; functionalist
account of, 28; instrumentalist
account of, 23; objectivity of, 20;
philosophy of, 16; pseudo-, 122
Scientific discovery, personal involvement and commitment in the
process of, 26
Scientific method, 16
Scientific and mythological thinking,
parallel between, 29
'Scientific theology', 272
Scientific theories, under-determination of, 19
Scientific world-views, comparison of
classical and contemporary, 61
Second Law of Thermodynamics, 34.
Selection, 93; group, 160–4; indi-
vidual or gene, 160–4; kin, 175;
natural, 50, 60, 102, 160, 164, 170;
role of behaviour of organism in,
168
Selection game, 101–2
Selection process, 101
Selection value, 101
Self, as agent, 132
Self-consciousness, of man, 138, 192–
193, 197, 204, 212, 217, 246, 338–
339, 353
Selfish gene, 161–4, 173, 175
Shepherd King, in relation to 'dom-
inion' of man, 283
Shiva, Nataraja, 106–8, 304; South
Indian representation, in bronze,
100
Sin, as a 'falling short', 192–3; as a
failure to realize potentiality, 193
Social anthropology, 27, 33
Social sciences, 33
Sociobiology, 162–4, 170–7
Sociology, 112, 117, 171–6, 369–70;
of knowledge, 17–18; of scientific
institutions, 18
Solar system, 59
Space, 52, 55, 66, 68, 360; absolute,
53, 55; Euclidean, 53
Space-time, 66, 70
Spirits, disembodied, 124
Statistical fluctuations, 101

Statistical knowledge, 58
Statistical mechanics, 97
Statistical thermodynamics, 58
Steady-state systems, 98, 260
Stochastic processes, 101
Struggle for existence, 164
Sub-atomic particles, 58, 66, 361
Suffering, 166, 182, 200, 246
Sun, as energy source, 258
Supernatural, 24, 123
'Super-nature', 122
Super-novae explosions, 65
Supervenience, 133
Sustaining, God's continuing creative work in, 78, 79, 80
Symbiosis, 258, 300

Taoism, 361–2
Technology, 309
Teilhardian theology, 338–9, 343, 345–6, 348, 356
Temporal lobectomy, 121
'Theological science', 371
Theology, changes in, 16–17; Christian, 17, 370–1; of nature, 23; as 'Queen of the sciences?', 367–71
Theology and science, relevance of science to theology, 23–7; and the sociology of knowledge, 17–22; 'warfare' between, 10
Theory autonomy, 117–18, 119
Theory of Relativity, 55, 360, 365
Theories of science, under-determined by the facts, 16
Thermodynamics, 97; laws of, 98; second law of, 326–8; of living organisms, 97, 210
Time, 52, 55, 63, 66, 79, 321, 360; absolute, 53, 55, 61; biblical words for, 332; 'carrier or locus of innovative change', 61; concept of, 321, 333–4, 348; as created, 55, 79–81, 333; 'end', 330–1; God's relation to, 80, 321–2, 333, 343; Newtonian, 61; 'primal', 330–1
Timothy, 1st Epistle to, 288, 332
Transcendence of God, 45, 75, 138, 139, 202, 204–5, 207, 239–44; of

human agent in action, 132–3, 139
Transcendence-in-immanence, 133, 139, 141, 211–13, 214, 230, 233, 306, 354
Trinitarian doctrine, 140, 143
Trophic levels, 258; of producers, 258; of primary consumers, 258; of secondary consumers, 258
Trophic models, 259
Truth, in natural science, a success in prediction and control, 19
Two Books, 3, 7, 11, 26, 46
Two-realm ontologies, 24, 25

Unconscious, 120; acts, 137–8
United Nations, Stockholm Conference on the Human Environment, 267, 294
Universe, basic given features, 70; 'cognizable', 68, 69; cognizing and self-cognizing, 65; cold early, 73; contingent, 68; continuity of, 75; centration of, 327–8; expanded consciousness of, 64; expanding, 327–8; formation of, 68; givenness of the parameters of, 71; history of, 69; immensity of, 51–2; Laplacian model of, 57; life of, 67; man's presence and emergence within, 68, 72, 75; man's involvement with, 68; meaning in, 89; Newtonian, 132, 365; oscillating, 73, 328; particularity of, 70; physical, 75; physical constants of, 69; potentialities of, 70, 87, 95, 103–4; -s, ensemble (or run) of, 68–9, (potentialities of), 70; 'the whole', 78

Values, 17, 154, 268, 312, (ecological) 269–70, 295, 300
Variation, mechanism of, 93
Velocity of light, 66
Vitalism, 118–19, 121, 167–8
'Void', 360

Westminster Catechisms, 190
Wisdom literature, 84, 257

Wisdom, of God, 45, 48, 143, 206, (Jesus as) 239
Wisdom of Solomon, 84, 143
Word of God, 13, 17, 45, 105, 143, 145, 205–6, 207, 231, 250, 289, 354
Work, man's, 310
World, as a closed system, 64; 'in God', 205–7, 238–9, 298; of matter (instrumental function of) 289–90, (symbolic function of) 289–90, 301; as a sacrament, 289–91, 301
'World 3', 131, 170, 177, 178
World Council of Churches, 76, 77, 256, 293–4

Yahweh, 41, 42, 82
Yamm, the god of the sea, 82

Zhabotinsky reaction, 99